REBEL QUEEN

Queen Caroline sketched at her trial by George Hayter.

REBEL QUEEN

The Trial of Caroline

Jane Robins

**SIMON &
SCHUSTER**

London · New York · Sydney · Toronto

A CBS COMPANY

First published in Great Britain by Simon & Schuster UK Ltd, 2006
A CBS COMPANY

1 3 5 7 9 10 8 6 4 2

Simon & Schuster UK Ltd
Africa House
64–78 Kingsway
London WC2B 6AH

www.simonsays.co.uk

Simon & Schuster Australia
Sydney

A CIP catalogue record for this book is available
from the British Library.

Hardback ISBN 0-7432-4862-7
EAN 9780743248624

Trade paperback ISBN 0-7432-4863-5
EAN 9780743248631

Typeset in Fournier by M Rules
Printed and bound in Great Britain by
The Bath Press, Bath

For Mum and Dad

CONTENTS

PREFACE

I have received a great deal of assistance whilst working on this book and would like to thank Her Majesty Queen Elizabeth II for permission to use the Royal Archives at Windsor, and the staff at the Royal Archives, in particular Jill Kelsey. Much of my research has been conducted in the Rare Books and Manuscript Rooms at the British Library; and the service provided by the staff there has been excellent. In addition, I am indebted to those at the London Library, the Guildhall Library in the City of London, the National Archives at Kew, the Newspaper Library at Colindale, Sheila O'Connell at the Department of Prints and Drawings at the British Museum, along with those at the Sheffield Archives and at University College London, which holds the Brougham papers.

I thank Tom Stuttaford for his brilliant suggestions and unwavering support, and am grateful to Helen Gummer, Tom McMahon, Lucy Kellaway, Emma Duncan, Julia Kreitman and Richard Ingrams. Ben Wilson was kind enough to read the manuscript and suggest several important amendments. Jasper McMahon subjected my prose to intense scrutiny, and his comments were invaluable. I also benefited from the wise editorial advice of my agent, Natasha Fairweather, and editor, Andrew Gordon, and the assistance of Edwina Barstow and Philippa Donovan.

On the home front, Vera Donovan, Louise van Lelyveld and the late Gina Christian helped me keep the show on the road. And I thank Josh Hardie for his excellent assistance with the research for this book. Finally, for her countless hours at the British Library acting as a first-rate researcher, fact-checker and subeditor I am immensely grateful to my mother, Molly Robins.

The narrative in this book is unusual in that it takes seriously the opinions of those eminent people alive in 1820 who feared a British revolution. There are two reasons for this. First, I have made the judgement that the fears were, to a degree, justified. Second, these sources serve to give a sense of the heightened anxiety in Britain about political convulsion. The forces of loyalism are not so well represented. These are well documented elsewhere and, in terms of the public debate of 1820, were largely hidden. Also, I use the press a great deal. Not as proof of what did nor did not happen, but because the newspapers and prints were part of the historical event itself. They contributed to the general frenzy.

A note on style. When using quotations from letters and diaries that were originally in French, I have translated them. For quotations I have, in general, reproduced the spellings used in the original material. There are some exceptions to this. For instance, when names have been spelled different ways by different people I have used just one spelling, as in the case of Louise Demont, who also appears in letters, newspapers, etc. as Dumont, Du Mont and De Mont. Pergami is often Bergami. Where short forms have been used such as & for and, and Q— for Queen, I have written the words out in full. Italics inside quotations represent underlining or emphasis in the original material. Elsewhere, any use of italics is my own. The transcript of the trial that I used was my own copy edited by Nightingale and published by Robins & Co in London in 1820, with some reference to the Hansard text in the British Library.

Jane Robins, 2006

PROLOGUE

Caroline, Queen of Great Britain, leaves her temporary home in St James's Square, London, and is greeted by a burst of cheers and 'huzzahs' that fill the air of the midsummer morning. Every part of the square is packed with the Queen's supporters. Some stare from the windows of nearby houses, others cheer from the rooftops, and everywhere people wave white handkerchiefs signifying purity and innocence. Cries go up of 'The Queen forever!' and 'God bless her!' This is the first day of the Queen's trial for adultery, the ordeal forced upon her by King George IV, who wishes to divorce his wife and strip her of her title.

The Queen steps into her carriage, which is drawn by six bay horses, and makes slow progress through the multitude towards the House of Lords, where she will encounter the 300 peers of the realm who are to judge her. She makes a strange sight and an unlikely heroine: a short, plump woman of fifty-two, swathed in black gauze and lace, and wearing an unusually tall hat adorned with outsized ostrich feathers. Her cheeks are crudely rouged and her eyebrows darkened to a smoky black, giving her once fair features a slightly fierce look. Along the route the common people are crammed into every space, shouting out their allegiance, and producing a clamour so loud that it can be heard inside the chamber. This is more than the braying of the mob. It is the overwhelming declaration of the lower and middle classes of London that they will not accept a guilty verdict. They have declared themselves hostile to the King and his ministers, and are prepared to tolerate the whole edifice of government only if the Lords support the people and the Queen against the King.

As Caroline enters the chamber, the Lords stand up. She responds by curtseying three times, and then takes her seat, arranging a voluminous white veil over her ample bosom and lolling in a manner that inspires the diarist Thomas Creevey to liken her to a popular doll called Fanny Royds, which has a big, round bottom, ensuring that it will always roll into an upright position. He also notes 'a few straggling ringlets on her neck, which I flatter myself from their appearance were not Her Majesty's own property'. The case against the Queen begins – an event so bizarre and so inflammatory that many people, including the Duke of Wellington, fear that it could lead to a British revolution, or civil war.

I

MARRIAGE

Amongst all things there is nothing that makes . . . [Princes] more
wilful than Carnal Love, and various affecting of voluptuous desires.

Cavendish's Memoirs of Cardinal Wolsey in *The Queen's Matrimonial Ladder,*
Hone and Cruikshank (1820)

In the winter of 1794 Caroline Amelia Elizabeth, Princess of
Brunswick, became engaged to George, Prince of Wales and 'first
gentleman of Europe'. The German Princess was a vivacious young
woman of twenty-six, as plump and gossipy as a kitchen maid, and
almost as poorly educated. Her informality was considered irregular
but attractive and her playful, extrovert nature – which sometimes
bordered on exhibitionism – made her an entertaining companion.
Caroline had acquired at least one admirer in the form of John

Stanley, a young Englishman who had visited the German court when she was fourteen years old. At that time the Princess had been, he said, animated and pretty, 'with light and powdered hair hanging in curls on her neck', and he had thought and dreamed about her 'day and night' for a year afterwards.[1] Thereafter, she made friends easily with those who liked her informal style, distinguishing herself by being witty and sharp, ever ready with a quick riposte. She was also generous and warm; and showed an unusual fondness for young children, often stopping them in the streets of Brunswick and arranging to visit them at home.

Princess Caroline's lively, open style, however, was not desirable in a wife. By eighteenth-century standards of behaviour she was too unpredictable, and had too little regard for etiquette. Her magnanimous spirit was not tempered by the desired female attributes of moral authority, discretion and delicacy – qualities considered by the British to be essential for the happiness of any family and, ultimately, the well-being of society at large. Instead, she liked to flirt, brazenly and without subtlety of manner, and it was rumoured that her governess followed her around at dances to prevent her embarrassing herself 'by indecent conversations with men'. The Whig aristocrat Lord Holland reported gossip that Caroline's morals were 'exceedingly loose' even for Germany 'where they were not . . . very nice about female delicacy'.[2] In short, she embodied the weaknesses but few of the strengths of a Jane Austen heroine. She talked when she should have been reserved, was reckless rather than considered and was said to be careless of her virtue.

It did not bode well that she was destined to become Queen Consort of Great Britain. Her future husband was the eldest son of George III, and first in line to the throne. On the death of his father he would become King George IV and Caroline would be elevated to a position in society without equal amongst women. Unless she could adapt to her new life in Britain, changing herself entirely, it was obvious that she would make a wholly unsuitable royal spouse. It did not help matters that the Prince of Wales was as fastidious as she was incautious and that he possessed an ego as powerful as her own.

George had chosen his wife in a hurry and had no idea of her attributes. He had not taken the precaution of meeting Caroline before proposing to her – but decided that she would do simply because she was German and a family member. Indeed, she was his first cousin, her mother Augusta being the sister of George III. The match also appeared attractive in terms of British foreign policy. The Princess's native Brunswick, although a small north German province, was allied to the greater power of Prussia. Prussia, like Britain, was resisting the march of the French republican army through Europe, and the British had long nurtured hopes of building an anti-French coalition with Britain and Prussia at the centre. In terms of her geopolitical attributes as well as her family pedigree, Princess Caroline seemed safe enough.

George was anxious to proceed quickly with the wedding because he was in debt and needed the money that would come to him upon marriage. Also, at thirty-two years of age, he was getting on, and the country had waited too long for a royal wedding, a Princess of Wales and, God-willing, an heir. He was not looking for a soul mate or lover, as he had mistresses for that purpose; he only required a wife. So he consulted his father, who, despite earlier protestations of distaste for marriages between first cousins, was pleased by the match. The King dispatched an old friend of George's, James Harris, Lord Malmesbury, to Brunswick to secure the marriage and escort Caroline back to England (there was no question of her declining his hand). The young woman's journey from Brunswick would not be without danger, as it would take her across territory that was threatened by the advancing French army. At this time much of the continent of Europe was alive with the sound of cannon fire and, in the aftermath of convulsion in France, the threat of revolution was everywhere.

Lord Malmesbury inspired confidence. He was a highly experienced, urbane diplomat who had served at the courts of Frederick the Great of Prussia and Catherine the Great of Russia, and who had distinguished himself by aiding a counter-revolution in Holland. On 20 November 1794 he arrived safely at the small Brunswick court and was shown great respect by Caroline's family. Later that day the King's envoy recorded his first impressions of the Princess in his diary. She had a pretty face, he thought, but it was 'not expressive of softness', her figure was short and 'not graceful'. Her 'good bust' and fine eyes made a positive impression, but he was unmoved by her fair hair and light eyebrows and could not help noticing that her 'tolerable' teeth were 'going'. Otherwise, he found her 'gay and cheerful, with good sense' and also 'vastly happy with her future expectations'.[3]

He was perturbed to hear from Caroline's mother, Augusta, that 'nothing could be so open, so frank and so unreserved' as the Princess's manner; and her father, the Duke of Brunswick, warned that while his daughter was no fool, 'she lacks judgement'.[4] The Duke's beautiful mistress, Luise von Hertzfeldt, took the English visitor aside. Caroline was not 'ill-disposed', she said, 'but of a temper easily wrought on'. She had '*no tact*'.[5] Malmesbury soon realised that the Princess and future Queen of England had no natural understanding or respect for the rigid codes of behaviour and self-restraint that would be required of her by the English court and her new husband. He was concerned by her unsuitability but, in a rare instance of poor judgement, decided against alerting the King and Prince of Wales to it. After all, he reasoned, his orders had been to arrange the marriage, not to question it. But he determined that for Caroline's sake he would try to educate her, to help her change her style and manners.

At dinner at the Brunswick court on 6 December, Malmesbury embarked on his mission. He listened as the Princess chatted happily, entreating him 'to guide and direct her' in matters relating to England and British society. Malmesbury's cold response was to recommend her to 'perfect silence on *all* subjects' during her first six months in England. Caroline did not take the advice well, and in the following days argued back. She told Malmesbury that she considered openness of character to be a good thing, and insisted that she liked to have warm relationships with the people around her. She added that she wished to be loved by the people of Britain. Malmesbury was, at all times, firm with her. The good opinion of the British, he said, could be obtained only if she made herself 'respected and *rare*'. She was wrong to want the love of the nation, but should instead seek to be respected and honoured. This could *not* be achieved by 'pleasant openness and free communication' but by a 'strict attention to appearances'. He urged her to mix affability with dignity as affability alone 'becomes familiarity and levels all distinction'. He advised her to subdue her 'cheerful and mixing manner', and tried to convince her that the life of the Princess of Wales was not to be 'one of all pleasure, dissipation and enjoyment'. 'My eternal theme to her,' he wrote, is '*to think before she speaks, to recollect herself.*'[6]

Caroline pressed Malmesbury to reveal whether, despite his reservations, he thought that she possessed the innate qualities to succeed at the English court. He replied with some sensitivity, telling her that she possessed beauty and grace and that the other essential characteristics which she lacked – prudence, discretion, attention, and most importantly *tact* – she could attain. 'Do I want them?' Caroline asked, still clinging to her view that her personality would charm those around her. 'You cannot have too much of them,' came the firm reply. 'I shall never learn this,' she said. 'I am too open, too idle.'[7]

Their conversations, as recalled in Malmesbury's diary, show Caroline to be a little in awe of her adviser and anxious that he should like her. But she was stubborn in her attitudes and slow to attain the discretion which he demanded. So, when she began to feel inappropriately fond of him, she did not keep the information to herself in a dignified manner, but blurted it out, confessing to Malmesbury that she thought 'too partially' of him and wished him to be her Lord Chamberlain and her mentor when she arrived in Britain. Shortly afterwards Malmesbury concluded that 'she has no *fonds*, no fixed character, a light and flighty mind', but was 'meaning well and well-disposed'.[8]

Caroline also hinted to Malmesbury that she had heard that the Prince of Wales was a womaniser, but assured him that 'I am determined never to appear jealous.' Malmesbury took the opportunity to set out his philosophy for a successful royal marriage:

I . . . entreated her if she saw any symptoms of a *goût* in the Prince, or if any of the women about her should, under the love of fishing in troubled waters, endeavour to excite a jealousy in her mind, on no account to allow it to manifest itself; that reproaches and sourness never reclaimed anybody; that it only served as an advantageous contrast to the contrary qualities in the rival; and that the surest way of recovering a tottering affection was softness, enduring and caresses; that I knew enough of the Prince to be quite sure he could not withstand such a conduct, while a contrary one would *probably* make him disagreeable and peevish, and certainly force him to be false and dissembling.[9]

Almost as if to test the Princess's ability to follow Malmesbury's sound advice, an anonymous letter arrived in Brunswick during his stay alerting Caroline and Augusta to the wiles of the Prince's current mistress – Frances, Lady Jersey. On 28 December the diplomat arrived at dinner to find mother and daughter unnerved and agitated by the letter, and anxious to receive his counsel. Lady Jersey was, indeed, an alarming prospect – a formidable society hostess, the mother of ten children and still as handsome as she was ambitious. The lady was also clever, witty and manipulative; indeed she had been an inspiration for Sheridan's poisonous Lady Sneerwell in *The School for Scandal*. In defending her elevated position at the Prince's court, she usually displayed the ruthlessness of a tigress guarding its young.

Augusta was sent into a melodramatic fit by the letter, and Caroline showed it to Malmesbury. He lent some calm to the situation by denouncing it loftily as an attempt to frighten the Princess with the idea that Lady Jersey would lead her into an illicit love affair, and might even provide her with a suitable man. But the English diplomat noticed, with some concern, that his theory failed to scare Caroline. So he told her bluntly that anybody who presumed to '*love*' her would be punished by death. He went on to impress upon her that should she surrender to a lover's advances, she too would be guilty of high treason and sent to the executioner. 'This startled her,' he recorded.[10] The Princess received a second shock on the same day with the arrival of a letter to her mother from the King of England, saying that he hoped his niece would not be too vivacious and that she would lead a quiet and retiring life.

On 29 December Caroline and Malmesbury left the Brunswick court and began their hazardous journey to England. Augusta was persuaded to accompany her daughter as far as the English Channel, although she was nervous about the dangers posed by the advancing French troops. As the party's carriages and horses left the town, a great crowd gathered in the streets and cannons were fired. The Duke became upset at parting with his daughter and instructed Malmesbury to look after her with the dedication of a second father. Caroline, though, was elated. In her excitement she elected to ignore etiquette and to ask Malmesbury to travel in her carriage. He, as always, was proper and dignified, and explained to the Princess that her suggestion was highly improper. She was unrepentant and merely laughed. Some days later, she again dismayed her 'mentor' with her lack of decorum when she had a troublesome tooth pulled. Caroline gave the tooth to a servant and asked him to show it to Malmesbury, no doubt believing he would be impressed by her ordeal. But he found the gesture 'nasty and indelicate'.[11]

He was also shocked by her haphazard toilette and the pride she took in being able to dress herself at great speed. He persuaded a lady-in-waiting to explain to her 'that the Prince is very delicate and that he expects a long and very careful *toilette de propreté*, of which she has no idea. On the contrary, she neglects it sadly, and is offensive from this neglect.' The next morning the Princess presented herself early and 'well washed *all over*'.[12] But the subjects of cleanliness and manners were not closed. Malmesbury continued to complain about her coarse petticoats and thread stockings, which, he observed, were never properly washed or changed often enough. He also had to urge Caroline to adopt more delicacy in her language.

He was impressed by her courage, though. When she learned that the French were close by, Caroline said she was not afraid and did not complain when she heard the sound of cannons. By contrast, her mother was troubled by nerves and asked to turn back for Brunswick. Malmesbury remonstrated with her, but Augusta argued that her brother the King of England would be angry if she were captured by the French. Malmesbury conceded that he would be 'very sorry' but told Augusta that, nonetheless, she must not leave her daughter. The Duchess eventually gave in. The difference between the mother's trepidation and the daughter's fortitude was stark, and Malmesbury concluded that, had it not been for a poor education, Caroline 'might have turned out excellent'. Her underlying strengths, he thought, were her generosity, her good humour, her bravery and her endurance. He observed that she 'had not a grain of rancour'.[13] In the round, though, her personality was flawed. He noted:

> that she has quick parts, without a sound or distinguishing under-standing; that she has a ready conception, but no judgement; caught by the first impression, led by the first impulse . . . loving to talk and prone to confide and make missish friendships that last twenty-four hours. Some natural, but no acquired morality, . . . warm feelings and nothing to counterbalance them . . . she has no governing powers . . . is naturally curious, and a gossip.[14]

The European journey took almost three months and was subject to long delays due to the war and bad weather. In the final stages the party became stuck at Hanover, and remained there for several weeks. Caroline stayed cheerful and busied herself trying to improve her faltering and imperfect English. She also endeavoured to learn the manners and customs of Britain. During their stay Malmesbury received a letter from the Prince of Wales, who was becoming impatient at the delay in the arrival of his bride. In his letter George mentioned that the Princess's ladies-in-waiting, including Lady Jersey, would meet her on arrival in Britain.

At seven in the evening of 28 March 1795 Caroline left behind her Brunswick life forever. Augusta was to return to the Brunswick court, while she and Malmesbury boarded the *Jupiter*, a 50-ton ship, for the crossing of the English Channel. A royal salute was sent up from the *Jupiter* and was returned by the accompanying British fleet. It was a clear evening and the ships, thought Malmesbury, made a fine sight. As for Caroline, she was entirely cheerful and pleasant, had 'no childish fears' and was 'all good humour'. In the morning when the ship set sail from Cuxhaven, the weather was 'charming', the Princess 'delighted' and the officers on board greatly pleased with her manners and good humour.[15] But before they arrived at the English coast the weather turned. A thick fog descended, forcing the ship's captain to cast anchor several miles off Yarmouth for fear of the flats. The *Jupiter* was delayed for three days, during which the Princess became unwell. Eventually, on 3 April, the sun broke through, allowing some progress, and at eight in the morning on 5 April, Easter Sunday, the party departed the *Jupiter* for the royal yacht *Augusta* and set sail up the Thames for Greenwich, where they disembarked in good weather at midday. However, the welcoming party had not yet arrived. Caroline was kept waiting for an hour by a lady-in-waiting named Mrs Aston, Lord Clermont, and Lady Jersey.

When she eventually turned up, George's mistress immediately sought command of the situation. She made derogatory comments about Caroline's muslin gown and blue satin petticoat and ordered her to change into a less flattering white satin dress which she had brought with her. She 'expressed herself in a way which induced me to speak rather sharply to her', wrote Malmesbury, but he allowed the change of dress to take place anyway.[16] He also stood by when Lady Jersey insisted that dollops of rouge be applied to Caroline's cheeks.

She then insisted on sitting next to Caroline in her carriage, saying that she could only face forward when travelling as facing backwards made her sick. This demand amounted to a gross breach of etiquette which would suggest to the world that the mistress of the Prince of Wales enjoyed a status equal to that of his wife. This time Malmesbury intervened, now opposing the Lady and telling her that since she must have known that riding backward in a coach disagreed with her, she ought never to have accepted the position of Lady of the Bedchamber. If she really was likely to be sick, he added, she could ride facing forwards in his own coach. 'This of course settled the business,' and for the journey to London Lady Jersey faced backwards, along with the Princess's recently acquired chaperone, Mrs Harcourt.[17] On the way Caroline began to chatter, telling her companions about herself and revealing that she had once been deeply in love with a man whom she could not marry because of her high birth — information that Malmesbury would have wanted her to keep to herself and which Lady Jersey could happily pass on to George. The Princess was probably nervous, and when anxious she invariably talked too much. At about half past two, the coaches pulled up at St James's Palace in London and Malmesbury informed the King and the Prince of Wales of Caroline's arrival.

George Augustus Frederick, future Prince Regent and George IV, was not the foppish idiot that he has become in the modern imagination. It was clear from an early age that he possessed a mean intelligence, and at the age of four he impressed those around him by choosing to 'lie and make reflections' when confined to bed by an illness. Like the seven brothers and six sisters who were to follow him, George received a strict and restrictive upbringing, with emphasis on duty, a fear of God, justice and prudence. With his brother, Prince Frederick, he was educated in the classics, Italian, German and French. One of his tutors, the Bishop of Lichfield and Coventry, drew up a plan of study which covered religion, government, law, history, mathematics, Shakespeare, Milton and Pope. He was also taught to play the cello, to draw and to appreciate fine art.

Charlotte Papendiek, a member of the royal household, thought that George, in adolescence, was a fine young man: 'His countenance was of a sweetness and intelligence quite irresistible,' she wrote. 'He had an elegant person, engaging and distinguished manners, added to an affectionate disposition and the cheerfulness of youth.'[18] But he was also vain. When he was eight his mother, Queen Charlotte, had given him sound advice which, in subsequent years, he frequently disregarded: 'Disdain all flattery,' she said, 'it will corrupt your manners and render you contemptible before the world.'[19]

By ignoring her counsel he allowed himself to become increasingly egotistical. He became resentful whenever he did not have his way, and 'seemed to act upon a practical conviction of all mankind being born for his exclusive use'.[20] In time, George became self-centred and small-minded, but it was never possible to forget entirely his innate talents, extensive knowledge and intelligence. The Duke of Wellington later described him as 'The most extraordinary compound of talent, wit, buffoonery, obstinacy and good feeling – in short a medley of the most opposite qualities with a great preponderance of good – that I ever saw in any character in my life.'[21]

At the age of sixteen he acquired a public image, and started a long career as a flamboyant figure on the political stage. He began to show signs of independence of spirit and rebellion, became attracted to improper company, and demonstrated a particular fondness for women and wine. When he fell in love with a 23-year-old governess, Mary Hamilton, he bombarded her with seventy-five passionate love letters. Miss Hamilton did not submit to his pleadings to share her bed, whereupon he switched his affections to a 21-year-old actress, Mary Robinson, who, on the promise of a steady income, was more obliging. A sixpenny print was published, which showed the young Prince gormlessly gaping at the actress, his coronet falling from his head. Other, more enduring, affairs were to follow.

The greatest of these began in 1784 with the announcement in the press that 'Mrs Fitzherbert is arrived in London for the season'. George spotted Maria Fitzherbert at the opera and begged to become acquainted with the 'angel' in a white hood. She was an attractive widow of twenty-eight years of age and he was now twenty-two. The Prince quickly became so infatuated with his new love that he constantly sought her out and refused to attend parties unless she was there. When she, a devout Catholic, repeatedly refused to sleep with him, George became virtually deranged with desire to possess her, and ultimately, in a fit of unbridled craving, acted out a melodramatic suicide attempt, stabbing at himself and producing a grisly display of blood. In this state, he begged his love to be his wife, put a ring on her finger, and afterwards told her that he 'look'd upon [himself] as married'.[22]

But Mrs Fitzherbert sensibly judged that George's word did not turn her into a married woman, and fled to Paris, refusing to communicate with him. Still he wrote to her, begging her to wed him secretly, despite advice that by marrying a Catholic he could never become

King; and when she failed to respond, he plotted to leave England and to hunt her down. Eventually she gave in, although she confessed that 'I know I injure him and perhaps destroy forever my own tranquility.'[23] Their marriage took place at dusk on 15 December 1785 at her house in Park Street, Mayfair, and was legitimate in canonical law, but unlawful by statute. According to the Royal Marriages Act, the Prince was not allowed to marry without the consent of his father. Several people, including Malmesbury, knew of the ceremony and Mrs Fitzherbert was treated with the respect due to a royal wife by society visitors to the extravagant homes that George made at Carlton House in London and at Brighton. Their relationship flourished, though not continuously, for the following sixteen years.

The public prints became increasingly fascinated with George's private life, sometimes getting their facts right, and sometimes not. James Gillray, Britain's leading satirical caricaturist, had caused a sensation by criticising the monarchy in artful, excoriating cartoons that were more sophisticated than anything the royals had been subjected to in the past. One Gillray print wrongly showed the Prince of Wales and Mrs Fitzherbert being married in a French church, the bridegroom happily ogling Mrs Fitzherbert's monumental cleavage. Another masterpiece entitled *The Morning after Marriage* depicted George and Mrs Fitzherbert in sprawling disarray in a bedroom – an overturned decanter, broken wine glasses and a broken candle lying on the floor, signifying shattered virtue. Horace Walpole wrote of the society scandal triggered by the affair: 'You are to talk of nothing else, for they tell me the passengers in the streets, of all ranks, talk of it.' Matters deteriorated further when in 1792 Gillray published his most vicious anti-George print of all. Entitled *A Voluptuary under the Horrors of Digestion*, it showed the Prince in vile puffed-up languor, wearily picking his teeth while the evidence of foul and debauched habits lay all around. By now he was grotesquely fat.

The newspapers were no better. In 1789 George was forced to buy up the *Morning Post* in order to suppress stories of his marriage, and in the same year he was vilified in *The Times* as a hard-drinking, swearing, whoring man 'who at all times would prefer a girl and a bottle, to politics and a sermon'. The paper declared that his only states of happiness were 'gluttony, drunkenness and gambling'.[24] The Prince's growing debts were a companion theme. In 1786 they were calculated at £270,000, and by 1792 had grown to a monumental £400,000. Much of his expenditure was on his homes at Carlton House and in Brighton, and on houses for Mrs Fitzherbert, who, for reasons of propriety, kept her own establishments. He decorated her house in Pall Mall at a cost of £50,000, while Carlton House became a palace of immense luxury and splendour. By 1794 his debts reached half a million pounds, and pamphlets had started to appear with uncompromising titles such as *John Bull starving to pay the debts of the royal prodigal*.

In this context, George began seriously to consider marrying again, this time in public with the full legitimacy of English law behind him. He knew that if he wed, his debts would be settled and his yearly allowance from the state increased to £100,000 from £60,000. In the past he had not felt compelled to marry formally and produce an heir, being content to delegate to his brother Frederick, the Duke of York, the job of providing the country's future monarchs. But, nine years after his 'wedding' to Maria Fitzherbert, she no longer dominated his life. He had become bored of her and her taste for domesticity, and had turned to the racier Lady Jersey, who thought her lover's proposed marriage an excellent idea. Mrs Fitzherbert might regard him as a bigamist, but she was now old news and her opinions counted for less than they used to. A German princess was required and, according to the Duke of Wellington, it was Lady Jersey who chose Caroline. She selected a woman, he suggested, 'of indelicate manners, indifferent character and not very inviting appearance, from a hope that disgust with a wife would secure constancy to a mistress'.[25]

When George heard that his bride had arrived at St James's he rushed along the palace corridors to greet her. Malmesbury was the only witness to their first meeting. 'I, according to the established etiquette, introduced . . . the Princess Caroline to him,' he wrote. 'She very properly . . . attempted to kneel to him.' George raised her, 'gracefully enough', and embraced her, but then with barely a word he walked off to a distant part of the room and called Malmesbury to him. 'Harris, I am not well,' he said. 'Pray get me a glass of brandy.' 'Sir, had you not better have a glass of water?' Malmesbury replied, upon which the Prince, 'much out of humour', let forth an oath, and said, '*No*; I will go directly to the Queen,' and away he went, to see his mother.[26]

Malmesbury returned to Caroline, who had been left alone at the other end of the room, and found her in a state of astonishment. She still found English difficult, and exclaimed in French, 'My God! Does the Prince always act like this? I think he's very fat and he's nothing like as handsome as his portrait.' Malmesbury assured the Princess that the Prince was simply 'a good deal affected and flurried at this first interview, but she certainly would find him different at dinner'.[27]

But the evening was worse. Caroline was forced to have her first meal with her future husband with Lady Jersey also at the table. The Princess seemed to be totally out of her depth, and instead of following Malmesbury's advice to hold her tongue and exude 'softness', she fell back on her most familiar behaviour and began to prattle in a way that she wrongly thought would impress the company around her. She appalled Malmesbury by expressing herself with 'rattling, affecting raillery and wit, and throwing out coarse vulgar hints about Lady [Jersey] who was present', constantly attempting 'cleverness and coarse sarcasm'. Lady Jersey responded with a superior and dignified silence, while the Prince was 'disgusted' at his fiancée's manners.[28]

Caroline later admitted to a lady-in-waiting, Lady Charlotte Campbell, that seeing George and Lady Jersey together had disconcerted her. She could be a slave of a man she loved, she said, but she did not love George and he did not love her and thus her situation was impossible to tolerate. To a more sympathetic heart than George's she might have appeared to be overcompensating for a sense of helplessness in an alien world, endeavouring to keep her pride by hiding her pain, albeit in the clumsiest manner. In practice, the Prince of Wales saw only vulgarity and felt only revulsion. Given this stormy juxtaposition of the couple's hostile emotions, it was unfortunate that their marriage was to take place just three days later.

On the morning of his wedding the Prince of Wales told his brother the Duke of Clarence, 'William, tell Mrs Fitzherbert she is the only woman I shall ever love,'[29] and steeled himself for the ordeal ahead by drinking so much brandy that he was noticeably inebriated during the service. The marriage took place in St James's Chapel and Caroline walked up the aisle wearing a dress of white silver tissue lined with ermine and encrusted with jewels. It was so heavy that she nearly fell over. She chatted enthusiastically to her attendants as she made her way to the altar. Matters were so apparently unhappy that even the correspondent of the *Morning Chronicle* noticed, reporting that throughout the wedding the Prince of Wales 'no doubt from an excess of sensibility, was uncommonly agitated . . . His voice in the responses was tremulous.' In addition, 'The Prince rose from his knees at the altar too soon, and the Princess followed his example; the Archbishop stopped the service. The King saw the dilemma and whispered [to] the Prince, who recovered his posture, and the service was concluded.'[30] It is quite possible that George was on the point of running away. He avoided looking at Caroline at all during the ceremony but threw glances to Lady Jersey, and when the Archbishop of Canterbury twice repeated the part of the ceremony which obliged him to be, henceforth, faithful to his wife, he shed tears. Lady Maria Stuart witnessed him looking 'like death and full of confusion'.[31]

The wedding night was a disaster. Caroline's version of events was that George, by then, was so drunk that he sank into a heap in the fireplace, where she left him. George's account of the wedding night, delivered to Malmesbury almost a year later, was as rude about her as she was about him – though both had a tendency towards exaggeration and we cannot be sure of the truth. She had scars on her neck and thighs, he said, and:

I have every reason to believe [that I was not the first], for not only on the first night was there no appearance of blood, but her manners were not those of a novice. In taking those liberties, natural on these occasions, she said, '*Ah mon dieu qu'il est gros!*', and how should she know this without a previous means of comparison. Finding that I had suspicions of her not being *new*, she the next night mixed up some tooth powder and water, coloured her shift with it . . . in showing these she showed at the same time such marks of filth both in the fore and *hind* part of her . . . that she turned my stomach and from that moment I made a vow *never to touch her again*. I had known her three times – twice the first and once the second night – it required no small [effort] to conquer my aversion and overcome the disgust of her person.[32]

As a result of these encounters Caroline, to the great joy of the King and Queen, became pregnant.

In these early days of her marriage Caroline acquired a press image that was as positive as her husband's was miserable. On her arrival in England the *Morning Chronicle* told its readers that 'her complexion is light and her face expressive and beautiful; she is under the middle size, and is *en bon point*' and observed 'an ease and condescension in her deportment which seem to rise from her natural disposition, and which more than any other charm engage the affections of the spectator'.[33] On 11 April, three days after the wedding, the paper reported a meeting between Caroline and her uncle, George III:

Her Royal Highness is most spritely and playful in her manners. On being presented to His Majesty, after kneeling and being raised, she took the King by the two arms with the most winning familiarity – and after eyeing him all round said – 'You are very like my dear Mama.'

The day after [during a garden walk] . . . Her Highness broke from the conductor who was leading her with the most respectful ceremony, and hooking the King under the arm, said with a smile: 'You shall be my beau and show me all the charms of the place.' The King was enchanted with a familiarity new to him . . .

George III was, indeed, very fond of his niece and was to retain his affection for her during the turbulent years ahead. The newspapers too were delighted by her, and charmed by her natural, open manner. The press liked her freshness and willingness to express emotion –

a striking contrast to the stiff formality of the rest of the English court. Their allegiance was significant in this uncertain age. The King and Queen of France had recently been sent to the guillotine, and the question of how royals should behave had become a pertinent one.

If the Prince of Wales thought that his marriage to Caroline would improve his press image, he was mistaken. Editors and reporters quickly returned to the old subjects of his lavish expenditure on fineries and his huge debts, which were repeatedly set in the context of the costs of the war with France, and the threat of the spread of revolution. This was an era in which views were expressed with large helpings of hyperbole. Nevertheless, when Lord Guildford was reported as believing Britain to be at the 'most awful and critical period' of its history, he would have been taken seriously by newspaper readers. On 28 April the newspapers carried long reports of a House of Commons debate on the state of George's finances, and asked whether Parliament should bail him out. 'When the cries of the starving poor were assailing us on all sides [Mr Grey] thought that the House would not be doing its duty by granting establishments to Princes with a profusion unparalleled,' reported the *Morning Chronicle*. Mr Curwen went further still, asking 'Gentlemen to turn their eyes to a neighbouring country, and recollect what brought on its great convulsions.' It was not tyrannical power that caused the revolution in France, he argued, but 'a lamentable negligence about the finances'. He might have added that the Prince's behaviour seemed otherworldly indeed when Tom Paine's republican *Rights of Man* was the best-selling pamphlet in the country, with sales close to 200,000 – and when the threat of invasion from France raised the possibility of a revolution in Britain.

In private the royal couple managed to tolerate each other during Caroline's pregnancy, although Lady Jersey's influence was as malign as ever, and the marriage was strained. On 7 January 1796, exactly nine months after the wedding, Caroline gave birth to 'an immense girl' who was named Charlotte. The new baby was welcomed into the world by her father, but did nothing to bring the couple closer to each other. Three days after Charlotte's birth George wrote out a will that, despite his continuing relationship with Lady Jersey, left all his property to 'my Maria Fitzherbert, my wife, the wife of my heart and soul' while to 'her who is call'd the Princess of Wales' he left one shilling. The long emotional effusion also stated that the mother of his child was to be in *no way* concerned in her care or education.[34] In March, George confessed to Malmesbury that he was contemplating a separation from Caroline.

By May the rift between the Prince and Princess of Wales and the casting of the Prince as the villain in his marriage was well established in the newspapers and prints. It was becoming known in society that Caroline was subjected by the Prince to harsh restrictions on her movements and activities. The landscape painter Joseph Farington was of the opinion that 'the whole royal family treat her with neglect, the Duke of Gloucester excepted'. The King had been Caroline's ally since she arrived in the country 'yet he has been so worked upon that he does not appear to notice her much'. As for her ladies, only Lady Cholmondely was a friend, 'the other Ladies particularly behave shamefully. Lady Jersey is supposed to be at the bottom of this.' George, though, was the worst offender, speaking very disrespectfully of his wife 'as to her person being unclean, with sores etc' and implying that he may not be the father of Princess Charlotte. In June, Farington reported that 'the behaviour of the Prince and Lady Jersey towards the Princess is spoken of as having been most scandalous'. The couple would spike Caroline's wine with brandy, according to the gossip, and then laugh at her for being drunk.[35]

In May 1796 the scandal exploded in the press. All the major London papers carried reports that Lady Jersey had intercepted a letter written by the Princess to her family in Brunswick and found that it included rude comments about herself and the royal family, and in particular referred to George's mother, Queen Charlotte, as 'Old Snuffy' — a reference to her fondness for snuff. The newspapers rushed to support Caroline. 'There are few crimes which, in the eye of morality, are more atrocious . . . than the concealment and opening of private letters,' proclaimed the *True Briton*. 'There cannot be a greater breach of faith and honour, than the opening of a letter designed for another person,' agreed *The Times*. Calls were made for the dismissal of Lady Jersey as a Lady of the Bedchamber, and countless criticisms were made of George, which could only add to his unpopularity. The *Morning Post*, for instance, insinuated that the Prince was shunning his baby daughter.

Several papers hinted that the Prince was jealous of his wife's popularity and wanted to keep her away from the public. Even the *Morning Herald*, generally sympathetic to George, took up the theme. On 3 June it wrote that Princess Caroline had received great applause from the public when she stood at the front windows of Carlton House, 'her infant in her arms'; in consequence of which, she had now been ordered to move the nursery from the front side of the palace to the garden side. The following day, the paper alleged that the Princess had been given 'the most positive commands' not to appear again at the opera that season, and that her obedience that Thursday had meant her: 'sacrificing her only amusement to the harsh and rigid demands of conjugal obedience'.

George and Caroline were now established in the press as reviled oppressor and pitiful victim in need of assistance. 'Nothing can be more honourable to the feelings of the English nation than its defence of a woman, who has thrown herself on its protection,' proclaimed the *Morning Herald*. *The Times* went further when it described the chivalry shown the Princess when she attended the opera. Echoing Edmund Burke's famous defence of Marie Antoinette, it reported: 'Were it possible any one should wrong this royal stranger, ten thousand swords were ready to leap out of their scabbards in her defence.' It was at the opera (which she continued to attend, despite the supposed ban) that impassioned support for Caroline was repeatedly shown, and then reported in the newspapers. 'The whole house rose, and for full a quarter of an hour maintained a continued acclamation of *"Bravo! Welcome! God bless the Princess! Long live the Princess!"*,' reported the *Morning Herald*. 'Her Royal Highness was very much affected and wept . . . the country knows her worth, participates in her affliction and resents her wrongs.'

In private, Caroline was utterly miserable. She complained constantly of her intolerable subjection to the presence of Lady Jersey and of the Prince's preference for his mistress's company to her own. She plainly felt humiliated, hurt and infuriated and her miseries were made worse every time she tried to make the best of things by travelling or making new friends. George railed against her audacity. He forbade her from making journeys of any length and from seeing anybody socially, other than suitable companions suggested by him. Those who saw Caroline at this time commented that she 'sees no company but old people put on her list',[36] and that 'the melancholy and anxiety in her countenance is quite affecting'.[37] Caroline confessed to a friend, 'I do not know how I shall be able to bear the loneliness.'[38] She also let off steam by gossiping about George. Her honeymoon at Kempshott, she said, had consisted of her husband's male friends drinking and gambling and 'sleeping and snoring' with their feet up on the sofas.[39] Lady Jersey was the only other woman there and the whole scene resembled a bad brothel much more than a palace. Caroline hinted to Lord Minto that George's loathing of her was founded in her knowledge of his own failings in bed.

George pressed for a separation and on 30 April 1796 wrote to Caroline from Windsor telling her that 'nature has not made us suitable to each other'. This was a formal declaration of his wish to part. Caroline had asked him to guarantee that she would never again have to sleep with him, even if the country desperately needed an heir; and George set down in writing that he would never again propose 'a connection of a more particular nature', even if an accident happened to Princess Charlotte.[40] The Prince's desire to leave the wife who he, by now, deeply loathed was inflamed further when on 24 May *The Times* reported a 'separation in high life'. This encouraged still greater support for Caroline, who attended the opera four days later. The 'House seemed as if electrified by her presence', according to *The Times*. 'Every hand was lifted up to greet her with the loudest plaudits. The gentlemen jumped on the benches and waved their hats, crying out *Huzza!*'

Then, on 2 June the *True Briton* railed against the 'unmerited ill-treatment' suffered by an 'amiable and accomplished personage'. The paper thought George '*incorrigible*', with a '*total disregard* for the opinions of the world'. Furthermore, he was doing more to promote Jacobinism than all the efforts of the kingdom's radicals. This was quite a claim, since there was much rebellious sentiment around in Britain at this time, some of it explained by the unpopularity of the war with France, some by rising bread prices. The radical London Corresponding Society was thriving, and radical meetings in London drew crowds reputed to be between 100,000 and 150,000 people. In 1794 the government had suspended *habeas corpus*, and repressive acts of Parliament were to follow, designed to stamp out sedition. Small wonder, then, that in this climate George was furious at a press image that suggested he was encouraging revolt, and formed a demonic obsession with the injustice, as he saw it, of his own vilification in the papers alongside constant reminders of Caroline's popularity. He could not understand the failure of everyone else to see that she was the 'vilest wretch this world ever was cursed with', a 'fiend', 'a very monster of iniquity'; in George's view there was 'no end to her wickedness'. 'She has flattered herself she could reduce me to such a situation as would give her a decided political superiority in this country,' he wrote.[41] He considered her capable of bringing down the entire royal family.

2

SEPARATION

Was it manly, when widow'd,
to spy at her actions;
To listen to eaves-droppers,
whisp'ring detractions?

The Queen's Matrimonial Ladder

The formal separation of the Prince and Princess of Wales was
opposed by the King, who remained fond of his niece and critical of his eldest son. George III put a high value on domesticity and
endeavoured to conduct his family life on principles that might set an
example to the country at large. He favoured loyalty, modesty, discretion and thrift within the family, and was repeatedly exasperated
by the Prince of Wales's disregard for these virtues. It was entirely

typical of their relationship that the father failed to convince the son to persevere with his marriage, and in 1797 George and Caroline parted for good.

The Princess went to live at Charlton in the suburbs of south east London, and then moved into Montague House in nearby Blackheath. In comparison with the high life at George's home at Carlton House, her new residence must have seemed provincial. Blackheath was dominated by the green space of the heath itself, which had windmills upon it and a smattering of new buildings going up at the edges. The local houses were designed for the families of rich young gentlemen of the upper and middle classes, and the community included many successful trade and business people, as well as navy men. But it was no centre of aristocratic society. Nonetheless, Blackheath did offer Caroline the opportunity to build a new life, at last selecting her own servants and ladies-in-waiting; entertaining when she liked, and choosing her own guests. She regarded George's letter of 30 April 1796 as a letter of licence, interpreting it as a recognition that she was free to live as she pleased. George had written, 'Our inclinations are not in our power, nor should either of us be held answerable to the other',[1] and for Caroline this was enough. She now considered her private life to be her own affair.

She encouraged society figures and influential politicians to make the journey from London to see her, and when they did so, she entertained them in her own idiosyncratic style. Guests at Montague House were invited to chat to her while she sat on the floor eating raw onions and drinking ale, and her parties would carry on until the early hours. Reverting to her old Brunswick self, she flirted outrageously, and was reputed to have a habit of leaving a dinner party with one of the male guests, taking him off to a private room, and not reappearing for several hours.[2] She hosted grand dinners, as well as informal gatherings at which she 'romped with [Princess Charlotte] . . . about the carpet on her knees',[3] and soon succeeded in establishing a mini-court that competed with her husband's more splendid and formal establishment. Her guests included French nobles who had fled Paris and now graced London society, amongst them the Prince of Condé, the Duc de

Bourbon and the Duc de Berri. Government ministers and politicians also visited Blackheath, aware that Caroline as the mother of the future Queen was a potential source of great political influence, and to counterbalance George's long flirtation with the Whigs. William Pitt came, as did the arch-conservative Lord Eldon and the future prime minister, George Canning, then a brilliant and ambitious young Tory. Some Whigs came too, including George's old friend Charles James Fox.

Some of these illustrious men, Fox in particular, may have attended Caroline out of mere curiosity, but Canning became a close friend. Like the Princess he was something of an extrovert, a talker and an enthusiast; he was to remain her ally for most of her life and his closeness to her was, in time, to cause him grave political embarrassment. He also found her sexually attractive and was constrained in his ardour only by the fact that he fell in love with another woman, Joan Scott, who was to become his wife. If it had not been for Miss Scott, thought Canning, 'I know not how I should have resisted, as I ought to do, the abundant and overpowering temptations to the indulgence of a passion . . . which must have been dangerous, perhaps ruinous, to her who was the cause of it, and to myself.' He did not name Caroline, but his words were written exactly at the point, late in 1799, when Canning had become a constant companion of the Princess and it is probable that he was referring to her. Shortly afterwards he confessed that he had eaten a last dinner with his amour which was 'not quite so blameless' as he had anticipated.[4] In 1800 he married Miss Scott, and the following year Caroline became godmother to the couple's first child.

In 1800 the dashing young society artist Thomas Lawrence stayed at Montague House for a number of nights and became another of Caroline's distinguished partners in flirtation. Then, in 1802, she became attracted to Sir Sidney Smith, a heroic naval adventurer in the style of the fictional Hornblower, who was entirely to Caroline's taste. In 1799 he had become famous by defending Acre from Napoleon Bonaparte, thus preventing him conquering the East. 'But wherever there is water to float a ship we are sure to find you [British] in the way,'[5] Napoleon said after Sir Sidney's triumph. Personally, Caroline's beau was flamboyant, vain and given to sartorial panache – at one stage he affected long mustachios. The Princess loved theatricality.

Sir Sidney was lodging with Caroline's neighbours in Blackheath, Major-General Sir John Douglas – who had been with him at Acre – and Douglas's wife Charlotte. Caroline befriended the little household. Lady Douglas, a good-looking, socially ambitious woman of low birth, became her constant companion, and for a time lived at Montague House. Sir Sidney, though, was more intimate still. The Princess 'is at present entirely wrapped up in Sir Sidney Smith', said Lord Minto in March. But by autumn he was cast aside in favour of a new love, Captain Thomas Manby. Although less well known than Smith, Manby had his own tales of naval derring-do to relate. In 1792 he had been part of an expedition to the north-west coast of America which had discovered a great many deserted villages, laid waste by a devastating epidemic of smallpox. By 1801, he found himself in the West Indies, engaged in bloody skirmishes with the French, and only in July 1802 had he returned to Britain as commander of the *Juno* and bearer of important dispatches on the state of the war. Manby's relationship with Caroline was resented by Sir Sidney Smith, who, according to Lady Douglas, had found the couple playing footsie under the dinner table. Caroline, at this time, became dangerously overt in demonstrating her sexual feelings for her sea-captain lovers, dancing about in their presence and 'exposing herself like an opera girl'. Echoing the advice of Malmesbury, William Pitt's niece, Lady Hester Stanhope, warned the Princess that 'it was a hanging-matter, and that she should mind what she was about'.[6]

Her men aside, Caroline's main preoccupation at this time was her fondness for children. She was an affectionate mother to Charlotte, a lively, hot-tempered girl, who in 1799 at the age of three was allowed to live near Montague House under the care of a governess. The Princess visited her daughter often, and Charlotte was regularly brought to her mother's home. But a single child was not enough for Caroline, and she began to acquire a larger family of 'protégées', becoming the protector of eight or nine poor children. They were sent to board with local foster mothers, the Princess supervising their education and upbringing. Little is known of the quality of life that she, in the long term, provided for these waifs, but her intentions at least were good. Then, in 1802, she adopted a three-month-old baby boy called William Austin, relieving his impoverished parents Samuel and Sophia of the 'burden' of his care. The child was provided with a nanny and a nursery at Caroline's home, and was from then on a constant, close presence in her family life. As a small boy he had blond hair, a cheeky look and an upturned nose – and the Princess appeared to dote on him. Caroline's detractors were prone to gossip about her idiosyncratic hobby, collecting children, but her own view was that 'everybody must love something in this world. I think my taste is the most natural and whoever may find fault with it may do it or not.'[7]

At Montague House the Princess of Wales put on a devil-may-care show of independence. As one of her ladies, Lady Charlotte Bury, later remarked: 'She had an aversion to dullness; and would have risked solid benefits to gratify her thirst for amusement for a few passing moments.'[8] But Caroline was happy in her quest for pleasure, enjoyed defying convention and, at heart, considered herself to be a good and generous person. She had no intention of changing, despite the disdain she received from the royal family and much of high society. The exalted Lord Holland thought that 'if not mad, she was a very worthless woman';[9] and even her supposed ally Mary Berry on meeting her wrote: 'Such an exhibition! But that she did not at all feel for herself, one should have felt for her. Such an overdressed, bare-bosomed, painted-eye-browed figure, one never saw.'[10] As for Caroline's home, Lady Charlotte Campbell thought it 'all glitter and glare and trick . . . altogether like a bad dream'.[11]

Most vicious of all, though, was her Blackheath neighbour Lady Douglas, who was fully encouraged in her venom by her husband Sir John. Before long Caroline had fallen out with her neighbours, barred them from her house and then grew incensed about their malicious gossiping. The Douglases, in turn, complained that Caroline had sent them anonymous letters clearly in her own handwriting, two of which included obscene drawings. One was captioned 'Sir Sidney Smith and Lady Douglas in an amorous situation', and the other (addressed to Sir John) 'Sir Sidney Smith doing Lady Douglas, your aimable wife'.[12] Then, as if matters were not bad enough, Lady Douglas asserted that Caroline had given birth to an illegitimate boy who now lived with her under the name of William Austin. In 1805 Lady Douglas's allegations were brought to the attention of George, who wanted nothing to do with the business, but was forced to act. The Prince's confidante, Lord Thurlow, advised him: 'Sir, if you were a common man, she might sleep with the Devil . . . But the Prince of Wales has no right to risk his Daughter's Crown and his Brothers' claims,' adding that, 'the accusation once made must be examin'd into.'[13]

The King reluctantly agreed that his niece's behaviour should be scrutinised, and in May 1806 a secret four-man enquiry was set up, which became known as the Delicate Investigation. Its four commissioners could hardly have been more eminent, comprising the Prime Minister, Lord Grenville; the Lord Chancellor, Lord Erskine; the Lord Chief Justice, Lord Ellenborough; and the Home Secretary, Earl Spencer.

Under oath, Lady Douglas gave an account of her erstwhile friendship with Caroline, whom she now described as 'a person without education or talents, and without any desire of improving herself'. She reported that the Princess had become a constant critic of all the royal family, dismissing them as 'very ill made' with 'plum-pudding faces, which she could not bear'. Caroline's friendliness to herself, she implied, was fed by lesbian desire. 'The Princess became so extravagantly fond of me that, however flattering it might be, it certainly was very troublesome,' and she would 'kiss me, take me in her arms and tell me I was beautiful, saying she had never loved any woman so much'. She would exclaim, '"your arms are fine beyond imagination, your bust is very good, and your eyes, Oh, I never saw such eyes" . . . In this manner she went on perpetually, even before strangers.' Caroline also, said Lady Douglas, tried to pressurise her into an illicit affair with Prince William, one of George's younger brothers, and suggested that she, Lady Douglas, must have slept with Sir Sidney Smith on the grounds that 'if ever a woman was upon friendly terms with any man, they were sure to become lovers'. Lady Douglas considered that 'it depended very much upon the lady'.[14]

Lady Douglas claimed that when she had been pregnant in 1802, Caroline had declared herself to be in the same state. 'I am with child,' the Princess is supposed to have told her friend, 'and the child came to life when I was breakfasting with Lady Willoughby. The milk flowed up into my breast so fast that it came through my muslin gown, and I was obliged to pretend that I had spilt something and go upstairs to wipe my gown with a napkin.' After this, said Lady Douglas, 'the Princess often alluded to her situation and to mine'. In October 1802 she saw Caroline 'dressed in a long Spanish velvet cloak and an enormous muff, but which together could not conceal the state she was in, for I saw directly she was very near her time'. Then, in January 1803, she visited her neighbour to find a baby sleeping on a sofa. 'Here is the little boy,' said the Princess of Wales. 'I had him two days after I saw you last; is not it a nice little child? The upper part of his face is very fine.' The Princess had said that if her secret were discovered 'she would give the Prince of Wales the credit for it, for that she had slept two nights in the year she was pregnant in Carlton House'.[15]

The Delicate Investigators next interrogated several of Caroline's servants. The attentions of Sir Sidney Smith were reported, along with the accusation that a housemaid, Mary Wilson, had 'found the Princess and Sir Sidney in such an indecent situation', and had been sworn to secrecy about it. Others cited amorous behaviour with George Canning, Thomas Lawrence, Captain Thomas Manby and Lord Hood. One servant claimed that a visiting doctor to Montague House had told her 'the Princess was with child'. Others testified that 'she grew lusty, and appeared large behind' during 1802, but became thinner at the end of the year. Fanny Lloyd, the coffee room maid, also reported a laundry woman saying that linen from Montague House 'was marked with the appearance of a miscarriage or delivery'. The washerwoman later confirmed that she thought the signs of a miscarriage were apparent.[16]

But under oath Mary Wilson could not remember seeing the Princess having sex and testified that she did not notice Caroline change shape in 1802. Neither did she, when she made the Princess's bed, ever have any reason to suspect that two persons had slept in it. A page, Thomas Stikeman, told the commissioners that Caroline had not looked pregnant, with the caveat that 'from her shape it is difficult to judge when she is with child'. Another servant, John Sicard, 'never had any suspicion of the Princess acting improperly with Sir Sidney Smith or any other gentleman'. Charlotte Sander, a maid, said, 'I am sure the Princess was not pregnant. Being her dresser, I must have seen if she was.' Several servants testified that William Austin's mother, Sophia, had brought her baby to Montague House when he was four months old, and Sophia Austin, when summoned, also swore that 'I know the child which is now with the Princess of Wales. I am the mother of it.'[17]

Recklessness was central to Caroline's personality, as was the great pleasure she took in shocking people; and it was entirely in character that she should pretend to Lady Douglas that she was pregnant. There exists an anecdote about her youth that may or may not be true, but which fits neatly with the idea that Caroline saw faking pregnancy as an enjoyable ruse. When she was sixteen, it is reported, her mother forbade her from attending a great ball in Brunswick. On the day of the celebration a messenger arrived to tell the Duke and Duchess that they must return immediately to their daughter. They did so and found her in bed, screaming. Her mother asked what was wrong and Caroline replied: 'I am in labour, and entreat you, madam, to send for an *accoucheur* immediately.' When the *accoucheur* arrived, the Princess was said to have wiped the livid colouring from her face and jumped out of bed laughing, and saying, 'Now, madam, will you keep me another time from a ball?'[18]

In July 1806, the commissioners of the Delicate Investigation delivered their pronouncements and found that 'there is no foundation whatever for believing that the child now with the Princess is the child of her Royal Highness, or that she was delivered of any child in the year 1802'.[19] But she was, nevertheless, condemned for her loose conduct with men, particularly Captain Manby, and thus left with a stain on her character and still the vilified subject of a society scandal. According to the political activist William Cobbett, 'low and infamous whispers' about her conduct reached people in America.[20]

Fortunately for Caroline, Thomas Manby was an honourable man. According to his brother, George, the two men had been staying at the Spring Garden Coffee House in London when an anonymous letter arrived offering Thomas up to £40,000 'if he would give or furnish such information as would convict the Princess of Wales'. The man bearing the note was, according to the barmaid, Colonel John McMahon, George's servant and ally. She said he later returned for an answer, but there was none. Manby burned the note in disgust.[21]

Newspaper editors tried to get hold of the report of the Delicate Investigation, but failed to find out anything other than the general gist of its conclusions. They were not deterred, though, from proclaiming their views in the strongest terms. A writer to the *Morning Post* argued in a published letter that the witnesses against Caroline were in reality informers who deserved to die. The paper's editors acknowledged that she had been found guilty of a '*general impropriety of conduct*', but believed these to be mere '*trifling and harmless levities* from which NO WOMAN IN THE LAND IS FREE'. Even those women who have the advantage of a supportive family to succour them cannot '*pretend to be wholly free from trifling levities*, which wicked malice can exaggerate into matter of scandal', declared the editorial. So what chance did Caroline have, when surrounded 'with the worst of sycophants . . . who are prepared to seduce for the purpose of betraying'?[22]

A few disagreed. William Cobbett, in his popular *Political Register*, argued that Englishwomen as a whole would never stoop to 'trifling levities', and to encourage them to do so would be foolhardy. 'I am not *the first* and I shall not be *the last*,' would be the self-consoling remark of every girl 'whose "levities" in the long run, compel her to appear before a justice of the peace,' he wrote.[23] Cobbett's stance, in turn, was widely deplored as 'unmanly' in its betrayal of the Princess. Manliness and chivalry were held up as British traits, and were to be called into service on Caroline's behalf throughout her life.

For the Princess, the ordeal was distressing; not just because of the humiliation involved, but because her eminent inquisitors had refused her the basic standards of a common court and proceeded with a disregard for natural justice. She knew royal adultery to be a capital offence. In theory at least her life was in danger; yet she had not been given the chance to appear before the enquiry and defend herself. Furthermore, she had no chance of an appeal, as the report's findings were devoid of any legal framework.

After eleven years in England, the Princess of Wales became gripped by a desire to go home to Brunswick, and was dissuaded only by the fear that fleeing the country would be taken as a sign of her guilt. Lord Minto wrote, 'I am really grieved for her. Her treatment from the beginning has been afflicting and insulting; and the prospect, instead of brightening, is more gloomy and threatening than ever.'[24] This grim year deteriorated further when in November 1806 her father, aged seventy-one, died from a wound one month after leading his troops into battle against the French at Auerstadt. Brunswick fell to the French, and was no longer a place of safety for Caroline, real or psychological. She was trapped in Britain.

3
REGENCY

false friends draw near,
Then spies gather round, and malignants appear;
And cajole, wait, watch, insult, alarm and betray,
Till from home, and her daughter, they force her away.

The Queen's Matrimonial Ladder

I n November 1810 King George III, nearly blind and distraught at
the death of his youngest daughter, Amelia, slipped into madness.
The terrible condition that we now know as porphyria caused him
great pain, and he began to issue forth 'a sort of wailing, most horrible and heartrending to hear',[1] which eventually subsided leaving the
old man living in a dream world, conversing with the dead and forgetting the living. He was to spend the rest of his days in a twilight

existence at his Windsor apartments, poised between life and death and in the care of his doctors.

In February 1811 the Prince of Wales, by contrast full of fleshy, tangible engagement with the world, took over his father's role and became Prince Regent. The political mood of the country was uncertain, with threats of rebellion and revolution resurfacing. The government had been particularly shaken by riots in London following the imprisonment of the political reformer Sir Francis Burdett in the Tower of London for championing press freedom and protesting against government oppression. Burdett, thanks to superb stage management, had been arrested while listening to his son translating Magna Carta from Latin. Riots ensued, and tens of thousands of people turned up to 'Burdett and Liberty' meetings, suggesting that anti-government sentiment was coming from a wider section of the populace than the motley bunch of malcontents who generally made up a London mob.

The government was worried. But George demonstrated little interest in grass roots politics, and made 'frequent applications to the liquor chest' to stiffen his poor resolve to deal with political matters.[2] His father had, during the previous fifty-two years, presided over a gradual decline in the power of the monarchy, a trend which, thanks to George's character, was now accelerated. The monarch could no longer initiate new measures without the support of his ministers or, increasingly, without favourable public opinion. He could, if he wished, influence or obstruct. But the Prince Regent was not assiduous in either and his ministers were largely left to their own devices. For the sake of stability, he kept his father's Tory administration in power, which was an immense disappointment for the Whigs. George had, for decades, allied himself with Whig politicians, made friends with them and given the impression that he would bring the party to power when he had the chance. The Whigs never forgave him for letting them down.

The Prince Regent's boredom with politics was more than matched by his engagement with the artistic and intellectual life of the country. He proudly declared that his Regency would eclipse Napoleon's rule in splendour, and in June hosted a magnificent fete for 2,000 people at

Carlton House, ostensibly in honour of the exiled French royal family, who turned up in force, but in reality to celebrate the Regency and demonstrate his own majesty. George sat beneath an illuminated crown bearing the letters GR, and presided over a table adorned with a fountain that flowed into long silver-lined channels spreading out on either side of him. Goldfish swam in the silver streams, which had little riverbanks made of moss, and sprouting flowers.

High society was impressed by the opulence of the occasion, and the London masses were invited in to admire the scene in the following days. At one stage the crowds were so dense that ladies found themselves 'almost completely undressed, & their hair hanging about their shoulders'.[3] Others, predictably, were outraged that money could be spent so thoughtlessly while the country was exhausted by the war with the French and the poor were struggling to pay for bread. 'It is said that this entertainment will cost £120,000,' complained the poet Percy Bysshe Shelley. 'Nor will it be the last bauble which the nation must buy to amuse this overgrown bantling of Regency.'[4] In fact, it cost less. But that was hardly the point – George's festivities gave an impression of monstrous excess.

The Princess of Wales was not invited to the party, nor did she expect to be. Nevertheless, she encouraged her ladies to accept their invitations and sent them off in her own carriage, a gesture of remarkable good humour given that, for her, the Regency signalled yet more distress. The King was no longer a useful ally for her, and she had no influence at all at the Prince Regent's court. At the same time, society was deserting her parties for George's more splendid offerings while he, despite his good fortune, was no more magnanimous towards her. His loathing was unceasing, and he began to impose tight restrictions on Caroline's access to Princess Charlotte, who was now in her teens and living under her father's supervision next door to Carlton House. He also decreed that Charlotte must, on her few permitted visits to the Princess of Wales, never come into contact with any of her mother's friends.

Indeed, Charlotte's social life was, on George's insistence, restricted to the company of a few approved governesses and ladies.

This was thought necessary not just because Caroline's influence might be damaging, but also because Charlotte was starting to develop some of her mother's traits. She was a lively girl who favoured a way of talking which was colourful, straightforward, and sometimes bordered on vulgar. More alarmingly, she was independent, sometimes impetuous and deeply resentful of the severe restrictions placed upon her. She was also 'a young lady of more than ordinary personal attractions'. At least that was the opinion of one Captain Gronow, who had seen her at a ball and had been charmed by 'the rich bloom of youthful beauty' in her complexion, while 'her eyes were blue and very expressive'. The very sight of her, he said, had filled him with national pride.[5]

By 1813, when Charlotte was seventeen, Caroline had become highly distressed by the long separations from her daughter insisted upon by George – her dismay perhaps stemming from maternal emotion, perhaps from frustration at her husband's dominance. Early that year she wrote to her lady-in-waiting, Lady Charlotte Campbell:

> I fear you have thought me very unkind not to have written to you before this; but I have been so annoyed about my daughter, Princess Charlotte, I have not had the power to tink of anything else. She was very unwell for some days, and though I begged hard, the Regent and the old stony-hearted Queen would not let me see her. To tell you God's truth, I know not how long I shall be able to go on bearing all my sorrows . . .[6]

In reality she was attempting to assuage her sorrows by seeking out some sort of political power. As she saw it, she needed to acquire some bargaining strength in the face of her husband's unrelenting persecution.

Caroline's choice of a political ally was Henry Brougham, and she could hardly have chosen better. Brougham was a leading Whig politician, a brilliant lawyer and fiercely ambitious. It was his aim to become the leader of his party and, eventually, prime minister. In 1813 he was temporarily outside of Parliament, and while away from the centre of power was spending his time attacking the Tories, in print, and by taking up anti-government cases in the courts. He was to act as Caroline's advocate for the next eight years.

Brougham's intelligence and breadth of learning had long marked him out. As a child he had been a prodigy, learning to read at the age of two. At sixteen he had a paper on the properties of light published by the Royal Society, and he later claimed to have discovered the scientific basis for photography half a century before anyone else. In 1802 he became one of the founders of the oppositionist *Edinburgh Review*, which was to have political influence for the following twenty-five years, and thereafter he became a vital ally and close friend of William Wilberforce, aiding him in his campaign against the slave trade. The enthusiasm with which Henry Brougham threw himself at an enormous range of subjects drew derision from less manic contemporaries. The historian Thomas Macaulay described him as 'a kind of semi-Solomon' who half knew everything from the cedar to the hyssop.

Those who saw him in debate were impressed by his sheer force. A friend, Henry Cockburn, wrote that Brougham 'could abandon himself to his subject and blaze as if he had been declaiming against Cicero in the forum'. Francis Jeffrey, another friend, was struck by the 'ferocious eloquence in which he scorched and blasted and overthrew all those who dared to give him battle'.[7] The journalist William Hazlitt, with typical hauteur, described Brougham's 'one considerable advantage in debate'. 'He is overcome by no false modesty,' he wrote, and showed no deference to others. 'He is absorbed in the pursuit of truth as an abstract inquiry, he is led away by the headstrong and over-masterful activity of his own mind. He is borne along, almost involuntarily, and not impossibly against his better judgement, by the throng and restlessness of his ideas as by a crowd of people in motion.'[8]

Others were struck by his extraordinary energy. Lord Holland thought his vigour equalled 'the stock of nine ordinary men',[9] and William Wilberforce told him he would 'never conceive it is any reason why you may not do a twentieth thing that you have already nineteen others on your hands'.

As an advocate Brougham had made his name on the northern circuit representing anti-establishment protesters and supporters of a free press. He had championed the Luddites and was now taking up sedition cases and opposing a barrage of libel actions brought by the Tory government against its detractors.[10] In 1812 Brougham had caused a stir nationally by defending the brothers Leigh and John Hunt, who edited the *Examiner* magazine, and who campaigned for parliamentary reform and an end to corruption in public life. The brothers stood accused of libelling the Prince Regent. In February they had termed him 'the Prince of Whales',[11] a reference to his vast girth. The pro-government newspaper the *Morning Post* replied with a sycophantic tirade of praise for the Prince. 'You breathe eloquence,' the paper declared. 'You inspire the Graces, you are an Adonis of Loveliness'.[12] The Hunts could not resist responding, declaring that 'this Adonis of Loveliness was a corpulent gentleman of fifty . . . a violator of his word, a libertine over head and ears in debt and disgrace, a despiser of domestic ties [and] . . . a man who has just closed half a century without one single claim to the gratitude of his country or the respect of posterity'.[13]

The Hunts were found guilty and were imprisoned, but only after Brougham had 'fired for two hours very close and hard into the Prince',[14] knowing that his speech would be reported in all the newspapers and that the case would doubtless bring George more harm than good. Indeed, Brougham was almost as much of a press manager as he was a lawyer or politician. In the 1807 general election he had organised the Whigs' press campaign, acting on his own maxim that 'nothing should be lost from want of suggestion'. Lord Holland noted that in the course of ten days Brougham was able to fill 'every bookseller's shop with pamphlets, most London newspapers and all country ones without exception with paragraphs, and . . . a large portion of the boroughs throughout the kingdom with handbills'.[15] In fact, Brougham was an early believer in the force of public opinion, and the power of the press to influence it. Caroline appears to have agreed with him.

Brougham saw Caroline's cause as a vehicle with which to continue his attacks on George and on his political enemies in Parliament. He also seems to have calculated that when Charlotte became Queen, and Caroline Queen Mother, he would be chosen as their (or, technically, Charlotte's) prime minister. He was not attracted to Caroline personally, but later wrote that, 'I really felt . . . that the conduct of the Prince had been such from the beginning towards his wife, and his later treatment of both mother and daughter so outrageous, as made it a duty to take their part.' On her side, Caroline was suspicious of Brougham and his intellectualism and judged him to be a schemer rather than a true sympathiser. Their relationship, in practice, rested on their being of use to each other. Caroline, nevertheless, often confided in Brougham and once confessed to him that, despite her complaints, she was in fact enjoying her 'warfare with the royal family' and having fun 'teazing and worrying them'.[16]

He also befriended Princess Charlotte. In defiance of her father, the Princess had become an enthusiastic supporter of the Whigs. By now, to the annoyance of the Prince Regent, she had become immensely popular and was cheered whenever she was seen in public. Charlotte became fond of Brougham and was heavily influenced by him – a development that could only irritate George further. But the Princess's relationship with her Whig adviser was, unlike her mother's, based on a genuine mutual attraction. At one stage she commissioned a small model of him, and confessed to her confidante Miss Mercer Elphinstone, 'I really do think Brougham the most delightful comforting person that ever [lived] for always he comes out with a little consolation amidst all intrigue.'[17]

Brougham cooperated with his old friend the reformer MP Samuel Whitbread to lobby on Caroline's behalf inside the House of Commons. Whitbread began making speeches setting out her complaints against George, while Brougham considered how best to manage the rest of her campaign. At length, he advised her to write George a letter designed both to state her case and appeal to public sympathy. He warned her that such a letter would result in retaliation from George, then with her consent he set about drafting it.

The letter, dated 14 January 1813, was long, emotive and political,

and signed 'Your Royal Highness's most devoted and most affectionate Consort, Cousin and Subject, Caroline.'[18] It was sent to George
and when he refused to respond, leaked to the *Morning Chronicle*,
which published it in full on 10 February.

> There is a point beyond which a guiltless woman cannot with safety
> carry her forbearance . . . If her honour is invaded, the defence of her
> reputation is no longer a matter of choice; and it signifies not whether
> the attack be made openly, manfully, and directly – or by secret insin-
> uation, and by holding such conduct towards her as countenances the
> suspicions that malice can suggest. If these ought to be the feelings of
> every woman in England who is conscious that she deserves no
> reproach, your Royal Highness has so sound a judgement, and too nice
> a sense of honour, not to perceive, how much more justly they belong
> to the Mother of your Daughter – the Mother of her who is destined,
> I trust at a very distant period, to reign over the British Empire . . . I
> am at length compelled, either to abandon all regard for the two dear-
> est objects which I possess on earth, mine own honour, and my
> beloved Child, or to throw myself at the feet of your Royal Highness,
> the natural protector of both . . .

The letter railed at length against the Delicate Investigation. Only a
dishonoured woman, it suggested, would have been treated as heart-
lessly as Caroline had been. The slur was 'fatal to the mother's
reputation': 'Let me implore you to reflect on the situation in which I
am placed without the shadow of a charge against me, without even an
accuser, after an inquiry that led to my ample vindication, yet treated
as if I were still more culpable than the perjuries of my suborned tra-
ducers represented me, and held up to the world as a mother who may
not enjoy the society of her child.'

The letter was re-published in most of the nation's newspapers and
caused a furore. Jane Austen read it, possibly in the *Hampshire
Chronicle*, which carried it on 15 February. The following day she
wrote to her friend, Martha Lloyd:

I suppose all the world is sitting in Judgement upon the Princess of Wales's letter. Poor woman, I shall support her as long as I can, because she *is* a Woman and because I hate her Husband – but I can hardly forgive her for calling herself 'attached and affectionate' to a man whom she must detest – and the intimacy said to subsist between her and Lady Oxford is bad. I do not know what to do about it; but if I must give up the Princess, I am resolved at least always to think that she would have been respectable, if the Prince had behaved only tolerably by her at first.[19]

The newspapers became obsessed with the royal marriage. Penny broadsides were sold to the lower orders on the subject, and pictorial prints abounded. Charlotte became temporarily angry with Brougham, and felt that he 'was stooping very low' by allowing Caroline's letter to be 'bought for six pence in every shop'.[20] He had, she said, provided her mother with 'very bad advice'. And the scandal only deepened when, on 13 March 1813, it became clear that Brougham had been correct in his prediction that George would retaliate. On that day the *Morning Herald* published the leaked depositions made against Caroline during the Delicate Investigation in 1806, including all of Lady Douglas's most damaging allegations. Brougham quickly organised the leaking of the testimonies in Caroline's favour, and the newspapers exacerbated the war within the royal marriage by declaring themselves either for Caroline or for George. In early March *The Times*, for the first time in its history, tried to reverse a decline in circulation by making a strategic editorial change based on public opinion. The paper declared for Caroline and immediately sales rose. The *News* supported her from the day following publication of her letter and in four weeks its circulation shot up by 27 per cent.[21] Lady Melbourne claimed that the coverage was so shocking that it became the 'fashion amongst ladies to burn their newspapers that the servants may not read of such improprieties'.

George's private response to Caroline's letter was to rush off with the findings of the Delicate Investigation to a number of elevated persons including the members of the Privy Council and the country's archbishops. Was it not reasonable, he demanded to know from them, that Charlotte should be protected from such an abandoned woman as her mother? At the end of February the response came; the great and the good considered it entirely appropriate that the Princess of Wales's contact with Princess Charlotte should 'continue to be subject to regulation and restraint'. Charlotte's sympathy immediately went to her mother and the two corresponded in secret. On 2 March Charlotte wrote to Mercer Elphinstone about the situation:

> We are afraid of writing often, and when we do it is always by a servant & sent at night. She continues to write in spirits and to hope I continue so, as she assures me all will go well with energy and fortitude. Why should she not feel so when she is innocent and has been *declared* so? [by the Delicate Investigation] I know that they are on *the watch* for *any letters* they can get hold of, *to her* or *from her*, and that they wish to institute a new investigation . . . and to criminate her if possible.

Charlotte said that her health was suffering 'from the *worries* and anxiety which is constant and unabated at present; so that my apitite and sleep are gone and I suffer much from headaches'.[22]

The episode ensured that Caroline was greeted ecstatically whenever she went out amongst the public, which had now become a source of considerable power for her. Brougham wrote that 'it is difficult to describe the sensation which the Report of the Secret Tribunal made wherever a knowledge of its contents reached'.[23] The politician James Mackintosh wrote 'all the world is with her, except the people of fashion at the west end of town'.[24] Public bodies started to write her letters of support, in the form of Addresses. Addresses were fast becoming a form of political expression for those who did not have a vote, and Caroline's responses were, similarly, of political significance. Brougham wrote many of these for her, expressing the Princess's faith in the wisdom of the British people, and her appreciation of their strong sense of justice – by implication as an alternative source of power to the King. There was no acknowledgement, though, that such sentiments expressed by a member of the royal family hinted at disloyalty of such great measure that it bordered on treason.

Towards the end of 1813 the rumpus subsided and another royal story gained the ascendant. On 12 December, at the wish of her father, Charlotte accepted a proposal of marriage from the Prince of Orange. But when the Princess discovered that her married life would entail going 'backwards and forwards constantly' between England and Holland, she became distressed, breaking into a 'violent fit of sobs and hysterical tears'. Brougham was also unhappy about the turn of events. He wanted Charlotte to remain in England in order that he could nurture his own personal and political relationship with her. In March 1814 he drafted letters for the Princess which insisted that she must never be forced to go overseas without her consent, and need not go at all in the early part of the marriage. In June, the concession was granted and crisis was, for the moment, averted.

That month London became the scene of magnificent festivities to celebrate the apparent end to the long war with France and the allied victory over Napoleon Bonaparte. Foreign heads of state, including the Prince of Orange, arrived in the capital for the entertainments and for a flurry of behind the scenes diplomatic activity ahead of the Congress of Vienna. This great convention of foreign ministers and kings would, it was hoped, redraw the boundaries of those countries of Europe that had been invaded by France and would put an end to French expansionism. In this context, the engagement of Charlotte to the Prince of Orange was seen as a triumph for the British Foreign Secretary, Lord Castlereagh, who wished to unite a new Kingdom of the Netherlands with Great Britain.

But the Grand Duchess Catherine of Russia, sister of Tsar Alexander I, was in town with political strategies of her own – and it did not suit Russia's interests that England and Holland should be so closely connected. Indeed, it was rumoured in society that Catherine's primary purpose in London was to disrupt the royal marriage plans. Lady Amelia Murray observed the Grand Duchess making a determined attempt to befriend Mercer Elphinstone with a view to influencing Charlotte. Catherine also, according to Lady Amelia, held a grand dinner at which she plied the Prince of Orange with champagne, knowing that he was to waltz in public with Charlotte later that evening. 'He was made tipsy,' she said, 'and of course the Princess was disgusted.'[25]

Catherine was a short, odd-looking woman with a puggish face. While in London she was presented to the Prince Regent, who muttered to Countess Lieven, the wife of the Russian ambassador, 'Your Grand Duchess is not good-looking.' 'Your Prince,' remarked the Grand Duchess to Dorothea Lieven a moment later, 'is ill-bred.' The atmosphere between George and Catherine became frostier still when the Grand Duchess announced that she intended to visit Caroline. Count Lieven threatened to resign if she did so, and Catherine backed down. As a consolation she befriended Charlotte, and in her letters to the Tsar praised the Princess's 'great intelligent eyes of pale blue', and the 'wit and doggedness in her nature'. She also applauded Charlotte's 'searching reasoning power, and manners so odd that they take your breath away . . . she looks like a boy, or rather like a young rascal, dressed as a girl'.[26]

On getting to know Charlotte, Catherine remained convinced of the undesirability of her engagement. It was rumoured that Charlotte felt more for the Duke of Gloucester than she did for her future husband, allowing the Duke of Cumberland to make the droll observation that, 'I was very much afraid that she would prefer the cheese to the orange.'[27] Charlotte denied the gossip, but nevertheless became increasingly doubtful about her marriage. She was also indignant at being kept away from the victory celebrations, while her fiancé attended them with gusto, and she was revolted when he again turned up to see her, drunk.

Then, at a dinner in honour of the Grand Duchess at Carlton House, Catherine's behaviour worsened. On arrival she insisted that the band should be made to leave, since music made her vomit. George tried to improve the mood by flattering her, but she was not impressed and later complained that she found him 'a man visibly used up by dissipation and disgusting rather. His much boasted affability is the most licentious, I may even say obscene, strain I have ever listened to.' The dinner deteriorated further when the Grand Duchess began making complaints about the strict discipline and seclusion that George imposed on Charlotte. He answered: 'When she is married, madam, she will do as her husband pleases; for the present she does as I wish.' The Duchess smiled as she trumped him: 'Your Highness is right. Between wife and husband there can be only one will.' 'From that evening,' wrote Countess Lieven, 'she and the Regent hated each other mutually, and the feeling remained to the end.'[28]

Tsar Alexander, the King of Prussia and Marshal Blucher then arrived in England. London was illuminated and crowds paraded the streets to celebrate the end to twenty years of war. In July, a service of thanksgiving took place at St Paul's Cathedral, attended by George, the Duke of Wellington, Blucher, royal dukes, peers and ministers of state, followed by a splendid fete held at Carlton House.

Caroline was incensed at being excluded from the celebrations and did what she could to attract the attention of the grand visitors, but with little success. Samuel Whitbread and Henry Brougham worked on her behalf, writing letters of protest at her exclusion to George's mother, Queen Charlotte, to George and the Speaker of the House of Commons, not forgetting to send copies to all the newspapers. Brougham also encouraged Caroline to attend the opera as often as possible, where she was greeted with cheers and applause. Of the royal guests, though, only the Tsar requested to see her, and George, through the Prime Minister, Lord Liverpool, told him that no obstacle would be placed in his way. In the end, though, Alexander backed out, preferring diplomatic good behaviour over the satisfaction of his curiosity. 'The treatment of the Princess has excited almost universal disgust,' wrote Lady Jerningham on 3 June, 'and I am told she was last night received at Covent Garden with unusual applause and "three hearty cheers for an *injured woman!*"'[29]

Caroline was mortified by her public humiliation and began, once more, to talk of leaving England to live on the continent of Europe. Brougham was deeply shocked. Caroline had proved to be an excellent means of stirring up popular sentiment against George and the government, and he did not wish to lose her. Worse still, he feared that the Princess of Wales would, when free of English constraints, indulge in behaviour so shameless that George would find it easier to divorce her. This might mean a second marriage and the possibility of Charlotte's claim to the throne being superseded by a male heir.

He put this scenario to Charlotte, who was quickly convinced that if she refused to marry the Prince of Orange and go to Holland, then her mother would be less likely to leave England. Charlotte's lady-in-waiting, Lady Charlotte Lindsay, wrote that: '[She] felt that both she and her mother should remain in England, and support and protect each other. In all the popular applause she has lately received, her name has always been coupled with her mother's, which seems to have had a great effect upon her.'[30]

To the dismay of George, Castlereagh and the rest of the government, Charlotte broke off the engagement, and wrote to the Prince of Orange explaining that she had become convinced that her interest was 'materially connected' with that of her mother, concluding that 'my residence out of this kingdom would be equally prejudicial to her welfare as to my own'.

The Whig diarist Thomas Creevey saw the letter and wrote to his wife: 'By God! It is capital. And now what do you suppose has produced this sudden attachment to her mother? It arises from the profound resources of old Brougham and is, in truth, one of the most brilliant movements in his campaign.'[31]

But Henry Brougham had not reckoned on the strength of Caroline's desire to escape. Against his advice, she bargained with Lord Castlereagh, promising to go overseas and stay away from Great Britain in return for an annual payment of £50,000. Samuel Whitbread heard of her action and told Brougham, whose 'convulsions in consequence were very strong'. Charlotte Lindsay, a close friend of Brougham's, burst into tears.[32]

Princess Charlotte was, unsurprisingly, dismayed by her mother's decision. At home in Warwick House during the following days, she was in a miserable mood when an order came from George that her chief attendants were to be taken away and replaced with others more to her father's liking. The Princess, maddened by the 'spirit of petty tyranny' around her, decided to bolt. On impulse she rushed from the house, ran across Cockspur Street, flung herself into the first hackney carriage she could find and drove to her mother's London residence in Connaught Place. When Charlotte arrived, though, she found that the Princess of Wales was not there, but at Blackheath. Caroline was immediately summoned, as were Brougham and Mercer Elphinstone.

The group arrived, along with Lady Charlotte Lindsay, and Charlotte took Brougham by the hands, saying, 'I have just run off.' She announced that her fixed resolution was to leave her father's house and to live in future with her mother. Brougham thought that she 'was in high spirits, seeming to enjoy herself like a bird set loose from its cage'. He explained that under the law her father, the Prince Regent, had absolute power to determine where she should live and told her that she must return to him. Charlotte was 'affected beyond description' by his opinion. 'I have told many a client he was going to be convicted,' Brougham wrote later, 'but I never saw anything like her *stupefaction*.'[33]

Caroline and Lady Charlotte Lindsay also pleaded with the Princess to return home, but she was resolute. George's brother, the Duke of Sussex, was sent for to help reason with her, as he had always been sympathetic to Charlotte's plight. Meanwhile, on discovering that the Princess was missing, the Regent's allies were also dispatched, the first to arrive being the Lord Chancellor, Eldon, followed by the Duke of York.

Brougham wrote in his memoirs that after a while Charlotte turned on him, and accused him of deserting her. He took her to the window, pointed to the park below, and explained that if she stayed, a great crowd would gather there in the morning to express their support for her, to be followed by troops who would be summoned to quell all resistance to the law of the land 'with the certain effusion of blood'. 'This consideration,' wrote Brougham, '. . . weighed upon her mind and induced her to return home.' In the early hours of the morning she left the house, climbed into a royal coach that was waiting outside and returned home to Warwick House accompanied by the Duke of York and her governess.[34]

Despite Charlotte's distress, Caroline remained determined to leave the country. Brougham made one last attempt to dissuade her, writing to her from York:

Depend upon it, Madam, that there are many persons who now begin to see a chance of divorcing your Royal Highness from the Prince . . . As long as you remain in this country I will answer for it that no plot can succeed against you. But if you are living abroad and surrounded by base spies and tools who will be always planted about you, ready to invent and to swear as they may be directed, who can pretend to say what may happen.[35]

But Caroline would not change her mind, and Charlotte was distraught. Mercer Elphinstone wrote on her behalf to Lady Charlotte Lindsay, who was now with Caroline: 'Let me entreat you to use every exertion of your influence for Princess Charlotte's sake, to induce the Princess not to make a long absence, which would be so ruinous, both to the interest of mother and daughter.'[36]

But Charlotte Lindsay was no more successful than Brougham. In the midsummer of 1814 Caroline made her preparations for exile, one of which was to send a message to the Prime Minister, Lord Liverpool, through her old friend George Canning. She would return to England immediately, she threatened, if any attempt at divorce were made while she was overseas. She would not countenance George being free to marry again or the prospect of interference in Charlotte's succession to the throne. Liverpool thought her letter fanciful and told Canning that he had read it 'with no little amusement'.

On 8 August 1814, Caroline left behind the eighteen-year-old Charlotte, and set sail from Lancing on the *Jason*. An observer of the scene, with more regard for sentiment than accuracy perhaps, reported that as she was leaving 'she condescendingly kissed her hands to the weeping females who stood on the water's edge, offering up many a prayer to heaven for her safety, and many a heart-felt sigh for her sufferings',[37] and according to other reports she was seen to shed a tear. But it is evident from her letters and conversations at the time that Caroline, now forty-six, was in fact in high spirits and optimistic about her continental adventure. She had selected a suite entirely to her liking, including Lady Charlotte Lindsay and Lady Elisabeth Forbes. Two vice-chamberlains, Sir William Gell and the Hon. Keppel Craven, were to be appointed – the former a writer on the antiquities of Greece, and the latter his close friend. Her old beau, Captain Hesse, was to be the Princess's equerry, Mr John Sicard her major-domo, and Mr John Hieronymus her messenger. She had also appointed a physician, Dr Henry Holland, to travel with her, along with her precious adopted boy, William Austin. And, in theory at least, she had plenty of money to finance her travels, although her allowance had been bargained down to £35,000 a year from the originally agreed £50,000. George was doubtless equally hopeful that Caroline's exile would prove a happy and thereby a long one. On hearing of her intended departure, he was rumoured to have raised a toast: 'To the Princess of Wales's damnation and may she never return to England.'

Once her mother left England Charlotte's life, contrary to her expectations, started to improve. In May 1816 she married Prince Leopold of Saxe-Coburg, a suave, charming but poor man with whom she was actually in love, and the couple took up residence at Claremont House in Surrey, an idyllic airy house which overlooked a Capability Brown landscape. 'We lead a very quiet and retired life here,' wrote Leopold, 'but a very, *very* happy one.'[38] He and Charlotte spent their time taking walks, driving out in the country, reading to each other and relaxing in each other's company. And Leopold's gentle and pedantic character proved a good counterbalance to Charlotte's strident impetuosity. One visitor to Claremont declared that the house was 'full of harmony, peace and love'.

During this time the Princess was on unusually agreeable terms with her father, visiting him at Brighton and Carlton House and confiding to her doctor that the Prince had, of late, been most 'affectionate and tender' towards her. The only tension in the atmosphere came from Charlotte's difficulty in maintaining a pregnancy. In the first year of marriage she suffered two miscarriages, before her third pregnancy, which reached full term – and this was a period during which she sometimes missed her mother greatly. At first the Princess had complied with instructions from the court that she should break off all contact with Caroline, but she could not hold out. She was under no illusions as to her mother's failings, but she refused to see her as the monster that George portrayed. Expressing a similar view to that of Jane Austen, Charlotte wrote that 'my mother was bad, but she would not have become as bad as she was if my father had not been infinitely worse'. On 10 October 1817, heavily pregnant and suffering from severe mood swings, she disobeyed orders and wrote to Caroline (at least, she may have done – there are some doubts about the authenticity of the letter):

> Why is not my mother allowed to pour cheerfulness into the sinking heart of her inexperienced and trembling child? . . . I have but one mother and no variation of place or circumstance can remove her from my mind . . . Should it be the pleasure of Providence that I servive the hour of approaching danger, I may at some future period be endued with power to restore you to that situation you were formed to embellish. But if an all wise decree should summon me from this sphere of anxious apprehension, not for myself but for my mother a pang of terror shoots across my bewilder'd brain . . .[39]

On 3 November Charlotte took a walk in the gardens of Claremont. As she returned to the house with Prince Leopold, she felt her first labour pains. She threw her bonnet and cloak on to a chair, dashed to her bedroom and Sir Richard Croft, London's most fashionable *accoucheur*, was summoned. A painful labour began, which was to last fifty hours. Sir Richard was concerned by its length and consulted his colleague Dr Sims, but together the doctors agreed not to intervene with the instruments that they had prepared for emergencies. Charlotte bore her ordeal heroically, sticking to her resolution neither to 'bawl nor shriek'. Prince Leopold ran back and forth between his own bedchamber and Charlotte's during the night, and at nine o'clock in the evening of 5 November, the birth took place. But the baby, 'a beautiful fine boy . . . very large', was stillborn.[40]

Half an hour after the birth, Charlotte began to haemorrhage. Then at midnight she became sick and complained of a singing noise in her head. Croft gave her a camphor mixture, but she brought it up. A little later he gave her twenty drops of laudanum in wine and water. At about a quarter to one she complained of a great uneasiness in her chest and difficulty breathing. Her pulse became fast, irregular and feeble, and she was in terrible pain, unable to remain a single moment in the same posture. Opiates and other medicines were given but she continued in this alarming state and, at two thirty in the morning of 6 November 'with a gentle sigh, she expired'. The Princess was two months short of her twenty-second birthday.[41]

Prince Leopold was stricken with unbearable grief. He forbade anyone from touching Charlotte's belongings, insisted that her bonnet and cloak remain on the chair in the hallway and that her watch not be moved from the mantelpiece. He wrote to the Prince Regent to tell him of the awful events and then retired to his bed-chamber. On receiving the news that his daughter was dead, the Prince Regent 'struck his forehead violently with both hands, and fell forward into the arms of the Duke of York' and he remained in pain and distressed for some time. 'All his thoughts and conversation turn upon the late sad event,' reported the diarist John Croker on 14 November. 'He never stirs out of his room, and goes to bed some-times at eight or nine o'clock, wearied out, and yet not composed enough for rest.'[42]

The news of the Princess's death reached the public at noon on 6 November, in a special issue of the *London Gazette*. The following morning the papers were published with heavy black borders, and along with the grim news they carried 'letters written from Claremont' containing 'painfully interesting details' of the Princess's demise. The public debate quickly became emotional, full of accusations of negligence on the part of the doctors, and of a cover-up. The *Sun* newspaper carried a letter 'On the necessity of a public inquiry into the cause of the death of the Princess Charlotte and her infant', and controversial reports of the cause of death soon followed in the leading London medical journals.[43]

On the streets, said Countess Lieven, people of every class were in tears, 'the churches were full at all hours, the shops shut for a fortnight and everyone from the highest to the lowest, in a state of despair which it is impossible to describe'.[44] Brougham wrote that 'it is difficult for persons not living at the time to believe how universal and how genuine those feelings were. It really was as if every household throughout Great Britain had lost a favourite child.'[45]

There followed a deluge of publications on the subject, aimed at every class of person. William Hone, a publisher of popular prints and pamphlets, released the *Authentic Memoirs of the Life of Charlotte* for sixpence, as well as the 'memoirs' of Prince Leopold. The *Authentic Particulars of the Death of the Princess Charlotte and her Infant* ran to at least five editions, and multiple printings of Hone's edition of the Princess's funeral and interment were also sold, along with a pull-out illustration of the funeral procession. Clergymen published their sermons on the Princess's death, eulogies were printed in their thousands and sold at a penny a time and an untold number of poems celebrating Charlotte as a saintly mother, as a Madonna and as England's Rose were sold. She became 'the Rose of England, nipped in the bloom', 'the fairest blossom of our isle' and 'a darling of virtue' adored for her 'moral loveliness'.[46]

From birth, Charlotte had been portrayed in the press and prints as the perfect result of a disastrous union – her private personality a pale, but infinitely more complex, shadow of her public image. Now, the grieving nation believed that it had known her well and had truly lost a loved one. The pamphleteer Charles Phillips felt able to write: 'Her youth – her beauty – her situation – the noble independence of her conduct – her disinterested selection of the man she loved – the simple unostentatious seclusion in which she lived – the pattern of domestic affection she displayed – her religious habits . . . these were qualities which it requires no rank to illustrate, and betrays no servility to almost adore.'[47] 'Never was a whole nation plunged in such deep and universal grief,' wrote Harriet Martineau many years later. 'From the highest to the lowest, this death was felt as a calamity that demanded the intense sorrow of domestic misfortune.'[48]

Letters and diaries from the period demonstrate the same over-whelming sense of personal misery experienced by every type of person. Jane Penrose of Fledborough in Nottinghamshire, the wife of a clergyman (and grandmother of Matthew Arnold) wrote: 'I believe there was never so general lamentation and there appears to be a universal gloom throughout the land. Everyone seems to mourn for her as a friend or relative . . . Mr Parry, tutor at the Duke of Portland's was here the other day, and he said he believed the least regret was felt amongst the aristocrats, because she was so extremely popular with the mass of the people.'[49]

And people remembered where they were when they heard the news. Mrs Penrose reports of a relative: 'One evening her maid came home and said to her "the ginger cost so much and the tea so much and the Princess is dead, ma'am."'[50]

There were dissenters from the woeful outpourings of the majority, but they were few. In private the Duke of Wellington thought Charlotte's death was a blessing to the country on the grounds that she 'would have turned out quite as ill as her mother',[51] and Lord Holland professed that 'little had appeared in this young lady to justify the inordinate grief at her death'.[52] The poet Percy Bysshe Shelley was practically a lone voice when, under the pseudonym the Hermit of Marlow, he published his misgivings at the public outpourings. He reminded readers that Charlotte was, in essence, an ordinary woman, without profound learning, who had 'accomplished nothing, and aspired to nothing and could understand nothing respecting those great political questions which involve the happiness of those over whom she was destined to rule'.[53]

The death of Charlotte in 1817 changed everything. George's descendants would not now inherit the throne of Great Britain, which, instead, would in time be passed on to Victoria, the daughter of the Duke and Duchess of Kent and niece of Prince Leopold. George, though torn apart by his personal loss, appears not to have minded much that future generations of monarchs would not be his direct descendants. And the death of his daughter had, for him, one positive consequence – he was now relieved of the bond of parenthood that he, technically at least, shared with Caroline. She could now be dismissed from his life entirely.

The Princess of Wales, meanwhile, no longer carried the status of a future Queen Mother. Politically speaking, she was deprived of her future. In the public mind she became fixed as a victim of fate, her sufferings now more terrible than ever.

4

TRAVELS

On searching for precedents, much to their dread,
They found that they couldn't well cut off her head;
And the 'House of Incurables' raised a 'Report'
She was not a fit person to live in *his* Court.

The Queen's Matrimonial Ladder

Three years before the death of Charlotte, Caroline had left England in the expectation of a more carefree life in Europe. She decided first to head for Brunswick, which, after the defeat of the French, had been restored to her family, and arrived at the province in August 1814 in high spirits. Her doctor, Henry Holland, travelled with her, and recorded in his memoirs that the Princess's upbeat mood was out of place with the 'grave decorum' of the formal little German court. It also jarred with the air of melancholy and 'grave simplicity' of her brother Frederick William, who was now Duke.[1] Frederick's sobriety was entirely appropriate, given the violent political upheaval that had befallen Brunswick, but was not amenable to Caroline, who saw her travels as a blessed release from the miseries of England, and a chance to be true to her exuberant self. She wished to be adventurous. So, after a fortnight, she said goodbye to her brother for the last time and departed. She had decided that Italy might be more to her taste, and journeyed south.

Italy at this time, and particularly Rome, was the destination of choice for European princes, soldiers made royal by conquest and displaced aristocrats. They were all waiting for the decisions of the Congress of Vienna, which was to begin later in the year. A new balance of power was to be created; and royal contenders were to be granted, or restored to, the courts of Europe. Caroline's amiable companion, Dr Holland, was intrigued by the great aristocratic names all around. When he was not indulging his favourite scientific pursuits – visiting the local volcanists, craniologists and geologists – he observed the celebrities. Charles IV of Spain was in Italy, he noted in his memoirs, as was the Queen of Spain and the Infante Don Paolo. A princess of Sardinia, a prince of Saxe-Gotha, and Louis the former King of Holland were also now in Italy, along with those persons from Napoleon's regime who had been able to cling on to claims for land as the French army was defeated.

The latter group appears to have attracted Caroline most. Like her, they were challengers to established, traditional monarchs and, like her, they did not respect the old order. But her reasoning would have been based on impulse not intellect, and it is most likely that she simply found Napoleon Bonaparte, and his connections, highly romantic. When she travelled through Berne she came across Napoleon's wife, the Empress Marie Louise, and befriended her. Long visits were exchanged. On one evening the Empress sang Italian and German songs, including Ferrari's 'L'Innamorata', and on another occasion the two ladies sang duets together. They got on so well that Caroline installed herself in the next-door suite to her new friend at a small

Swiss inn.[2] It is not known whether they discussed Marie Louise's exiled husband.

The Princess of Wales also travelled through Lausanne, where she appears to have been particularly informal. Hearing that a little ball was taking place at a house opposite the Golden Lion inn, she asked for an invitation. 'After dancing with everybody and anybody,' one witness observed, 'she finished up by dancing a Savoyard dance called a fricassée with a nobody.' A lady present was reported to be so distressed by the Princess of Wales's unfettered gaiety that she wept and declared the honour of England to be compromised.[3] Not long afterwards, Lady Bury claimed to have seen her at a party in Geneva 'dressed, *en Venus*, or rather not dressed further than the waist'.[4]

By the end of October 1814, she had arrived in Rome, where her new *joie de vivre* was noticed at a great ball held in her honour. Here she danced with 'indescribable abandon', wearing an unusual sheath dress, fastened beneath the bosom and 'without the shadow of a corset'. The garment had no sleeves, and so exposed her arms, of which she was very proud. Moreover, 'a shawl floating in the air did not succeed in making the costume decent even to the eyes of the Roman ladies, who were themselves not particularly scrupulous in the matter of dress'.

It was in this outfit, and in this flamboyantly carefree mood, that Caroline met and was attracted to another guest. Lucien Bonaparte was the excitable and volatile younger brother of Napoleon. He had recently been created an Italian prince by the newly restored Pope, assuming the title of Prince of Canino. He also possessed a palace filled with works of art, which he made open to Caroline and her suite; and he hosted a ball and concert for her which was 'magnificent in the assemblage of the Roman nobility there, including seven or eight Cardinals'. 'We saw much of the members of the Bonaparte family then at Rome,' wrote Henry Holland. Caroline was, at last, enjoying the lifestyle that she had always felt should, by rights, be hers.[5]

At this time Lucien Bonaparte was in contact with his brother on Elba. The two men had been estranged for years, but now messages were being sent secretly from Rome to Elba, and a reconciliation was soon achieved. Lucien, despite his new royal status, saw the Congress of Vienna as establishing a coalition of kings of the old order which would subject France to a return of tyranny. He met the agents of Napoleon in Rome, along with those of Joachim Murat, one of Napoleon's most able generals and now King of Naples, to discuss the best means of France and Italy rising up to fight for liberty – a plan which required the escape of Napoleon from Elba.

Caroline may or may not have been aware that something was up. Either way, her inclination was to travel next to Naples, and into the company of Joachim Murat, hero of Marengo, Austerlitz and the Spanish campaign; veteran of the great retreat from Moscow, and husband of Napoleon's youngest sister, Caroline Bonaparte. Napoleon, on Elba, is reported to have described Murat as the most brilliant man he had ever seen in battle, and considered it 'a really superb sight to see him fighting at the head of the cavalry'.[6] For the Princess of Wales, the King of Naples was an impossibly exciting figure. Dr Holland describes him as a tall and masculine person, with handsome features which exuded good nature and 'a rude energy and consciousness of physical power'. His black curly hair tumbled over his shoulders, and he wore a hat which was 'gorgeous with plumes'.[7] He was also a man of strong passions, a spirited child of the revolution, and was splendidly courageous. Back in 1796 he had so distinguished himself in battle that he was given the honour of carrying captured flags back into Paris.

Joachim Murat, however, had many detractors. He was considered shifty and unreliable in negotiations, and capable of betraying two sides of a conflict at once in pursuit of his own ambition. The Tsar stated bluntly what many thought: 'He is a *canaille* who has betrayed us all.'[8] In recent times, Murat had defected from Napoleon to the allies in an effort to hold on to Naples and secure further possessions in Italy. But now, like Lucien Bonaparte, he was scheming in favour of France and Italy, and against Austria and Great Britain. He, too, was in contact Napoleon, using a network of spies to send and receive messages. Like Caroline, Murat was emotional and determined, but no intellectual.

The Murats showed the Princess great hospitality, inviting her to the opera and to their frequent balls and masquerades, where she joined them in the English country dances which had lately come into fashion. The Princess was delighted by the Murats, and on 15 December wrote to Lady Charlotte Lindsay: 'The King and Queen are both very clever, and very good-natured indeed to me, and very fond of my society. I live entirely with them, and go to dinner alone with them constantly.'[9]

Caroline told Mr Moses Hoper, whom she had left in charge of her financial affairs in London, that she believed the society in Naples to be better than that at Paris. And, thanks to the reasonable cost of living, she considered that, 'I shall make a much greater figure here than the Queen of England in London.'[10] She was delighted to be able to buy three fine gowns, one in satin and two in velvet, for a mere twenty pounds.

Her interest in culture was weaker than her appetite for entertainments, but she did visit Pompeii, and also ascended Vesuvius in the company of young Dr Holland. They witnessed a 'sudden explosion of flame' from the volcano and burning stones were shot into the air. The doctor perceived that this was 'a pleasurable excitement to one of her temperament, always courting rather than shunning bold and hazardous chances, whether of personal or political danger'. His impression of the Princess was, in fact, remarkably similar to that of Malmesbury twenty years earlier. Dr Holland writes: 'There was a strange sort of irrational bravery in the character of . . . [Princess] Caroline, leading her to disregard all common precautions . . . even where personal risk and suffering were concerned. She had certain talents and quick perceptions, as well as some really generous affections.'[11] He regretted that these virtues had not been nurtured by a good education and happier marriage.

Britain's Foreign Secretary, Lord Castlereagh, was somewhat shocked by Caroline's behaviour, which was a severe embarrassment to Britain. He was in negotiation with European leaders, in particular with Prince Metternich in Austria, about the future of Naples. He did not trust Joachim Murat, and was sensitive to widespread demands that he be removed from the throne in favour of a more dependable man. The Prime Minister, Lord Liverpool, was equally suspicious of Murat, having learned in December that he 'is active and on the move',[12] and equally angry at Caroline's decision to court him. He had written to her back in September, advising that she live anywhere in Italy other than Naples, given that England and Naples were not at peace, only an armistice existing between them.

The Duke of Wellington, then ambassador in Paris, considered Murat's power in Naples so serious that he wrote to Liverpool proposing a British military campaign to topple him. 'If he [Murat] were gone,' Wellington argued, 'Buonaparte in Elba would not be an object of great dread.'[13] These were difficult days for Liverpool, who was highly conscious of 'the combustible state of the interior of France'. If war were renewed, he warned Lord Castlereagh, 'it would very probably plunge Europe again in all the horrors from which we have had the credit of extricating it'.[14]

Like others in the government, it seemed, Castlereagh had been so keen to see Caroline leave England that he had given little thought to how she might behave once she had her freedom. But when she ventured beyond Brunswick, he did, at least, ensure that he secured intelligence on her activities, lest they threaten national security. In advance of the Congress of Vienna, the continent was awash with espionage. The Germans, Austrians, British, French and Russians were all spying on each other – and information on Caroline was scooped up along with everything else. Cardinal Consalvi in Rome passed reports on the Princess's conduct along to Castlereagh, while Metternich siphoned-off Caroline intelligence to Castlereagh's brother Lord Stewart, who was the British Ambassador in Vienna.

George, also, ordered his spies to follow Caroline, less for political reasons than to furnish him with evidence that might secure a divorce. To circumvent his British ministers, George, as Regent of Hanover, asked his Hanoverian minister in London, Count Ernst von Munster, to appoint a man to spy in Italy primarily on the behaviour of the Princess of Wales, but also on the seditious elements in the region. Munster approached a former Hanoverian chamberlain, Baron Friedrich Ompteda, a conscientious man who was most eager to please his political masters, and told him 'to approach as near as he can to the Princess and write an exact account of her conduct'.[15] Munster stressed that 'if that conduct is not as it ought to be, it is extremely important to obtain sufficient proofs to legitimate the fact'. Ompteda was to report to Munster, and Munster was to report to George. Nobody in the British government was to know about the intelligence with one exception, Lord Castlereagh.

With the dedication of a municipal policeman, Ompteda followed Caroline to Naples and infiltrated his way into her company. The Princess was aware of intelligence activity all around, and wrote to Lady Charlotte Campbell saying, 'Believe me, Naples is currently crawling with spies', but she did not suspect that Ompteda was, in her case, the principal offender.[16] On his part, Ompteda filed long reports back to Munster, suggesting that Murat 'was raped by the Princess' on the grounds that 'it is impossible to find another word to describe the excess of her extravagance'.[17] But he was soon to be on the trail of a larger story, suspecting that Caroline had been having an affair with her friend Captain Hesse and had now ditched him in favour of her Italian courier, one Bartolomeo Pergami. Lord Sligo, also in Naples, engaged in a little freelance spying of his own, and sent back to London a report to be passed on to George and Castlereagh. He, like Ompteda, thought Hesse had been dropped and at first wrote, 'I don't know who is rogering the Princess now.' This, however, was soon updated with a report that Pergami was very much favoured within Caroline's establishment. 'In short,' he wrote, 'I think it very likely that he does the job for her.'[18]

Pergami was a soldier, and had fought in the recent wars on the side of the French. He was six foot three with a fine masculine physique, a mass of curly black hair and a luxurious dangling moustache. In appearance he was not dissimilar to Joachim Murat, although at thirty he was far younger and sixteen years Caroline's junior. Unlike Murat, he had no huge reputation, but he was not without an air of soldierly romance, and it was rumoured that he had once killed a senior officer in a duel.[19] According to one report he had first met Caroline in Milan, when he presented himself at her hotel, dressed in the uniform of the

Italian Hussars and bearing a letter of introduction. Nobody was around in the lobby, so the elegant soldier ventured inside, where, in the saloon, he discovered a woman struggling to disentangle her long dress from a piece of furniture. He bent down, skilfully released the dress, stood up again and politely asked to be directed to the Princess. 'I am the Princess,' replied Caroline, whereupon Pergami went down on one knee to present his letter of introduction. He was hired, pretty much, on the spot.[20]

At the start of 1815 Caroline, in Naples, began to retreat from the company of the Murats and spend more time at home in the company of Pergami, whose job included waiting on her at table. Ompteda painted watercolours of him to send to Munster and thence to George, and in his reports described Pergami as 'a sort of Apollo, of a superb and commanding appearance . . . his physical beauty attracts all eyes', and it is indisputable that at this time Pergami was Caroline's favourite, and the recipient of her constant attention.[21] It was a disappointment to the assiduous spy, however, when he heard a report that as a consequence of war injuries Pergami was 'wholly deprived of the means of satisfying a woman'. Ompteda was anxious to confirm the fact and promised Munster that he would try to make 'an ocular inspection'. In any case, he was certain that London would be happy with his report that Caroline had become the talk of Naples. 'Her unguarded conduct, especially towards men, exposes her to scandalous suspicions,' he wrote, '. . . in a town where chastity has never had much of a ministry.'[22]

It did not help Caroline's reputation that the most important members of her household were quitting. William Gell and Keppel Craven were both starting to find Caroline's social extravagance trying and had other travel plans, while a lady-in-waiting, Lady Elisabeth Forbes, had also decided to leave. Dr Holland remained and Lady Charlotte Lindsay was to arrive soon, but only for a temporary visit. Caroline was left with too few English members of her suite to satisfy general notions of respectability. The steward, Hieronymus, remained, along with a Swiss lady's maid, Louise Demont. Pergami supervised the hiring of two more Italian servants, Maurice Crede and Theodore

Majocchi. This helped ease the difficulties of running the Princess's household, but it did nothing to recover her reputation.

On 5 March 1815 Caroline and her suite attended a grand ball given by the Neapolitan Minister of Finance, Count Mosburg. The Neapolitan aristocracy attended, along with several distinguished foreign guests. One of these was the Countess Walewski, Napoleon's mistress, who had recently arrived from Elba with the couple's young son. Dr Holland wrote that 'her sudden presence at Naples, and certain other collateral incidents, excited suspicions without defining them. It was that vague whisper which often precedes some event close at hand.' [23]

The sense of expectation at the ball was heightened when Count Mosburg was suddenly summoned from the room, then quickly returned. He went up to Joachim Murat, and then Caroline Bonaparte, both of whom were halfway through an English country dance. Intelligence was whispered into the royal ears, then both immediately disappeared, and the ball was brought to an abrupt end. The information in question was that Napoleon Bonaparte had escaped from Elba on 26 February.[24] His destination was France, where he intended to raise a huge army and return to power. Napoleon did not want military support from Murat, other than the supply of a few ships in Elban waters. Instead he wished him to play a diplomatic role in endeavouring to keep Austria out of the war. But Murat, whose unpredictability sometimes bordered on instability, was late in supplying naval support to Napoleon, and instead started to make preparations on his own behalf for conflict in Italy.

The British government was forced back into war, and was understandably anxious for Caroline to leave Naples immediately. For once, she complied with their wishes. Lucien Bonaparte, according to a contemporary report, saw Caroline at the time of the Mosburg ball, and being as indiscreet as she, confidently boasted that Napoleon would be at Grenoble on 6 March, at Lyons on the 8th and in Paris on the 15th, when there would be eighty thousand men under his command.[25] Ompteda, highly excited by Caroline's closeness to the Bonapartes, sent long reports to London suggesting that she had somehow been involved in the escape plan. Quite rightly, little credence was given to his judgements, which, as his commitment to his task intensified, became increasingly fanciful. Apart from anything else, Caroline had by the end of her four months in Naples fallen out with the Murats, implying in a letter to her friend Mary Berry that they were somehow contributing to the loss of her good name. Disillusioned, she told Miss Berry that she had had enough of Naples and was 'very anxious in deed' to return to Britain 'as soon as a certain Great Gentelman shall be save out of this great world in the *next*'.[26]

Her travels took her next to Genoa where she cheered up instantly, finding the town as glorious as she had once thought Naples. Here she paraded the streets in a carriage that had been given her by Murat, in exchange for an old Dover coach which she possessed. The Comtesse de Boigne, a French royalist, was in the town, and saw the Princess riding in:

> a kind of phaeton constructed like a sea-shell, covered with gilding and mother of pearl, coloured outside, lined with blue velvet and decorated with silver fringes. This was drawn by two very small piebald horses driven by a child who was dressed like an operatic cherub with spangles and flesh-coloured tights, and within lounged a fat woman of fifty years of age, short, plump, and high-coloured. She wore a pink hat with seven or eight pink feathers floating in the wind, a pink bodice cut very low, and a short white skirt which hardly came below her knees, showing two stout legs with pink top-boots.[27]

In front of her rode a tall and handsome man, presumably Pergami, on a little piebald horse, dressed and making gestures like Murat.

In Genoa, Caroline gave the Comtesse the impression that she was still – or once again – in the 'full fury of her passion' for Murat and for all things Napoleonic. She tried to persuade Lord William Bentinck, commander in chief of the British troops in Italy, that the British army should fight with Murat's Neapolitans, and made a long speech to the Comtesse's father on the certainty of Murat's military success, his approaching support for Napoleon, and 'the triumphs which awaited them'.[28] Caroline wrote at this time to William Gell, saying she was pleased with Genoa, and declaring in her own idiosyncratic idiom that, 'I ride in the woods every day upon a delightful donkey which gives one a great appetite as Beef and Mutton is equally good to that of John Bull in England. I feel very comfortable and settled here for some time.'[29]

But, of course, she was not, and soon left for Milan, where she went to many 'fine fetes', and, she told Gell, she attended a 'very superb Court Ball' which was 'without any etiquette, nor red cushions or great chairs which I always remember with much terror at *some ex-courts*, the dreadful balls which poor me was obliged to witness last Winter'.[30]

In Milan, Caroline made a significant new appointment to her household. Angelica, Countess of Oldi, was an unsophisticated lady and, despite her title, not well educated. She spoke no English or French, and appeared not to possess any identifiable characteristics which made her suitable as a lady-in-waiting for the Princess of Wales. Nevertheless, she was soon employed as such, since she came with a high recommendation from her brother, Bartolomeo Pergami. He had now risen from the post of courier to that of equerry, and general manager-in-chief of the Princess's household. In practice, the Countess of Oldi was not required to undertake any of the tasks normally required of a lady-in-waiting, and these were ably executed by the Swiss maid, Louise Demont. Secretarial work was undertaken by Joseph Hownam, a seaman whom she had taken up when he was a child, and who had come from England to join her household. Caroline described her new employee as 'always merry and placid and never makes any difficulty to travel even without a servant. She is a married woman; her husband has been in the Austrian Army – a very good old family from Venice. She is young and really good-looking.'[31]

More travelling ensued. At Ravenna she saw 'the Tomb of Dante and all the other curiosities' and shortly afterwards 'the finest alfrescoes I ever beheld in my whole life'. But, she declared mournfully, 'I am very well and comfortable, but never happy! Which I never can be more in this wicked world being made such dreadful experiences of friends and friendships. All illusion is gone and I only live for the day!'[32] The letter appears to reflect a sudden bitter mood rather than her general demeanour, which was still flamboyantly affectionate towards Pergami. Lady Charlotte Campbell was with Caroline at this time and wrote that, 'I live in fear every moment of having the horrid stories confirmed before my eyes.'[33] Her letters home convinced both Lady Charlotte Lindsay and Henry Brougham that Caroline and Pergami were enjoying an active sex life. 'Nothing,' thought Lady Charlotte Lindsay, 'could be worse than the state of things.'[34]

Then, in midsummer Caroline bought a house of her own naming it the Villa d'Este. It was a grand establishment on the edge of Lake Como, with grounds that spread out across a steep hill at the back of the house, and which were peppered with little follies including a Temple of Minerva and miniature battlements. Caroline described it to William Gell as 'romantic, superb, [with] a great many variety of amusements . . . I have seven barges with boats and all sorts of useful appendences for the Lac'.[35] The new purchase became a curiosity for British travellers in Italy, who were able to hire a boatman to row them past it. The house was 'neither very magnificent nor very pretty', according to one English tourist, while 'the grounds also seemed to have been laid out in rather . . . worse taste than usual', even for Italy, 'with sham towers, walls and fortifications'. And, from his boat on Lake Como, he made a little pencil sketch of the scene to send home.[36] Caroline planned a great many improvements, despite receiving letters from Henry Brougham stating that her finances were in a parlous state, and planned the building of a new road to the local town.

Just before Caroline moved into Villa d'Este, however, the great events unfolding on the battlefields of Belgium were to intrude upon her domestic life. On 16 June her brother, the Duke Frederick William, was killed leading his 'Black Brunswickers' into battle at Quatre-Bras, to be forever remembered as a military hero. Two days later Wellington, with the vital assistance of Marshal Blucher and his Prussian troops, led the allied armies against Napoleon at Waterloo, and the Emperor was brought down for good.

As for Joachim Murat, when Napoleon escaped from Elba, he instigated a plan to lead Italian troops into battle against Austria with a view to removing Austria from the region, and creating a unified Italy under his own rule. His army quickly occupied Rome and Bologna, but was routed by Austria at Tolentino on 2 May. The Austrians advanced on Naples, and the Bourbon King Ferdinand IV was restored. Murat escaped to France, and offered his help to Napoleon, but this was rejected out of hand, as he was no longer trusted. Later Napoleon regretted his decision, and even thought he might have won at Waterloo had Murat led the cavalry.

Caroline's old friend now dreamed of returning to Italy with a new army, and sailed for Calabria with 250 armed men. A storm broke up the little flotilla, and eventually he landed at Pizzo with only 30 soldiers and, as it turned out, no popular support. Murat was swiftly taken prisoner, and on 13 October was tried by court martial under one of his own laws for disturbing the public peace, found guilty and shot within the half hour. He met his fate with his usual courage, and is buried at Pizzo. We do not know when the news of Murat's death reached Caroline, or what her reaction was. But her spirits were clearly low when she wrote to Lady Charlotte Campbell a few weeks later. 'Nothing in the world do I care for,' she lamented, 'save to pass the time as quickly as I can, and death may hurry on as fast as he pleases – I am ready to die.'[37]

Death would have to wait, however, because Europe was at peace again, and Caroline was planning another trip, this time to the east. She set off late in 1815 with a small entourage, including Pergami, William Austin and Joseph Hownam, but not her old friends Gell and Craven. Hownam was miserable about the special treatment received by Pergami. 'A handsome head, it is true,' he wrote in his diary, 'but without almost an atom of education, not even ease of manner, wearing an insolent stare, fitted to the circumstance.'[38] Caroline, he noticed, was entirely preoccupied with Napoleon and his fame, and the party's first destination was Elba for an inspection of the Emperor's former island prison.

An Englishman saw her there, and wrote to London describing her behaviour. Caroline, he said, had examined Napoleon's palace with utmost attention, admiring especially those rooms identified as

Napoleon's favourites. Then she went into the saloon where his portrait was still on display and said, in front of everyone, 'Napoleon, I salute you – I always had and have now the greatest esteem for you.' She spent the night at the palace and, when she left, took away a billiard cue as a souvenir.[39]

Caroline, for this first part of her journey, was on board the *Leviathan*, under the command of Captain Thomas Briggs, who was to take her next to Palermo. Caroline boasted of her captain, who, she said, 'has been at Constantinople with Lord Elgin in former times', but relations between the two were not, in practice, good.[40] The Princess insisted on Pergami sitting next to her at dinner and, despite the objections of both Captain Briggs and her friend Hownam, would not back down. She visited Palermo briefly, and then set off for Messina, where the arrangement with Briggs came to an end. The party transferred to the *Clorinde*, under the command of a Captain Pechell, who was no happier than Briggs about having Pergami at table. The argument was resolved only when he was told that he need not dine with the Princess at all, that she would provide her own cook and dine at her own table during their journey. With this arrangement in place they departed for Syracuse in January 1816.

In Sicily the Princess managed to secure two honours for Pergami – the first an Order of Malta, which was offered by the Grand Master to the Englishmen in her suite but purloined for the Italian, on the grounds that they, as Protestants, could not accept. The second, a barony, came with the purchase of an estate on his behalf. Pergami's elevation to the nobility meant that he was now, technically at least, senior enough to accept a promotion to the position of chamberlain to the Princess of Wales.[41] Caroline also devoted some time to resolving the problem of, as she saw it, uptight British naval captains, by commissioning Captain Vincenzo Garguilo to take her on the next leg of her travels in his three-masted trading ship, or *polacca*. The ship was fitted up to her specifications, and had its name changed from the *Industria* to the *Princess Charlotte*.

In April 1816, the Princess set sail for north Africa and arrived at Tunis, where she accepted the hospitality of the bey, and entertained a hope that she might help release a number of imprisoned slaves being held in the country, which, largely due to luck, she was able to do. It happened that the English fleet was sailing for Tunis with the same intent, and as the new friend of the bey, Caroline was able to mediate between him and the English naval officer in charge of the operation, Lord Exmouth.[42] The impression she made on his Lordship, though, was reputed to be unfavourable. 'She dined at the Admiral's table,' the journalist Charles Knight was told, 'and left an impression that will never be forgotten. Her talk was of such a nature that Lord Exmouth ordered the midshipman to leave the cabin.'[43]

Caroline wrote from Tunis:

> After I had visited Sicily for the sake of the antiquities I came here and had the pleasure to release a great many slaves . . . I am quite in aston-ishment that all the wonderful curiosities of Carthage, Utica, Savonny, Udinna never have been taken much notice of . . . I can assure you the soi-disant Barbarians are much more real kind and obliging to me than all the civil people of Europe for which reason I shall certainly remain with them as long as I can . . . I am quite a philosopher and go my own way and do not more trouble myself about anybody, nor what these foolish tongues may say about me or not. I am in perfectly good health and spirits and I have all the hearts of the people at Tunis, which proves their good taste . . . I never have been so happy in my life . . . I am living a perfect enchantment. The dear Arabians and Turks are quite darlings. Their kindness I shall never forget.[44]

But she was not as free from the civil people of Europe as she might have thought. She was seen visiting Tunis by a judgemental Englishman, who published his observations in the *Bristol Mercury* that December – and it seems from his description that her taste for flam-boyant outfits had not abated. Her dress was of scarlet velvet, cut low both at the front and back, and reached only the knees; the sleeves were just two inches long, while on her legs she wore red thigh-length boots. The observer was not impressed by 'a wig (which is curled at the sides nearly as high as the top of the bonnet), artificial eye-brows (nature having denied her any) and false teeth . . . She appears very ignorant and coarse in her manners and indelicate in her conversation . . . She walks, bows, twirls a stick, and gesticulates like a man, and after visiting the harem spoke of the customs there without reserve.'[45]

This report concurs with others, some of them doubtless gossip and without foundation, that reached Britain during and after her travels. Joseph Farington noted in his diary that the Princess of Wales had been observed 'assuming the dress of a man – [she] has discharged petticoats and wears trowsers'.[46] The artist John Constable also said he had heard that Caroline had been spotted wearing 'a man's hat and had a coloured handkerchief round her neck. She had short petticoats and Hessian boots. Her appearance was very masculine.'[47] And Mary Wollstonecraft Shelley, the wife of the poet and creator of Frankenstein's monster, was told by a friend that he had seen Caroline wearing 'a black pelisse, tucked up to her knees, and exhibiting a pair of men's boots. A fur tippet that seemed as if it would cover ten such – a white cap, and a man's hat set on sideways.'[48]

Caroline next rejoined the polacca and made her way to Malta, the island of Milos and then Athens, which was reached on 8 May 1816. Next she visited Corinth and Constantinople, and then on to Acre, scene of the heroic battle won by her old friend Sir Sidney Smith. She next set out overland with Hownam, Pergami, William Austin and a few others for Jerusalem, now seeing herself as 'a good Christhinne'. She rode on a donkey, travelled by night because of the heat, and rested during the day.

The group arrived at Nazareth at three in the morning, spent the day visiting holy sites, and continued on their journey in the evening. Eleven camels followed them, sent by the Pasha of Acre, and carrying enormous tents and other equipment which he provided. Next they journeyed to Jerusalem, having acquired a large crowd of pilgrims who joined the group. The Princess, still riding the donkey, arrived at the holy city in the evening of 11 June. Hownam wrote in his diary: 'It would be impossible to paint the scene. Men, women, children, Jews, Turks, Arabs, Armenians, Greeks, Catholics and infidels, all came out and received us crying *"Ben venute!"* as many fingers extended towards the royal pilgrim with "that's her".' His emotions, he said, 'mixed up of fatigue and religion were almost solemn and certainly laughable'.[49]

A few days later, Caroline was asked to nominate members of her party to be dubbed Knights of the High Order of Jerusalem. She suggested William Austin, Pergami and a servant named Michele Schiavini, who all took an oath declaring that they were of noble birth and would give up their property for the defence of the Holy Catholic Apostolic religion, if needs be. They were then given boots and spurs, and the 'épée of Godfrey of Bouillon', which they wore around their waists. Another ceremony took place, in which the Princess founded the Order of St Caroline and bequeathed upon Pergami the honour of Grand Master. The order, in the form of a red cross on a lilac and silver ribbon, was to be worn by 'all the faithful knights who have had the honour of accompanying her on her pilgrimage to the Holy Land'.[50] This was the high point of her great Mediterranean journey. The Princess was at last wearying of travel and wished to return home to Como. On 15 August 1816 she arrived at Rome, where she was received by the Pope. She then returned to the Villa d'Este, where a shock awaited.

When Caroline had left on her Mediterranean excursion her 'friend' Ompteda had panicked. His intelligence on Caroline had been severely criticised by London, and particularly by the Vice-Chancellor, John Leach, on the grounds that it was all hearsay and insinuation, and devoid of copper-bottomed proof of adultery. Witness depositions were required and, most importantly, 'English witnesses are to be preferred.' An English member of Caroline's household, William Burrell, had already and of his own accord started to make scandalous revelations about her lifestyle, which were duly conveyed to George. The Regent was appreciative, but far more 'evidence' of such respectable provenance was needed if he was ever to secure a divorce.[51]

Desperate to collect some devastating and incontrovertible evidence, Ompteda decided to bribe one of Caroline's servants, Maurice

Crede, to hand over the keys to her bedroom. His aim was to snoop there while she was away and, if necessary, to wait for her return and then burst in on her one night in the hope of discovering her with Pergami in flagrante. His subterfuge, though, was discovered when Crede told all to Caroline in the hope that an honest confession would prevent him from losing his job. The Princess wrote a long letter to her old friend George Canning about Ompteda, and another to Princess Charlotte. And to William Gell she lamented, 'I can never more receive strangers in my House, since all such plots [are] going on.'[52] Crede was dismissed, and the faithful Joseph Hownam challenged Ompteda to a duel. Ompteda attempted to wriggle out of the challenge, but eventually agreed to meet Hownam at Mannheim in Germany. He waited there with his second, but Hownam did not show up. The sad series of events resulted in Ompteda writing to Munster resigning as a spy.

Caroline resolved that Ompteda's betrayal would not stop her from enjoying herself. 'I have a charming theatre at my house and very often we play French charades and Italian operas,' she told Gell. 'I go on horseback every morning. I have a great many people in my House, constantly, and very excellent society, and we are all very merry indeed.'[53] And her lifestyle continued to shock, as Byron, writing from Venice, informed his publisher John Murray in January 1817:

> The general state of morals here is much the same as in the Doge's time – a woman is virtuous (according to the code) who limits herself to her husband and one lover – those who have two, three or more are a little *wild* – but it is only those who are indiscriminately diffuse – and form a low connection – such as the Princess of Wales with her Courier . . . who are considered as overstepping the modesty of marriage.[54]

According to one British gossip who visited Italy, several of Caroline's friends reported seeing her 'in the most disgusting undress, along with Pergami'. Moreover, local parents 'forbid their children going near the House, and one priest earnestly exhorted his flock to abstain from entering it, as they would avoid contamination'.[55]

As was usual, Caroline did, in time, tire of the Villa d'Este. And, as was her habit, she accumulated a mass of debts. So she eventually sold up, and in August 1817 moved to the Villa Caprile near Pesaro. This was smaller than the Villa d'Este, and less exposed. Caroline hoped that here she might avoid curious English travellers and, more specifically, George's spies.

The Princess was delighted with her new villa, which, while less grand than her Como palace, had pretty gardens and a little open-air theatre in which she staged recitals from French plays. She bathed in the sea, and wrote to Gell declaring that she was very happy with her new, more modest style of life. Pergami remained her constant companion, and his family now filled the house. His sister the Countess of Oldi remained in the suite and had been joined by Pergami's mother, generally referred to as Madame Mère, his little daughter Victorine, brother Louis and cousin Bernardo. Pergami's wife, however, was not invited to join her relatives.

Caroline, at this point, was enjoying life as an honorary Italian. Her English servants had all departed, and she rarely saw English travellers. Overwhelmingly her main connection to her old life in Britain came via Charlotte – and Caroline had written to her daughter since the early days of her exile. She could not decide whether she would return to England when George became King, but was plainly attracted by the prospect of going back when Charlotte, in time, became Queen. She also seemed thrilled at the news of Charlotte's marriage, despite the fact that she was not invited to the wedding, and also by her daughter's pregnancy. In October 1817 she wrote proudly to Lucien Bonaparte, 'I can tell you that I will soon be a grandmother; I had the most satisfactory news from England on the health and happiness of my daughter.'

Her peace was to be disturbed in the most brutal way. When Charlotte and her baby died, George refused to write to Caroline to tell her of the dreadful news. To do so would break his promise to himself that he would never communicate directly with his wife again, and so it was left to Prince Leopold to send the letter. But he was so debilitated by grief that he delayed in doing so. In the meantime, George did write to the Pope – and the courier carrying the message happened to pass near Pesaro, was intercepted there, and brought to the Princess's house.

In his diary, Joseph Hownam wrote of a letter arriving by messenger in the early hours of 30 November 1817. He learned the bad news, and was anxious about how to break it, fearing that on seeing a letter Caroline would assume 'that it was a messenger of good tidings rather than the harbinger of death'. Presently, he knocked on her bedroom door and 'said I wished to speak to her if she would permit me. In a few minutes she came out.'

'Well, Hownam, what is the matter that you wake me?'
I said, 'I have something, madam, to communicate to you.'
'What is it?'
'A King's messenger arrived this morning.'
'Ah, Princess Charlotte is delivered.'
I remained silent.
'She is ill!'
'I am afraid she is, madam.'
'Dangerously so?'
'From what I can learn from the messenger I think . . .' A pause.
'Has he letters?'
'Yes, madam.'
Turning very pale, she said, 'My God Hownam, what is the matter?'
She paused a little, then tears came into her eyes and she said, 'Well, my dear Hownam, I am prepared for the worst, give me the letter.' I put it into her hands . . . She seized it, and seeing the black seal, 'My God, she is dead, poor Charlotte!' She opened and read it, and giving me the letter, 'It is just so, Hownam, poor dear Charlotte,' and cried a great deal. I endeavoured all I could to encourage her. 'Well,' she said, 'she will never know all the torments her poor mother has suffered or will suffer, it is probably better. This is not only my last hope gone, but what has England lost?'[56]

Soon afterwards the Princess wrote to Lady Charlotte Campbell, 'I have not only to lament an ever-beloved child but one most warmly attached friend and the only one I have had in England.'[57]

In Britain, George's appetite for divorce was undiminished. In August 1817 a great bundle of evidence regarding Caroline's behaviour had been handed to Sir John Leach, the Vice-Chancellor, who on reading it, recommended that 'proper researches should be made in the countries where the Princess had resided' to find further information 'as might exclude all doubt with respect to the character of her conduct'.[58] As a result of this George, in the summer of 1818, decided to press once more for the evidence which he needed to set himself free of his marital ties; and set about establishing a properly managed, well-funded commission dedicated to securing credible witnesses and sworn affidavits to prove Caroline's adultery. Ideally, he would have liked her to be charged with high treason as a result, but legal technicalities got in the way, since adultery on foreign soil was not as damning as that in Britain; and, in any case, his ministers found the idea of charging the Princess of Wales with a capital offence unpalatable. Divorce, though, seemed to George entirely achievable.

The Prince secured Lord Liverpool's support for the new body, soon to be known as the Milan Commission, and appointed the loyal John Leach as chairman. Leach had become a close, confidential adviser to George, and was as vehemently in favour of a divorce as his master wished him to be. As a lawyer he was, according to Brougham's old friend Samuel Romilly, possessed of 'considerable powers of argumentation', but lacked legal knowledge and in judgement was 'more deficient than any man possessed of so clear an understanding that I ever met with'.[59]

Brougham despised Leach, declaring him 'moderately learned' in his own profession, but 'beyond it . . . one of the most ignorant men that ever appeared before the bar'. Brougham wrote that Leach's worst quality was his 'unhesitating and overweening confidence in his own opinion, which exceeded that of any other man, and perpetually led both himself and his clients astray'. He damned Leach for his 'uncontrolled conceit' and a 'contracted understanding that saw quickly and correctly very near objects, and disbelieved in the existence of all beyond'. In short, according to Brougham, the Prince Regent could not have found a worse ally. Though they were both acute men, Brougham maintained, they were utterly blinded by the Prince Regent's 'passions' and 'the conceited arrogance that inspired the vulgar adviser'. Brougham was, of course, a biased observer, but he was voicing a fairly common view.[60]

Leach's devotion to duty could not be faulted. He appointed a team of two members, William Cooke and James Brown, and one agent, John Powell, to be dispatched to Italy immediately. The trio, aided by another agent named Vimercati, established themselves at Milan in September 1818 and set about seeking out anybody who had come into contact with the Princess during her travels, and interrogating them. Their general approach was to leave no stone unturned and, because of their feverish activities, Caroline soon came to know of the new investigation – although she was never officially informed of it. Many of her former servants made statements, including a courier, Giuseppe Sacchi, a coachman, Giuseppe Restelli, and a particular favourite of Caroline's, Theodore Majocchi. Most worrying for the Princess, though, was the testimony of her maid, Louise Demont, who had observed her mistress at close quarters for most of her Italian and Mediterranean journeys. Rumours soon circulated suggesting that the witnesses were being paid handsomely for their evidence, and gossip had it that anyone who had set eyes on Caroline could sell their story to the Englishmen in residence at Milan.

In London, Henry Brougham continued to exercise some responsibility for Caroline's affairs, and grew alarmed when in 1818 Joseph Hownam called on him. Caroline's old friend was taking leave from her household, partly to travel and to see his family, but chiefly because he could no longer endure working alongside Pergami. The 'baron', as he was now known, was running Caroline's residence with total autonomy and with a degree of self-regard that Hownam found intolerable. Pergami, moreover, had control over the Princess's accounts and Hownam had become convinced that she was being swindled. All of this was relayed to Brougham, who decided that, as a matter of urgency, an emissary should be sent to Pesaro to check up on Caroline and to establish just how vulnerable she was in the face of the Milan Commission. The departure of Hownam, Brougham believed, had made matters worse than ever, since his presence at Pesaro had 'kept up the little respectability' that remained there.

Brougham selected his younger brother, James, to visit Italy and report back to him, and by March 1819 James was happily ensconced at Caroline's villa, from whence he wrote his brother a long letter entitled 'General Appearance of Things'.[61] He thought the house 'more of a cottage than a palace', although it was home to sixty-three live-in staff, who were part of a total entourage of eighty. Forty-eight horses were kept in the stables, some of them 'the finest Arabian', and all of them good. He also noticed a regular guard of fourteen soldiers allowed Caroline by the Pope, who, along with Cardinal Consalvi, 'are extremely civil to her'. 'The stile of the whole thing is more *hospitable* and *plentiful* than dignified, elegant or even comfortable,' he wrote – adding a note in the margin: 'Wine which is quite impossible to touch – ordinaire.' His overall tone was not snobbish but friendly, and he reported that Caroline constantly had guests, generally twelve or more, at dinner. He thought her 'well liked and respected all over the country . . . generous and charitable'.

Unlike Hownam, James Brougham thought Pergami 'a plain, straightforward, *remarkably good sort of man*' who was very active, 'understands figures well and superintends everything'. However, the baron, 'a tall, good-looking fellow, about 35', enjoyed an undisguised status within the household that was entirely scandalous. 'His picture in every room – the child [Victorine] is a daughter of his and calls him Papa and *her Mamma*! And she is as fond of it as if it were her own – Everything is "le Baron".' At a grand dinner held on 14 March, thirty guests ate their food from plates marked with Pergami's arms. 'Certainly the whole thing tells badly,' concluded the visitor. '*His* house and grounds, *his* plate, *his* ordering everything, he even buys her bonnets, this I saw, and all his family quartered upon her!!!'[62] His dismay increased the longer he stayed, and in a further letter he told his brother:

they are to all appearances man and wife, never was anything so obvious. *His room* is close to hers, and his *bedroom* the only one in that part of the house. The whole thing is apparent to every one, tho' perhaps there might be difficulty in proving the fact to find her guilty of high treason, yet I should think all the circumstances being stated would completely ruin her in the opinion of the people of England, that once done, the Prince might get a divorce, or at any rate prevent her being Queen.[63]

The Milan Commissioners, meanwhile, were struggling with the large numbers of potential witnesses turning up to give evidence of questionable use. William Cooke wrote to John Leach complaining that 'Persons of inferior condition, such as Boatmen, are offering to testify to having seen the Princess and Pergami in a Boat together upon the Lake, or in the same carriage without attendants, or walking Arm in Arm, without being able to speak to the circumstances'.[64] The evidence of Louise Demont, however, gave rise to greater expectations. 'Mad'elle Demont's examination . . . has occupied parts of twenty-two days. It was necessary to allow her time for recollection and not to fatigue her by too long attendance at one sitting,' the Milan Commissioners informed Leach. With some excitement they added that the deposition of Demont amounted to 'a clear narrative of the most important facts, described with extraordinary accuracy' and supported the evidence of Theodore Majocchi, 'with whom she had no possible means of communication'.[65] In March the depositions of forty-four people were sent to London.

In the spring of 1819, Caroline became seriously worried about the activities of the Milan Commission, and at one stage told James Brougham that she would agree to a divorce in return for a substantial financial settlement. Then, she intimated, she would continue to live peacefully at Pesaro with her Italian 'family', staying away from Britain for good. 'I never saw a person so eager about anything as she was about this,' wrote James Brougham. 'Her mind was quite made up to go thro' with it.'[66] Caroline's wishes were conveyed to London, where Henry Brougham consulted George's old friend Lord

Lauderdale about the way forward. The two men concluded that no divorce would be possible unless Caroline would admit adultery. The law did not allow divorce by consent, and a parliamentary bill in effect exempting the royal couple from legal restrictions on the rest of society was out of the question. James Brougham told Caroline that she might get a separation by mutual consent, though not a divorce. 'She said that was doing nothing. She seemed so anxious, and spoke so confidentially that I asked her whether she would consent to allow . . . that she had been guilty of infidelity – to which she answered "that is impossible".'[67] This left Henry Brougham with the firm view that Caroline would be happiest staying away from England in return for a substantial pay-off.

But George had decided that for him a separation was not good enough, only a divorce would do. His motivation stemmed, it seemed, not from a wish to remarry but simply to be wholly disconnected from his wife. He could not tolerate the idea of her ever becoming his Queen, and argued that the Milan Commission would soon report. Proceedings against Caroline must surely follow it.

Lord Liverpool and the government disagreed. The Cabinet wished to avoid a damaging public inquiry, and was keen to persuade the Prince Regent to settle for a separation. In essence the Cabinet and Brougham agreed that compromise was best – and on 14 June 1819 Brougham wrote to Lord Hutchinson suggesting a deal, and asking him to put certain recommendations to Caroline: 'that she shall agree to a formal separation, to be ratified by Parliament . . . that she shall renounce her right to be crowned in the event of a demise of the Crown . . . and shall henceforth take some other style and title, as that of Duchess of Cornwall . . .'[68]

In return she would receive her current annuity for the rest of her life. The Princess of Wales, Brougham told Hutchinson, would, in all probability, have no desire to return to England now that Princess Charlotte was dead. He also stressed that such a deal would be highly beneficial to the country if it 'prevents the manifold evils of a Public Inquiry into the most delicate matters connected with the royal family'.[69]

Brougham assured Lord Hutchinson that he was presenting the case to Caroline, putting it 'in the manner most likely to give it effect' but, disingenuously, warned that the Princess of Wales had 'made no direct proposition herself'.[70] Then, oddly, he did nothing. For reasons of his own, he failed to inform Caroline that the Cabinet supported the proposals. The most likely reason for his silence is that he wanted to stoke the government's fear that she might return at any minute, and thus not only provide the climate for even better terms for Caroline, but also ensure that all his strategic options on his own account were kept open. It is hard to know exactly what his game plan was, but plain to see that Henry Brougham liked to be in a strong bargaining position with the government, and adored being at the centre of the political stage. From both viewpoints, it suited him that the Caroline situation remain unresolved.

In July the Milan Commission made its report, which was presented to the Cabinet. The ministers surveyed the mountain of evidence, but noted that most of it was supplied by 'foreigners, most of them not above the rank of menial servants'.[71] Moreover, they still found the idea of issuing formal proceedings against Caroline unpalatable, raising the spectre of sordid allegations being traded in public between the Prince and Princess of Wales and risking the corruption of public morals. In the end, the Cabinet disappointed George by concluding that although imputed adultery had been established, 'so long as she continued abroad and held no higher station than that of Princess of Wales, it was thought expedient to abstain from any public proceeding on the subject'.[72]

Nevertheless, in Italy Caroline was squaring up for an almighty confrontation. She set her own agents to work to find out which of her acquaintances and servants were betraying her and, as Brown wrote on 30 September, 'Every engine is now at work on the part of the Princess. Her emissaries are all activity and abound here.'[73] She also alarmed the English spies by talking about returning to England in order to settle the matter for good, and spent the summer away from Pesaro; a move which gave rise to rumours that she was, indeed, about to leave Italy. In September, the London newspapers started predicting her immediate arrival. James Brown was forced to write to London reassuring his masters that Caroline was still safely in Italy, but confessing his anxiety that she might nevertheless depart at any moment.[74]

On 6 October he wrote again warning that Italy 'is teeming with plots and intrigues' and that Caroline was leaving. 'The Princess has *this day* demanded and received her passport *for France*,' he told George's aide, Sir Benjamin Bloomfield. 'She is to travel with one made out in the name of the Countess Oldi,' and is heading for Calais. Then 'she is to appear in London with whatever she may be able to cull from [amongst her entourage] . . . that may pass for something resembling a gentleman. Her agents in the mean time are all activity . . .' A few days later Brown sent a package to London containing intercepted correspondence from various members of Caroline's household, including Pergami.[75]

Caroline was, in fact, on her way to Lyons, where she hoped to meet Henry Brougham to discuss the prospect of a settlement. She arrived in the town on 12 October, causing, once again, profound concern to the British government, which was now terrified that she was en route for England. Castlereagh's brother, Charles Stewart, wrote to her making it clear that if she ventured as far as Paris she would not be received by the court of the French King. She was furious, and doubtless tempted to proceed to the French capital for the sake of defiance. But she stayed in Lyons, waiting for Brougham, and when he turned out to be too busy with domestic politics to make the journey, she packed her bags and went south to Marseilles hoping for milder weather. Here she toyed with the idea of going to England but ultimately settled on going back to Italy and her congenial life at Pesaro. At the end of January 1820 she set sail, putting in at Monaco due to bad weather, and then resuming her journey and arriving at Leghorn in February. It was here that she learned that King George III had died on 29 January, and that she was now Queen Consort of Great Britain.

5

QUEEN

And when in great need of protection she stood,
She found a Knight-errant in Alderman Wood

Brave Alderman Wood, published by Catnach (1820)

It was no surprise that Caroline intended to be a 'people's Queen'. From the moment of her engagement to George she had shown concern about her relationship with 'the people', and Malmesbury, in the winter of 1794, had been horrified at her wish to be *loved* by them. Her husband had been jealous of her popularity with the masses, and at the height of the Delicate Investigation scandal of 1813 she had appealed to 'the people' when she published her grievances in the London newspapers. Now, on becoming Queen in January 1820, she invoked the people once more, directly appealing to the masses to support her, to be a source of power in her struggle with her husband. The newspapers published a letter from her pointing out that the 'genuine nation' desired her return to England.[1] Who exactly constituted this 'genuine nation' was unclear, but it certainly did not include George, his ministers or high society. By 1820 she was using 'the people' as a term of opposition to the establishment.

Caroline had read the London newspapers, corresponded with a few London friends, and was in fact well informed about the political climate in England. Thanks to public knowledge of the Milan Commission, her popularity had been building in recent months and on becoming Queen she was thrust back into the limelight of the British political scene. Once again hearts went out to her as the victim of George's cold cruelty. Henry Brougham told Thomas Creevey that 'she is extremely popular' and that the cry at the proclamation of the new reign on 31 January was not for George, but 'God save the Queen!'[2] The editor of the *Morning Chronicle* knew all this, he claimed, but had not dared to put it into his paper.

The Queen left Leghorn and returned to Pesaro and the bosom of the Pergami family to consider her options, communicating by letter with her British advisers. She was in good health, she told her friend William Gell, and was feeling the benefits of a change of air. In this positive spirit she now had to decide, for good or ill, whether to carry out her threat and go to England to fight for her rights as Queen or to settle for the 'simple' Italian life that she claimed to love best. We do not know whether Pergami encouraged her to go or stay, or whether her feelings for him were still strong. The only hint on the subject comes three months later, in April, when George's spy James Brown reports that 'she appears wholly wrapped up in his presence and more fond of him than ever'.[3]

But we do know that Henry Brougham wrote telling her to set out immediately for Brussels or Paris or Calais, and to send for a yacht to take her to England.[4] It is possible that he truly wanted her to come back, but probable that he simply felt that by looming large across the Channel, Caroline would frighten the British government into paying her handsomely to stay in Europe.

Throughout 1819 Caroline had constantly seemed on the point of returning to Britain. In July she had asked Lady Charlotte Lindsay to be ready to meet her at Dover, and told her bank, Coutts, that she would be back by September. In August she thought of writing to the newspapers about her intentions, and in September she had said she would need a frigate for Dover the following January.[5] And before the old King's death that month, she professed herself to be always ready to start for England.[6] All this had some ring of true intention about it but, in the light of the Milan Commission, mostly seemed like a loud cry for, if not help, then for acknowledgement and respect.

But now the decision was real, and in making up her mind two separate influences weighed hard with Caroline. The first was the torrent of insults that were coming her way from diplomats and aristocrats who refused to acknowledge the royal status of someone they regarded as vulgar and, thanks to George's rejection of her, illegitimate. She had not forgiven the British government for blocking her being received by the French King when she had visited France. Her father and brother had both been killed in battles against Napoleon, and it was just that she should be welcomed at the French court. The snub was deeply hurtful.

But now, on becoming Queen, the humiliations were even greater. In March Caroline went to Rome, where she had always been a welcomed guest, only to suffer by the hand of Cardinal Consalvi, the head of diplomatic affairs. Consalvi had been friendly to Caroline in the past, but now his sources led him to believe that Caroline was soon to be stripped of her title as Queen. When she arrived in the city in February 1820, he behaved towards her in a manner that was offensive and cruel, refusing her a guard of honour unless she deigned to receive one as Duchess of Brunswick rather than Queen. At the same time, he denied her an audience with the Pope, which she should have been granted as a matter of course. Moreover, he was rude in his letters, referring to her as 'this royal person'. Caroline was bewildered, angry and in tears. She had imagined that her new title would put an end to the sort of treatment she had received in France, and would entitle her to a degree of respect.

The English ladies in Rome at the time followed Cardinal Consalvi's lead and did their best to avoid the Queen. Elizabeth Foster, the Duchess of Devonshire, condemned her as a 'wretched woman',[7] and Mrs Canning, the wife of her old friend George, and mother of her godchild, preferred the morals of the Duchess to those of the Queen and stayed away. Only in April, when letters from England persuaded the Duchess that 'the Queen is to remain Queen',[8] did she put her signature to the visitors' book that Caroline left in the great hall of her shunned house in Rome. Caroline wrote to William Gell complaining about 'this worldly cardinal' and to Lords Liverpool and Castlereagh asking why she was obliged to submit to such 'great insolence'.[9]

The slights made her inclined to fight back, and to return to Britain. But there were other influences on her, too. She appears to have listened to those Britons who had remained her allies; the self-appointed champions of 'the genuine nation' who had backed her against George seven years earlier. These were radical and reforming politicians and agitators who, in the aftermath of the French Revolution, demanded political change in Britain; men who detested the 'rotten boroughs' in Parliament, who demanded universal male suffrage and had been influenced by Tom Paine's best-seller of 1792, *The Rights of Man*. For them, Caroline was useful, a royal figurehead who could be used to attack the excesses of the King and his corrupt Parliament.

The Queen was plainly no political thinker. But she was attracted by those she saw as romantic rebels. Just as all things Napoleonic appealed to her, so did the British radicals, who, to her mind, were like her – outsiders battling against the entrenched power of the oppressor. George served as a pillar of monstrosity for both, and the printmakers in early 1820 depicted the new King, overblown and arrogant as ever, either as in cahoots with the supposed suppressors of the people, Castlereagh and Sidmouth, or as the dastardly enemy of Caroline – who was now portrayed as 'truth' and 'justice'.[10]

Caroline's greatest friend and champion amongst the radicals was Alderman Matthew Wood, the son of a West Country serge-maker. As a young man Wood had moved to London, where he went into the druggist trade and City politics. In 1802 he was elected to the Common Council of the Corporation of London, and in 1815 became Lord Mayor. He was re-elected in 1816, making him the first man in several hundred years to serve two consecutive terms. The honour came about partly because Wood was a genuinely hard worker – in 1816 he had complained to the Home Secretary Lord Sidmouth that there were so many destitute people in London that he was processing two hundred cases of vagrancy a day. But the second term was also a recognition of Wood's ability to balance his ardent campaigning for political reform with a hard line against the violence that occasionally surfaced amongst London's revolutionaries and hardliners.

In December 1816, Wood had distinguished himself when a radicals' meeting at Spa Fields in east London turned into a riot. A speech by the thunderous Henry 'Orator' Hunt was disrupted by a group of revolutionaries, followers of Thomas Spence, who marched through Clerkenwell and Smithfield to Snow Hill, where they murdered a gunsmith and plundered his shop. They then set off for the City, firing shots as they went, and finally arrived at Mansion House where Wood confronted them. He later told his fellow aldermen, 'Two fellows levelled their Musketts at me. I said, "Fire away, you Rascals." One of them fired.' Despite being unarmed, the Lord Mayor managed to apprehend the rather ineffective ringleaders before the military arrived.

In London, Matthew Wood was far more radical and popular than the government, and consequently was much maligned by his opponents. Sidmouth saw him as an extremist rogue force, George referred to him as 'that beast Wood' and Henry Brougham put him down as a 'blockhead'.[11] The fact was that these were politically turbulent times and Wood's popularity and independence of spirit seemed threatening.

Caroline probably met Matthew Wood for the first time in 1813, in the midst of the public fuss over the findings of the Delicate Investigation. That year the Common Council of the Corporation of London publicly expressed its 'horror and indignation' at the 'odious and wicked conspiracy' which had been directed at Caroline's life and honour.[12] Wood saw a political opportunity and took a lead in proposing that Caroline be sent an Address offering her the support of the City of London. And, as was usual practice with such things, the Address would be presented to her in person by the aldermen.

Caroline, says Samuel Romilly, 'appointed Kensington Palace as the place at which she would receive it, that the procession might pass all through London; and she fixed on a Monday, that being with a great many inferior workmen a sort of holiday'. Accordingly an 'immense crowd' turned up for this highly manufactured political occasion, during which Caroline accepted the Address from the aldermen, and gave her response.[13] This voiced her gratitude to the City, and conveyed a promise to impress on Princess Charlotte that when she became Queen she should remember the City's support of her mother. The event, particularly the drafting of her response, demonstrates that Caroline was taking political advice in 1813, definitely from Brougham, and quite possibly from Matthew Wood as well.

Wood next turns up in an astonishing letter written by Caroline in 1815, and now in the Royal Archives at Windsor. On 11 April of that year the Princess of Wales wrote from Italy to her London agent Moses Hoper asking for one hundred pounds to be paid from her own funds to her old friend, the reformer Samuel Whitbread, for his children's schooling, and 'another one hundred pounds to Alderman Wood for his children's school'.[14] Caroline had a generous spirit, but she was not strong on follow-through, so it is possible or even probable that the sums were never paid. Nonetheless, the Princess of Wales was offering to finance the radical Lord Mayor of London – an enemy of the Tory government and her husband – to help pay for his sons to go to Winchester, a leading public school. This was an outrageous political act.

Caroline was not devious or cunning, and she had no real interest in political philosophies. Most likely, she simply sympathised with Wood and wished to help him educate his boys. If she could demonstrate her gratitude for his support in 1813, that was fine. And if Lord Sidmouth and George were to learn of her act and be shocked, well all the better. She loved to shock. She may also have been nurturing a political ally, anticipating that he might be of use in the future.

In any case, it seems likely that Caroline and Matthew Wood kept in contact and met up in Italy in 1818. That year he sent his fourth child, William, now fresh out of Winchester, to spend two years studying in Geneva. In September, the Wood family went to visit William, and on the 6th the young man wrote to a friend, 'My father only stayed here till Tuesday last: he then set off for Chamounix, and intended to proceed as far as Milan. He will return in three weeks' time . . .'[15]

Three weeks in Milan without the rest of his family? Matthew Wood arrived in the Italian city in the very month that the Milan Commissioners arrived to start collecting evidence against Caroline, and it is highly likely that he visited his old friend, the Princess of Wales. If they did meet, then the occasion must have consolidated their relationship; for in the spring of 1820, when Caroline was trying to decide what to do, she turned to Alderman Matthew Wood and made him her closest adviser in England.

She also at this time corresponded with the radical MP, Sir Francis Burdett – a unique character in the House of Commons, distinguished by his long, lean figure, upper-crust manners, legendary love affairs and controversial political views. As a young man, he had lived in Paris, witnessed the early days of the French Revolution, and then returned to Britain with a mission to fight tyranny wherever he found it. His long rhetorical speeches were as hard to stomach for the Whig and Tory old guard, as were his single-minded campaigns for press freedom and political reform. He became popular in the country, and was sometimes referred to as the most popular man in Britain. Caroline was never as close to Burdett as she was to Wood, but he was her sort of man – idiosyncratic, unrestrained and charming – and in 1813, during the Delicate Investigation scandal, he had given her his wholehearted support, comparing her misfortune to that of Marie Antoinette. Addressing the people of Westminster, he asked, 'Is it not curious to observe that those persons whose sensibility was so alive to the misfortunes of the Queen of France, who thought all England and all the world should draw the sword to avenge her injuries, have no sensibility alive, no commiseration awake, to the injuries of the innocent and calumniated Princess of Wales?'[16]

The image of Marie Antoinette was to be used in this way, on Caroline's behalf, again and again throughout her life, by political campaigners and by newspapermen. Burdett kept in touch with the Princess while she was in Europe, and during that time became increasingly distracted from grass-roots activism and ever fonder of the more patrician business of hunting. However, in 1819 he returned to the political fray, becoming entangled in an event which was to cast a vast shadow over British political life, and to set the context for Caroline's entry on to the political stage – the Peterloo massacre.

In 1819, Britain was in the midst of a slump in trade and suffering high unemployment, and radical agitators throughout the country organised a series of mass meetings to protest about living conditions. Tension was high, and warnings of revolution reached the Home Office almost daily. 'Nothing but ruin and starvation stare one in the face,' wrote the Stockport reformer, Joseph Johnson, 'and I believe nothing but the greatest exertions can prevent an insurrection. Oh that you in London were prepared for it.'[17] Several of the meetings went ahead without incident. But the greatest, which took place on 16 August in St Peter's Field, Manchester, attracted 60,000 people – nearly half of the local population – to hear the booming declamations of Henry Hunt. It terrified the authorities with its military-like level of organisation.

Nervous local magistrates and military commanders got together 300–400 Special Constables, and many hundreds of soldiers – army and yeomanry, cavalry and infantry, along with a number of two-pounder guns. Violence, said the Home Office, was to be used only as a last resort. However, the Manchester Yeomanry prepared for the event by having their sabres sharpened, while the Home Office minister Henry Hobhouse instructed local magistrate James Norris that the Cap of Liberty must not be raised 'with impunity', and stated that the militia should aid the civil authorities if necessary.[18]

The crowds, when they arrived, marched with a discipline that alarmed the authorities; and were accompanied by bands and carrying banners bearing slogans such as 'Annual Parliaments' and 'No Corn Laws'. Women turned out in force and hundreds arrived in women-only delegations, or in the case of those from Stockport, as a Female Union. Women from Royton carried a flag reading 'Let us die like men, and not be sold like slaves', while other female protesters were abused and told to go home to their families.[19] Every so often, someone in the crowd marched by wearing a Liberty Cap, and a few were reported to hold staves. The authorities reacted to the immensity and spirit of the crowd by agreeing that Orator Hunt should be arrested, and the Yeomanry cavalry were sent in amongst the crowd to do the deed.

But the operation was not conducted smoothly – one horseman yelled out, 'Have their flags!' and the soldiers rode amongst the people, sabres thrashing about, and horses swerving dangerously. Eleven people died, and several hundred were seriously injured. Samuel Bamford, surveying the scene afterwards, wrote:

> over the whole field were strewed caps, bonnets, hats, shawls, and shoes, and other parts of male and female dress; trampled, torn and bloody . . . Several mounds of human beings still remained where they had fallen, crushed down, and smothered. Some of these still groaning; others, with staring eyes, were gasping for breath and others would never breathe more. All was silent save those low sounds, and the occasional snorting and pawing of steeds.[20]

The Home Secretary, Lord Sidmouth, responded by conveying to the Manchester magistrates the commendation of the Prince Regent on their prompt and decisive action, while, on the other side of the political divide, new fire inflamed the belly of the outraged, aggrieved radical movement. Sir Francis Burdett, for his part, read the accounts of the carnage in the newspapers and wrote a letter to the electors of Westminster condemning this terrible use of a standing army in time of peace. 'What, kill men unarmed, unresisting: and gracious God women too!' he exclaimed. 'Disfigured, maimed, cut down and trampled on by Dragoons. Is this England?' He then called upon the gentlemen of England to head public meetings throughout the United Kingdom to prevent the country from falling into a 'reign of terror and blood'. He asked whether the meetings would be met by military violence, but proclaimed, 'A man can die but once and never better than in vindicating the laws and liberties of his country.'[21]

The letter was published in all the leading newspapers, and the government's response was to declare that Francis Burdett be charged with seditious libel. Orator Hunt, too, was to be tried; but the government resisted all demands for an impartial inquiry into the events. The cases against Burdett and Hunt were to come before the courts in the spring of 1820, so it is small wonder that when Caroline started talking about the wishes of 'the people' at some time between Peterloo in August 1819 and the trials of the following year, her words seemed politically charged.

William Cobbett, an off-and-on enemy of Burdett, was another towering figure on the political scene. Unlike Burdett he was a self-made man of modest origins, but like him he was a charismatic egotist and born self-publicist who believed that Britain must secure the reform of Parliament, throwing out the boroughmongers and widening representation of ordinary people. Cobbett was also a true patriot who attacked the government and the Regent in order, as he saw it, to strengthen Britain and to restore to its people their ancient rights and liberties. In 1816, in response to hunger and unemployment in the countryside, he published a short, cheap version of his weekly paper, the *Political Register*. Known, to Cobbett's delight, as 'twopenny trash', it became an immense success. As never before, Cobbett was making a clarion call for parliamentary reform in a mass-circulation paper. Laws intended to put seditious writers into prison soon followed. In 1817 Cobbett fled to America. In 1819 he returned to England with a mission to re-establish himself in British political life and quickly realised that Caroline's cause might be of use.

Cobbett's physical presence was remarkable. He was tall and portly with, according to Hazlitt, a 'good sensible face – rather full, with little grey eyes, a hard, square forehead, a ruddy complexion with hair grey or powdered'. He dressed as a gentleman farmer might have done a century earlier, on occasion sporting 'a scarlet broad-cloth waistcoat with the flaps of the pockets hanging down'.[22] His dress sense was appropriate, for Cobbett in his radicalism chose to romanticise the established facts of the past rather than pursue utopias of an imagined future.

He must have read Caroline's submissions to the London papers with interest, since he too appealed to the 'genuine nation'. He had never met the Queen but, after opposing her in 1806, had become a convert to her cause and supported her in 1813, when the findings of the Delicate Investigation were made public. His commitment was tested during a miserable stay in Newgate prison in 1810–1812 on a sedition conviction.

Anne Cobbett, William's daughter, said that, at that time, an acquaintance of George 'told Papa that if he would be silent on the subject of the Princess he would be let out. Papa said he would promise nothing, but act when the time came, as he might think proper,' and remained incarcerated.[23] Anne reports that her father's health did not suffer in Newgate, but his temper did, and that from then on he broke a habit of never talking about politics in society. 'After Newgate he talked of little else. He was so angry at being ill-used.'[24]

In early 1820 Cobbett leapt into action, starting a new newspaper. Then, when the King died and an election became due, he ran for Parliament in Coventry. The newspaper sold few copies at the time, thanks to Sidmouth's laws, and the election did not provide Cobbett with a seat. However, Caroline's cause started to look like a fruitful political opportunity – and Cobbett began to write in her favour in his *Political Register*. Indeed, throughout 1820 he was to devote nearly two thousand pages of the *Register* to her.

On 15 February Anne, as canny as her father, wrote that 'a Queen's party is forming'. Her observation was significant. Until now, the main problem for Britain's radicals was that they could never agree about tactics or philosophy, and factionalism was rife. Some favoured slow, peaceful change. Others demanded more dynamism. Some thought parliaments should be elected on an annual basis, while others thought such short terms unworkable. Now, though, those disagreements might be forgotten. The Queen's cause was becoming so popular, and being taken up by so many different types of people, that the radicals sniffed the possibility of, at the very least, causing serious damage to the government. For once they were broadly united. Paradoxically, the Queen was supported as much by republicans, albeit with some cynicism, as she was by gentle reformers. She was to be made the representative of 'the people'. And 'the people' were, for once, not a vague concept deployed by the establishment to rally the forces of loyalism. They were, instead, fast becoming an antagonistic body. And the Queen, as their figurehead, made the perfect symbol of opposition to this unpopular monarch and his government. As the *Manchester Observer* was to put it later that year: 'There has long been wanting in England a centre of union to all the friends of liberty.' Caroline was to fill that gap.

6

EXCLUSION

All the people are of one mind – that Revolution has pervaded the Continent and will succeed here.

Home Office spy (1820)

George, on becoming King, devoted his waking hours to consideration of one urgent policy objective, namely that of divorcing his wife and preventing her from being crowned Queen. As he saw it, his reign would be intolerable if Caroline were to play a part in it; and he was determined that she should have none of the rights and privileges due to a Queen Consort. In early February he became seriously ill with a chest infection, and was feared to be close to death. But he was soon well enough to call for all the prayer books in Carlton House, and to spend many hours ploughing through them in search of a precedent for his first political act as George IV – a demand that Caroline's name be removed from the liturgy at Sunday services. Her very existence annoyed him, and the thought that she be prayed for, along with him, in every village church was impossible to contemplate. As the Tory MP John Wilson Croker put it, the subject had 'taken a wonderful hold of his mind'.[1] Castlereagh wrote that it 'haunted his imagination and distracted his rest'.[2]

The King's power, of course, was restricted, and whilst he might attempt to force his wife's name out of the Church without the support of his Cabinet, it was preferable to have it. Lords Liverpool, Sidmouth, Castlereagh and Wellington were all remarkable men – but this was not their finest hour. They opposed a royal divorce, and were against the removal of the Queen's name from the liturgy, but they were weakened by the government's unpopularity and its bludgeoning attacks on any action deemed seditious. The Peterloo massacre had been swiftly followed by the infamous 'Six Acts' which cracked down on the cheap press and banned public meetings of more than fifty people – and in early 1820 the Liverpool ministry seemed isolated from the populace and dependent on keeping favour with the King. The Prime Minister Lord Liverpool was cast as the grim figurehead of repression, the Home Secretary Lord Sidmouth as its architect, and the Foreign Secretary Lord Castlereagh as a bloody-minded enemy of the common man. By association, even Lord Wellington, the hero of Waterloo, found his popularity waning. All round, the government had a defensive air about it.

George, amongst his prayer books, continued to search for his precedent, but failed, and it was Croker who, in a moment of inspiration, provided the justification for removing Caroline from Sunday prayers. 'If she is fit to be introduced to the Almighty she is fit to be received by men,' he argued, 'and if we are to *pray* for her in church we may surely bow to her at court. The praying for her will throw a sanctity round her which the good and pious people of this country will never afterwards bear to have withdrawn.'[3] The ministers caved in, and in defiance of the Archbishop of Canterbury an order went out on 12 February demanding that the clergy of the United Kingdom did not mention the name of the Queen when praying for the royal family in church on Sundays. Most clergymen were happy to oblige, but made themselves unpopular in doing so.

Many in the press and public took instant offence. The fourteen-year-old Elizabeth Barrett was moved to record the event in her diary. 'At this period, when the base & servile aristocracy of our beloved country overwhelm with insults our magnanimous and unfortunate Queen,' she wrote, 'I cannot restrain my indignation, I cannot control my enthusiasm – my dearest ambition would be to serve her, to serve the glorious Queen of my native isle.'[4] The newspapers were more restrained in their language, but made their opinions clear. As early as 1 February *The Times* proclaimed that now Caroline was Queen Consort of the United Kingdom she was 'entitled to her state and establishment'. Then, on 14 February, the paper published its views on the liturgy. 'Extremely sorry we shall be,' it opined, 'if political differences insinuate themselves into our worship.'

Four days later *The Times* carried the shocking news of the assassination of the Duc de Berri in Paris, raising the fear that revolutionary sentiment might once more be stirring in France. On the same day the paper reported a disturbing incident at Drury Lane. At the end of the previous evening's performance of music and odes, 'God Save the King' was played, but was interrupted when a group of radicals in the gallery 'showered down from their elevation a profusion of printed papers into the pit'. When examined, the papers were found to carry an additional stanza to the national anthem, to be sung at the end:

> God save Queen Caroline!
> May our great power divine
> Bless our good Queen!
> Confound her enemies
> Make her fame pure to rise
> Hail'd by a nation's cries
> God save the Queen!

'If the motive of this proceeding,' said *The Times*, 'was to sow dis-
sension' it was 'wretchedly miscalculated'. The audience, it reported,
was unmoved and did not burst into song.

Spurred on by his triumph on the liturgy, George now went back to
his ministers demanding more concessions. Could Caroline be tried
for high treason? he asked. No, said Lord Liverpool, it was out of the
question. Well then, it has to be divorce, insisted the King, encouraged
by John Leach, the commander in chief of the Milan Commission.[5]
But divorce, said Liverpool with the unanimous support of the Cabinet,
would be extremely hazardous, not least because any evidence of the
Queen's adultery would have to be supplied by foreigners of low birth.
Worse still, a divorce case would have to be held in public, and revelations would be made that were offensive to public decency 'and likely
to disturb the peace of the country'.[6]

George wouldn't budge. Surely there was enough 'evidence of
criminality'[7] on the part of the Queen to make a divorce a perfectly
straightforward affair? The testimonies of the Milan witnesses, he told
Liverpool and the others, were so consistent that the fact that they
were foreigners was immaterial. He did not express much concern
about public decency, which, presumably, could look after itself.

The ministers persisted in trying to make him change his mind,
asking him to permit negotiations with Caroline aimed at paying her
off to stay out of the country. This was not good enough for the King,
who feared that under such a deal his wife would still be able to return
to England at any time and destroy his peace. He stood firm, and
threatened to sack the entire Cabinet if it continued to resist him. The
ministers in turn dug in, considering it utterly reckless to expose
the government and monarch to 'the dangers *of a public trial in
these factious times*'.[8]

Indeed, the Cabinet had half a mind to resign and on 13 February
Lord Sidmouth admitted that 'the government is in a very strange,
and, I must acknowledge, in a precarious state'.[9] On the same day
Castlereagh confessed that he thought the government, 'virtually dis-
solved',[10] and rumours of a government resignation quickly spread
around London high society.

Charles Greville, Clerk to the Privy Council, recorded in his diary that resignations were in fact offered and that the King had, in response, 'treated Lord Liverpool very coarsely and ordered him out of the room'. He also snapped at the Chancellor, Eldon, 'My Lord, I know your conscience always interferes except where your interest is concerned.'[11] George was, clearly, in a huff. 'His agitation is extreme and alarming,' wrote Croker. 'He eats hardly anything – a bit of dry toast and a little claret and water.'[12] In the end, though, George's ability to find a new set of ministers willing to do his bidding was almost non-existent, since the Whigs were as opposed to a divorce as the Tories, and both the King and his government knew it.

On 14 February the argument reached its climax. Lord Castlereagh had a five-hour audience with George which began with a three-hour speech from the King extolling the virtues and the necessity of a divorce. But Castlereagh was known to be brilliant in private negotiation, and was altogether a superior man to his monarch. Unknown to most of the hostile British population, his lofty air was underpinned by a strong morality and, though he lacked the King's easy charm, he was able to wear down opponents by persistence, knowledge and conviction; William Wilberforce was so wary of Castlereagh's negotiating skills that he insisted on dealing with him by letter. George was not given to feelings of inferiority, but he was facing a man who had already proved himself one of the greatest Foreign Secretaries in British history and, by the by, had retained his proud good looks while the King had lost his.

The details of Castlereagh's response to George's tirade are unrecorded, but we do know that he aimed directly at the weak underbelly of the King's case. George seemed to be blind to the fact that Caroline would, in court, be entitled to a defence of 'recrimination', allowing her to argue that his behaviour had been as bad as hers, if not worse. Did the King not realise how embarrassing this could be to him? How it would allow a field day of comment on his 'neglect and ill-usage' of his wife? That it would almost certainly cause his case to fail? Castlereagh catalogued George's less-than-private affairs with

'his several mistresses from Mrs Fitzherbert downwards', in the knowledge that royal womanising was, even now, in full throttle and that
he was in the process of dumping his amour of the previous years,
Lady Hertford, for another plump woman of mature years, Lady
Conyngham. Henry Hobhouse wrote in his diary that Castlereagh 'left
the King in a subdued tone of mind'.[13]

Three days later George wrote to the Cabinet, capitulating. He
would now agree to a proposal being put to Caroline to pay her
£50,000 in return for a promise to stay abroad. This compromise, he
complained, required a 'great and painful sacrifice of his personal feelings'. However, if the Queen did not accept the proposal, as he
suspected she would not, then it would be the duty of the Cabinet to
support to the utmost 'every measure which will be required for the
due maintenance of the Dignity of the Crown – the interests of the
Public – and the personal honour and feelings of the King'.[14] In short,
if Caroline did not agree to the deal, George was to get his divorce
case. The Cabinet lost no time in moving events forward, and called
for Henry Brougham, whom Caroline had now appointed as her official legal representative – her Attorney General. Brougham told the
ministers that he would counsel the Queen to stay abroad, with the
warning that 'she was a woman of such strong passions' that he could
not guarantee that she would follow the advice.[15]

On 18 February Parliament met. In the Commons Joseph Hume, a
leading, able and 'lynx-eyed' radical MP, caused a stir by asking after
Caroline's welfare. Would the Queen continue to receive the annuity
granted her until the death of George III? Castlereagh gave a brief
answer, assuring the House that her interests would be granted proper
consideration. Three days later, in the middle of a debate, Joseph
Hume rose again, this time with a more fiery and overtly antagonistic intervention. He urged Parliament to deplore the treatment that the
government had accorded the Queen. When George III had died, he
asked, why had no message of condolence been sent to Caroline? Or
for that matter any message of congratulation on becoming Queen?
Was she to continue to live abroad supporting herself by alms? Was
her fate no concern of Parliament? The Whigs did not follow this

radical lead. They were biding their time, and did not rush to make Caroline an anti-Tory, anti-George cause. Even Henry Brougham, who was prone to run away with himself in argument, kept his language mild and controlled. The Hume intervention, though, thrust into the open the connection between Caroline and the radicals. The London newspapers reported it and some published messages of support for the Queen.

Then, on 23 February, an event occurred which for a short time diverted the nation's attention away from Caroline. A gang of revolutionary conspirators met that evening in a small hay loft in Cato Street, just off Edgware Road in London. They were armed with guns, swords and daggers, and plotting to murder the entire Cabinet. Led by Arthur Thistlewood, a notorious rebel and follower of the eighteenth-century revolutionary Thomas Spence, the 'diabolical ruffians' were a bunch of discontented ideologues and misfits. At least one of them, George Edwards, was a government spy. The gang intended to storm a Cabinet dinner party at Lord Harrowby's house, kill the diners, and then set fire to the City's army barracks, seize the artillery, take over the Bank of England and the Tower of London, throw open the gates of Newgate and finally put into place a provisional government. One gang member, Ings, vowed to cut off the heads of the government's two most hated men, Lord Castlereagh and Lord Sidmouth, and had brought along two haversacks and a long knife for the purpose. Their heads were then to be carried on pikes through the slums of London. Wellington later claimed that he was to have been the victim of Thistlewood himself.

Through Edwards, Lord Sidmouth knew about the plot in advance, and the Cabinet debated what to do. Castlereagh was in favour of going ahead with the dinner at Lord Harrowby's. The Cabinet should be armed, he argued, and should fight it out in hand-to-hand combat with the revolutionaries. But the Duke of Wellington's cooler approach won the day and the politicians met elsewhere, while a small band of police officers advanced on Cato Street. When the policemen entered the Cato Street loft, however, Thistlewood rushed at an officer named Richard Smithers, stabbing him through the heart with his sword and killing him almost instantly. Thistlewood then ordered the lights to be turned out, and in the confusion, several men escaped. The ringleaders were soon rounded up, and Ings was discovered to be hoarding a stack of gunpowder, fire-balls and hand grenades.

Lord Sidmouth was convinced that the attempt to overthrow the government was part of a nationwide, organised plot, and George, who had a particular fondness for his Home Secretary, was of a mind to accept his view. He praised Sidmouth for his zeal and vigilance in 'the detection of crimes which have brought our land to the condition heretofore reserved only for revolutionary France'.[16] In the wider political world, the Cato Street conspiracy was used to further different causes. Richard Rush, America's representative in London, noted in his diary that government opponents saw the plot as resulting from Sidmouth's repressive laws. Criticism of the government, they said, could no longer be expressed openly through the cheap press, and was forced to find 'modes more dangerous'.[17]

Some newspapers dared to print seditious sentiments. The *Manchester Observer* said Englishmen, of course, abhor assassinations, but if on offering up their 'humblest petitions for redress they receive only thrust of the bayonet and blows of the sabre', a blatant reference to Peterloo, then who knows to what lengths they may be driven. What weapons might they take up in 'combating an enemy who himself tramples on all the ties which have heretofore bound men together in civil society'?[18] The Home Office had its eye on the paper, and also on the similarly outspoken *Leeds Mercury*.

Richard Carlile's radical paper the *Republican*, by coincidence, published a long editorial on 'the Queen' just two days after Cato Street, making Caroline's cause seem like just another dimension of the broader political picture. 'As men struggling to be free,' the paper argued, 'we feel it an imperative duty to support this injured woman.' It was not a matter of the rights of royalty that she should be championed, but one of standing up for an ill-used wife. 'The more the Queen is persecuted and reviled by the court Sycophants the more she will reign in the affections of the British people,' it continued. The public would ensure that (unlike her husband) she will not 'need a troop of guards with drawn swords to protect her, nor a carriage that is bullet proof'. Indeed, 'she has nothing to look to for protection but the mass of the people'.[19]

By 'the mass of the people' Carlile meant the lower classes, which were also the focus for Sidmouth's suspicions. And those suspicions were never more aroused than now. One of the Home Secretary's spies in Manchester reported that the activities of the radical committees there had intensified in the aftermath of Cato Street and 'there is good reason to believe that they contemplate some explosion at no very distant period'. The imminent trials of Francis Burdett and Henry Hunt were also causing 'a considerable ferment in the minds of the lower classes'. Moreover, reported the informant darkly, 'the influx of strangers and the assemblage of small parties in the street has much increased, and a well-known look of defiance is very observable'.[20]

In London other spies infiltrated seditious meetings regularly held at the Mulberry Tree pub in Bull Street, Moorfields, where 'the hopes of a *Revolution* in France, Spain and England was *publickly expressed*', and a debate was held asking '*Whether the French Revolution has tended to ameliorate the condition of society*', with arguments in favour of the benefits of all revolutions being expressed with 'extreme violence'. The coffee houses were 'assuming a bolder tone of sedition than in . . . [the] past', claimed a London informer and the revolutionary radicals were trying to forge alliances with the editors of the 'corrupt and seditious press' in Manchester, Birmingham, Glasgow and Dublin.[21]

Unsolicited warnings, many of them anonymous, flooded into the Home Office, alongside those from paid informers. 'The blow is to be struck suddenly,' wrote a 'moderate reformer' from Wakefield. 'Revolution is the word – arms are to be taken from those who have any in their possession; Pikes to a considerable amount in number . . . have been made and spread over the whole face of the country, those who make the least resistance are to be put to Death.'[22]

On 7 March, in the House of Lords, Lord Sidmouth defended the necessity of keeping the Six Acts, telling peers that 'the constitution of

England was in greater danger than it had been in any other time since the accession of the House of Brunswick to the throne'. Lord Grenville agreed that 'nothing could equal the imminence of the peril which impended over the country', while the Whig leader Earl Grey spoke against the Acts, declaring that they 'took away the protection allowed to free discussion, and aimed a blow at one of the most valuable rights of Englishmen such as the most arbitrary Minister in the most arbitrary times never proposed to Parliament'.

Lord Sidmouth's unpopularity at this moment was deep and widespread. Death threats arrived at his office most weeks, along with other poisonous hate mail. 'It is not possible to be hated more than thou art hated by us,' spat an anonymous correspondent. 'We thirst not after blood but after Liberty, Liberty of which we have been so basely robbed . . . but remember Caesar's warning, remember Caesar's fate.'[23] Sidmouth, privately a kindly, courageous and learned man, refused to be cowed by his post bag – and pressed on with the honest view that to crush sedition quickly and decisively was essential in order to prevent Britain from slipping into chaos.

The Cabinet, for the most part, supported his tough line, as did George, who regarded Sidmouth as his chief commander in the war against tumult and revolution, and who dubbed him 'the Duke of Wellington upon Home Service'.[24] Wellington himself saw the danger as a serious one and urged Sidmouth to organise, without loss of time, the whole of the militia of the United Kingdom into a comprehensive fighting force in case domestic rebellion should break out.[25]

The prospect seemed real enough to the people of Glasgow, who woke up on the morning of 2 April to find revolutionary proclamations on display throughout the city calling on the people of Scotland, England and Ireland to rise up and effect a revolution by force. It recommended the proprietors of large factories to suspend operations, and told the common people not to go to work. The call to revolt was authored by a committee for the organisation of a provisional government. The weavers of Glasgow and Paisley stayed away from work, as did the colliers, the iron founders, the wrights, masons and machine makers. The cotton mills went still during the course of the day and the streets became full of gazing crowds waiting for the revolution to begin.

The magistrates soon assembled a large military force and warned the people that rebellion would be put down. The revolution failed to materialise – but three days later, on 5 April, a skirmish broke out at Bonnymuir between forty to fifty radicals armed with muskets, pikes and pistols and the cavalry. The military won the battle with little difficulty and no loss of life. Sidmouth's intelligence network was, as usual, busy, and arrests of revolutionaries or potential revolutionaries were made in Glasgow, Renfrewshire, Lanarkshire, Dumbartonshire, Stirlingshire and Ayrshire. Trials were scheduled for July and August, and were to result in the execution of three men, and the deportation of about twenty others.

The uprisings of early 1820 did not, thanks to the vigilance of the authorities, come close to a full-blown rebellion. But they were serious enough to cause the government grave anxiety. All around the country there were, undoubtedly, groups of malcontents planning unrest, with some degree of coordination. Thus far, when they had tried to put their violent plans into action they had been stalled by a failure to swell their numbers at the crucial moments, and by the effectiveness of government spies. The Scottish rebels had hoped that the whole of Glasgow would rise up, and a simultaneous rebellion planned in Huddersfield in Yorkshire failed when its leaders converged on an agreed meeting place where the River Colne joined the Calder and found only 200, not the expected thousands of men, ready to fight. The *Leeds Mercury* believed a successful revolt in Huddersfield was to have been the signal for an uprising 'throughout all the manufacturing districts in the Kingdom, extending even to Scotland'. The general feeling in Cabinet was that the rebels had been put down thus far, but that the country remained unsafe.

In March and early April, in the midst of all the disturbances, a general election took place and Caroline made her allegiances known to her friends. On 13 April she wrote to William Gell from Pesaro: 'The elections are going on extremely well for the Opposition. Young

Whitbread is for Brentford and Hobhouse for Westminster; in short all gone on well.'[26] Whitbread was the son of her old friend Samuel Whitbread, who had taken his own life in 1815, while John Cam Hobhouse was a dedicated reformer who was to become one of her keenest supporters. In the same letter she said she would be in Calais by the first or second of May.

At the same time her difficulties were revealed to the English public with the leaking to the newspapers of a more literate, more detailed version of a letter she had written to Lord Liverpool on 16 March. The public learned of her humiliating experiences when snubbed by foreign dignitaries, of her demands made to Lords Liverpool and Castlereagh that her name be inserted into the liturgy, as well as her insistence 'that orders be given to all British Ambassadors, Ministers and Consuls that I should be received and acknowledged as the Queen of England'. She informed the British public that she had demanded a palace to be prepared for her, and declared, 'England is my real home, to which I shall immediately fly.'[27]

The date of Caroline's arrival was now a matter of intense speculation, particularly in London. The Lord Chancellor, Eldon, said 'great bets' were being laid, and that: 'Some people have taken fifty guineas, undertaking in lieu of them to pay a guinea a day till she comes, so sure are these that she will come within fifty days.' For his own part, Eldon predicted that 'she will not come *unless she is insane*'.[28] Meanwhile, the Queen was applauded at dinners and public occasions across the city. The lawyer and journalist Henry Crabb Robinson attended the theatre on 26 April but found it hard to hear the performance. 'A fellow cried out from the shilling gallery – "The Queen!"' he wrote in his diary. 'The allusion was caught up, and not a word was heard afterwards.'[29]

A day or two earlier, Matthew Wood had been guest of honour at a dinner to celebrate his success in the general election, in which he retained his seat representing the City of London. *The Times* carried a report of the occasion, stating that a toast was raised to the King, and then a second proposed for 'the Queen and all other branches of the royal family'. This was drunk, according to the paper's witness, 'with the most enthusiastic expressions of applause'.[30] Quite possibly the greatest pleasure in this toast was felt by Wood himself, for by this time he had become the Queen's closest confidante in England, and was urging her to come to England at once. Lady Anne Hamilton, a former lady-in-waiting to Caroline, wrote imploring her to follow Wood's advice. Advisers close to the King's ear, she said, doubtless meaning Brougham, were using 'specious reasoning' to persuade her to stay in continental Europe. Caroline should instead put her trust in 'he' (Wood) who was 'better acquainted with the public feeling' and who would be 'incapable of compromising Your Majesty's interests' in favour of 'ambitious views of his own'. She must 'take counsel from the people of England', who would ensure the safety of her life and liberty.[31]

On 15 April, Caroline wrote to Matthew Wood proclaiming in her usual free-form grammar and spelling, 'The 30th April I sal be at Calais for certain: my health is good and my spirit is perfect.' She added: 'I have seen no personnes of any kind who could give me any advise different to my feelings and my sentimons of duty relatif of my present situation and rank in life.'[32] Decoded, this letter implies that Caroline was now relishing the idea of fighting for her rights, and that she would tolerate only those who supported her decision to engage in battle. Lady Anne Hamilton was at the forefront of those who encouraged her, writing to her again in May: 'Again and again . . . I beseech Your Majesty to come with all speed to receive the blessings of your subjects.'[33]

If Lady Anne and Matthew Wood had known of the travelling companions that Caroline had selected for her journey towards England, they would have been delighted. A new chamberlain by the name of Olivieri had been signed up, as well as a Captain Vassalli. Both men alarmed the Milan Commissioner, James Brown, who warned London that they 'are of violent democratical principles which in fact are the politics encouraged and prevalent in the whole of her suite'.[34]

At Geneva Caroline was to include Matthew Wood's son William in her entourage, and the Alderman set about maximising his influence.

He launched into a frenzy of activity attending to one remaining commitment in England before he could sail for France to meet the Queen – attendance at the executions of five of the Cato Street conspirators. Wood had become convinced that their actions had been spurred on by George Edwards who was not just a government spy, he thought, but an *agent provocateur*. With the consent of the condemned men he quizzed them on the subject in the moments before they took their places at the scaffold.

They were hanged before a great crowd. John Cam Hobhouse wrote in his diary: 'The men died like heroes. Ings perhaps too obstreperous in singing Death or Liberty and Thistlewood said, "Be quiet Ings; we can die without all this noise."' Once dead, the mens' heads were cut off and paraded before the crowd, who booed and hissed not the traitors, but the hooded executioner.

Matthew Wood next made a plea in the House of Commons for George Edwards to be tried for treason, on the grounds that his part in the conspiracy had been active. But Sidmouth ensured that his agent was spirited away out of the country to the Channel Islands, and Wood decided that his battle against the government should now proceed on one front only – through Caroline. In this he felt the same as many other activists. After the execution of the Cato Street conspirators, observed the journalist Charles Knight, 'there was only one chance of a convulsion', and that lay with the Queen.[35]

Matthew Wood sailed for France in order to accompany Caroline to England. He was determined that she should not, at the last minute, accept any deal proposed by the government, and so was particularly keen to reach her before Henry Brougham did. It was his mission to be at the side of the Queen of England as she entered London, to show the world that the Queen and radicalism were walking arm-in-arm.

7

BROUGHAM

They neglect and proscribe her;
She threatens returning – they then try to bribe her!

The Queen's Matrimonial Ladder

The Queen could not have chosen a more able Attorney General than Henry Brougham. While she had been away on her European travels, he had been consolidating his position as the Whigs' brightest star, enthusiastically campaigning for favourite causes such as the education of the poor and the abolition of slavery. He was now well established at the reforming end of Whig politics and also, thanks to hyperactive socialising, had great influence with the traditionalist Whig aristocrats. He was not accepted as their social equal by any means and his fierce intellect got in the way of his popularity. But he was listened to and, to a degree, he was feared. The Queen, like others, had conflicting feelings about him. She did not like him much and was not sure that she could trust him. But she was aware that he was a brilliant politician, lawyer and publicist.

She did not know that in her absence Brougham had experienced a number of debilitating attacks of exhaustion, or deep depression, which could render him incapable of work. He hid these episodes as far as he could by retreating to his home in the north of England until he was better and could again appear in public. We know how frightening the attacks were from an essay written by Brougham which reveals his understanding of depression. 'The active powers were first affected,' he wrote, 'all the exertions of the will becoming more painful and more difficult.' The inertness next crept over the intellectual faculties, 'the exercise of which became more distasteful and their operations more sluggish'. In 1815, he experienced a particularly deadening attack which caused him to '*ache all over*', made him unable to work for four months and prompted his friend Thomas Creevey to question his sanity. After this, Brougham was constantly alert to his susceptibility to breakdown, and once confessed that, 'I really always reckon on each night being my last.'[1]

His method of staving off the black dog was to keep himself busy and to hope for the best. He did this in his private life as well as his public, first through a liaison with the fashionable courtesan of the period, Harriette Wilson, who counted the Duke of Wellington among her clients. Then, in 1816 he began an affair with Caroline Lamb, sister-in-law of the more famous Caroline Lamb who was Byron's lover. Lamb, known in the family as 'Caro George', caused a scandal by leaving her husband and running off to Brougham, who was on holiday in Geneva. Her lover's attraction lay more in his spirit, intellect and wit than his looks, for, despite looking incredibly beautiful in a portrait by Thomas Lawrence, he had a strange uneven face and an enormous nose which bulged at the end. The courtesan Julia Johnstone thought him an 'antidote to the tender passion . . . his features apparently stamped on a toad-stool and his eyes like marbles floating in mortar'.[2]

The Geneva encounter did not go well. Brougham found his new love as dull as he did Switzerland. 'Ennui comes on the third hour,' he wrote, 'and suicide attacks you before night.'[3] Lady Frances Shelley, who encountered him on this trip, found him disengaged from his surroundings, and living inside his own head. William Hazlitt had observed that Brougham's mind was so active that 'it appears to require neither repose or any other stimulus than a delight in its own exercise'. Lady Frances wrote:

> He hates travelling, abhors Switzerland and the Swiss generally, scoffs at fine views, does not go to see anything if he can avoid it. He by choice travels at night, and passes the day in writing letters. He wishes himself back in England, and yet has no intention of going there. He stays in places where he has no reason for staying and is always dissatisfied. It is evident that great talents are of no use, without a little sunshine of the mind![4]

Whilst on the continent he made a detour and visited Caroline at Lake Como. Little is known of what happened at their meeting, but it does not seem to have affected the nature of their relationship; they remained tied to each other by bonds of necessity, not affection.

When back in Britain, Brougham made it his aim to consolidate the various anti-government forces in the Houses of Parliament. This was a tough undertaking, as the aristocratic 'high Whigs' of his party had little in common in policy terms with the group of radicals and reformers that included Sir Francis Burdett, John Cam Hobhouse and Joseph Hume. Brougham was also on a quest to make himself the leader not just of his party, but of the country, as the next prime minister. All in all, he made a hash of it. His causes, which included tax cuts and prison reform, failed to win the hearts of the high Whigs, while he equivocated on the great issue of the day, the thorough reform of Parliament and extension of the franchise, and so disappointed the radicals.

In March 1816, he further damaged his chance of taking the Whig leadership by an embarrassing display of self-aggrandisement that was probably due to some sort of manic episode. He told the radical

Francis Place that he was on the brink of offering himself to the nation with the words, 'I am willing to take the charge of this Government, to reform the Parliament, and to change the whole of the present ruinous system.' Two nights later he made a speech in the Commons that amounted to little more than an intemperate and personal assault on the Prince Regent, making special note of George's lack of concern for the sufferings of his people and his profligate way of life. His tirade offended almost everyone. 'He could not have roared louder if a file of soldiers had come in and pushed the Speaker out of his chair,' said Charles Western, a back-bench anti-Tory squire who witnessed the event and thought it a 'damn'd impudent speech' which 'will *never* do'. 'I have often marvelled at the *want* of sense, discretion, judgement and common sense that we see so frequently accompany the most brilliant talents,' he wrote to Creevey, 'but damn me if I ever saw such an instance as I have just witnessed in your friend Brougham.' As for Brougham's ambition to be leader, 'for that he is DONE NOW'.[5] Brougham's old friend Samuel Romilly thought that, with all George's faults, it was 'absurd to speak of him as if he were one of the most sensual and unfeeling tyrants that ever disgraced a throne'. Brougham's use of words, he wrote in his diary, was better suited to describe the latter days of the Emperor Tiberius. He had made one of the worst mistakes of his political life.[6]

In the following years Brougham tried to redeem his reputation by playing a leading role in the Commons, and his gutsy, fiery speechifying was the main reason for the Prime Minister's complaint to George that 'we are exposed to the most acrimonious, systematic and persevering Opposition that I ever recollect to have seen in Parliament'. His attacks on government ministers during the repressive clampdown on writers in 1817 and in the aftermath of Peterloo were particularly ferocious. But they did not secure Henry Brougham the Whig leadership. The high Whigs still regarded him with suspicion. He was too unpredictable and too ambitious.

Now, thanks to his appointment as Caroline's Attorney General, he was at the centre stage of politics and determined to play his hand well. But his efforts in the spring and early summer of 1820 were clumsy bordering on incompetent. Perhaps he was juggling too many objectives. Caroline's interests, his own interests, those of his party, and the benefit of the country were all of importance, and Brougham's mind did not tend towards simplifying the difficult, he was better at making simple issues complex. 'Brougham has hated always the broad Turnpike roads of life,' observed his friend Sydney Smith, and he arrived at his goals 'by crossing the country over hedge and ditch'.[7] These rambling ways make any attempt at inference of his purpose from the nature of his acts a hazardous business.

When charged by Liverpool to negotiate with Caroline and to persuade her to accept a deal, he had been slow to act, urging the Queen to head towards Calais, but not rushing to meet her. So, for about four months Caroline had been in the dark about the government's proposals. It seems that, during this time, Brougham could not make up his mind whether the Queen should stay in Europe, or come to England. 'It would be *frightfully dangerous* for her to come here all at once,' he had told Lady Charlotte Lindsay on 18 February. 'All now depends on her coming to Brussels or some near and handy spot. If she arrives plump on you at Paris, make her either stay there or at Calais till I come out to her.'[8]

It was only in late April that he became aware of Alderman Wood's profound influence on Caroline, and began to demonstrate some appearance of urgency. He then wrote to Lord Hutchinson, a personal friend of George's, saying that he had heard that Wood was off to the continent, ostensibly to see his son William in Paris but, thought Brougham correctly, in reality to meet Caroline. He feared Matthew Wood's strategy and advised George's people to launch a smear campaign against the Alderman in the press. 'I am clear that Carlton House ought in Monday's newspapers to put in all manner of hurts and squibs against him,' he wrote. 'This may keep her from listening to so great a blockhead, if well done and quickly.'[9]

This is a fine example of Brougham acting in the manner of a modern-day spin doctor, keenly aware of how to use the press. It was precisely the sort of tactic that the Whigs, in promoting their own interests, relied on Brougham to deliver. But they did not want a

master of such distasteful practices as a figurehead, let alone prime
minister. On one occasion Brougham tried to persuade the party's
most respected leader, Lord Grey, of his approach. 'I don't mean that
things should be undertaken from mere love of popularity,' he argued,
'but it is a good assisting reason, when they are excellent in themselves.'[10] For parliamentarians, it was an idea whose time was still to
come – and Grey did not embrace it.

While Brougham was fretting about Matthew Wood getting the
advantage over him with Caroline, he was also considering a little bargaining with George's government on his own behalf. Some time that
spring he asked for promotion for himself and his colleague Thomas
Denman to King's Counsel – in other words, silk gowns, and a guarantee of more income. Then, he intimated, he would ensure that all
the hurdles blocking a deal with Caroline would somehow be swept
away.[11] George Canning, Caroline's old friend and now a member of
the Cabinet, thought the wish should be granted as a matter of
urgency. Henry Brougham, he believed, was wondering whether 'he
has not a better game before him in fighting the Queen's battle than in
conspiring with us to keep the peace'. And the silk gown given or
promised at once 'would have fixed him'.

Brougham's interests, Canning pointed out, would be well served if
he were to lead Caroline into battle, since the 'hostile discussion' of
the row between the King and Queen would without 'the slightest
doubt' overthrow the government. Lord Liverpool, the Prime
Minister, was persuaded of Canning's argument and in favour of
granting the silk gown, but his wish was blocked by the Chancellor,
Lord Eldon, who loathed Brougham and found his presumption
offensive. It is possible that the gown was offered in the end. But it was
too late – Brougham's strategy had moved on. In early June he left for
the continent and Caroline, but by the time he reached her, Matthew
Wood had already been with her for a week, lobbying her to proceed
to England. As Brougham put it later, the Queen's close advisers were
'speaking in the name of the multitude, and would advise her to throw
herself on them for protection'.[12]

Caroline's trip across Europe, meanwhile, had been interrupted by a spell of sickness. First, as she expressed it to William Gell, 'I have been in bed with a Rheumatique complaint in my left leg.' Then, 'I was taken very unwell with a most dreadful spasm in my stomach.'[13] This, she thought, would mean that she would be unable to get as far as London, and would mean turning back for Italy before the autumn. However, in true Caroline spirit, this was all forgotten by the end of May, by which time she had made her way to Villeneuve-le-Roi where she composed and sent a letter to Lord Liverpool saying she would arrive in London next Saturday, '3thd of Juin'. 'I desire also that the Earl of Liverpool will give proper orders that one of the royal yachts should be ready at Calais for bringing me over to Dover,' she continued. And then she demanded to be informed of 'his Majeste's intentions what residence should be allotted to me, either permenant or temporary use'. The letter was signed, rather sarcastically, 'I trust that His Majeste the King is perfectly recovered from his severe illness. Caroline, Queen of England.'[14]

Brougham would have been horrified at her crude way of expressing herself, and had he been close to Caroline at the time would doubtless have drafted something far more elegant. But the letter arrived in London and the King's friend, Lord Hutchinson, like most courtly types, was aghast at her tone. 'It is impossible for me to paint the insolence, the violence and the precipitation of this woman's conduct,' he wrote to Bloomfield. He went on:

> She has really assumed a tone and hauteur which is quite insufferable, and which nothing but the most pure and unimpeached innocence could justify . . . We have at length come to a final and ultimate issue with this outrageous woman. She has set the King's authority at defiance, and it is now time for her to feel his vengeance and his power. Patience, forebearance and moderation have had no effect upon her. I must now implore His Majesty to exert all his firmness and resolution: retreat is impossible. The Queen has thrown down the gauntlet of defiance. The King must take it up.[15]

It was Hutchinson who, it was decided, should travel with Brougham to see Caroline. Together they would try to persuade her to stay in

Europe, with the offer of £50,000 a year if she agreed. 'I was the bearer of a proposition that she should have all the rights of Queen-Consort, especially as regarded money and patronage,' wrote Brougham later. 'Lord Hutchinson was the bearer of an intimation that on her coming to England all negotiation must cease.'[16] The message was plain. If she set foot in England, all the government's weaponry would be used to destroy the Queen. The evidence of the Milan Commission would be released, Caroline would be accused of adultery and divorce would follow.

The Queen had now reached St Omer, a town near Calais in northern France. Brougham and Hutchinson arrived there on 3 June and checked into two separate hotels. Brougham went out in search of the Queen and found her at a third hotel in the company of Matthew Wood and 'surrounded by Italians'. Lady Anne Hamilton, a woman of radical sensibilities, was there too. Brougham, who had received in writing the detailed terms of the government's proposals back in April, still did not pass them on to Caroline. Instead, he introduced Lord Hutchinson as the government envoy who would negotiate with her.

Hutchinson was taken aback. He had expected to take a secondary role to Brougham in the negotiations and did not have a written copy of the deal – so, in his hotel room he drew up something from memory, sending it on to Brougham and Caroline in the afternoon of 4 June. The £50,000 was mentioned, as was the stipulation that the Queen must stay abroad or face the consequences. Indeed he quoted Lord Liverpool as saying that the decision 'is taken to proceed against her as soon as she sets foot on the British shores'. But he also wrote that 'the Queen is not to assume the style and title of Queen of England, or any title attached to the royal family of Great Britain'.[17] This was harsher than the government's true intention to offer some other title, though not Queen.

There was no chance of Caroline accepting such terms. She was taking advice from Alderman Wood, who saw the £50,000 as a bribe, and argued that any acceptance of the money would amount to an admission of guilt on the adultery charge. And, in any case, she was still smarting from the unbearable insults levied at her by foreign diplomats, particularly those from Cardinal Consalvi in Rome. She was not, as they had termed her, Caroline of Brunswick, she was Queen Consort of Great Britain; the government's proposal was in her view insulting and humiliating. At five o'clock on 4 June she gave her answer: 'Mr Brougham is commanded by the Queen to acknowledge the receipt of Lord Hutchinson's letter and to inform his Lordship that it is quite impossible for her Majesty to listen to such a proposition.'[18]

Hutchinson scrambled to rescue the situation, asking Brougham for a more detailed explanation for the Queen's refusal and offering to negotiate a more favourable settlement after liaising with London. But he was too late. Caroline was already saying her last goodbye to Bartolomeo Pergami and was stepping into her carriage. Her refusal to negotiate was to be considered heroic, and a public meeting of her supporters at the Crown and Anchor tavern on the Strand in London expressed, in the grandest terms, the nation's mood:

> the conduct of her Majesty at St Omers in rejecting with indignation the Proposal made to her, of bartering her Honour for money, deserves our warmest praise: And we consider that her Majesty maintained the Dignity of the British Nation and the honourable Character of her Sex in braving every insult, daring every danger and encountering every difficulty, rather than she would suffer the Nation's wealth to be made the purchase of her Dishonour, and the price of Banishment from the Country of which she is the rightful Queen.[19]

This saviour of British honour was now bound for Calais, her coachmen driving on fast through heavy rain.

Brougham, who had watched Caroline leave from a hotel window, sent a note on after her, urging her to 'reflect calmly and patiently upon the step about to be taken'. She should, he said, accept any pledge by government that she should be received abroad by British diplomats 'according to your rank and station'. She should not go to England.[20]

He pleaded with her not to listen to Matthew Wood and others who 'will be found very feeble allies in the hour of difficulty'. And if, despite his advice, she were to travel to England, then she should go in the most private and 'even secret' manner possible. 'It may be very well for a candidate at an election to be drawn into towns by the populace,' he wrote, but not for the Queen, and he felt it necessary to state very plainly that any such exhibition would be 'both hurtful to your Majesty's real dignity and full of danger in its probable consequences'. Caroline, of course, did not listen. Her mind was made up.[21]

Hutchinson was furious with both Brougham and Caroline. 'Before our arrival she had organised everything for stage-effect,' he wrote to Sir Benjamin Bloomfield. 'Her chief performer was that enlightened mountebank Alderman Wood.' He considered that he, the government and the King had been 'entirely out-generaled' and concluded that the 'violence and the determination of this woman have had the effect for the moment of wisdom and arrangement and she has completely succeeded in all her plans'.[22]

In the eyes of many of his friends and colleagues Brougham had, all along, connived at the breakdown of the negotiations – in fact wanting his client to face a divorce case, regardless of her own interests or those of the country. His friend Thomas Denman says otherwise. In his memoir, Denman claims that Brougham considered resigning as the Queen's Attorney General when he realised that she was heading for England, and that he supposed she would then give the position to Matthew Wood. The worldly wise Thomas Creevey, though, was sceptical. He recalled a conversation with Brougham which had occurred shortly before Brougham's dash to St Omer. The two friends had been discussing who might be the next Whig prime minister: 'He thought himself more likely to be sent for to make a Ministry than anyone else, how clear it is that the accomplishment of this divorce was to be the ways and means by which his purposes were to be effected.'

In any case, the result for Brougham of his failure in St Omer was that nobody now trusted him. Lord Liverpool's confidence had been entirely betrayed, while those in Caroline's entourage, especially

Alderman Wood and Lady Anne Hamilton, kept up an unceasing campaign to 'foment her jealousy of him'.[23] It took little persuasion to convince the Queen that Brougham was unreliable, and as she returned to England she put herself entirely in the hands of the politically motivated rabble-rouser, Matthew Wood.

8

AGITATION

If she is mad enough or so ill-advised as to put her foot upon English
ground, I shall from that moment, regard Pandora's box as opened . . .

Castlereagh to Prince Metternich, 6 May 1820

Caroline set foot on English soil at Dover at one o'clock on 5 June
1820 and was greeted by noisy crowds and the grave reverber-
ations of a royal salute. She conducted herself with some dignity, her
manner and figure 'perfectly befitting her exalted station', and walked
among her supporters with 'a firm step, a composed manner and a
smiling but steady countenance'. At least these were the impressions
of the *Times'* correspondent at the scene, who thought her in good
health, 'her blue eyes shining with peculiar lustre'. 'Well-dressed
females, young and old' saluted her, he noted, with exclamations of

'God bless her: she has a noble spirit: she must be innocent.' The shops in Dover were all closed that happy Monday and, reports a second witness, the windows above were 'filled with females waving their handkerchiefs'. A third heard the Queen declare herself now to be 'in a land of freedom'.[1]

When the crowds made it impossible to proceed on foot, Caroline, with Matthew Wood and Lady Anne Hamilton, climbed into a handsome open carriage, while local men set free the horses and then pulled the vehicle along themselves – the very act that Brougham had feared. A band marched in front, playing loudly, and two large banners were held aloft by local tradesmen bearing the words 'God save Queen Caroline'.

Presently she reached her hotel where a guard of honour at the door caused a change of mood. People in the crowd started to hiss and cry out, 'No soldiers!' The senior officer at the scene, Major Lockyer, later reported that an attempt was made 'to take away the arms from some of my men, which they with the greatest difficulty resisted'. The soldiers were forced to retreat inside and, following the request of Matthew Wood, ordered to stay away from the crowds. 'The treatment we received was shameful', thought the Major, and 'it was with the greatest efforts I could use to prevent my men from retaliating upon these aggressions'. In his view, Caroline's followers were no benign crowd, but 'the mob'.[2]

The Times, though, judged that the crowds at Dover represented the view of 'public opinion' at large and captured the public mood. A leader writer expressed his disgust that no royal yacht had been provided to bring Caroline to England and asked: 'Is she not – we put it to every English bosom – is she not a brave woman, thus unprotected, thus obstructed in her journeyings, to force her way to us, through a thousand impediments, and in spite of sanguinary threats, in contempt of treacherous offers, to claim her rights as Britain's Queen?'[3]

The paper compared her to William the Conqueror, Henry VII and William III, pointing out that when these illustrious kings came to Britain they had the advantage of a train of armed followers. 'But this

woman comes arrayed only in native courage and (may we not add?)
conscious innocence; and presents her bosom, aye, offers her neck to
those who threatened to sever her head from it, if ever she dared to
come within their reach.'[4]

This was fighting talk. In taking up Caroline's cause, asserting
her innocence, and dramatising the dangers she faced, as well as
her courage – the editor of *The Times*, Thomas Barnes, was
now challenging Lord Sidmouth and the government. We will be
independent on this, he was saying, and see if you do anything to stop
us. The Six Acts were still on the statute books, along with other
measures designed to suppress the press.

On the evening of her arrival at Dover, the Queen set off towards
London, staying overnight at the Fountain Hotel in Canterbury. The
following day, the party once more took to the London road; Caroline
faced forward in her carriage with Matthew Wood sitting at her side.
Lady Anne Hamilton was in the opposite seat, travelling backwards.[5]
The seating arrangement was highly provocative, which Caroline
must have understood – London's high priest of radicalism was at the
Queen's side, for all to see. As Countess Lieven put it in a letter to her
lover, Prince Metternich of Austria: 'What a to-do, what dangers!' A
huge section of the public supported the Queen, she said, and thought
her 'a pure and innocent victim'. Matthew Wood, meanwhile, 'manages
the Queen and also manages the London populace'. He would, she
imagined, 'make a fine use of his influence'.[6]

People had started to gather at the side of the road to London at
about three o'clock, and Caroline's carriage was greeted joyously by
large crowds. At Deptford, Union Jacks were strewn across the road
and the huge crowd at Blackheath resembled a great continental fair.
At Shooters Hill people of all ranks gathered, some arriving in an
array of 'barouches, chaises and other vehicles filled with respectable
and decent women'. William Cobbett and his daughter Anne were
amongst the crowds there and waved a bough of laurel as they
watched the Queen pass by 'in a miserable half-broken down carriage
covered with dust, followed by a post chaise and a calash'.[7]

When Caroline reached the outskirts of London the weather, which had been rainy, became fine and rays of sun shone through, increasing 'the splendour of the scene'. The carriage was thrown open, and the Queen could now be properly seen dressed in a black gown with a fur ruff, and a black satin hat adorned at the front with a few high, luxuriant feathers. It was a look that, during the coming months, she was to make her own. Amidst cheering and shouting she made her way to Matthew Wood's house in Mayfair and the crowd swelled beneath the windows, hustling and pelting all passers-by who refused to salute. Caroline soon made an appearance and acknowledged the loyalty of the people. The *Times*' reports assumed a golden glow, professing the sight of Caroline sporting herself on the balcony 'with a deportment perfectly graceful' amounted to 'the most splendid pageant, the most imposing theatrical exhibition'. Genuine delight 'seemed to pervade all ranks of spectators at this instance of condescending kindness'.

High society was equally fascinated by the Queen's arrival. The gentlemen's clubs in St James's Street were illuminated, as was Burlington House and some others in Piccadilly – the display of lighted candles demonstrating either support for Caroline, or simply a strategic decision to appear to support her rather than have their windows smashed by the mob. The novelist Fanny Burney told her friend Mrs Lock that 'all London now is wild about the newly arrived royal traveller',[8] and countless letters and diaries written that week express the same opinion. Countess Lieven described London to Metternich with the words 'What a stir, what excitement what noise!' 'The mob,' she said, 'streamed through the streets all night making passers-by shout, "Long live the Queen!"'[9]

Lord Eldon thought support for Caroline could be broken down along class lines. 'The lower orders here are all Queen's folks,' he told his daughter, but, 'few of the middling or higher orders, except the profligate, or those who are endeavouring to acquire power through mischief.'[10] Sarah Lyttelton, eldest daughter of Earl Spencer, agreed that only the lower orders believed in the Queen's innocence, but that did not stop her from being irritated with the government for handling Caroline's concerns so badly.[11] Many in higher society took a 'plague on both their houses' view, and many women expressed Jane Austen's earlier opinion that *she* may be bad, but he made her so, and *he* is worse.

Mary Shelley wrote: 'It is too great a stretch of the imagination to make a God of a Beef-eater [a reference to her manly outfits], or a heroine of Queen Caroline – but I wish with all my heart downfall to her enemies, and that is no great stretch of compassion.'[12] Her husband's view was similarly knowing. The nation, as a whole, was for the Queen, he thought. And making 'her Sacred Majesty' into a heroine demonstrated the 'generous gullibility' of the English. He wished no harm to Caroline, he said, even if she had 'as I firmly believe, amused herself in a manner rather indecorous with any courier or baron'. But he saw it as one of the 'absurdities of royalty' that a vulgar woman with tastes which 'prejudice considers as vices' should be lionised merely because she 'is a queen, or, as a collateral reason, because her husband is a king'.[13]

If the lower orders did believe in her innocence, it was sometimes a stance of convenience. Mostly, like Mary Shelley, they wished to see the Queen as a thorn in the side of George and his unpopular ministers; and in the light of George's profligate behaviour they saw Caroline as a victim anyway, regardless of whether her purity was less than total. Brougham and others heard cries from Caroline's crowds of 'three cheers for Mr Austin, the Queen's son', her supporters seeming not to care whether or not their heroine had, in fact, committed High Treason and was the mother of William Austin; Canning, meanwhile, thought it quite evident 'that the question of guilt or innocence enters for nothing in the general public feeling'.[14] The Duke of Wellington appeared to suspect that the crowds believed the Queen to be guilty when, on one occasion, he was confronted by a gang brandishing pickaxes and demanding he declare his support for Caroline. 'Well gentlemen,' he is said to have told them, 'since you will have it so, God save the Queen – and may all your wives be like her.' (Although some historians attribute the witticism to Lord Anglesey.)

While the question of the Queen's innocence was a source of widespread entertainment, the politics of Caroline's return were a source of anxiety. Speculation was everywhere. How dangerous is the mob? How motivated by radicalism? How organised? And some questioned whether her cause might be the spark to ignite a revolution. The drama was heightened during the three nights following Caroline's arrival in London, when the mob passed through the streets knocking on doors and demanding that people illuminate their houses 'for the Queen!' or have their windows smashed. Countess Lieven refused to comply, and regarded her broken windows with an air of heroic calm. Lord Exmouth was more excitable and rushed out of his house brandishing a sword and a pistol.

Sidmouth's house was attacked on three consecutive nights. On the third occasion the Home Secretary happened to be arriving home in his carriage with two colleagues, Lord Eldon and the Duke of Wellington, also inside the vehicle. Sidmouth said he wished to get out, despite the furious rabble outside, but the Duke of Wellington, in a commanding voice, was heard to say, 'You shall not alight, drive on.' The crowd then attacked the carriage, and according to a witness, one window, possibly that closest to Wellington was 'shivered to atoms by a stick or stone'. The vehicle returned later accompanied by a small group of the Life Guards.[15] Lady Hertford, George's recently discarded mistress, also had her windows in pieces, which seemed unfair as his current lover, Lady Conyngham, was spared. The mob's intelligence on the subject was, presumably, out of date.

Plenty of observers were ready to declare that the crowds on the streets were careering towards rebellion. 'Depend upon it, the house is tottering,' announced the *Black Dwarf* magazine run by the prominent radical activist Thomas Wooler, 'and all the exertions of the ministerial mob can not prevent it from falling.'[16] Letters arrived at the offices of Cabinet ministers containing dire warnings of the people allying themselves 'with all such brave fellows as Thistlewood' as revenge for the 'foul conspiracy' against the Queen.

Government informants, meanwhile, claimed that the radicals had set up a 'Liberal alliance' and appointed a 'Directory Committee' in London to seek out the 'most efficient means of carrying on sedition', and suggested that the disaffected were in a defiant mood. Lord

Carlisle wrote to Liverpool warning that unless the government restored Caroline's good name, the radical cause would 'deprive us . . . of all the means of maintaining good order and of upholding the Constitutional government of the country'. He feared that the government would 'fling the country into a raging fever', concluding: 'While there is a moment left, Do not pass the Rubicon.'[17]

Death threats against ministers were received almost daily – from around the country, but with a heavy bias towards London. Letters piled up marked 'Plot against Lord Sidmouth', or 'Threat to the life of Lord Sidmouth' or 'Lord Castlereagh' or 'Threat to assassinate the King'. And the cry of 'No Queen, no King' became a common one.[18] The Reverend Crowther was, at the end of June, put on trial for saying it in public. The Reverend Thomas Chamberlayne of the Rectory in Charlton, Kent was more law-abiding, but received a note representing 'all the lower and middling class of people' demanding that he read out the Queen's name in prayers. 'If you do not choose to comply,' wrote the authors, '. . . you will damned soon have your house about your ears.' Spies, he was assured, would be in church the following Sunday.[19]

Countess Lieven confided in Metternich: 'I am very much afraid we may reach the crisis which I have long feared.'[20] Lady Jerningham found the spirit of the time 'most alarming', and feared that the country 'is nearer disaster than it has been since the days of Charles 1st',[21] while Lord Grey, the Whig leader in the Lords, feared 'a Jacobin Revolution more bloody than that of France'.[22] Lord Eldon wrote to his daughter in less frightening terms. There 'is certainly an inclination to disquiet among the lower orders', he admitted; but he thought the situation stable on the grounds that the 'inclination', as he put it, 'is so well watched'.[23]

A few days later, though, an incident occurred which could only add to the government's unease. On 15 June, the 3rd Regiment of Guards, stationed in the King's Mews, mutinied. The men had complained of too much work, too little pay and of being overcrowded in their barracks. Three days earlier a private was heard to say to his fellow soldiers: 'The Queen is going to the Tower.' The answer came:

'If she does the King will have blood for supper and a bloody Quantity too.' Signs of insubordination followed, then on the fifteenth, nine of the men who had been on duty at the King's Drawing Room refused to give up their ammunition. Huzzas were given for the Queen, and the next morning the battalion was marched out of London, heading for Portsmouth where they would be under cover from heavy naval guns. That night the London mob assembled by the barracks and would not disperse until the Riot Act was read and the Life Guards charged them. The rest of the regiment was sent to Portsmouth two days later.[24]

The incident coincided with a show of popular support for the Duke of York, George's popular younger brother. The Duke, it was intimated, would make a better monarch than the cowardly King, who dared not show himself in London. The Duke of Wellington's confidante, Harriet Arbuthnot, wrote in her diary that the Prime Minister, Lord Liverpool, had said 'that the aversion to the King was rising to the greatest possible height, that the Guards in London were all drinking the Queen's health and had the greatest possible contempt for the King, from thinking him a coward'. He thought that, if needs be, the King should 'go over to Hanover for a time while the storm here blows over, and have a regency here' under the Duke of York.[25]

Lady Cowper wrote to her brother Frederick Lamb expressing her fears about the soldiers, who, she feared, 'are all in her favour'. 'They also have an idea that they swore allegiance to G[eorge] third, and owe him [George IV] nothing.' If the people rise to support the Queen, she asked rhetorically, will the army 'with their discontents march against them?'[26] Her concerns were widespread. James Mills, an English gentleman of conservative leanings, expressed it in print – the British, he felt, loved the monarchy and the nobility but if Lords:

will drag a Queen of these realms, and such a one as our present Queen, whose sufferings have made the *hearts of the nation* as the *heart of one man*, then will the consequences be on their own heads. Castlereagh may calculate upon the support of the army to degrade the Queen, against the wishes and the will of the people; but I will tell him, not one hair of her head falls to the ground, by the consent of the brave soldiers who owe her allegiance as their rightful Queen.[27]

The Duke of Wellington, meanwhile, was alarmed by the turn of events, and wrote a memorandum to the Prime Minister expressing his 'greatest anxiety respecting the state of the military in London'. He was most disturbed by the fact that neither the government nor the commander in chief of the army had had any knowledge of the discontent in the 3rd Regiment of the Guards until several hours after the outbreak of mutiny. Although he believed much of the army was to be relied upon, he could not rule out the possibility of another mutiny at any time: 'Thus, in one of the most critical moments that ever occurred in this country, we and the public have reason to doubt in the fidelity of the troops, the only security we have, not only against revolution but for the property and life of every individual in the country who has anything to lose.'[28]

The government was depending on the troops for its protection against insurrection and revolution, he said, and particularly relying on the fidelity of the three thousand Guards. He urged the government 'without the loss of a moment's time' to set up a police force or military corps in London which should be 'of a different description' from the regular military force. Then, he reasoned, mutiny in the regular force would cease to be of such importance.

The Home Office did not take up Wellington's idea; nonetheless Sidmouth shared his concern. Alarming reports from informants and the public continued to arrive at his office, some of them well researched and others verging on the hysterical. A letter to Liverpool was typical of the general tone: 'Be assured the soldiers are not to be depended on where the Queen is in question,' warned the writer in a shaky hand. 'Let the soldiers there [near the Queen] be well observed; for Heavens sake, My Lord, do not despise this hint.' Another warned that a 'dreadful calamity' would result if the subject of the Queen was not put to rest, as 'there is a train of powder through the Kingdom . . . and a particle would cause an explosion'.[29]

Many of the anonymous letters received at the Home Office, as would be expected, were from mad people. Nonetheless there is enough evidence of wider public opinion to suggest that the uncertainty was fairly widespread. It was part of the regular gossip among well-born ladies with connections in London, and was reflected in comments by those who were one step removed from the centre of power, such as Charles Greville, a clerk to the Privy Council who thought it 'doubtful how far the Guards can be counted on' if the Caroline affair was to erupt in public disturbances. And the socialite Henry Luttrell joked that the state of the army was such that 'the extinguisher is taking fire'.[30] The politician William Fremantle, a former army man, observed that 'there are some ale-houses open where the soldiers may go and drink and eat for nothing, provided they will drink "Prosperity and health to the Queen".'[31]

Such reports amounted to a good deal more than gossip. By 1820 Britain had experienced more than 20 years of threats that a rebellious outbreak would spark a national convulsion and test to breaking point the loyalty of the armed forces. During this period the country had become a nation at arms, thanks to the war with France. From 1798 to 1805 Napoleon's main strategic aim was to invade Britain, and Britain's response was to build a military of an unprecedented size – from 60,000 men in 1791 to about 400,000 at the height of war-time activity, with as many again in the reserves. Alarmingly, the government had never been entirely sure that significant numbers of this militarised population would not, at times of economic distress, defect to an invading army that promised republicanism. Such a prospect was unlikely, since the national character was defined in part by hostility to France, but it was not impossible.

Now, though, the demon French had been conquered and Napoleon was an emasculated figure imprisoned on the remote island of St Helena in the South Atlantic. Britain was finally at peace, and her soldiers were laid off in their tens of thousands. As a result, society was run through with men trained in the use of arms, many of whom had found it difficult to find work in difficult post-war conditions. The reduced army, meanwhile, was prone to showing great distaste when its orders were *not* to fight a foreign enemy, but to quell its own people. As Wellington reminded Liverpool, the sergeants and corporals of the Guards were 'of the class of the people and liable to be influenced by the views and sentiments of the people'.[32] That influence could only be intensified by the likelihood that any large crowd now included the soldiers' former comrades-in-arms, veterans of the Peninsular War, of Trafalgar and Waterloo. It was also the case that army officers used to serving under men who had distinguished themselves in battle did not enjoy reporting to civilian magistrates. It was humiliating. And it was now hard for Sidmouth and his Tory colleagues to argue, as they had done during the war, that public demands for political change were unpatriotic, and conversely, that it was a soldier's patriotic duty to quash politically motivated rebellion.

The early nineteenth century had brought forth a heady mix of uncertainties. It was in this general climate that John Wilson Croker had remarked three years before Caroline's return to Britain: 'If there should arise any division in the royal family, it will be the match to fire the gunpowder.'[33] Now she was back. And the diarist Charles Greville put words to a common feeling: 'It is impossible to conceive the sensation created by this event,' he wrote. 'Nobody either blames or approves her sudden return, but all ask, "What will be done next? How is it to end?"'[34]

9

ACCUSATION

The general opinion of the country is that the Ministers
must destroy the Queen, or themselves be destroyed.

The Traveller, September 1820

The King, meanwhile, was delighted by his wife's return to
England. Her arrival meant that, at last, he could unleash legal
proceedings against her and seek a divorce. All along he had believed
her to be guilty of adultery, but judged that she would turn up in
Britain and fight the charge nonetheless. His ministers, by contrast,
had misjudged Caroline, and had bargained that she would stay on the
other side of the English Channel and negotiate. 'Our fault,' the Duke
of Wellington said later, 'was in not believing she would leave Italy,
and our unwillingness to look the thing in the face.'[1]

On 6 June, as the Queen was parading in the streets of London, George dispatched Lord Liverpool to the House of Lords and Lord Castlereagh to the Commons, each bearing a 'message from the King' declaring that the Queen's arrival had forced him into handing over painful 'disclosures and discussions' about her conduct. Parliament, he was confident, would proceed accordingly. The 'disclosures' comprised the vast mass of evidence which had been collected by the Milan Commission, and was now inside two sealed Green Bags. The first was placed before the Lords by Liverpool and the second – a replica – before the Commons by Castlereagh. The government's view, as put forward by the two ministers as they deposited the Green Bags, was that each House should set up a secret committee which would examine the evidence against the Queen and advise on the action to be taken.

In the Commons, Thomas Creevey spoke immediately after Castlereagh had delivered his bag. 'From the reign of Henry VIII downwards it had not been the custom of Parliament to interfere with the Queen of England,' he declared. Then, to great cheers from the opposition benches, he made fun of the 'indescribable alarm' of the government party, asserting that fifteen ministers had failed to come to Parliament the previous night as they were at home protecting their property from the Queenite mob and were thus 'busily employed in arming against one poor, weak, defenceless woman'.

Sir Robert Wilson, a radical and a military man, spoke next for the Queen, followed by Archibald Hamilton, brother of Lady Anne. The removal of Caroline's name from the liturgy, he complained, had shown a predetermination on the part of the ministers to condemn the Queen without a trial. Then, after a brief contribution from Caroline's newly appointed Solicitor General, Thomas Denman, Brougham spoke. Until now, he said, he had refrained from telling the Queen's side of the story. But the arrival of the King's message and the Green Bags made the continuation of his silence impossible, he told the House, and the time was approaching when his lips would 'be unsealed from that state of silence which he had hitherto imposed upon them'. His words, which were reported in the newspapers the following morning, could only prompt speculation about how far he would go in defending the Queen. Would he, for instance, expose the underhand methods the King had used to spy on his wife? And would he reveal all he knew of the King's infidelities, and of his first marriage to Maria Fitzherbert? The latter point was of great interest. If Brougham were to succeed in proving George's marriage to Mrs Fitzherbert a valid one, then the King, who was by law forbidden from marrying a Roman Catholic, might even be removed from the throne. This was not far-fetched. Mrs Fitzherbert had applied to the Pope for his view on the matter, and the Pope had advised that she was indeed married.

The following day Brougham arrived at the Commons bearing a message from the Queen, the main thrust of which was to object to any proceedings held in secret, and to plead for an open investigation 'in which she may see both the charges and the witnesses against her – a privilege not denied to the meanest subject of the realm'. She protested at the many ways in which the government had presented her to all the world as a guilty woman, citing the liturgy issue, the refusal of a royal residence, the slights from English diplomats and the foreign powers that followed their lead. These actions by the ministers, she said, could be justified only if she had already faced trial and conviction. The message was loudly cheered as Brougham read it out.

Brougham was convinced that Caroline's case could bring down the Tory government, and the directness of his attack reflected his confidence. But the Whig hierarchy was not yet ready to agree with him. The high priest of Whig society, Lord Holland, judged the Queen's alleged adultery as far too grubby an issue to be of real political interest, and regretted that the whole world from the 'Prime Minister to the scavenger in the streets' was agitated by the arrival in Britain of 'an ugly mad woman'. 'For the life of me,' he wrote, 'I can feel no interest and little curiosity about these royal squabbles, degrading no doubt to all concerned and disgusting and tiresome I think to the bystanders.'[2] Also, he admitted, prominent Whigs had no confidence whatever in Caroline's character. The Whig leader in the

House of Lords, Lord Grey, meanwhile, had determined not to make a party political issue out of the Queen's case. On principle, he would judge it on its merits.

In the Commons, Castlereagh rose to answer Brougham. He would not disclose the contents of the Green Bags, he said, but he would say this: that the charges were 'grave and serious' and that they came from individuals who were ready to back up their allegations by their personal testimony – i.e. at a trial, or any process resembling a trial. Of course, he said, no guilt could be attached to the Queen unless it was the result of a full public examination. Then he proceeded to attack her for not listening to her counsel (presumably a reference to Brougham's faltering attempts at compromise) and instead succumbing to 'base and pernicious interference' (a clear reference to Matthew Wood). If she thought she would be supported by the agitation of the country, he declaimed she would experience 'nothing but regret and disappointment'. She had allowed herself to become the dupe of 'wicked and dangerous men'. The motion was then put that the Green Bag papers be presented to a secret committee.

Brougham responded. Caroline, he argued, was supported by nothing other than 'conscious innocence', 'moral vigour' and 'strong faculties'. And her reception in Britain had convinced him that 'the House as well as the country would not be satisfied with anything less than a full and public disclosure'. He complained that a secret committee would be a departure from the normal practices of law. Any person subjected to such a proceeding might see their character 'destroyed and blasted', and yet have no opportunity to call any witness for the defence. Still, such a measure was worthy of such a 'ricketty and shattered administration'. And, after the dreadful treatment the Queen had received, he continued:

> Could you wonder that any person, but more especially a woman, and still more especially this woman, born a princess, niece to Frederick of Prussia, niece to George III, daughter to the heroic Duke of Brunswick, and consort to his present Majesty, the first sovereign in

Europe; could you wonder that this exalted female should feel acutely when the ministers of her own country ventured to treat her with indignity?

He could not finish without making one more plea for negotiation in order to 'spare the country the dreadful consequences of investigation'. In his view the calamity ahead should be avoided if possible 'for the sake of the wives and daughters of all who loved decency, morality and who recollected when, but a few years since, the opening of a newspaper was regarded with fear and disgust by the father of every modest and well conducted family'. This was a reference to a royal scandal in 1809 involving an affair between the Duke of York and an actress named Mary Anne Clarke.

The atmosphere in the House became charged as the next speaker rose. Those present knew that George Canning, who was now a prominent figure in the Tory Cabinet, had, as a younger man, been scandalously close to Caroline, and had possibly been her lover. Canning now informed the House that he was torn. As a privy councillor, he said, he was close to his sovereign, but to Caroline 'he owed and he gave unabated esteem, regard and affection'. And after wishing that a trial could be avoided, his next best hope was that 'she would come out of the trial superior to the accusation'.

Brougham, he argued, had misrepresented the government ministers as the Queen's accusers. In fact they were simply acting from a sense of public duty. 'So help me God,' he continued, 'I will never place myself in the situation of an accuser towards this individual.' If it had been in his power, he said, if he had been in any other place than on the government benches he 'would have been all ardour and affection (if he might use the term) in her service'. He would have made 'any personal sacrifice' to avert the present calamity and hinted that he would have been 'not only willing but anxious' to resign, if he thought that Caroline would be spared as a result. He concluded by announcing that it was his intention to take no further part in the proceedings against the Queen. He would absent himself entirely.

George, according to Henry Hobhouse, was furious at the way his government was handling his affairs. He disliked the secret committees as much as Caroline, wanting all the allegations against her to be made public as soon as possible. He was beside himself with indignation at Canning's contribution, and told Lord Liverpool that Canning should resign from the Cabinet. 'Lord Liverpool did not hesitate to declare that his own resignation would follow,' Hobhouse wrote in his diary.[3] This merely served to set George thinking about how he might rid himself of Liverpool, and he pressed Lord Sidmouth very strongly to take over as prime minister. Sidmouth said that nothing would induce him to accept, and refused to comment when George wondered out loud whether the Duke of Wellington might oblige. Instead Sidmouth advised the King to stick with Lord Liverpool, advice that reflected a widespread view within Cabinet that the government's chances of survival were shaky.[4] George Canning, it was mooted, was quite capable of defecting to the Whigs and, in so doing, bringing the ministry down. George also made tentative efforts to sound out Whig leaders such as Lord Holland, George Tierney and Lord Grey, but to no avail – unsurprisingly, they would offer him no more succour on the Caroline question than the Tories.[5]

The King's confidence in his ability to control the situation seems to have been puffed up by being cheered as he entered the Chapel Royal the day before his meeting with Sidmouth. He was then, recorded Hobhouse, 'led by the sycophants around him to believe in his own popularity'. The Cabinet thought the royal self-regard dangerous given that, in reality, the lower orders in the capital as well as the country, and particularly the women, were in favour of the Queen, and the cry of 'No Queen, no King' was gaining popularity. The ministers thought that the King should be 'undeceived on this point', and Sidmouth spent one and three quarter hours trying to convince him of the disaffection of the common people. George, to his credit, thanked the Home Secretary for his candour in telling him the truth.[6]

In the meantime, the Commons led the way for one last attempt at negotiation. On the evening of 7 June, Brougham wrote to Lord Liverpool saying that the Queen, in deference to the House of

Commons, was prepared to receive further proposals from the government. Liverpool answered by referring her back to the £50,000 offer he had mentioned to Brougham in 1819 and reiterated later. This, though, got the government nowhere, and it was resolved that progress might be made if each side appointed two people as negotiators. The King's representatives were to be the Duke of Wellington and Lord Castlereagh, while the Queen chose Lords Fitzwilliam and Sefton, but the arrangement was stalled when Fitzwilliam refused to cooperate unless Caroline's name was restored to the liturgy immediately. 'This of course was quite impossible,' wrote the pro-government Harriet Arbuthnot in her diary, and 'the Queen finally chose Mr Brougham and Mr Denman'.[7]

The negotiators had five meetings, but made little progress. Then a new factor emerged in the form of the intervention of a monumental voice representing piety and the moral view – William Wilberforce. At fifty-nine years of age, Wilberforce had long since achieved his historic victory in securing the abolition of the slave trade and was now a hero of philanthropy and a political grandee – highly regarded, if slightly mocked for his high-mindedness; Francis Burdett liked to refer to him as 'the honourable and religious member'.

Wilberforce's diary reveals that his conscience was sorely troubled by the dispute between the King and Queen, and it was through his efforts in the Commons that an adjournment on the secret committee debate was secured, thus buying time for a compromise agreement. Shortly afterwards he dispatched his son with an earnest letter to the King begging him to restore Caroline's name to the liturgy, suggesting that if he did not give way then 'the country would be in a fury and perhaps the soldiers might take the Queen's part'. On 15 June Wilberforce wrote to his wife: 'I fear lest it should please God to scourge the nation through the medium of this rupture between the King and Queen. If the soldiery should take up her cause, who knows what may happen – and is it very improbable? O Lord, deliver us!'[8]

He was soon assured that a climbdown by George was impossible, and that the Cabinet was now prepared to stick by the King on the liturgy point, to the extent of making it a resignation issue. So, in the cause of peace, he switched to trying to persuade Caroline to bear the burden of a compromise – hoping that she would accept a deal sweetened by a guarantee that she would keep the name and rights of a Queen and be granted a royal frigate, but would give in on the liturgy issue. Brougham, he writes, encouraged him to believe that Caroline would accept and on 22 June Wilberforce proposed a resolution in the Commons recommending the Queen not to insist on all her claims.

The debate attracted a packed chamber and public gallery – Charles Greville said he had never seen the Commons so crowded. Much lauded contributions were made by Castlereagh, Brougham, Canning and Denman. But it was Caroline's radical ally Sir Francis Burdett who attracted most attention. He equated her valour with that of the Duke of Wellington, said she possessed ten times the nerves of the government ministers, and drew the usual attentions to her sufferings at the hands of George. He also, surprisingly, hinted that she was to be championed whether she were guilty or not: 'If . . . goaded by insult and driven almost to madness, she had acted improperly, no man who harboured a principle of honour in his breast would not shed a tear for her misfortunes – but he would not at the same time pursue her with the arm of vengeance.'

He was interrupted at this point by loud cheers. He was against Wilberforce's compromise he said, on the grounds that the Green Bag – 'this Pandora's box' – should never be opened in any case. As far as the general public or 'the people out of doors' were concerned, they would believe Caroline 'pure and spotless as the snow' even if she were in fact 'crimson-dyed in guilt', as the Green Bag represented her.

Burdett's arguments did not persuade the majority of MPs. The resolution was carried by 394 votes to 124 and on 24 June Wilberforce, dressed in full court costume, went with three other Members of Parliament to Caroline's residence in central London. The parliamentarians were jeered by the crowds outside, who despised Wilberforce for wanting the Queen to compromise or, as they saw it, to accept the King's bribes. Nonetheless, he showed 'proper insensibility' to their lack of courtesy, and presented Caroline with the proposal. Despite Brougham's assurances, she rejected it without a moment's consideration. 'Her manner was extremely dignified,' wrote Wilberforce, 'but very stern and haughty.' As he left, the crowd became so threatening that Henry Brougham feared for his old friend's safety and accompanied him on his homeward journey.[9]

His failure, thought Wilberforce, was deeply regrettable for the country, but at least his conscience was clear. 'Whatever ensues,' he wrote, 'it will always be a consolation to me to reflect that I have done my best to prevent all the evils that may happen.'[10] Caroline's rejection of the compromise, thought her former lady-in-waiting Lady Charlotte Lindsay, was foolhardy. She put it down to the continuing influence of Matthew Wood and to Caroline's susceptibility. 'The weakness of her adversaries makes her rash,' she told her friend Mary Berry. 'She thinks that everything that embarrasses them [the King and his government] must be for her advantage, not recollecting that they may all fall to the ground together.'[11] Her boldness made some people suspect that Caroline was insane. 'Some think she is a little deranged, but I fear not sufficiently so for Bedlam,' wrote Lady Jerningham. But, deranged or not, 'she lowers royalty'.[12]

Caroline's rejection of Wilberforce's proposal was a clear signal that the Queen had no intention of turning back from the brink. She had the people behind her, the support of her radical friends, and she would use any allegiances available to fight her case. All the evidence suggests that, like her husband, she wanted stark confrontation, and was less worried than he by suggestions that the royal battle might drag the country into chaos or even, as the scaremongers suggested, civil war and the end of the monarchy. Indeed, her personality was such that she was more likely to relish the high drama of popular unrest than be subdued by it. She enjoyed risk.

It was now inevitable that the two Green Bags would be opened and the activities of the secret committees would go ahead. The House of Lords had already voted for the investigation and had merely been awaiting events in the Commons before moving – now there was nothing to stop them. On 26 June, Caroline made one last protest against secrecy, and in favour of being heard in public. She wrote to

the Lords complaining that an enquiry without her, her counsel or any
of her witnesses, who were still in Italy, would be a crying injustice.
She asked the Lords to listen to her counsel at the bar 'this day', and
confided to her friends that if they refused to hear Brougham, she
would go down to the House of Lords in person the following day.[13]

Brougham and Denman were, in fact, allowed to speak in support
of the Queen's message, and urged that the Lords' secret committee
should suspend proceedings until the witnesses had arrived in
England. In the course of his speech Denman delighted the Lord
Chancellor Lord Eldon by insinuating that the present crisis was the
fault of John Leach, the instigator of the Milan Commission. Leach,
he implied, was hyping up the evidence against Caroline to win the
King's favour, and thereby Eldon's job as Lord Chancellor. Denman
adapted *Othello*:

> Some busy and insinuating rogue,
> Some cogging, cozening slave, to get some office,
> Must have devised this slander.

The Lords were not to be swayed by the two lawyers and on 27 June
they voted down a motion put by Lord Grey, the Whig leader in the
Lords, proposing that the secret committee idea should be dropped.
This removed the last obstacle in the way of the investigation – the
Green Bags were opened and their sordid contents earnestly examined
by fifteen peers of the realm. Walter Scott, the novelist, wrote to his
friend Lady Abercorn telling her he suspected many people of being
'privately glad we are to have the reading of all the scandal, especially
now that we have made [some show of] decent reluctance to it'.

Scott thought the country in the midst of a fascinating drama that
demanded resolution. Since the discussion has gone so far, he wrote,
'I cannot see why these two great personages should remain, the one
under the suspicion of subornation of perjury, false accusation and I
know not what, and the other under a charge of infamy and guilt,
without the public knowing which is right, which wrong.'[14]

George Canning, meanwhile, had been in a state of some anxiety about his own delicate position. As he had declared to the Commons, he felt it necessary to withdraw support for his government colleagues at this time, and to ensure that he had no association with any proceedings against the Queen. But his action, he believed, did not go far enough; honour demanded that he proffer his resignation from the Cabinet. He met Lord Liverpool and made his offer, but the Prime Minister urged Canning in 'the strongest terms' to change his mind. As he had told the King, he was convinced that Canning's resignation would bring with it 'the most serious evils and inconveniences' and might 'lead to the immediate dissolution of the Government'.[15]

Liverpool's persuasive entreaties were successful, and when George Canning went to see his monarch on Sunday 25 June and tendered his resignation, it was not accepted. After the meeting George gleefully told those around him that Canning had disclosed his belief in the truth of the evidence of the Queen's misconduct. The King further boasted to the Duke of Wellington that he had almost made Canning confess to his former 'extreme intimacy' with the Queen. Henry Hobhouse wrote in his diary: 'The King believes, and probably with great reason, that C[anning]'s intimacy with the Queen has gone to the utmost extent.'[16] It had also been the view of Lady Bessborough, who, in 1806, had talked to Canning on the subject. He 'neither own'd nor denied,' she said, 'but on the whole I am staggered and afraid it is in great part true'.[17] Castlereagh too wrote, 'He was, no doubt, one of the many favoured.'[18]

But this was not the view of everyone. Mrs Arbuthnot, who was no admirer of Canning or Caroline, thought the King was wrong[19] – and Canning's biographers are unsure on the subject. Either way, he clearly felt it would be intolerable that, having been Caroline's close confidante, he should now turn accuser. He also had his own political ambitions to think about. At this time Canning was anxious to take over Castlereagh's position as Leader of the Commons and had told Liverpool so. Liverpool, meanwhile, offered him Lord Sidmouth's job at the Home Office, but Canning refused on the grounds that this would require too much involvement in the King's battle with his wife. Better, he thought, simply to absent himself from the political scene, and pursue his ambitions when the Caroline affair had blown over. He was also grieving for his eldest son, nineteen-year-old George, who had recently died after a lifetime of illness; and in the circumstances he thought it best to leave the country for a while and tour Europe with his wife, Joan.[20]

On 4 July the secret committee of the House of Lords made its report. Its chairman, the Earl of Harrowby, rose in the chamber and declared that the testimonies in the Green Bags deeply affected the honour of the Queen, and attributed to her conduct 'of the most licentious character'. These charges, said the Earl, seemed to be calculated to affect the dignity of the Crown and the 'feeling and honour' of the country. The committee had reached the conclusion that the charges should now become the subject of a 'solemn inquiry' which should be conducted through a 'legislative proceeding'. Lord Liverpool responded by saying that a Bill would be brought in the House of Lords the following day.

The *Morning Chronicle* declared that the secret committee's report would be unsurprising to anyone who had given a moment's reflection to the subject. 'Everyone has heard,' ran the editorial, 'that persons of all ranks and situations of life, from Hanoverian barons down to the lowest scum of Italy, had been employed to beset the Queen,' and it was by the evidence of these treacherous individuals that the charges against her were to be supported. Journalists, it declared, had a special duty to total impartiality in reporting everything that was to follow.[21]

The next day the Lords met to hear the terms of a Bill of Pains and Penalties against Caroline, or 'an Act to deprive her Majesty Queen Caroline Amelia Elizabeth of the Title, Prerogatives, Rights, Privileges and Exemptions, of Queen Consort of this Realm, and to dissolve the Marriage between his Majesty and the said Caroline Amelia Elizabeth'.

The Bill took note of Caroline's employment of Bartolomeo Pergami, 'a foreigner of low station', and asserted that a 'most unbecoming and disgusting intimacy' had commenced between the couple. It referred to the way Caroline had raised Pergami to a 'high station' and bestowed on him 'extraordinary marks of favour and distinction' and conferred on him a fake order of knighthood. The Queen had, it said, conducted herself towards Pergami with 'indecent and offensive familiarity and freedom, and carried on a licentious, disgraceful and adulterous intercourse' with him. The Bill should be enacted in order 'to manifest our deep sense of such scandalous, disgraceful and vicious conduct on the part of her said Majesty, by which she has violated the duty she owed to your Majesty, and has rendered herself unworthy of the exalted rank and station of Queen Consort of this Realm'.

A Bill of Pains and Penalties was as rare a measure then as now, only one having been enacted in the previous 200 years. Lady Cowper disliked the idea of it intensely. 'It is such a foolish hobble to have got into,' she wrote to Frederick Lamb, 'and if it goes on I do think we shall have blood shed before it passes the Commons.' Moreover, 'A Bill of Pains and Penalties is an awkward name, it sounds to the ignorant as if she was going to be fried or tortured in some way.'[22]

In reality, the measure amounted to a trial through Act of Parliament. Caroline was to be declared innocent or guilty according to a simple majority of votes from the 300 or so peers, but was not to receive the basic rights enjoyed in a normal court of law – she was not, for instance, to know in advance who would bear witness against her, a right due every defendant held on a criminal charge. Earl Grey voiced another reservation. It seemed, he said, as if the House of Lords itself had assumed the character of a prosecutor in a case which it was about to try – that is, that the peers were to be both prosecutors and judges.

The Times went further, condemning the Bill as a 'violation of the law of God'. The law of divorce, it pointed out, separates a pure man from an impure woman but it 'does not allow, nor ever has allowed, nor ever can allow, of the separation of two impure people at the option of either'. It fell short of labelling George as impure, but declared that if Caroline's behaviour were examined, but not her husband's, then the 'sacred solemnity of the marriage contract' would end at once. In short, the Bill was not simply a political act of revenge, it was also a challenge to the very fabric of society, undermining the institution of marriage, which was at its heart.

Throughout July, Countess Lieven wrote to her lover Prince Metternich, explaining that she had a deep inside knowledge of events, and enjoying the peculiar Englishness in the manner of society's obsession with the King and Queen:

> I know a great deal more than the interested parties, for I am treated so much as an Englishwoman by both sides that nobody minds talking in front of me. The English, silent and cold about everything else, are particularly talkative and frank about their own affairs. They have not got the knack of ordinary conversation, and do not take the trouble to talk to you, if you want to talk of trivial things; but boldly propose the most intimate question and they are on their own ground. Above all, argue . . . and they appreciate you much more than you could have hoped at the beginning of the conversation.[23]

She was, indeed, well regarded in society, and accepted as a confidante by both Whigs and Tories. It was thanks to her impressive social skills that she was able to write to Metternich in a style that injected flirtatious intimacy into what was, in essence, a diplomatic briefing. She told him that, as the Bill was on the point of being announced, 'the Queen is doing more mischief than ever' and the situation in the military was still precarious. 'The army is disaffected and taking up the cause of the Queen. If she has the people on her side, and possibly the army too, what is left?' On 8 July she wrote, 'The Duke of York . . . boasts of sometimes spending three nights running at his office. He is not making plans of campaign. What is he doing?' And on 10 July: 'The radical families are already urging the populace to take up arms in defence of the Queen; and she herself . . . makes an appeal to the people. On such occasions, delay is the worst policy; they [the government] should strike quickly and decisively; that would daunt the mob . . .'[24]

Alarm in Britain was heightened by new revolutionary fervour on the continent, which was now threatening the conservative international order created by Metternich and Castlereagh at the Congress of Vienna. In Spain Ferdinand VII was overthrown following a mutiny in the army, and a new constitution established; and unrest quickly spread to Portugal. In Naples, meanwhile, a popular revolt forced a reluctant Ferdinand I to grant a constitutional monarchy. 'The lower classes have been taught to know their own power, and that the armed force . . . is the only counterpoise on the side of the rich which prevents their will from becoming law,' wrote Sir William à Court in Spain, in a letter to Lord Castlereagh. Then, at the end of July, the Foreign Secretary received a report from Colonel Browne at Milan, indicating that 'the infection from Naples' had travelled there, and that the coffee rooms were more crowded than usual and full of desperate talk. 'Constitution and insurrection are in every one's mouth,' he wrote, continuing:

> I cannot, perhaps give your lordship a better idea of the extent to which the question of the Queen is mixed up with politics here than by mentioning that a leader of the democrat party said in society a few evenings since, 'The Queen of England *shall* triumph'; and two or three questions of a similar nature are all that are now wanting to restore the rights of man, and to rid us of all our tyrants at once.[25]

Caroline, meanwhile, was chiefly concerned with getting through the ordeal immediately ahead. She was distressed by her heavy reliance on Henry Brougham and spent much of her time debating whether or not to sack him. On one occasion she was seen pacing about her room repeatedly exclaiming, 'If my head is upon Temple Bar, it will be Brougham's doing!'[26] In public she assumed the air of a tragic heroine. Referring to George, she said pointedly that as '[we] shall not meet in this world, I hope we shall in the next'. Then, according to *The Times*, she pointed her hand towards heaven and, with great emphasis, added: 'where justice will be rendered me'.[27] In truth, she wanted *victory* rather than justice, and settlement in the worldly present, not the remote hereafter.

PUBLICATION

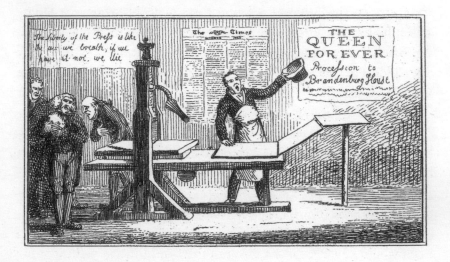

Public opinion in favour of reform 'is growing too large for the channels that it has been accustomed to run through'

Robert Peel (1820)

William Cobbett now directed his formidable energy towards turning the Queen's cause into a campaign for political reform. The imminent Bill of Pains and Penalties was, in effect, the trial of the Queen of England for adultery. It was hard to imagine an event more sensational, or more ripe with political opportunity. For any activist the trial was a chance to capitalise; but for Cobbett, with his fabulous way with words and his determination to shape history, it was a wonderful gift.

Before the trial opened in August 1820 he combined forces with a street-wise radical activist named William Benbow to launch an attack on the House of Lords. Together they produced a cheap pamphlet called *A Peep at the Peers*, which put a figure on each peer's income from the public purse, and exposed the degree of nepotism among the aristocrats; the powerful message being that the Lords, like the rest of government, was corrupted by patronage and was, therefore, biased and incapable of being an independent judge of the Queen. *A Peep at the Peers* was the boldest of descriptions of Cobbett's great enemy, which he termed 'Old Corruption'. The sordid establishment made the British state rotten, he asserted, and the need for change unarguable. The publication was ostentatiously dedicated to Queen Caroline.[1]

Cobbett's objective was primarily political – but he also needed *A Peep at the Peers* to provide him with cash. He and his long-suffering family were still struggling to recover from the political and financial costs of their recent exile in America, and were now waiting to appear before the bankruptcy courts. William's daughter, Anne, confessed that, due to poverty, 'Papa, John [her brother] and I often dined on cauliflowers or salad. But we were in high spirits. I, for my part, think Papa would never have got through that hard time so well, if it had not been for the Queen's Affair.'[2] Fortunately the pamphlet sold astoundingly well, and became a much appreciated personal triumph to help Cobbett recover from electoral failure in Coventry. He later claimed that *A Peep at the Peers* had sold more than 100,000 copies at twopence each, and 'was in every village of the kingdom'.[3] After a gap of four years, he was firmly back in the business of writing mass-circulation political commentary.

The success provided a good start for the next stage of Cobbett's plan of action. He wished to graduate from merely editorialising about Caroline to securing a place at the heart of her entourage – in her war room, managing her campaign. He found it frustrating on the outside, particularly since he believed that her current advisers were failing her. Henry Brougham, he thought, was too motivated by manoeuvring on his own behalf within Parliament, and too ready to accept a compromise that might bring peace to the country and with it dishonour to Caroline. Alderman Matthew Wood, like Cobbett, was true to the radical cause, but lacked the necessary rhetorical skills to represent the Queen in print. Moreover, Wood was a powerful figure in London, but Cobbett had a following nationwide. He was not a man to underestimate his own talents, and plainly felt that the Caroline affair, if handled properly, that is, by him, would become a pivotal moment in the history of political reform.

In June he started sending letters to Caroline imploring her not to give in to Parliament and begging her to reject the £50,000 'bribe' to leave the country. Instead she should follow his advice – stay firm and recognise that her power lay in the force of public opinion. In a letter of 8 June he pointed her to the 'thousands and hundreds of thousands whose hearts beat with anxiety for the Queen', and who 'implore her to beware of insidious and perfidious advice'. Two days later he informed her that already the windows of the print shops were 'exhibiting her Majesty's person attired in royal robes, with a Crown on her head and a sceptre in her hand'. On 15 June he wrote informing Caroline that her enemies were now cowering: 'They see that public opinion in her Majesty's favour is too strong to be safely set at defiance.'[4]

'Day after day Papa addressed these letters to her,' wrote Anne Cobbett. Lady Anne Hamilton took them in, or told Caroline of their contents. But it was Matthew Wood who watched over all activity at the Queen's door and he 'took no notice of Papa'. The Alderman was guarding his position as the Queen's closest adviser, and did not relish the idea of the mighty Cobbett moving in. But Cobbett did not give up. He carried on sending his missives, relentlessly drawing Caroline's attention to the power of the people. Her Majesty, he wrote on 25 June, 'should be informed that her strength and safety lie in public opinion; that the Parliament will do nothing for her except as it is influenced by the public opinion'.[5]

Caroline did not, as yet, reply, although she believed, with or without Cobbett's help, in maximising public sentiment in her favour, and using it for her own ends. Now she went further and attempted physical identification with the poor and oppressed by travelling about in a modest coach, staying in an ordinary house and mingling regularly with the masses; with a fine theatrical sense, she exhibited herself as the embodiment of wretchedness and suffering as experienced by a royal personage. In July, John Cam Hobhouse wrote to his friend Lord Byron, who was in Italy, telling him that the Queen was living at 'a little lodging' and 'drives out with two hack horses before and a bouquet of blackguards behind her carriage', adding that their acquaintance, Hoby the boot maker, said 'it made him weep to look at her'.[6]

The Times felt it necessary to warn Caroline against rendering herself 'too common' by constantly appearing in public, but felt that she was forced into going out by having no opportunity to exercise at her small house, other than to run up and down stairs. The paper described her current abode at 22 Portman Street as a 'hovel' and concluded that it was not 'that the Queen of England is too often seen out of her house, but that her Majesty has not a proper house to hide her head in'. To Cobbett it must have seemed that, through her actions, Caroline was playing her part admirably.

He and Benbow kept up their enthusiastic campaigning throughout the early summer. Cobbett wrote long articles in his weekly *Political Register* trying to bring round all manner of social groups to Caroline and the radical cause. In June he addressed an article to 'the Reformers', declaring that Caroline had 'opened the eyes of hundreds of thousands who were blind before her arrival; and, therefore, all the oppressed part of the nation ought to feel great gratitude towards her'.

He held her up as a pillar of morality and heroine to the common people, who 'almost universally' lived moral lives. The upper classes, by contrast, were following her case in order to revel in all the concocted salacious revelations to come. It was the 'reptiles in Bond-street, filthy with snuff and blinded with whiskers' who wanted her to face a trial and thus 'enliven the circle of their gaming tables and their stews and their other infamous places of resort'.[7] In Cobbett's world the ordinary people of the country, not the repulsive socialites and the politicians, were the essence of Britishness, the true patriots.

Cobbett's arguments were shot through with the moral power that came from the appropriation of the language of patriotism for his cause. Waterloo and the defeat of Napoleon had made this possible. Like other radicals, he could now attempt to rally 'the people' using the rhetoric of patriotism without seeming to jeopardise national security. And he set about his task with great enthusiasm, using arguments that would appeal to the emerging working classes without alienating the growing, similarly disenfranchised, middle classes. Similarly, he set about defining 'the people' as a large and inclusive entity calling for political reform, going so far as to appeal to women – who were generally ignored by the radicals. Cobbett doubtless sensed that women were rallying behind the Queen, and he set about portraying her not simply in passive terms, as a victim of oppression, but as a symbol of female fortitude, rising above her scheming advisers:

> All her conduct has upon this great occasion been marked by that *decision*, *promptitude*, and *sharp-sightedness* for which strong-minded women are always more remarkable than men. They see *quicker* than men of equal comparative mind; and they are more *rapid* in following their thoughts by acts. In cases where great *suspicion* is necessary, they far surpass men. They penetrate more quickly and more deeply into all machinations against them. A bungling hypocrite may deceive a man; but it must be a clever scoundrel indeed that dupes a woman of any mind.[8]

Cobbett was no feminist – but he had a magnificent facility for conjuring up the appropriate arguments to win over any particular group when he needed to.

His colleague, William Benbow, was cruder. He sold his own pro-Caroline wares using sensationalism rather than fancy rhetoric. Benbow was a shoemaker from Manchester, who had changed trade and had recently opened a print shop near Cobbett on the Strand. He had been a rabble-rouser in every near-revolutionary crisis since 1816 and by 1820 was well established in a new career as a grubby street agitator. He was now anxious to cash in on the Caroline affair by publishing any piece of writing, however crude or obscene, that might make him a profit, or in his own words assist him 'in stirring up public opinion' on behalf of Caroline and 'freeing her from the fangs of her blood-thirsty enemies'. He began by producing a raft of quasi-pornographic writings and squibs about Caroline and George, and the whole of the Caroline sensation. He depicted the secret committee as 'Doctors, Bishops, Judges, Generals and Statesmen at Hard work, or a Shitting Committee', showing them emptying their bowels into a stinking, bloated Green Bag.[9]

George was portrayed, and not just by Benbow, as a ram-like being with muttonchop whiskers, mutton being a play on words that meant both female genitalia and slut. One Benbow squib was entitled *A Peep into W[indso]r Castle, after the Lost Mutton*, and did not hold back on ribald rhymes depicting George frolicking with his various mistresses. A print entitled *K[in]g Cupid in the Corner – Playing Bopeep* was just as base, showing Lady Conyngham in her petticoats, breasts exposed and legs apart, with the fat mutton face of George peering out from under her underclothes and uttering: 'Peep-bo – ah! Ha! Ha! Am not I a cunning fellow, the Queenites will never think of finding me in this Paradise.' Lady Conyngham replies: 'Oh! What a happy retreat, to cherish and cover so charming a fugitive, the very essence and model of perfection.' The 'Adonis of loveliness' was thus reborn.[10]

Benbow's imagery was reproduced everywhere, and in even cruder terms. A Mr Wilson of the Royal Exchange, for instance, published a *Peep at the Pavilion, Or Boiled Mutton with Caper Sauce*, and began with a rhyme depicting the Prince of Wales in pursuit of 'the lost mutton' in the form of Maria Fitzherbert. George, it proclaimed:

> Sallied forth in to Sussex, his anguish to lighten
> Believing the MUTTON had stray'd down to B[righto]n.[11]

Benbow, at the same time, orchestrated an inflammatory radical campaign by plastering the streets of London with subversive placards; the

most infamous of which were posted on 3 July with the words 'Proposal
to Murder the Queen' in a huge and blazing headline; such techniques
were used on the streets, but not yet by the respectable newspapers. The
poster described Caroline's forthcoming trial as a way of ensuring her
death, and concluded: 'Englishmen, look well at these things . . . Will
you stand by? Will such monsters [as George and the ministers] dip their
hands in the blood of a woman; an INNOCENT WOMAN; and INNOCENT
AND INJURED QUEEN.'[12] Another entitled 'Brutal Abuse of the Queen'
took a similar theme, and together the placards suggested a plot to
stab, boil or behead Caroline. Benbow, unlike Cobbett, had no regard
for the sensibilities of respectable citizens, or building a broad concept
of 'the people' as a body in opposition to the ruling elite. He preferred
to stir up the passions of the mob with extremist, sometimes Jacobinical,
slogans.

The Queen's reaction to such dangerous political mischief might
have appeared seemly; in that she appeared to ignore it. In truth, it is
more likely that Caroline was enjoying the agitation. Indeed, according to Anne Cobbett, she was financing at least part of it. The Cobbett
family published placards throughout the Caroline affair, Anne states,
which were posted up on walls everywhere. 'John [her brother] used
to carry the copy over to Benbow and leave him to have it done.' The
placards were paid for with money supposedly from Cobbett's
Register and no accounts were kept. Matthew Wood, confessed Anne,
gave her father the money, 'but there was no charge made; it was an
understood thing what the money was for. We did not keep any of
these in the house, we were afraid'.[13] The well-connected Harriet
Arbuthnot recorded that since arriving in Britain, Caroline was
rumoured to have spent £8,500, which, according to Brougham, had
been 'plundered by Alderman Wood'.[14] In effect, then, Caroline herself, possibly without her knowledge, was financing the two seditious
troublemakers, Cobbett and Benbow, as they poured out vast amounts
of personal, sentimental, radical and obscene tirades in her favour.

Not that Benbow was fussy about where his income came from. He
also took bribes from George's men to suppress his own publications,
and received more than £200 from them during 1820. But he felt no

duty to act as he had promised, and published anyway, sometimes using the attempted government 'suppression' as a selling point.[15] He was, moreover, extremely successful and, as Caroline's trial approached, his shop on the Strand became a focal point for the Queenites. A contemporary print shows Benbow's shop selling not just overtly Caroline squibs, including *A Peep at the Peers*, but also displaying prominent advertisements for Cobbett's *Register*.[16] Government spies watched Benbow's shop – earlier in the year both he and Cobbett had been cited in a list of rebel leaders who were 'endeavouring to seduce the people' – and branded it the most profane and seditious in the capital.

A third printer, William Hone, had established an office on Ludgate Hill, just to the east of Cobbett's and Benbow's premises. He was unlike them in character, lacking their flamboyance and bombast. As a boy he had received no formal education but had learned to read by studying the Bible. Now a man of forty he was introspective and deeply moral, simply dressed, modest and possessed of a serious demeanour. For the previous fifteen years he had thrown himself, heart and head, into campaigns against injustice, protesting against the horrific conditions in lunatic asylums, the hanging of people for the most trivial offences and the brutal press gangs of the period. His most controversial work, though, spoke against corruption of government and for political reform and the freedom of the press.

In 1817, when William Cobbett fled to America, he had asked Hone to join him – but Hone stayed behind to face the repressive laws of Lord Sidmouth. That year he defended himself in three high-profile government-sponsored libel cases – winning them all. The victory briefly turned him into a national hero. But, like Cobbett, he was constantly beset by financial crises. He set up magazines and social welfare projects that failed, and buckled under the pressures of supporting his family, from time to time finding himself in the bankruptcy courts. So it was always helpful if he could combine a cause with a profit.

Solvency became an achievable objective when, in 1815, Hone began a partnership with the illustrator George Cruikshank, who was twelve years his junior, but ambitious and obviously talented. Cruikshank later drew a picture of the two men sitting opposite each other at a simple wooden table, pens in hand and chatting to each other as they worked. The drawing evokes a spirit of fraternity and creativity. Their relationship was, in essence, an easy one – though occasionally marred by Hone's seniority, which allowed him to pocket most of their income. Hone wrote affectionately of Cruikshank's late hours and womanising; and of his tendency, when he had drunk too much gin, to tell his boss to 'Go to Hell.' Cruikshank was brilliant at drawing the targets of the couple's satires, and particularly George, in lurid ways that invited ridicule and disdain whilst avoiding the oppressive libel laws. Hone, at the same time, wrote carefully, rejecting stark phrases that might earn him a prison sentence, but in fact leaving the reader in no doubt of his message.

At the beginning of 1820 he published a one shilling pamphlet called *The Political House that Jack Built*, with thirteen illustrations by Cruikshank, who was paid half a guinea for each. Hone composed a rhyme deploring Peterloo and celebrating the defiance of the press against the Six Acts. He portrayed an oppressed people calling for reform, relying on the press for their power, but opposed by corrupt judges, soldiers prepared to sabre peaceful demonstrators, politicians levying intolerable taxes and most grotesquely George, or 'the Dandy of Sixty' – the monstrosity who, while:

> Britain's in tears, sails about at his pleasure;
> who spurned from his presence the Friends of his youth,
> And now has not one who will tell him the truth.[17]

The force of the words was, as usual, underpinned by a Cruikshank drawing, this time showing an obese George with drooping mutton-chops; his chest dripping with medallions and finery, an entirely repulsive figure.

Hone deserves the accolade of forefather of the modern tabloid newspaper editor. He employed great skill in setting out Cruikshank's illustrations, designing the page and choosing headlines. And he maximised his print runs by having Cruikshank make his etchings not on copperplate, which could make only a thousand or so prints before wearing out, but on end-grain blocks of tough boxwood. Woodcuts were generally made from cheaper cuts of the wood and used for crude drawings printed in shorter runs on ballad sheets and one-penny broadsides. Copperplate, by contrast, was expensive and used for upmarket prints, out of the price range of most people. Hone and Cruikshank pioneered a middle course. Their woodcuts were of top quality, could be used many times, and produced prints at an afford-able price. *The Political House that Jack Built* sold more than 100,000 copies.[18] Hone made close to £1,000 and, despite the anti-press laws, the government, as Hone had calculated, chose to avoid its own embarrassment and did not prosecute. Charles Knight, the editor of the *Windsor and Eton Express*, wrote that pamphlet buyers everywhere 'rushed to Hone', favouring him over his rival, Cobbett.

William Hone later claimed that he was in no rush to join Cobbett and Benbow in cashing in on Caroline. He plainly approved of the Queen, considering her to be a 'frank, open-hearted, unsuspicious woman . . . shrewd, witty, sarcastic and gay – and so disloyal as to speak what she thinks'.[19] But, he asserted, her trial came at an awkward time. He relates that during 1820 he was taking stock of his recent life and thinking of quitting political pamphleteering in order to write a book. He was, he said, 'very sore' at the libel trials that he had endured, and particularly aggrieved that he was prosecuted while George Canning, who also wrote parodies, had found 'place and power'. 'I wanted to write a *History of Parody*,' and, 'I was reading in the British Museum for that purpose.' Whilst there, some of Caroline's 'chief partisans' (he does not name them) approached him and asked him to support her in print: 'I refused for some time, till at last they said, "The Queen expects it of you" – and I felt I could no longer refuse, but it troubled me very much. I had gone there to be quiet and out of the way of politics, about which my mind had begun to misgive me – that is, as to my interference with them. Observe, though God has changed my opinions about religion, I have not changed my politics.'[20]

On his way home from the Museum, Hone, thoughtful and 'a good deal out of sorts', stopped at the window of a toyshop and, gazing into it, noticed a toy called 'the Matrimonial Ladder', showing the different stages of a marriage. This was to be his inspiration; during the next few days he adapted the idea for a pamphlet on Caroline, called *The Queen's Matrimonial Ladder* – describing the fourteen stages of the royal marriage – from 'Qualification', in which a fat, slobbering George is, circa 1795, already 'in drink and o'ertoppled by debt', through 'Acceptation' in which Caroline 'all youthful and gay' is soon overcome by cares and a 'husbandless bride-bed'. 'Accusation' shows George holding the Green Bag up to Caroline, whilst being poked in the bottom by the Devil; and the final stage, 'Degradation', has the defeated King being led away to the 'jeers of the world!' The pamphlet went on to sell forty editions in 1820, outstripped the success of *The Political House that Jack Built* and was soon being advertised in the London newspapers as '*the most rapidly selling Production ever issued from the Press*'.

Hone's biographer, Ben Wilson, points out that he was far more enthusiastic about joining the radical and Queenite protests than he later liked to admit, partly because he was determined to avenge his persecutors of 1817 – and Hone's brilliantly crafted publications of 1820 are additional evidence of his genuine commitment to the Queen's cause. Like Cobbett, he presented his arguments in terms of public opinion, putting great emphasis on the press as the people's most powerful and gutsy representative. 'Publication', in Hone's design for the *Matrimonial Ladder*, became a vital stage of the royal marriage; and an accompanying Cruikshank drawing depicted the press in the form of the *Chronicle*, the *News*, *The Times*, the *Examiner*, the *Traveller*, the *Statesman* and the *Star* all blasting George, whilst Caroline sat untroubled. Hone's words were equally pointed:

> Scorned, exiled, baffled, goaded in distress,
> She owes her safety to a fearless Press.[21]

Hone wrote that soon after the first edition was published he was approached by a person who offered him £50 to suppress the pamphlet. 'I refused,' he wrote, 'and was offered up to £500. I said, "Could you not make it £5,000? Even if you did, I should refuse it."' George Cruikshank, by contrast, saw his work in business, not moral, terms and on 19 June signed a receipt for £100 'in consideration of a pledge not to caricature His Majesty in any immoral situation'.[22] In practice the deal did not restrict him much, although he kept to the letter of it. He was still able to depict George in a multitude of undignified and ridiculous postures and, indeed, build a career portraying the King variously as Henry VIII, an enormous baby, a whale, a green bag and a teapot; the latter coalescing George's grotesque body shape with that of a dome on the Brighton pavilion.[23]

The Matrimonial Ladder reached its thirteenth edition by August and Hone and Cruikshank were fired up for more. They would meet with the writer William Hazlitt at the Southampton Coffee House in Chancery Lane to discuss their next squibs. Hazlitt recalled that on one occasion he tried to explain an idea to Cruikshank, who dipped his finger in his ale glass and traced something in beer on the table, asking, '"Is that what you mean, sir?"'[24] The way was now open for Hone and Cruikshank to do what they did best – not to make direct or dogmatic political attacks, but to undermine the throne by tearing to bits the so-called dignity of the King, directing their barbs at George's weakest personality traits; his monumental self-indulgence, his un-British, unmanly pampering of his person, his debauchery, extravagance and profligacy. At the same time, they would hold up Caroline as a paragon of womanly virtue and representative of an oppressed nation.

At the height of the press activity in her favour Caroline decided that she needed a political adviser closer to the centre of Westminster politics than was Matthew Wood. On 2 July, aware that the secret committee was about to report on the contents of the Green Bag, she sent for Sir William Grant, a Master of the Rolls, who had been an adviser to her in earlier times. She explained to him that some of her close advisers wished her to accept the £50,000 offer to leave Britain. This would, she said, amount to submitting to degradation, which she never would do. Sir William, rather impertinently, replied that 'degradation was comparative' and 'might be the consequence of persevering in the course she had adopted'. He also remarked that the £50,000 might no longer be on offer. Caroline said she thought 'all would be adjusted' if she could only have an interview with the King, whom she 'could remind of circumstances which no one else could lay before him'. Sir William expressed 'great doubt' about whether this could be arranged and said that, in any case, he was not the right person to do it.

Caroline then told him that since George Canning was no longer active in the government, he would be able to be her agent – and asked Sir William to visit her old friend, which he did. Canning, at this point, disappointed the Queen by answering that he had not actually resigned. Instead he had, with George's consent, simply absented himself from the whole affair, and would be at liberty to visit Caroline only if the King gave his permission. This, he added, was 'impossible for him to ask'. Sir William took the bad news back to the Queen.[25]

In the wake of Canning's refusal, Caroline gave up her attempt to approach George through an intermediary, and instead sought help from the government's most dedicated political enemy, William Cobbett. Matthew Wood was no doubt irritated by her decision, but Cobbett's endless criticisms of the quality of advice the Queen was receiving, both from Wood and Brougham, must have eventually taken root in Caroline's mind. And she now needed help managing a new source of political activity – the 'Addresses' that were arriving at her door, and the replies to them which had to be drafted. These Addresses were, like those sent during the Delicate Investigation scandal, messages of support from diverse groups of people, which, once received, were often published in the daily newspapers. In 1820, far more so than in 1813, they served as a potent form of political expression for those who were formally disenfranchised.

Matthew Wood and, more often, Henry Brougham had both drafted Caroline's responses. Cobbett had found both men's efforts inadequate, and reserved particular venom for, as he saw it,

Brougham's political timidity. It is likely that Caroline agreed. Henry Hobhouse had heard that in early July she had rejected two responses written by Brougham to an Address from the City of London. Shortly afterwards, on 15 July, she gave the job to Cobbett.[26] Of all the Addresses, some arriving with tens of thousands of signatures, that from the City of London had special significance. The City was Matthew Wood's domain and was a constant reminder to the government that power in the capital was not based in Parliament alone. The City had a separate means of political expression in the form of the Common Council, its own law-enforcement bodies, and it was prone, from time to time, to flirt with radicalism. Right now, it represented 'Londoners and the Queen' in opposition to the King and government. Other Addresses arrived from the citizens of Nottingham, the citizens of Southwark, from Preston, and from householders of Westminster, the last spearheaded by Caroline's old allies, the radicals Sir Francis Burdett and John Cam Hobhouse.

The Queen's responses, until now, had been clear reflections of Brougham's desire that Caroline separate herself entirely from the country's politics, and in particular from the reformers, radicals and their campaigns. The Queenites of Nottingham were thanked for their affectionate sentiments but assured that 'I cannot mix political animosities with my just cause.'[27] Similarly, the inhabitants of Preston were told by Caroline that her object was the 'vindication of my honour', a sacred duty that would be fulfilled 'without making myself a party to the political divisions that at present exist'.[28]

From 15 July the responses, in the hands of Cobbett, became overtly and controversially radical. On 29 July Cobbett published an open 'Letter to His Majesty the King'. Even if the King did not see this letter, he wrote optimistically, 'half a million people may'. Then he set about explaining why the Queen was a radical.

In Britain, he said, a radical was treated like a traitor, and jailed for his politics, even though 'the radicals ask for nothing that is not strictly according to the laws and constitution of their country. They are injured and oppressed men who ask for *legal redress*.' He wrote of the right of British men to representation if they were to be taxed, and of

the laws that forbade the selling of parliamentary seats. Reform and
the abolition of the boroughmongers, he told the King, would bring
about the *implementation* of the law, not defiance of it.

The Queen, he said, was in a similar situation to the radicals. 'They
have had spies set upon them, and the Queen has had spies set upon
her. Green Bags and Secret Committees were their lot, these too have
been the lot of her Majesty.' The Queen, he said, now demanded open
trial, and so did the radicals 'when sent to the dungeons by Sidmouth'.
Now the Queen was deserted by society and Parliament, it was small
wonder that she turned to 'the *people*' for protection. And she had
common cause with the people – who were honourable, and not traitors or revolutionaries. If, however, there are dangers of revolution,
the King should blame Castlereagh and the rest of the repressive government. 'Her Majesty knows by this time,' he wrote, 'what is meant
by the word *Radical*.'[29]

It is unlikely that Caroline was, in practice, au fait with radical texts,
or much interested in the radical cause, but, more than ever, she identified radical men as her allies; and from this moment the public
pronouncements made in her name took on a bolder political rhetoric.
When, on 1 August, the inhabitants of Sunderland presented an
Address to her, all restraint was gone. 'The public welfare is at this
moment intimately identified with the preservation of my rights and
dignities as the Royal Consort of his Majesty,' she proclaimed, her
words most likely written by Cobbett. She added:

> General tyranny usually begins with individual oppression . . . [and]
> If the highest subject in the realm can be deprived of her rank and
> title – can be divorced, dethroned and debased by an act of arbitrary
> power, in the form of a Bill of Pains and Penalties – the constitutional
> liberty of the Kingdom will be shaken to its very base; the rights of the
> nation will be only a scattered wreck; and this once free people, like the
> meanest of slaves, must submit to the lash of an insolent domination.[30]

The Queen's overtly political message was reinforced by two friends
who had recently become close confidantes, and regular visitors to her

home. The first, Dr Samuel Parr, was a prominent curate, teacher and pamphleteer whom she had known since 1814. He was a 'character' of the time, and was often cast as a paler version of Samuel Johnson who, through bad luck, lacked a Boswell. The comparison, though, was more justified in terms of Dr Parr's willingness to share his opinions in good company, than in the quality of his aphorisms. He was an amiable man, who admired Caroline and who had conveyed his outrage when the Queen's name was dropped from the liturgy by recording his sentiments, for all to see, in the prayer book of Hatton Church, where he had been resident minister for nearly thirty-four years. 'Whensoever I pray for *all* the royal family,' he wrote, 'I shall include Queen Caroline as a member of it. Though forbidden to pronounce her royal name, I shall, in the secret and sacred recesses of my soul, recommend her to the protection of the Deity.'[31]

Others, such as the Reverend Mr Gillespie, a Scottish army chaplain, agreed with Dr Parr's sentiments and said, 'Bless also the Queen' out loud at services; for his boldness he was soon placed under military arrest by his commanding officer. But such clergymen were in the minority, and many followed the liturgy instructions with some enthusiasm. According to Lord Holland, 'their industry in disseminating the filthiest tales about the Queen and their haughty displeasure at every popular movement on her behalf, disgusted and irritated their flocks. Never since the period of Charles I were the English people so estranged from the Established clergy as on this occasion.'[32] Perhaps Dr Parr was trying to redress the balance.

When Caroline arrived in England, Parr journeyed to London, offered her his services and found her as friendly as ever. She was, he wrote later, 'possessed of a good understanding, of a noble and lofty spirit, of a warm and benevolent heart; gay, lively, open, unsuspicious in her temper; pleasing, though not strikingly beautiful in her person'.[33]

He, also, was slightly odd-looking, having round, chubby facial features, and a bald head that was sometimes covered with an obvious wig. Caroline liked Samuel Parr, perhaps because he was almost as informal and open as she, and appointed him her senior chaplain. He would probably have been accepting of her unconventional style, unlike most of high society. Lady Jerningham, for instance, that summer spread the gossip that a young painter whom Caroline liked had been ordered to draw or paint her, but found her in her room 'on the ground without shoes or stockings, eating a potatoe'. He asked her to 'take some other attitude', said Lady Jerningham, but 'she laughed at his prudery'. Samuel Parr was not the type of man, particularly at the age of seventy-four, who worried about such things. Indeed, he was similar to Caroline, in that he enjoyed controversy and thought of himself as a free spirit.

Parr introduced Caroline to an old friend, the Reverend Robert Fellowes, philanthropist and former editor of the *Critical Review*. Fellowes, heavily influenced by Parr, became another author of Caroline's responses. Like Cobbett's compositions, his were radical and unsparing. High society, including George, was bemused and a little shocked that intelligent and respectable individuals such as these had put themselves at the centre of Caroline's campaign.

Cobbett was surely thrilled by his new political platform, and Brougham horrified. Cobbett intended to go further still; in August he wrote a 'Letter from the Queen to the King' which, once signed by Caroline, was leaked to all the newspapers and published by them on the sixteenth, the day before her trial was to start. His aim was 'to stir the people up'.[34]

The letter was uncompromising. Caroline – in Cobbett's words – complained of 'the unparalleled and unprovoked persecution' which 'has been carried on against me under the name and authority of your Majesty'. She decried the 'wound given to public morals' caused by 'the indulgence of your Majesty's inclinations' and criticised a royal court which had become a place of 'low intrigue and scurrility' in which 'spies, Bacchanalian tale-bearers and foul conspirators swarmed'. Her indignation, she professed, 'was lost in pity for him who could lower his princely plumes to the dust'.

The King's every action was determined by his desire to persecute her, and his friends chosen according to their willingness to be her enemies. 'To calumniate your innocent wife was now the shortest road to royal favour; and to betray her was to lay the sure foundation of boundless riches and titles of honour . . . Your Cabinet was founded on this basis.' As the object of George's cruelty:

> I had one consolation left; the love of my dear and only child. To permit me to enjoy this was too great an indulgence. To see my daughter; to fold her in my arms; to mingle my tears with hers; to receive her cheering caresses, and to hear from her lips assurances of never-ceasing love; thus to be comforted, consoled upheld and blessed was too much to be allowed me. Even on the slave mart the cries of 'Oh my mother, my mother! Oh! my child, my child!' have prevented a separation of the victims of avarice. But your advisers, more inhuman than the slave-dealer, remorselessly tore the mother from the child.

At the moment of Charlotte's death, she lamented, 'you saw me bereft, forlorn and broken-hearted; and this was the moment you chose for re-doubling your persecutions' by setting up the Milan Commission. The injustice of the Bill of Pains and Penalties was obvious. In practice this was to be a court of law in which the King was the plaintiff, and the judge and jury his placemen. 'I demand a trial in a Court,' she said, 'where the Jurors are taken impartially from amongst the people and where the proceedings are open and fair . . . And I will not, except compelled by actual force, submit to any sentence which shall not be pronounced by a *Court of Justice*.' She concluded:

> Having left me nothing but my innocence, you would now, by a mockery of justice, deprive me even of the reputation of possessing that. The poisoned bowl and the poniard are means more manly than perjured witnesses and partial tribunals; and they are less cruel, inasmuch as life is less valuable than honour. If my life would have satisfied Your Majesty, you should have had it on the sole condition of giving me a place in the same tomb with my child: but, since you would send me dishonoured to the grave, I will resist the attempt with all the means that it shall please God to give me. CAROLINE, R.[35]

The letter was unique – an unprecedented confrontational public condemnation of a king by his queen, and the sensation it caused was
immense. Cobbett later claimed that an astonishing two million copies
of the letter were published in Britain and nearly half a million printed
in America.[36] The pro-Caroline newspapers rallied to her side, *The
Times* declaring the composition as 'calculated to rouse every generous and manly moral feeling'. The pro-government papers professed
outrage. The *New Times* condemned the Queen's message as 'ostensibly addressed to the King, but really to the mob. Its true object is to
rouse the mob to action.' The paper's writers thought the letter both
seditious and treasonable and trusted 'that every loyal man will be prepared to cut down the Insurrection the moment it is attempted'.

The Cobbett family were afraid that the letter might land William
in prison again. Anne Cobbett writes that 'we were in absolute terror'
when it first appeared in the newspapers; and states that it was the
Queen's threat to 'resist' being dishonoured which frightened the
authorities. Together, the family feigned ignorance of the authorship
of the letter. Anne describes the visit of a 'young Mr Bryant' who,
'came over to us with one in his hand, and read it out with great feeling. Papa and I affecting wonder and admiration all the while. He the
writer, I the copyer. Papa got up and went away and tore up his rough
copy.'[37]

When asked directly on the subject, Cobbett's standard reply was:
'*I* believe it was written by Alderman Wood.'[38] In fact, the chances
that the government would have dared to prosecute Cobbett were low.
A legal confrontation would have inflamed the public temper. And, in
any case, all resources were now being directed towards the main
event – the opening of the trial of the Queen in the House of Lords.

11

THE LORDS

The British flag, that waves in view,
Protects us from abusers,
And arms, that fought at Waterloo,
Defend suborned accusers.

The Royal Letter-Bag, published by Thomas Dolby (1820)

The government was preparing for rebellion. In the early hours of Thursday 17 August, the first day of the trial, carpenters erected heavy wooden barriers near the Houses of Parliament, which, it was hoped, would hold back the mob. And from seven o'clock onwards the troops and the police marched into Westminster and took up positions at strategic points. The Foot Guards, the Life Guards and the 6th Dragoons took their places. At half past nine the soldiers of the

Surrey Mounted Patrol rode over Westminster Bridge and then paraded down Parliament Street, Whitehall and Charing Cross before stationing themselves close to the House of Lords. Westminster Hall was packed with reinforcements from the Coldstream Guards, along with field guns. Gun boats patrolled the Thames.[1]

The demonstration of force was astounding, and largely the result of the lack of a useful police force which might be used for crowd control. In these times of political uncertainty the British government relied on armed soldiers to quell unrest, thus constantly raising the spectre of state violence against British civilians. On this day in August, it seemed that any provocation of the army into action against the people in London might easily turn into a bloodbath infinitely worse than that at Peterloo, and with more dire consequences. Equally, if the army was not reliable, as Wellington feared, and split into two factions – for and against the Queen – the outcome might be similarly catastrophic. The *Courier* newspaper, which was the puppet of the King and the ministry, noted on the eve of the trial that troops in London had been hooted and hissed and had sticks thrown at them. The soldiery, it said, should not be expected 'to passively submit to be pelted by a disaffected rabble'.[2]

The sentiment was provocative. That week processions were taking place in remembrance of the Peterloo massacre – in Manchester itself as well as Bolton, Blackburn, Ashton, Oldham, Stockport, Royton, Middleton, and Macclesfield. And as the north demonstrated against the government, the whole of politics began to be seen through the prism of this imminent trial. 'Troops are moving in every direction upon London,' reported the *Manchester Observer*. 'What an eloquent confession is this, of the injustice about to be committed against the Queen! . . . Whenever power is exhibited, it is a fair presumption that right is menaced.'

As the military gathered, so did the common people – with 'persons of every description' filling the streets in anticipation of watching the ministers, the peers and of course the Queen process to the Lords. By nine o'clock the crowd had become 'one uniform compact and unbroken body' filling the whole of the area from Westminster to Charing

Cross and St James's Square. Most of the people were respectably dressed, and the windows and roofs of the houses were full of 'fashionable and respectable' spectators, mainly women, who 'manifested the greatest anxiety for the approach of the Queen'. But the mob and the radicals were present too. Samuel Waddington, a popular radical activist, paraded about with a Green Bag mounted on a long pole, to the delight and encouragement of the crowds. The Green Bag had, by now, come to represent not just the oppression of the Queen, but all that was corrupt and wrong with the British Parliament.

The heavy troop presence consoled Harriet, Lady Granville, who from the comparative safety of her London house confessed to her sister Lady Morpeth that her nerves were unsettled by the 'extreme peril we are all in'. But 'if the Guards are steady', she wrote tremulously 'nothing can be safer'.[3] Lord Grenville was similarly worried that 'the crisis is certainly such as this country has not seen for more than a century', but was reassured that the troops in London were the 'best regiments' available and 'accustomed to act against the Radicals', being 'exasperated against them'.[4] The governor of the Bank of England was fretting about the safety of the Bank, and the Reverend Webber at Westminster Abbey confessed to Lord Sidmouth his fears that the Abbey might come under attack. He had, he told the Home Secretary, taken every precaution that would not 'betray appearance of alarm'.[5]

Some of the most vociferous of the crowds had packed themselves into St James's Square, where Caroline had taken a house for the duration of the trial; and not just any house but that next door to Castlereagh's. The Foreign Secretary was now, apart from the King and Sidmouth, the most loathed man in the country, and Caroline's choice was a controversial one, apparently designed to stir up the emotions of the mob. Castlereagh maintained his usual intrepid coolness and wished to stay put, despite the dangers. It was only with the greatest difficulty that he was eventually persuaded to shut up the windows of the house and make up a bed for himself at his office, away from the epicentre of the hostile Queenites.[6] His retreat allowed Caroline to preside, symbolically at least, over that part of London that extended from St James's Square, ran past George's residence, Carlton House, on Pall Mall and south to the Houses of Parliament. In short, in appearance, the Queen and the people had taken possession of that part of the kingdom which was the heart of its government.

A number of wagons lined the edges of St James's Square and these were filled with women who had paid a shilling each for their places. In front of the wagons and carts hundreds of people were squashed together, all hoping for a glimpse of the Queen. By nine o'clock the square 'presented almost one solid mass of human beings', and the windows and balconies all around were filled with ladies.[7] Some intrepid souls made it on to the roof tops. Soon after nine the Queen went to her window and showed herself to the supporters outside. 'Her appearance and deportment called forth from the surrounding multitude the most unbounded marks of applause' wrote the *Times*' reporter on duty. When Caroline withdrew a great shout went up of 'The Queen! The Queen!' until she came to the window again. Her carriage stood outside the house; not the ragged calash of the previous weeks, but a grander state carriage harnessed to six handsome bay horses. It was soon joined by another which brought Matthew Wood and Lady Anne Hamilton along with Caroline's old friends and chamberlains, Sir William Gell and the Hon. Keppel Craven, who had both travelled from Naples. Sir William had come at the expense of his health, since he suffered badly from gout; but he had been receiving a pension of £200 a year since 1815 from Caroline, and felt he should show her his gratitude. Keppel Craven's objective was primarily to provide companionship and care to Sir William.

In the streets leading to Parliament the crowds, while waiting for the Queen, were entertained by the arrival of Caroline's judges – the Lords. Some turned up alone, others in groups. George's more popular brother Frederick, Duke of York, rode through the Horse Guards soon after nine o'clock and received great cheers – partly, presumably, because the crowds would prefer him as their monarch, and partly in sympathy, as his wife had recently died. Augustus, the Duke of Sussex, who had, in the past, been a friend to Caroline, was also welcomed with loud huzzas.

For the most part the crowds applauded the opposition peers, and jeered the ministers and ministerial allies. As the Duke of Wellington came by on horseback he was hissed and shouted at and, according to Lord Holland, one man stepped in front of the rest, clenched his fist and 'with great emphasis and anger' repeated the word *Ney* three times; a chilling reference to Napoleon's commander, Marshal Michel Ney, who had been shot for treason in 1815. Wellington's 'horse made a little start', wrote Creevey, 'and he looked round with some surprise. He caught my eye as he passed, and nodded, but was evidently annoyed.'[8] Lord Holland fancied that the mass of the people that morning had a dangerous look about them, and that 'their countenances seemed to indicate design, determination and revenge'. He thought they called out 'with such marked indifference that it was difficult not to suspect that they had some more serious undertaking in view'.

At a quarter to ten an immense cheer went up as Caroline began her journey to the House of Lords, with Lady Anne Hamilton at her side. Their carriage moved slowly due to the great mass of people pressing in close. The Queen was dressed in black in mourning for the Duchess of York. 'Her Majesty's appearance was commanding and dignified,' reported the ever loyal *Times*. 'She repeatedly bowed to the people, who rent the air with their acclamations: her countenance, though pale and seemingly careworn . . . had yet an expression of great dignity and fortitude.'

In Pall Mall her carriage passed by Carlton House. At this point the applause became louder still and the sentinels on duty, after a moment's pause, presented arms, to the joy of the crowds. The procession then moved through Cockspur Street, Charing Cross, the Admiralty and Whitehall and turned into Parliament Street, where, according to *The Times*, 'the universal emotion produced' was 'impossible to describe'. The ladies present 'universally waved their handkerchiefs, and thousands of voices exclaimed, "God bless her!" as she passed'. At St Margaret's Church the pressure of people became so great that the barrier gave way, and the masses rushed forward to accompany the Queen 'to the very threshold of Parliament'.

Caroline entered the Parliament building, and then the chamber of the House of Lords. She seemed 'evidently much affected' by the scene of the peers rising and treating her with more respect than she had ever received in Britain before. She took her seat on the right hand of the throne, 'lolling back in her chair, with an easy air of indifference'. She was accompanied by Lady Anne and Sir Archibald Hamilton who stood close to her throughout the day – or, as Creevey put it, Lady Anne Hamilton 'for effect and delicacy's sake . . . leans on brother Archy's arm, tho' she is full six feet high and bears a striking resemblance to one of Lord Derby's great red deer'.[9]

The first business of the House was to recognise those peers who through ill health, foreign travel, age, their Roman Catholicism or the death of a close relative, were to be excused from attending the trial. The list included Lord Byron, whom Caroline dearly hoped might return from Italy and support her. She had pressed Byron's friend John Cam Hobhouse to try to persuade him to come, which Hobhouse did, urging him to testify as to the manners common in Italy. For the moment, however, Byron arrived in London only on a wave of gossip to the effect that he had been spotted in this place and that. Lady Caroline Lamb, for one, refused to believe that he was not in the country. But the fact was that Byron was deterred from coming by a long-running feud with Henry Brougham. Should he come to England, he wrote, his first task would be to challenge Brougham to a duel.[10] The position of the distinguished lawyer Lord Erskine was less complicated. He was excused attending the trial on the grounds that he was seventy years of age, but said that he wished to anyway, if his health permitted it.

Then the Lord Chancellor, Lord Eldon, rose and announced that he had received a letter from the Duke of Sussex asking to be excused 'on account of the ties of consanguinity which existed between him and the parties'. His brother the Duke of York then pronounced that his own claims for leave of absence were stronger still, presumably because of the death of his wife, but he would not 'suffer any private feelings to deter him from doing his duty, however painful it might be'. The Duke of Sussex was duly excused, while the Duke of York sat down to business; but Sussex's withdrawal was not popular with the mob, who, according to Lady Granville, later became angry and thought him a 'shabby fellow, who won't vote either way'.[11]

The House now came to the second reading of the Bill of Pains and Penalties, the first reading having been a formality. Lord Leinster stood up and in a 'purely Irish tone' put the immediate motion 'that the said order be now rescinded'; a proposition which gave the Lords the chance to dismiss the Bill out of hand and, given that they were not about to do so, allowed for the initial support for the Bill to be measured. A vote was taken, and Lord Leinster's motion dismissed by 206 votes to 41. The Lords were evidently keener to serve their King than give in to the sentiments of the crowds, their resolve being interpreted both as the action of the monarch's craven placemen and, from the opposite perspective, of brave resistance to mob rule. The few who voted with Leinster included the doyen of Whig society Lord Holland, but not the party's leader in the Lords, Lord Grey, nor Caroline's trustee, Lord Fitzwilliam.

Shortly afterwards the Duke of Hamilton addressed the Attorney General, Robert Gifford, who was, in effect, acting as chief prosecutor in the case against the Queen; or, looked at another way, for the plaintiff. 'In a most excellent manner,' Hamilton demanded to know whom he was representing. Whose instructions was he receiving? Gifford was embarrassed; he shifted and shuffled about and was apparently unable to answer the question. The Duke put the question again, and Lord Liverpool intervened to help Gifford, but did not answer clearly, and made no mention of the King. George's presence, however, must have been keenly felt. Matters moved on, with the Lords, in the absence of precedents, making up much of the procedure.

The time now came for Henry Brougham to make his debut as the head of the Queen's defence team; a moment anticipated with much anxiety by his friends. There were several reasons to doubt that he would be on good form. He had fallen out quite badly with Caroline in the weeks before the trial. At the same time, it was clear that he harboured grave doubts about her innocence. 'He had received from various quarters the most sinister reports,' wrote Thomas Denman, who would never forget the solemn manner in which Brougham had confessed his anxieties before the trial began and said: 'So now we are in for it, Mr Denman.'[12]

It was also known by Thomas Denman and others close to the case that Brougham had recently succumbed to one of his dreadful attacks of 'fatigue and anxiety'. When his doctor had advised that a change of air 'was absolutely necessary' he had retired to the country and as recently as 7 August had been warned that he must stay there 'to the latest moment possible'. Any attempt to resume work before a recovery in Brougham's health, thought his doctor, might produce consequences 'very serious to his constitution'.[13] It was in these shaky circumstances that Brougham embarked on his opening speech.

The thrust of his argument was that the Bill was wrong *in principle*. It was a private law, he said, introduced for the sole purpose of punishing an individual. Such black proceedings were not unknown in law, but were repugnant to every sound principle of jurisprudence and were known to the Romans as *privilegia odiosa*. Furthermore, the current bill was an *ex post facto* law – 'it suffered a deed to be done and afterwards pronounced upon its innocence or its guilt'. Even the worst of laws of this nature, he continued, passed at other dark moments of history, including those 'relating to the wives of Harry VIII', were, when compared with this case, 'regular, consistent and judicial'.

Why had Caroline not been impeached? he asked. Then, at least, she would have had the benefit of a real judicial proceeding with some specification of the charges; and the list of witnesses against her would not have been withheld, as they were now. The Bill, he argued, was also inexpedient. 'Was the succession or its purity endangered, or was there even a possibility of it being put in jeopardy?'

And then he threatened the King: 'I put out of view at present the question of recrimination . . . I should be most deeply and I may say with perfect truth unfeignedly afflicted if, in the progress of this ill-omened question, the necessity were imposed upon me of mentioning it again; and I should act directly in the teeth of the instructions of this illustrious woman.' At this moment he pointed dramatically at Caroline who sat immediately below him. 'I should disobey her solemn commands if I again used even the word recrimination without being driven to it by an absolute and overruling compulsion.'

In fact few doubted that Brougham was raising recrimination in order to make it clear that, if he thought it necessary, he *would* use it in the Queen's defence. Society once again ruminated on what the nature of the recrimination would be. Would he produce absolute proof of the King's marriage to Maria Fitzherbert? Or, perhaps, subpoena Mrs Fitzherbert, forcing her to testify? She had fled to Paris fearing that he would do just that. Rumours began to circulate that Brougham had secured some devastating evidence against George; and were only to be inflamed by a subsequent speech by Thomas Denman in which he called recrimination 'the most important right belonging to a consort'.

The House adjourned at four o'clock and the Lords departed; once more to face the mob. The crowd again pressed around the Duke of Wellington and, according to *The Times* he was regaled by calls of 'We must have the Queen – no foul play, my Lord!' and 'The army for ever, my Lord!' One person who was, like the Duke, on horseback, rode alongside shouting out 'The Queen and the Army!' Caroline, when she appeared, seemed 'somewhat exhausted by the fatigue and anxiety she must have sustained throughout the day', but found the energy to bow repeatedly to her followers before she returned to St James's Square, where the crowd remained until late. Caroline left them at six o'clock and returned in her private carriage to Brandenburgh House in Hammersmith to the west of London, which was now her main home. At two o'clock in the morning, however, she got up to inspect some papers that had at that moment been delivered by her courier. He had come from Rome, bringing news of high-ranking individuals offering to come to England immediately to testify on her behalf. She sent the papers on immediately to William Vizard, a solicitor based in Lincoln's Inn who was coordinating her case.

After the day's events, thought Lord Holland, the people were in more benign spirits, and had lost their earlier threatening tone. Lady Granville was less sanguine and confessed that 'I cannot help looking out of [the] window and spying out for ill-looking men.'[14] Thomas Creevey went to his club, Brooks's, and found that his fellow Whigs had pronounced Brougham's speech as magnificent and that, for once, having recovered his health, he was a hero amongst them. Whilst there, Creevey came upon Lord Grey, who was so impressed by Brougham that he predicted that the Lords would throw out the Bill 'before Saturday fortnight'.[15] The following morning *The Times* praised Brougham's speech for its 'fervid eloquence, powerful reasoning, intense thought and glowing language, every word of which will be eagerly read and long remembered by the country'.

On 18 August the mob was quiet, to the relief of Lady Granville. Inside the House, Thomas Denman, as Caroline's Solicitor General, made his own opening speech, reinforcing much of Brougham's earlier message. The Queen attended and was 'as before quite tranquil and unmoved, retiring to sleep during a great part of the day', prompting Lord Holland to compose a droll rhyme which was soon repeated in prominent London houses:

> Her conduct at present no censure affords
> She sins not with peasants but sleeps with the Lords.[16]

Later in the day, when Caroline returned to the rooms that had been provided for her in the Lords, she found Thomas Denman already there. She greeted him with the words, 'My God, what a beautiful speech!' Denman wrote later: 'I was reposing, much fatigued, on one of the sofas and had thrown my wig on the other. When she entered I expressed great distress at having taken so great a liberty with her room, and she answered me laughing, with an allusion to what I had been saying about the preamble of the bill, '"Indeed it is a most unbecoming familiarity".'[17]

Denman's speech was well received. Lady Granville said it had caused a sensation 'amongst the country gentlemen' and thought the day 'went decidedly against the government'.[18]

Now that the trial was actually under way, the rumours regarding Caroline's guilt or innocence were legion. Sara Hutchinson, friend of

Wordsworth and love object for Coleridge, had heard of a conversation between Sir Francis Burdett and Caroline, and was eager to spread the news. In a private meeting before the start of the trial, she said, Sir Francis had asked Caroline:

> Had she raised this Pergami from a menial condition to be her Chamberlain –
> The Queen had answered – *Yes*
> Had he, as was reported, slept in the same room with her?
> *Yes*, said Caroline, *she was afraid of being poisoned*.

A good joke, thought Sara Hutchinson, who was *not* a Queenite, to fear being poisoned 'while asleep'. She wrote that no one believed the Queen actually to be innocent 'not even *The Times* newspaper itself' and she had heard gossip that Caroline was subsidising the paper by buying up £500's worth of copies a week. 'She is a true Messalina,' she wrote, 'and the indecencies are they say more horrible than any thing that can be conceived; far worse the Lords say than simple Adultery in its worst shape.'[19] Harriet, Lady Granville, reported that 'Lady Spencer says there is an English sea captain who can prove everything. Lord Westmorland says so also.'[20] Lady Jerningham also thought 'everything that is improper and indecent can be proved', but observed that 'if the offence does not meet the letter [rather than the spirit] of the law the rest is all *Fudge*'.[21]

Brougham, meanwhile, went about London causing amusement in society circles by asserting that he believed his client to be 'pure in-no-sense' while, at other times, hinting at the possibility that, despite appearances, she had never actually committed adultery. 'Brougham says he has Pergami's b———x in a bottle,' John Cam Hobhouse wrote to Byron, 'others swear he is a woman.'[22] Brougham's hint at Pergami's impotence reflects the contents of a letter he had received that August from a surgeon who had attended Caroline on her travels.

> In various conversations which I had with Mr Pergami, he recounted the hardships he suffered in the Russian campaign, and in particular

consulted me for pain and debility of back, loins and hips; he felt, as he expressed himself, as if those parts were frozen and rendered him perfectly indifferent to women, in short, that he had lost all desire for the sex ever since his sufferings in the Russian campaign.

Caroline, meanwhile, was reported to have told friends that 'she never committed adultery but once, and that was with Mrs Fitzherbert's husband'.[23]

The opening of the trial brought into sharp relief the division between those in high society who were prepared to visit the Queen, thus risking their reputations, and the majority who preferred to shun her. Prominent Whig men, led by Brougham and Denman, came to see her, while Tories stayed away. But the real story of Caroline's non-acceptance in high-class circles lies with the women. A number of Whig 'ladies of quality' including the society hostess Lady Jersey, the daughter-in-law of Caroline's *bête noire* of the 1790s, were anxious to visit the Queen but were afraid to do so.

Denman thought that Henry Brougham could and should have led the way by sending his wife to meet Caroline back in June. Brougham was on good terms with many influential Whig ladies, and might have influenced them, but did not. A report was spread that Lady Jersey confidentially asked him for advice, and that he 'exhorted her to abstain from calling'. 'The truth of this is unknown to me,' wrote Denman, 'but it is certain that when the newspapers inserted Lady Jersey's name and that of Lady Fitzwilliam among the visitors at the Queen's miserable residence in Portman Street the statement received a formal contradiction.'[24]

Thomas Denman's wife wished very much to call on the Queen, but he begged her to wait until Mrs Brougham had done so, 'dreading that such scenes of vice and debauchery would be proved as would overwhelm with shame any woman who had formed any acquaintance with the criminal'.[25] Caroline's former lady-in-waiting, Lady Charlotte Lindsay, whose relationship with Brougham was both close and flirtatious, was similarly terrified. She disapproved strongly of Caroline's allegiance with Matthew Wood and the radicals, and was scornful of those who thought the Queen's appearance in England proof of her innocence. Anybody who knew Caroline better, she thought, 'cannot but foresee the ruin and disgrace that she is bringing upon herself, and the probable confusion into which she is plunging the country'.[26] So, when Caroline had landed at Dover, Lady Charlotte took the advice of her friends and fled London to the country. She wrote in her diary: 'The appearance of deserting an old friend is so repugnant to my nature, that I confess it was not without some difficulty that I resolved upon this measure; but I am perfectly satisfied, upon reflection, that it is not only the safest, but the most honourable conduct that I could pursue.'[27]

Charlotte Lindsay writes that she had considered sacrificing her own good name, and visiting Caroline whose conduct, she claimed, was 'notoriously disgraceful in the eyes of all Europe'. But one fact propelled her in the opposite direction. She did not, she wrote, trust in Caroline's friendship. Indeed, she thought hers 'not a character capable of real friendship', giving in too much to caprice and 'while appearing to consult and trust me, she would in fact be guided by the counsels of mischievous and foolish persons, as long as their counsels agreed with her own inclinations'. So Lady Charlotte felt, on balance, that she was morally bound to retreat to the country and to save her reputation. She knew, however, that an ordeal awaited; she would soon be summoned to London to give evidence at the trial.[28]

Aside from Lady Anne Hamilton, the only woman of consequence to visit Caroline was Anne Seymour Damer, a famous and talented sculptor who had, earlier in life, endured a scandal of her own when her husband had committed suicide and left her with monstrous debts. Mrs Damer's intimate friendships with other women also caused gossip; by 1820 she had been in a relationship with Caroline's friend Mary Berry for some twenty years. Unlike Caroline, she had no exhibitionist leanings and did not embrace controversy for the sake of it. Whilst the Queen had a reputation for vulgarity and self-indulgence, Mrs Damer was cultivated, self-possessed and independent. She shared Caroline's interest in Napoleon, had visited him in Paris when he was at the zenith of his power, and had presented him with a bust of Nelson and one of Charles James Fox. In return, he had given her a diamond-encrusted snuff box.[29]

On her death in 1828 Mrs Damer ordered that her private papers be destroyed, and we cannot know why she chose to reject society and publicly display her friendship with Caroline. Most likely, given Anne Damer's personal history, she simply believed in the Queen's cause, liked her and sympathised with her. Unlike her peers, she was brave enough to follow her own instincts, declaring herself for the Queen even before she had heard the prosecution case. The rest of female high society was reserving judgement; well-born women evidently valued their reputations above all else. They were not inclined, as were the lower classes of women, to show solidarity with a persecuted wife, or to close their eyes to the probability that Caroline was guilty of the charges against her.

12

PROSECUTION

let the ceremony
Take place of the uglification of the Queen

Percy Bysshe Shelley. *Oedipus Tyrannus;
or Swellfoot the Tyrant* (1820)

The prosecution's case against the Queen opened on Saturday 19
August. The multitude again filled the streets of London, men and
women together declaring their support for Caroline and hoping to catch
a glimpse of her. 'Where the devil they all come from, I can't possibly
imagine,' wrote Thomas Creevey, 'but I think the country about London
must furnish a great part.' However, the people were to be disappointed,
as the Queen had decided to stay at home rather than listen to the sordid
speechifying of her accusers. Lady Cowper wrote to Frederick Lamb: 'I

believe she knew Saturday was a bad mob day and did not like to see her-self ill-attended, so she has saved herself for Monday.'[1] But the poor attendance was more wishful thinking on Lady Cowper's part than real.

Inside the House, the Attorney General Sir Robert Gifford rose to address the 300 peers who packed the scarlet benches and the bal-conies. The 41-year-old Gifford had been promoted to Attorney General the previous year, having made his name as a prosecutor in prominent sedition trials. In 1817 he had acted for the Crown in a notorious case against James Watson, who was charged with imagining the King's death. The jury, presumably because of the preposterous nature of the crime, acquitted Watson. But later that year Gifford was successful in a case of high treason against a group of armed Nottinghamshire rioters who, after rampaging to the cry of 'Roast-beef and ale, and a fresh government', were convicted and executed. Then, shortly before the Queen's trial opened in 1820, he led the prosecution of the ill-fated Cato Street conspirators. This record put him firmly on the side of conservatism, if not oppression, in the great national debate. The Queen's legal team, by contrast, was made up entirely of lawyers who had defended in sedition and polit-ical libel cases, and who were champions of press freedom and political reform. The physical presence of the dozen or more lawyers in the Lords was commanding – they all wore long wigs and voluminous black gowns, which fluttered as they reached for papers or whispered confidences; in all they resembled two dark conspiracies of ravens, one for King and Tories, the other for Queen, Whigs and the people.

As Gifford began to speak, a storm broke outside, and claps of thunder rumbled around the chamber giving his words a portentous air that was much remarked upon in the public prints. 'There is a cou-plet about it,' Countess Lieven told Metternich:

> Accusation in thunder,
> And proof in the dark.[2]

The Attorney General said he would prove the Queen's adultery by demonstrating that at Naples Caroline had ordered Pergami's room to

be moved close to hers and had banished William Austin from sleeping in her apartment, as he had done in the past. On 9 November 1814,
she had dismissed her female servants and had spent the night in the
bedroom of her lover. This, he maintained, was the beginning of a
five-year affair.

Gifford drew the peers' attention to Caroline's behaviour at a ball at
the house of Joachim Murat, the King of Naples. She had, he said,
changed her outfit during the ball in the presence of Pergami, and no
one else. Moreover, he was 'instructed to state that the dress worn by her
Royal Highness on that occasion was of a most indecent and disgusting
kind'. Later on she changed again, and appeared with 'her courier, her
menial servant Pergami', both of them dressed as Turkish peasants. The
Queen, he suggested, had brought disgrace upon the British nation.

Around this time, the servants had noticed that whenever the Queen
rose in the morning, Pergami appeared too. Moreover, she took breakfast with him in her apartments, despite his lowly status as her courier
and her *valet-de-chambre*. On one occasion Pergami had been kicked
by his horse and was confined to his room. A servant was assigned to
look after him. 'I am instructed to state,' said the Attorney General,
'and it will appear in evidence, that, after her Majesty entered the
room, this man could distinctly hear them kissing.' At this point a
'buzz of surprise' was heard throughout the House, this being the first
instance of actual physical intimacy between the Queen and her servant. Pergami, he asserted, entered Caroline's room at all times with
absolute, assumed freedom 'until at last he became the lord and master
of her establishment'. As a result, the Queen soon found herself with
no English lady in her suite.

At Genoa, Pergami was Caroline's constant companion 'in all her
rides and walks', and had a bedroom near hers. Indeed, the Queen's
bed seemed rarely to have been slept in, while Pergami's 'bore evident
marks of having been occupied by two persons'. Pergami was a married man, Gifford reminded the peers. He told them about Pergami's
daughter Victorine, who was taken into Caroline's household at the
age of three, along with his sister, brother and mother, though not his
wife. In May 1815 a second Pergami sister, the Countess of Oldi, was

incorporated into the suite – 'a woman of vulgar manners, totally un-
educated'. This person became a companion to Caroline, taking on a
role formerly occupied by British ladies such as Lady Elisabeth
Forbes, Lady Charlotte Lindsay and Lady Charlotte Campbell.

As the English quitted her service, he said, there was less reserve in
her attention to Pergami. This was particularly the case at the Villa
d'Este after he was promoted to chamberlain, and on Caroline's journeys across the Mediterranean. Pergami's cabin would always be close
to the Queen's, and she would walk arm in arm with him on deck,
calling him 'her dear' and 'her love'. Indeed, she 'played with him so
familiarly' that no doubt could remain in their Lordships' minds, 'but
that an adulterous intercourse alone could justify the attentions, or
account for the familiarities of her Majesty'.

The Lords' working day came to an end, and the House would have
to wait until Monday to hear the remainder of Sir Robert Gifford's
speech. In the meantime, however, the British people had the satisfaction of reading the verbatim report of the trial carried by the
Sunday papers. For most, this was their first exposure to the lurid
details of the allegations against the Queen, and Gifford's words produced 'a great effect on the public mind'.

The Sunday papers, even more than the dailies, were increasingly
drawn to scandal-mongering and scurrility, and were characterised by
moralists as corrupting influences on the mass of the people. Nineteen
different Sunday papers were published in London alone, publications
such as the *Examiner*, *Bell's Messenger*, the *Observer*, the *News* and the
Sunday Times were becoming so popular that their readership
amongst tradesmen and the middle classes of the metropolis was
'almost universal' – raising fears that their 'seditious' messages were
destabilising the nation. As one correspondent to Lord Sidmouth
put it:

I am, my Lord, convinced that those Sunday Papers have done more
mischief, in the way of spreading Radicalism, and engendering evil
spirit and crime, than all the other disaffected publications put
together . . . They form a rallying point for the disaffected, and

Princess Caroline of
Brunswick. Some
found her attractive
and charming, but she
was not beautiful.

George, Prince of
Wales as portrayed
by James Gillray. He
was also described as
the 'Prince of
Whales' and a 'fat
Adonis'.

The Prince Regent as he wished to be seen, heroic and splendid.

Princess Charlotte. The Duke of Wellington thought that, had she lived, she 'would have turned out quite as ill as her mother'.

The Queen at her trial.

Henry Brougham, whose intelligence, wit and wiles determined the fate of the
Queen and the nation.

The trial of Queen Caroline in the House of Lords. Lord Grey is standing to question the unfortunate Theodore Majocchi. The Queen looks on.

8

Bartolomeo Pergami, devoted servant.

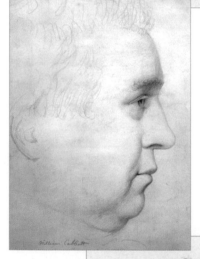

9

William Cobbett. He worked to ensure that the Queen's cause was taken up in 'every cottage in the Kingdom'.

10

William Hone and George Cruikshank. Their squibs and pamphlets acted as a popular press.

The Prime Minister, Lord Liverpool. He
was unable to control the King or
the country.

The Home Secretary. Lord Sidmouth
was deluged with hate mail and warnings
of revolution.

Thomas Denman, the Queen's dutiful
Solicitor General.

Alderman Matthew Wood, the 'beast'
who made the Queen a radical.

'The Radical Ladder'. This loyalist print was published a few days after the Queen's death.

The funeral procession of Queen Caroline. A battle between Life Guards and mourners broke out in Hyde Park, leaving two men dead.

would-be revolutionists and assassins – They draw the idle on Sundays to the . . . public houses, in which places of vile resort there is more treason hatched than in any other in the country.[3]

Another writer was so dismayed by the corrupting effect of the Sunday papers that he was moved to publish a pamphlet on the subject. On the lowest estimates, he calculated between 200,000 and 300,000 people in London alone were readers of the Sundays. He thought about five people read each paper (other estimates have been put as high as 15 or 20) 'not to speak of the many readers of each separate newspaper found in public houses, ordinaries, tea gardens and other places of Sunday resort'.[4]

For the proprietors and editors of these publications, the Queen's trial was a great blessing. It was also a money-spinner for those who made their entire week's earnings selling the Sunday papers, or traders such as 'hairdressers, pastrycooks, greengrocers and others', who opened on Sunday simply for the profits to be made from selling the papers as a sideline. Sales on 20 August must have been particularly good thanks to the trial and the helpful decision of the Queen to ride out from Hammersmith in her state carriage and parade herself through Knightsbridge, Hyde Park, Green Park, St James's Park, over Westminster Bridge, back over London Bridge and into the City of London, before returning to Brandenburgh House. The *Courier* lamented the Queen's disregard for 'ordinary notions of modesty' in showing herself in such a manner, particularly since the 'disgusting disclosures' made by the Attorney General were now 'very generally circulated'.[5]

The distressed pamphleteer would, doubtless, have agreed. He lamented the violation of the Sabbath caused by the worldly reports of criminal trials and theatrical performances, and decried 'the disquisitions upon politics – prepared, for the most part, by obscure and mercenary writers, who are utterly ignorant of the first principles of a science upon which they speak with such an unmeasured and unseemly confidence'. In addition, the evil done by the Sunday papers 'does not end with the corruption of Londoners on the Sabbath itself, as the papers are then distributed about the country to do their political mischief in country places. We are not therefore (like the child) to fancy that when the thunder-cloud has passed over our own heads, its danger is at an end.'

He pointed out that the Sunday papers arrived the same day in Brighton soon after midday; and the same placards which announced their contents in London were sent with them and publicly exhibited in the Brighton shops. The clock, he thought, must be turned backwards; postulating that the women of Britain were, perhaps, the people to do it: 'Let an humble and unassuming female learn, that by inducing the father of her youth, or the husband of her bosom, to cast a Sunday Newspaper out of his house, she may perhaps be eventually found to have been the instrument of having saved a soul, and occasioned joy in heaven.'[6]

But, during Caroline's trial at least, newspaper sales were rising rapidly. Perhaps women were encountering male resistance when they tried to ban them from the home, but it is more likely that they, like the men, were avid readers of all the filthy revelations which were becoming daily fare.

On Monday 21 August, Sir Robert Gifford resumed his assault. He informed the Lords that Caroline had bestowed various honours on Pergami, procuring for him the title of Knight of Malta and a higher title still, namely that of Baron della Francina. Thereafter she always addressed him by the title of Baron. Caroline, he said, had allowed herself to be painted in the character of Mary Magdalen, 'with her person considerably exposed', and was also drawn as a Turkish woman. A picture of Pergami in Turkish dress was also drawn, and then presented to him by Caroline; an act of favour which, according to Gifford, demonstrated that 'the most criminal intercourse' had taken place. Any other interpretation was 'impossible'.

He cited many more suspicious incidents which took place during the Queen's Mediterranean journey. At Athens an Englishman had come across Caroline and Pergami sitting together 'in an alcove', Pergami behaving entirely as if they were of equal rank. At Ephesus, Caroline was seen sitting on an old travelling bed that she took with her on her journeys, 'Pergami being seated on the floor near her.' At

Ann, in Syria, she had ordered a tent to be put up and a bed put in. 'Her Majesty was seen in that bed undressed, Pergami sitting in his shirt sleeves, almost undressed, on the side of the bed. Some time after he was observed coming from the tent *en déshabillé*, her Majesty being still undressed and in bed.' And so it continued.

In Jerusalem, said the Attorney General, the Queen had created the Order of St Caroline and made Pergami 'the Grand Master'. This caused a laugh to sound out in the House. Then Gifford described what was to become 'the tent scene', a theatrical highlight of the trial. When Caroline boarded the polacca at Jaffa for the voyage back to Italy, he explained, she had ordered a tent to be put up on deck for her to sleep in, and had been joined there by Pergami. He described how, in broad daylight and in front of the servants, the Queen would sit on Pergami's knee 'embracing and toying with him'. If she acted like that in the open day, 'how do you suppose she acted when alone with Pergami, and when the veil of night had removed all delicacy?' Moreover, on several occasions during her voyage Caroline had taken several baths 'and on these occasions she was attended, even while bathing, by Pergami, and by Pergami only!'

Sir Robert's speech did not go down particularly well, even amongst those who loathed Caroline, such us Henry Edward Fox, son of Lord Holland. He thought it 'ill-delivered and wretchedly put together'. Lady Harriet Granville agreed. Others took the view that, whatever the Queen and Pergami had done was their own business because of the formal separation with George as long ago as 1796. The famous 'letter of licence' of 30 April 1796 was republished, reminding the public that George had put in writing that, 'Our inclinations are not in our power, nor should either of us be held answerable to the other.' For the most part, high society maintained its disapproval of the Queen's behaviour, but was also disgusted by George's audacity in subjecting her to the trial. His adultery dated back to the time of their marriage, and his conduct was brazen. Her 'misbehaviour' occurred only after their separation, and in obscure foreign parts, or on ships in the middle of the Mediterranean.

William Cobbett, meanwhile, examined the written reports of the

Attorney General's speech 'with a sincere desire to come to a just conclusion' and wrote a grand, though hardly sincere, *Answer* which he
addressed '*to the People of the United Kingdom*'. This was published by
Benbow in a threepenny pamphlet and concluded that 'the charges are
false'. The Attorney General, he wrote, had argued that Caroline and
Pergami were acting, from November to March 1814–1815, day and
night, like a 'pair of Turtle Doves, continually billing and cooing'.
How come this had not been noticed by the honourable English persons at that time in Caroline's entourage – people such as Lady
Charlotte Lindsay, Lady Elisabeth Forbes, Keppel Craven, Sir
William Gell, Dr Holland and Captain Hesse? 'Where were their eyes
and ears? They were living in the *same house*; under the same roof;
and yet *they* never *saw*, or *heard*, anything about these open and fla-
grant and shameful doings!'

How was it that Lady Charlotte Campbell had joined Caroline at
Genoa without noticing that she was living in a style 'which would
excite a blush even in a brothel'? She was with the Queen from March
1815 to May or June 1816, he wrote. 'What! Was she all this while in
the same house with the Queen without *hearing* of the *adulterous intercourse*?' All this is impossible, he continued. 'There is no man living
who would believe it.' In reality, he said, 'the Queen's character and
conduct are an honour to the country'. Cobbett later claimed that a
hundred thousand copies of this *Answer* were sold.[7]

Leigh Hunt, editor of the *Examiner* (and one of the Hunt brothers
who had been defended by Brougham in 1812), wrote to his friend
Percy Shelley: 'At present we are all in a pretty turmoil about the
Queen. Her trial has commenced and either the evidence against her
is perjured beyond all the perjury in Italy and Ireland to boot, or else
she has been playing most princely vagaries indeed.' He thought the
proceedings delightfully destructive of the legitimacy of the monarchy and wished that the Queen 'recriminates, as it is hoped and
announced she will'. Then he offered a view that was commonly held,
in fear by some and in hope by others. 'The whole thing,' he wrote,
'will be one of the greatest pushes given to the declining royalty that
the age has seen.'[8]

13

FOREIGNERS

It was the very dregs and sediment of Italian treachery, concocted by the aid of English gold.

Robert Huish

The witnesses against Caroline, mostly Italians, and of the servant or trader classes, had been arriving in Britain during the previous few weeks, and were having a miserable time. One batch of eleven men and a woman landed at Dover in early July and while they were in the custom house having their luggage examined were set upon by a mob of local people. The crowd 'beat them most unmercifully, venting all the while', with women taking the most violent part. The militia had to be called out to restore peace, and the Italians were able to leave the town only by stealth and avoiding the main road to

London. News of the attack reached Italy where, it was reported, several other witnesses refused to set out for England 'not liking the pelting and hooting with which their immaculate countrymen were lately received'. Unfortunate Italians already resident in England were said to 'quake, lest the mob should massacre them as spies'.[1]

At one stage the Italian witnesses were shipped out to Holland for their own safety, and returned only when a protected residence had been found at Cotton Garden in Westminster. This location quickly became infamous, and was depicted in the public prints as a filthy cauldron of Italian depravity, lies and treachery. In the narrative that was unfolding, shaped by the popular prints and public opinion, the Italians were forced into the role of traitors to the Queen – and the worse they were, the more deserving and heroic she became. They were cowardly and despicable; had no honour or pride, but were 'crafty, venal and officious – naturalised to crime – outcasts of credulity'.[2] She, meanwhile, remained 'virtuous and fair'; and the victim of loathsome maltreatment. To be spied upon was bad enough. But to be betrayed by these foreign devils of low birth was monstrous.

The demonisation of the Italians served to stoke up patriotic pride. Britons at this period considered themselves to be the greatest nation on earth, a fact not simply acknowledged in British hearts, but proven on the battlefields of Europe. The defeat of Napoleon and the French amounted to a great deal more than the victorious outcome of a clash of armies and navies. It signified the superiority of the values of Britishness – honour, courage, the willingness to champion a just cause, fair play, straightforwardness. These virtues surfaced endlessly in the one-penny news-sheets and ballads on sale in the streets in 1820, and were championed in terms as fulsome as those used in condemnation of the Italians for traits that were decidedly un-British. There was no shame in insulting the Italian witnesses, they were considered fair game. But this was not xenophobia in the sense that the foreigners were feared; there was no dread here, just utter contempt.

The much paraded un-Britishness of the Italians took several forms. They were Roman Catholics and therefore particular enemies of a nation that had, for centuries, defined itself not just as Protestant, but anti-Papist and prepared to fight any Papist threat. (Catholic emancipation was a feature of the political agenda during this period, but it was firmly shelved during the turmoil of 1820.) One pamphleteer caught the spirit of the popular sentiment: 'The filthy sewers of Italy disgorge a living leprosy upon our throne and slaves and spies [are] imported from a creedless brothel,' he wrote. 'Their very churches [are] scenes of daily assignation! – their faith is form – their marriage ceremony a mere mask for the most incestuous intercourse . . . Away with them any where from us – they cannot live in England – they will die in the purity of its moral atmosphere.'[3]

Besides, Britain was a manly nation and Italy feminine, like the old enemy France.[4] The Italian witnesses were depicted as 'effeminate in manners – sensual from their cradles', colluding in the government's un-British, unmanly act of persecuting the Queen. As stated in one of the hundreds of pro-Caroline publications on sale:

> The Ministers – even Wellington
> Is, sculking, through the back-door gone,
> And folks, indignant, cry he's no man,
> Who thus makes war upon a woman.[5]

It was an affront to John Bull that the wretched Italians were the instruments of the British King and his government. The image of a monarch and his lackeys using foreign weapons in an assault against the honest British people was hard to resist, and made all the more potent by the fact that Cotton Garden was situated between Westminster Hall and the Thames – virtually in Parliament itself. The witnesses were housed in temporary buildings that had been erected for the now postponed Coronation; and the symbolism was wonderful. There was no greater celebration of majesty than that at a Coronation, no greater proclamation of the King's place at the heart of the nation, no better excuse for George to display his magnificence to the people. And what did the nation see instead? A king unable to be crowned because of his dishonourable persecution of his wife, and the buildings erected for the Coronation filled not with the trappings

of splendour but with despicable foreign villains. In such circumstances
the patriotic response was to support the Queen, and that patriotism
was reinforced by the distasteful image of the Italians being defended
not just by George and his government, but by the British soldiers
who guarded Cotton Garden. A rhyme, published as though written
by an Italian witness inside Cotton Garden, caught the spirit:

> The British flag, that waves in view,
> Protects us from abusers,
> And arms, that fought at Waterloo,
> Defend suborned accusers.[6]

The full satire, published as *The Royal Letter Bag*, was so popular that
it went into its sixth edition within two weeks of going on sale.

John Cam Hobhouse thought the witnesses so degraded that he
told Byron that 'nothing will be believed which is said by Italians'.[7]
The mainstream press also portrayed the Italians as liars and cheats.
Lord Nelson, Britain's greatest hero, had – it was reported – dismissed
Italy as 'a country of fiddlers and poets, whores and scoundrels'.
Meanwhile, those close to the witnesses, such as James Brown, who
was still in Milan channelling them through to London, were similarly
unimpressed. Italian witnesses, he told his bosses, should be carefully
observed at all times, as it was 'almost impossible that an Italian can
keep his own counsel'.[8] Henry Brougham characterised Italy as full
of 'intriguing men and abandoned women', where 'false oaths' are a
natural consequence of the 'culture of gross ignorance and a super-
stitious faith'.[9]

The Times published an editorial about 'these Italian locusts', and
Lady Granville remarked that Britain, or John Bull, looked upon the
Italian witnesses as 'so many bugs and frogs'. She thought it amusing
to pass on an anecdote originally told by Lord Holland. The official
put in charge of looking after the Italian witnesses, he had said, was a
dandy and when visiting the Italians one day took a moment to adjust
his cravat. The Italians mistook the movement of his finger across his
neck to mean that their throats were to be cut. 'They set up a horrid

yell,' reported the delighted Lady Granville, 'and plumped down on their knees, crying "Misericordia!"'[10]

At the same time satirical prints, selling at anything from a few pennies to several shillings, depicted the Italians as low crooks. The Green Bag was often shown with Italian witnesses popping out, or as bags of rotten grain with the witnesses inside and the ministers as rats gnawing at the tatters.[11] It was generally assumed by the public that the Italians had accepted government bribes. In reality, Castlereagh and Liverpool had not authorised bribes, but anecdotal evidence on the ground suggests that their instructions were sometimes ignored. An Italian friend of Caroline's wrote to her from Lugano, telling her to be very cautious when writing to Italy, and to write to good friends only, as 'spies and infamous agents' were everywhere trying to get possession of her letters. Indeed:

> they have gone so far as to endeavour to corrupt me with gold – they have just offered me two hundred gold louis . . . you can imagine my indignation at such a proposition – all the gold in the world would not be sufficient to make me betray a friend . . . be sure that the witnesses of our Canton are dearer to them than any others, and there are immense sums of money for that purpose.[12]

In London the public prints suggested that the witnesses be lodged in the Tower of London for their protection , and anti-Italian songs were for sale from street-sellers at a penny each, with rhymes such as:

> No nice degrees Italians know,
> They think no crime a sin, Sirs;
> But boldly swear whate'er they're told,
> And *lie* through thick and thin, Sirs![13]

And in the House of Lords, the Attorney General was forced to include in his opening remarks a plea for the peers to accept mere Italians, and menial Italians at that, as credible witnesses. He recognised that the Lords, as Britons, were likely to feel their superiority over other nations, but such sentiments, he argued, should not prevent them giving credit to witnesses merely because they happened to be foreigners. And the Queen, above all, should accept the evidence of foreigners, since it was she 'who caressed foreigners' and gave them the most distinguished places about her.

Inevitably, there was a great sense of anticipation when the first witness for the prosecution, the Queen's Italian servant, Theodore Majocchi, was called for examination on Monday 21 August. Caroline had arrived in the chamber a few moments before, walking with a 'more decided step' than usual, as she was announced with drums and trumpets. She curtseyed to the peers, bowed to Denman and to Brougham, the latter giving her 'a cold and distant acknowledge-ment', and then took her seat, which was about three yards from the bar, providing her with a close view of the witnesses. Twenty-eight-year-old Majocchi, a young man from the province of Lodi, was now led to his position. Throughout his manoeuvre, Henry Edward Fox was watching the Queen closely, observing that she 'almost trembled' and frequently clenched her hand and opened it 'as a person under great emotion'. Then, when she saw Majocchi, a robust man with large whiskers and bushy hair, she 'sprang up with the rapidity of lightning, advanced two or three steps, put her left arm a kimbo, and threw her veil *violently* back with her right. She looked at him steadily for about two or three seconds during a dead silence; she then exclaimed in a loud, angry tone, "Theodore!" and rushed out of the House (followed by Lady Anne Hamilton).'[14]

Thomas Denman recorded her exclamation as 'Theodore! No! No!' and a minority thought she said not Theodore but *traditore* – Italian for traitor. In any case, her outburst caused a sensation. Henry Edward Fox thought that 'nothing but madness' could account for it. He was convinced that it was a prepared scene and claimed that Sir Thomas Tyrwhitt, Black Rod, had said in advance that Caroline would be in the chamber only for a few minutes. 'Poor maniac!' he wrote. 'The effect it has produced is far from being of use to her. Everyone felt disgusted at her impudence and convinced of her guilt . . . They say she means to kill herself. I should not be surprised.

A woman capable of what she has done today can do anything violent or disgraceful.' Sara Hutchinson was more condemnatory still, maintaining that 'the Queen did not expect to see him [Majocchi] then – she believed him dead – poisoned'. Caroline, she imagined, had organised other killings too.[15]

The Times pronounced the event a 'burst of agony' on the part of the Queen, and claimed that placards headed 'Flight of the Queen from the House of Lords' and declaring her action to be a proof of her guilt, had been issued from 'some vile printing press' in 'the purlieus of Fleet Street'. The paper was happy to state that the placards were 'instantly torn down by the people'.[16]

After Caroline's departure, the Solicitor General, John Singleton Copley, began his examination. Majocchi confirmed the bedroom arrangements of Caroline and Pergami at Naples and said that Caroline had visited Pergami when he was in bed with an injured foot, having been kicked by a horse. The Queen had remained alone with him in his room on two separate occasions and Majocchi had heard 'whispering'. He did not mention the 'kissing' that the Attorney General had promised in his opening statement. Majocchi testified that at Genoa the couple had taken breakfast together, and maintained that Caroline had been lifted on to an ass by Pergami, an act which required him putting his hands around her waist. He had then 'held her hand while she rode, as if to prevent her Royal Highness from falling'. There was an intimacy between them, he said. He explained how in Milan Caroline's suite had swelled with the arrival of new Pergamis, including little Victorine, and confirmed that no 'English lady of honour' remained. On several occasions Pergami's bed 'appeared as if he had not always slept in it', and he had once seen Pergami going to the Queen's room dressed only in 'his morning-gown, with stockings and drawers'.

While travelling around the Mediterranean, Majocchi had seen Pergami kiss Caroline on the lips before leaving her to go shopping in Messina. Everywhere, he said, the arrangement of the bedrooms had allowed the couple to visit each other without being seen, and he had once seen Caroline sitting on a bed, with Pergami at her feet. He confirmed the Attorney General's assertion that on the homeward journey aboard the polacca, the Queen had slept in a tent on deck, which contained a sofa and a travelling bed. Copley asked:

Did the Princess sleep in that tent generally on the voyage from Jaffa home?

She slept always in it during the whole journey.

Did anybody else sleep in the same tent?

Pergami.

On the deck?

On the deck.

Did that take place every night?

Every evening.

Were the sides of the tent drawn down so as to shut them in entirely?

When they went to sleep the whole was enclosed.

Did they use a lantern or lamp in going to bed?

Yes.

After they were undressed and prepared to go to bed, what was done with the light?

Sometimes Pergami told me to take away the lamp when he made the bed, and sometimes he came and put the lamp out with his hand between the deck and the tent.

Were the beds regularly prepared every night?

Every night.

Do you remember where the Princess bathed on board the vessel?

Yes; in her own cabin.

Who assisted her at the bath?

The first time I carried the water into the bath, and then Pergami came down and put his hand into it to try the temperature: then he went upstairs and handed the Princess down, after which the door was shut, and Pergami and the Princess remained alone in the cabin.

Did the bathing take place more than once?

More than once, as well as I can recollect.

Do you remember at any time, when Pergami and the Princess were below in the cabin with the bath, being called upon to supply additional water?

I do; two pails; one of hot, and the other of cold water.

Who took the water in?

I went with the water to the door of the cabin, and Pergami came halfway out of the door and, taking the water, went in.

*Do you know whether, when you took the water, the Princess was actually
in the bath or not?*

I cannot know that.

Soon afterwards the House adjourned. Lady Granville declared that
Majocchi had given 'strong evidence without embarrassment or hes-
itation',[17] but Henry Edward Fox thought that the evidence so far was
not strong enough to convict her. The only material point, he wrote,
'is the going together into the bath'.[18] The radical weekly, the *Black
Dwarf*, thought the evidence flimsy at best. 'At Milan, the Princess
used to ride out sometimes, and the witness saw Pergami put his hands
round her waist – to do *what*, good reader? Why, in good sooth, to lift
her upon the ass! . . . At Milan and Venice also, the Queen and
Pergami walked arm-in-arm, and Pergami frequently sat with her at
table. Very unceremonious, we confess; but where is the criminality?'[19]

The paper's editor, Thomas Wooler, plainly took the view that the
lesser sin of undignified behaviour was no proof of the crime of royal
adultery. Others, particularly society stalwarts such as Countess
Lieven, would have forgiven adultery if only Caroline had managed
her private life with good taste and discretion, much as she conducted
her affair with Prince Metternich. The Queen's table manners, rough
speech, and her familiarity with servants were, in their eyes, the unfor-
givable part of her conduct.

The Queen's legal team were, meanwhile, dismayed by their client's
fit of melodrama upon being confronted with the first witness.
Denman reports that Caroline 'was copiously bled that night' and
appeared to be traumatised when she took her seat in the House of
Lords for the resumption of the prosecution evidence the following
day. 'I never saw a human being so interesting,' he wrote. 'Her face
was pale, her eyelids a little sunken, her eyes fixed on the ground, with

no expression of alarm or consciousness, but with an appearance of decent distress at being made the object of such revolting calumnies, and a noble disdain of her infamous accusers.' At this point, if not before, Brougham and Denman decided that she should stay away from the trial as much as possible. 'We did not think it proper for her to give her attendance during the whole investigation,' records Denman, 'but advised her to be absent except when required for any particular reason.'[20]

But Caroline obeyed her lawyers only when she felt like it. At the House of Lords on Tuesday 22 August she watched with interest as John Copley resumed his interrogation of Majocchi. The Italian servant was asked to recall accompanying Caroline and Pergami when travelling through Bavaria, and was questioned as to whether he remembered finding a bottle in their carriage. Yes, he said. Was the bottle usually in the carriage when the couple travelled together? Yes it was. The bottle was three or four inches wide in diameter and, according to Majocchi, was used for Pergami 'to make water in'.

The Solicitor General next asked Majocchi about a man by the name of Mahomet who had joined Caroline's entourage at Jaffa and afterwards lived at the Villa d'Este. Mahomet, confirmed Majocchi, had performed a dance called a Guioco in front of Caroline, and to demonstrate its nature to the Lords he moved his body up and down 'with a sort of dancing motion, occasionally extending his arms and snapping his fingers, as if using castanets in a fandango, and exclaiming "*vima dima*"'. Majocchi was asked to 'describe the Guioco from beginning to end', and did so by pulling up his trousers and resuming the dance. The interpreter, a man named Spineto, said that their Lordships could see the motion made, and could judge for themselves what it was. Brougham intervened to claim it was a curtsey, and several peers called out 'No! No!' The Solicitor General then asked if Mahomet had done anything 'to his trowsers with his hands', the answer came, 'No'. *The Times* in an editorial the following day concluded that Majocchi had included suggestive hand movements in his depositions to the Milan Commission, that he did not corroborate in the House.

'We regret to be obliged to insert filth of this kind, and send it forth before the world,' the leader went on. 'The nation has His Majesty's ministers to thank for the inundation of obscenity with which they are overflowing it.' The ministerial paper the *Courier*, by contrast, thought the Queen's supporters the guilty parties. 'We have again the painful task of noticing the gross depravity of the mob in hissing and hooting the Duke of Wellington and the Marquis of Anglesea,' it complained on 23 August. 'Those distinguished heroes, to whom the country owes so much, treated the rabble with proper contempt.' The filth and depravity, whilst thrilling, it seems, to Lady Granville, who had 'been doing my duty, reading the debate', was starting to turn the stomach of Princess Lieven, who asked her husband to read the newspapers to her and, she told Metternich, 'what he does read gives me a fair idea of what he misses out'.[21]

The time had now come for Brougham's cross-examination of Majocchi. After a few preliminaries, he asked:

In the Queen's house at Naples where did William Austin sleep?
I do not remember [*Non mi ricordo*].
Will you swear he did not sleep in the next room to her Royal Highness?
I cannot remember.
Where did Dr Holland, her Royal Highness's physician, sleep?
I do not remember.

It was quickly evident that the witness had been carefully schooled to give answers to set questions, but was unable to respond well to anything that he had not rehearsed. Brougham moved in:

Was it not the Princess's constant practice, on the voyage [whilst in Egypt], *to throw herself down in the middle of the day for repose, without taking off her clothes?*
I do not know: to that I paid no attention.
Will you take it upon you to swear that during the whole of that voyage the Princess ever took off one stitch of her clothes?

After her Royal Highness had dismounted from . . . [her] horse, she undressed herself to rest.

What part of her clothes did she take off for that purpose?

Her upper garment, her gown.

Do you mean to say that her Royal Highness took off her gown, or a surtout or cloak in which she might have been riding?

That I do not remember.

Was there not a cloak which she used to throw over herself, on dismounting, before she went to rest?

That I do not remember.

. . . Were there sheets and blankets on the sofa in the tent, on which a person could go to bed, taking off his clothes, as in Europe?

I placed the bed and some feather pillows and then retired.

You did not put any sheets or blankets on it?

I do not remember.

Was it exactly so with the sleeping in the tent on board the polacca?

I do not remember.

. . . Will you swear you ever saw, either during the land journey in Palestine, or the voyage by sea home, one stitch of bed-clothing upon the beds?

I do not remember.

. . . Have you not sworn that it was your duty . . . to make the beds?

When we arrived I placed the tent, and then I went out.

You told us who made the beds at night; who removed them in the morning?

I do not remember.

Will you swear it was not yourself?

I do not remember.

Did you happen to see William Austin rest in the tent in the same way?

I do not remember.

Do you know where the Countess of Oldi slept?

I do not remember.

. . . Where did you sleep yourself?

I sometimes slept on a sofa below.

Where did the maids sleep?

I do not remember.

Majocchi repeated the Italian phrase *Non mi ricordo* more than 200 times, and was entirely demolished by Brougham. The phrase was repeated in all the newspapers and prints and became a national joke. William Hone produced a best-selling pamphlet called *Non mi Ricordo!* which sold at sixpence, and had on its front page a picture of George with his droopy jowls bearing black flowing Italianate whiskers, standing at the bar and failing to remember his own name. A parody of Brougham's cross-examination of Majocchi was printed inside.

The thinness of Majocchi's evidence, in the view of Wooler's *Black Dwarf*, was reduced to nothingness by the fact that he was an Italian and a servant. Remember, the paper advised, the testimony of the British *knight* and *lady* Sir John and Lady Douglas, who had perjured themselves in 1806. Lady Douglas's evidence 'was all a lie! An odious damned lie!' She had submitted to the pressure of 'the same parties' (the King's agents) who were now forcing pathetic calumnies out of poor Italians. And to drive home the point, Wooler republished the lurid allegations of Lady Douglas. 'Now what is the Italian's tale to this?' he asked. 'Less than the shadow of a shade!' The current allegations against the Queen were, as before, the product of a foul conspiracy.

The *non mi ricordo* incident appeared to fill Brougham with confidence, and from now on he taunted the Lords whenever he had the chance. 'He never opens his mouth without insulting the peers,' reported Countess Lieven. 'He plagues them; he lies to them; he is as impertinent as he possibly can be,' safe in the knowledge that they could not retaliate. Normally, she told Metternich, the Lords had the right to 'send an insolent counsel to the Tower', but Brougham was protected by his status as a Member of Parliament in the House of Commons. Any attack on him would amount to an attack on the Commons, and the peers did not want to antagonise the Lower House for fear that it would then reject the Bill and bring about a general election. This the government would avoid at all costs, 'for if there were an election the new House would be Radical'.[22]

On 23 August the Queen, with Lady Anne Hamilton at her side, again attended the trial, on this day discarding her long white veil in favour of a peach-blossom satin hat with a luxuriant white feather. Over her shoulders she wore a light blue scarf with 'a gay border'. In short, she had brightened herself up. The next witness to be called was a ship's mate of about thirty years old named Gaetano Paturzo, a man 'of shabby appearance'. Thomas Denman rose to ask what religion the witness professed and, as he expected, learned that Paturzo was a Roman Catholic. Denman then asked when the witness had last taken the sacrament, telling the House that he wished to establish that, according to the Roman Catholic religion, 'no oath is binding unless taken within a certain time after confession and after receiving the sacrament'. He was overruled, and the witness sworn in. Denman's theological nonsense had served its purpose – to remind the peers of the witnesses' vile religion. Paturzo confirmed the proximity of the bedrooms of the Queen and Pergami on various occasions. He had seen the couple sitting together on a bench near the main mast of their ship, he said, 'the Princess sitting in his lap with her arm around his neck, over his shoulder'. Overall, his evidence was less damning than Majocchi's. On cross-examination, Thomas Denman tried, but failed, to show that Paturzo had been rehearsed and bribed.

The following morning the prosecution produced the master of the polacca, Vincenzo Garguilo. He testified that Pergami and Caroline had spent time inside their closed tent both during the day and at night. The Queen was accompanied by Pergami not just for her baths, he said, but 'for everything she did'. Even when she went below to use the water closet, Pergami went with her. He had seen the Queen and Pergami sitting together on a ship's gun and kissing each other. Garguilo was cross-examined by John Williams, a junior member of Brougham's legal team, who – as Denman had – endeavoured to show that the witness had been bribed. Garguilo admitted he had been paid by British officials, but testified that the amount was less than the loss to his business caused by his absence. He had, he said, spent five days in Naples 'endeavouring not to come here', but had been ordered to come against his will. The bribery charge, while strong in the public mind, was not sticking in the House of Lords.

On 25 August the King's lawyers called to the bar Thomas Briggs, the commander of the *Leviathan*, the ship used by Caroline for the first part of her long journey. It was Briggs who had objected to Pergami eating at the Queen's table, and the defence team must have been nervous about his testimony. In advance of the trial they had tried to sound him out, and had written to him asking for a meeting in London. But Captain Briggs's reply had been terse and did not bode well. He said he did not plan to come to town, and wished to enter into no correspondence on the subject with the Queen's representatives. The anxiety of Brougham and his colleagues could only be increased by Briggs's status as an Englishman and, by nature, a credible witness.[23]

Under examination, Briggs said he had seen Caroline and Pergami walking arm in arm on the ship, and explained that Caroline had altered the room arrangements so that Pergami's cabin would be next to hers. Then, after counsel for both sides had concluded, the time came for any of the peers who so wished to put a question to the witness. Lord Ellenborough rose and asked two questions that the defence lawyers had failed, or feared, to put:

Did the witness see any improper familiarity between the Princess and Pergami?
No, I saw none.
Had you any reason to suspect any improper freedom or familiarity between them?
No.

George's witness had, when pressed, delivered evidence in support of Caroline – and a moment of great relief for her team.

The next witness was Pietro Cuchi, an innkeeper from Trieste, who had, it emerged, spied on Caroline and Pergami through a keyhole in a secret door when they had stayed at his establishment, the Black Eagle. The door was hidden behind a large canvas which had a cut in it at the appropriate spot. On three or four mornings he had seen Pergami leaving Caroline's bedroom at around eight or half past eight wearing a 'dress made in the Polish fashion, with some gold lace on it, which came from the waist down behind'. Besides this he wore 'drawers', and a garment which was 'at once stockings and pantaloons; but I cannot precisely say, for I was looking out through the keyhole of my room'. On his feet were 'some strings' that, according to the interpreter, were used to fasten the drawers.

The Solicitor General then asked:

Did you make any observations on the bed assigned to Pergami?
Yes I have.
Did that bed appear to have been slept in?
Never.
I wish to know whether, after Pergami went away, you made any observations on the sheets of the bed?
The sheets were put on the bed clean, and were taken away clean.
How many pots de chambre *were there in the Princess's bedroom?*
There were two.
Were they both made use of?
I say yes.

His testimony also made clear – as had that of other prosecution witnesses – that if Caroline and Pergami were actually sleeping in the same room, then the Countess of Oldi, who often slept close by, must have known about it. Speculation was in the air over whether the defence would dare, when the time came, to call the countess as a witness.

Many of the Lords were now convinced that the Queen was guilty, but the general public was not impressed and remained robustly and vociferously Queenite. Day after day *The Times* carried reports of the Queen's crowds, alongside descriptions of Caroline's appearance and demeanour. On 24 August, she had paraded before the cheering multitudes dressed in a white satin hat with a 'superb plume' of white ostrich feathers and wrapped 'in an ample grey cashmere shawl'. Women especially 'seemed to set no bounds to their enthusiasm' and many of them 'rushed forward in spite of the utmost efforts of the police officers to restrain them'. At the same time the windows and balconies were once again 'crowded with ladies who appeared to vie with each other in demonstrations of regard towards her'. On her return at the end of the day the scene was equally spectacular. Besides the 'immense crowds' on foot 'the whole space from Parliament Street to Charing Cross was literally filled with coaches, wagons etc, all covered with people'. Pall Mall was nearly as crowded; in St James's Square the Queen's carriage was for some time unable to move.

In the midst of all the pro-Caroline fervour, the unfortunate Marquis of Anglesey rode out from the House of Lords, accompanied by Wellington. The Iron Duke rode off, but Anglesey remained among the 'great concourse of people' and called out, 'Why do you hiss me?' According to Robert Huish, an early biographer of Caroline, he was answered by loud shouts of 'The Queen! The Queen!' With great aplomb Anglesey called back: 'If you want me to do anything contrary to my conscience I must tell you I would rather you ran me through the body!' His bold challenge, however, 'called forth loud cheers from the crowd'. Happily for him the mob's intentions were not, for the moment at least, violent, and they quickly resumed their cry of 'Queen!' 'The gallant marquis,' wrote Huish, 'losing all patience, put spurs to his horse and left them.'

Days like these ensured that Lady Granville, like many other society gossips, was still obsessed with the spectacle, feeling that it added to the richness of London life, and staved off the terrible peril of ennui. She passed on to Lady Morpeth the comment of a friend who 'proposes having the royal family tried by turns, one every August'. The denigration of the monarchy had, indeed, become a hugely popular pastime for those in society households who opposed the Queen, but were fixated by her case, and also for the thousands of people on the streets who seemed elated, and occasionally euphoric, as they continued to pitch their will against that of the King.

14

WOMEN

See the women lay aside their softness, and *unsex* themselves, to sail in the storm of rebellion

A Warning Letter to His Royal Highness the Prince Regent.
Rev. Lionel Berguer, 1819.

'Is the Queen really a woman?' Countess Lieven asked Metternich. Her question reflected a fascination in society at large with Caroline and her trial that went beyond mere curiosity as to how it would all end. Her behaviour *as a woman* was particularly intriguing, and was made all the more so in late August when it became clear that the next witnesses against the Queen were to include two females. Betrayal by Italian men was one thing; the treachery of *female* servants another. It would take the action in the House of Lords into

204

private places, laying open the intimacy of the relationship of the Queen with the ladies who waited upon her, and permitting public scrutiny of the Queen's bedroom.

Outside the House, Dorothea Lieven warmed to her theme. No real woman, she suggested, would indulge in such 'disgusting' behaviour, let alone sit there listening to all 'these things being said and proved against her'.[1] The Russian Princess's letters read not as the genuine thoughts of one too sensitive, or too moral, to be exposed to tales of the Queen's love life. Instead, they are the words of an intelligent and sophisticated woman wishing to remind her distinguished lover of her detestation of vulgarity. She was typical of many high-born ladies with Tory leanings in regarding Caroline as a disgrace to her sex – the revulsion at the Queen's behaviour having little to do with her sexual activities, and everything to do with the way she flaunted herself. She was unreserved, indelicate and coarse, quite the opposite of the qualities of femininity prized in society. Countess Lieven, by contrast, wished men to know that she was intelligent and sexual (or at least sensual), but she conducted herself with discretion, humour and grace. For her it was intolerable that 'that woman' was bringing royalty and Parliament so low. 'How can the House of Lords, uniting as it does all that is most dignified and most exalted in the greatest nation in the world, lower itself by listening to such vile trash? . . . Worst of all, how could statesmen have allowed things to come to such a pass?'[2]

Countess Lieven could not side with Caroline, as Jane Austen had done, 'because she *is* a woman', since she saw the Queen as letting down her sex and, in doing so, betraying her class. She was incensed at the House of Lords *lowering* itself – an anger that was made deep, doubtless, because the upper house of the British Parliament was so much more than a legislative and judicial body – it was the bastion of the nobility. If the Lords somehow had a right to be there it was largely because of the superior values that went with good breeding, and the Queen was a spectacular affront to those virtues. Her behaviour was 'disgusting' and it was dangerous too.

By contrast, if Caroline had conducted an affair with discretion and with someone of her own class it would have been a relatively benign event, despite the fact that the Queen's adultery (on British soil at least) was still regarded in law as high treason. Gossip and probably a scandal would have ensued, but not political convulsion. In practice, aristo-crats' extra-marital affairs were so numerous as to be regarded as almost de rigueur and illegitimate offspring were regularly incorpo-rated into family life. Several of George's mistresses had borne him children who grew up in high society without a ripple of moralistic concern surrounding them. In 1816 Pamela Fitzgerald had described the practice beautifully when she asked a friend: 'Emily, does it never strike You, the vices are wonderfully Prolific among Whigs? There are such countless illegitimates, such a tribe of children of the mist.'[3] Caroline's friend Lady Oxford famously had so many offspring by different lovers that they became known as the 'Harleian miscellany' – a reference to her family name of Harley.

An image of this sexual liberty is provided by Countess Lieven her-self who, on one occasion, attended a party at Lord Castlereagh's country house at which discrete sexual encounters seemed to be the norm:

> While we were dancing, those members of the party who had some sentimental preoccupation went for a stroll. It was a dark night; the little paths were well screened with thick laurel bushes; and the great majority of the guests gave us the slip . . . In the end, the ball-room was occupied only by little girls, dancers of the calibre of my husband and the master of the house, a few old women and myself.[4]

But such a giddy way of life could not, some felt, last forever. The tone of contemporary diaries and letters sometimes indicates a feeling that with the end of the Regency period a way of life might be coming to an end; that a British revolution or some other profound societal change was looming. Perhaps a style of living that had turned scandal into an art was possible only in a rare and short-lived peacock of a society. If so, for those such as Countess Lieven, Caroline's actions presaged not just danger but also regret.

Lady Jersey, a formidable society hostess, was in the minority in openly supporting the Queen (although Whig ladies were more prone than Tories to be pro-Caroline). She exhibited the female qualities of sensibility and fragility in doing so, and proclaimed herself deeply affected by Caroline's sufferings. But she was ridiculed for her efforts, either because she overdid her displays of emotion, or because her views were unacceptable. According to Lady Granville, Lady Jersey 'cries all the time she is talking' about the Queen, although she was very amiable when she forgot 'as she frequently did, her despair'.[5] Countess Lieven meanwhile complained to Prince Metternich that 'Lady Jersey has become so violent that she is at daggers drawn even with the Holland family . . . Poor woman, she is quite frenzied – she ought to go out and cool herself off in the rain.'[6]

Lady Derby, according to Lady Granville, was at the head of a rare group of aristocratic women who affected to know nothing of the trial 'as if there were no such things as Queens and newspapers'. One distinguished female, when asked about the Caroline affair, was reported to respond: 'I know nothing about it. I am aware that there are such people as Pergami and Ricordo, and that is enough for me.'[7]

Outside the aristocratic classes, women were predominantly for Caroline – and often vehemently so. The supporters who greeted her everywhere she went made this obvious. Women often made up much of the crowd, and on at least one occasion they were seen to outnumber men by three to one – thus swelling the numbers and ensuring that the Caroline demonstrations were, by far, the largest protests of public feeling of the period. Women shaped the character of the crowds, declaring themselves strongly partisan by wearing white, or white favours, and waving white handkerchiefs. These were symbols of Caroline's innocence, but even more so of female purity. Set against the imagery of Italian treachery and the manliness of Britishness, women were presenting themselves as the source of the British virtues that men took from the home on to the public stage. It was women's role and duty to keep men virtuous, and to instil the nation's values in its children. Now, through the attacks on the Queen, women as a whole were under attack and, therefore, British virtue itself was threatened. The very fabric of the nation was at stake.

Such arguments were not hysterical. In the eyes of many women, the charges against Caroline were trumped up by evil and politically motivated men. And for them it was unacceptable that the stronger sex should be oppressing the weaker, throwing aside all notions of chivalry, and defying the bond between the sexes that gave women social rights (though little legal protection). It was man's duty to protect the female, and if he failed to do so then he was breaking a fundamental social contract. Such sentiments were set out particularly eloquently in a pamphlet of 1820 published, and probably written, by William Hone. It was sold under the title *The King's Treatment of the Queen Shortly Stated to the People of England* and was reprinted in several editions:

> The cause of her Majesty is the cause of every woman in England . . . Should it become the fashion amongst us to degrade the female sex – to trample on those softer and finer affections, which are the springs of social love, and the bonds of social society – if this shall happen, what will become of women? . . . They will be turned out of doors – they will be cast upon the world. Deprived of all their honours, and of all their influence – the tenderness and respect that are now felt for them, will be felt no more – they will be no longer the partakers of our joys, and the sharers of our confidence. Their very charms – their very virtues, will only excite unmeaning jealousy, and unmanly persecution.[8]

In a reversal of the creation story, Hone has turned the man, George, into the perpetrator of the deadly sin that requires all men and women to be cast out of the Garden of Eden. The monarch's behaviour towards his wife, if followed by his subjects, would put an end to all social harmony, since woman, once 'cast out' into the manly public world, would be rejected by men. This is what happens when women enter the workplace as they have 'in other countries, to perform every low and menial office'. (He seems not to mind that his pamphlet would have been read aloud in taverns frequented by working men with working wives, and sometimes by working women too.)

The message to women is, be as you are, passive and virtuous, and we men will, in theory at least, make you into goddesses safeguarding the nation's virtue. Alternatively, be cast out, enter a man's world and suffer the chill of competition which, given woman's fragile nature, would amount to 'unmanly persecution'. Put another way, this would be a sexual revolution and it would have dire consequences: 'Revolutions in manners are as frequent as revolutions in government; and whilst an example is held up to every ruffian in the land to abuse and insult the wife that he promised to cherish and protect, is it reasonable to apprehend the degeneracy and decay of our national morals? But heaven forbid this worst of all revolutions – man changes his nature when woman changes her place.'

To drive home the point, Hone writes a fulsome eulogy to women, assuring them their goddess-like status in the current social structure:

Of that exalted being, I do not wish to speak extravagantly, but I cannot speak of her without enthusiasm – she is at once the blessed source of our existence – its noblest ornament – its sweetest solace, and its highest pride. In her mind no selfish thought is wont to enter – in her heart no impure feeling reigns – all goodness – all devotion – she is the creature of pity, tenderness and love – the centre of all that is noble, generous and true . . . To her we are indebted for the first sentiments of virtue, as well as for the first nourishment of nature – and her we are bound to defend even to the last effort of our strength.[9]

Hone ends, like dozens of other authors that year, by raising the enduring image of a Queen who was failed by men, who found no chivalry in a world turned upside down – Marie Antoinette. Paraphrasing Edmund Burke he predicts that 'ten thousand swords shall leap from their scabbards to avenge even a look that may threaten her with insult'.

Moreover, the King's lifestyle was seen by the public as monstrously disdainful of domestic ties and domestic responsibility. He had failed to provide his wife with any sort of family home, and instead had turned his husbandly duty of protection on its head – he had betrayed, attacked, bullied and slandered his wife. What had happened to chivalry? It was a concern for every woman who relied on the protection of a husband for all aspects of her well-being. Eight thousand women from Nottingham who demonstrated in favour of the Queen were impressed by Caroline's 'powerful recommendations to protection' and wrote: 'Your father is no more, your brother fell in battle, the chief solace of your cares, your amiable daughter, was soon, too soon, snatched away – and your great protector, our late, venerable Monarch, soon followed her.'[10]

The spirit of Charlotte was repeatedly summoned. The late Princess remained an icon of domesticity and represented the type of female virtue that women of the middle classes held dear. Caroline, said the Nottingham women, could rely on the 'brave people' to save her from 'domestic persecutors'. The response expressed the Queen's joy that 'the hearts of so large a portion of my own sex are vibrating with emotions of affection', and trusted that the large majority of British women would 'consider the honour of her Majesty as reflected upon themselves'. Women, she said, would know best 'how to appreciate the slanders by which I have been assailed and the indignities by which I have been oppressed'. And to an earlier group of women she had responded: 'When my honour is attacked, every loyal Englishwoman must feel it as an imputation upon her own.'[11]

Lady Granville was perplexed at the attitude of the lower orders of women and asked her children's governess, Miss Trimmer, why the English people were not 'staggered' by some of the facts that had come out about the Queen. Miss Trimmer replied that the firm belief of the masses was that 'the King had sent a number of people for the purpose of assassinating her, and that Pergami was her only sure and tried protector, and that consequently if he had been half an hour absent from her, she would have been murdered'. Alderman Wood, she explained, encouraged the same impression by walking up and down in front of Brandenburgh House 'armed with pistols and telling the people that without such precautions she would not be safe an hour'. Miss Trimmer personally knew of several working women who had gone to visit the Queen, including 'a better sort of housemaid' who had travelled to Hammersmith on top of a stagecoach, and found Caroline's house 'a very gay sight'. Whilst there she did not become tired or weary, since plenty of gin and gingerbread was for sale on the lawn. A man had come out and read something, which she failed fully to comprehend, 'all she knew was that it was exceedingly improper'. In her usual tone of delighted outrage Lady Granville wrote: 'So much for the present Court of her Majesty.'[12]

At George's court women's marches and Addresses were a source of mirth – and the anti-Caroline cartoonists portrayed the participants as ridiculously dressed, with ballooning bosoms and comical manners. Sometimes they were presented as little better than prostitutes. The *New Times*, a pro-government paper, for instance, mocked the women in a satirical piece about a petition from the debauched 'United Sisterhood of Fleet St and Drury Lane'. In reality, the female Queenite protestors came from a wide section of society. There had never before been a time when women, en masse, had protested in such numbers or such a manner. And it is probable that there were, in fact, prostitutes amongst them – indeed the Home Secretary had received a wild anonymous letter warning him to be on the alert 'for God's sake' since there were 'about one thousand four hundred prostitutes of the lowest order in Westminster who take the part of the Queen . . . urging the men on to Mutiny and call Queen for Ever'.[13]

The pro-government paper the *Courier* tried to convince its readers that the female demonstrators were not, as *The Times* would have it, respectable and 'elegantly dressed' ladies. 'We . . . have not been so fortunate to *see* these ladies,' it stated. But, if they were 'really visible we must beg leave to express our doubts of their "respectability". Indeed, we should very sincerely lament the degradation of the female character in this country, if we did not know that there is a designed exaggeration in all these descriptions.'[14] Any truly modest and virtuous female, according to the *Courier*, would not involve herself with Queenite protest. The paper also carried letters on the same theme. One from 'a lady of Bath' declared that those 'ladies of Bath' who sent an Address to the Queen were not ladies at all. Another mentions that the ladies who signed the Address were 'in the lowest situations', and a third suggested that the ladies who presented the Marylebone Address refreshed themselves on the way to Hammersmith with 'a thimbleful of Hodge's best'.[15] The *Courier*, though, was a minority voice. The mass of the evidence points to all sorts of respectable women protesting for the Queen, albeit that they were more likely to be housemaids, seamstresses, and governesses than society hostesses.

As the trial advanced, Countess Lieven could only become more disgusted, Lady Granville more gossipy and Lady Jersey more distressed; for the two women witnesses about to be called were to give specific and sordid descriptions of Caroline's most private activities. Female modesty was to be surrendered in the pursuit of justice. Never mind that this justice was, as Dorothea Lieven observed, nothing but a 'solemn farce'.[16]

In the afternoon of 25 August Barbara Kress was sworn in and the Attorney General established that the young woman had been married for three years, lived at the Post-Inn Carlsruhe and was a Lutheran. She remembered the Queen's visit to the inn, she said, and testified that Pergami had arrived first and arranged for the narrow bed in Caroline's room to be replaced by a wider one. The Lords' day ended there, and the examination continued the following morning. Kress said she had come upon Caroline and Pergami sitting together on the Queen's bed, and that Caroline had jumped up. The chambermaid had retreated from the room, frightened, but had been in the room at other times to make up the bed.

'Did you at any time,' asked the Attorney General, 'see anything on the sheets?' Kress replied, but her response could not be heard, and the King's interpreter and the Queen's started talking between themselves. The Queen's interpreter emerged from the huddle to tell the Lords that the word the witness had used could not be interpreted in English, and the King's interpreter was directed to state what word, in German, she had used. 'She says,' he replied, 'that when she made the bed the sheets were *wuste*.' The Queen's interpreter cut in to remark that the word might mean 'in disorder'. The proper meaning was 'waste', he said, 'it is an adjective'. From the floor of the House Lord Hampden offered that *eine Wuste* means a desert. After more discussion on the subject the King's interpreter was directed to ask the witness to explain what she meant. 'She is at a loss what to say,' he replied. 'She says *stains*.' The examination continued:

> *What sort of stains were they that you saw?*
> As much as I have seen, they were white.
> *Are you married?*
> Yes.

Here Kress became agitated, and began to weep. A glass of water was brought, and some minutes' pause followed until she recovered herself. She was then asked what she thought the stains were, answering:

> I did not inspect them so narrowly. What I have seen is, that they were white.
> *Have you ever made the beds of married persons?*
> Yes I made all the beds in the house in general.
> *What was the appearance of the marks you saw on Pergami's bed?*
> You will pardon me, I have not reflected on this.
> *Were they dry or wet?*
> They were wet.

Brougham's cross-examination produced no surprises, and Barbara Kress stepped down. Lady Bessborough thought the chambermaid's evidence the strongest so far, and her friend Harriet Arbuthnot, a committed Tory and close friend of Wellington, was convinced that proof of adultery had now been secured. 'All one can say is,' she wrote in her diary, 'if the Whig Lords do not consider the disgusting details they have heard *proof*, the Whig ladies may in future consider themselves very secure against divorces, for it would be impossible to conceive a case in which more proof could be established.'[17]

Several more male Italian servants gave testimony, one of whom had seen Pergami and the Queen peek under the fig leaves of statues of Adam and Eve in the garden at the Villa d'Este. Another had witnessed the lewd dancing of Mahomet who, he said, had made a 'kind of roll' with the front of his breeches during his dance. Caroline had watched him and laughed. The Marquis of Landsdowne asked what the roll was meant to represent and was told 'it seemed as if it was the membrum virile of man'. Lord de Dunstanville asked whether Mahomet always made this movement while he danced, and was told that he did.

Next to testify was Louise Demont, Caroline's former maid. Creevey noted that 'she is the smartest-dressed of *femmes-de-chambre* but neither the youngest, nor the prettiest'. Even before she appeared, Demont had achieved nationwide notoriety, being demonised in the press, and cast as a wicked traitor to her mistress. In Market Rasen women gave a party with tea and cakes and burned her in effigy. The men, meanwhile, as in numerous other villages, burned Majocchi. The Swiss maid was regarded as worse still than Lady Douglas, and both women were smeared by the suggestion that they were about to engage in the unwomanly act of telling not just lies against their mistress, but lies of a disgusting and sexual nature.

Demont was sworn in on 30 August and was examined by John Copley, who established that she had joined Caroline's suite on a five-year contract at Lausanne, and travelled with her to Italy.

At Milan Caroline had engaged Pergami as her courier, she said, and shortly afterwards the company had travelled to Naples. Until then William Austin, who was at that time twelve or thirteen years old, had slept in the Queen's room, but Caroline had suddenly declared 'that William Austin had become too big a boy to sleep in her room, and he must have a chamber to himself'. On the second night in Naples the Queen had arranged the rooms so that she and Pergami might have access to each other's without being disturbed. That evening she had attended the opera, but returned early and went straight to her bedroom, telling Demont that William Austin must be forbidden from entering 'because she wished to sleep quietly'. She sent Demont away quickly and 'was extremely agitated'. The following morning she appeared at eleven o'clock, for her not an unusual time. She had not, though, followed her normal practice of sleeping in her small travelling bed, choosing instead another, much larger, bed.

Demont testified that while at Naples she had seen Pergami leaving his bedroom and heading for Caroline's:

What was the state of Pergami's dress at the time you saw him . . . going towards the bedroom of her Royal Highness?
He was not dressed.
When you say he was not dressed, what do you mean; what had he on?
He was not dressed at all.
Do you remember what he had on his feet?
Slippers.
Do you remember whether he had any stockings on?
I saw no stockings.
Had he on anything more than his shirt?
Nothing else.

She told the Lords that at Joachim Murat's ball in Naples Caroline had decided to discard her outfit, that of a Neapolitan country woman, and reappear as the Genius, or the Muse, of History (a figure usually represented crowned with laurels, holding in one hand a trumpet and a book in the other). She had been alone with Pergami while she changed into her Muse costume, a process that took about three quarters of an hour. Later on, she changed again and, in public, walked arm in arm with Pergami, both of them dressed as Turks.

Caroline, on leaving Naples for Rome, she said, had left behind most of her English suite. The party spent two months at Genoa where they were joined by Pergami's brother Louis, his sister Faustina, his mother and his daughter Victorine. The next stop was Milan, where Pergami's other sister, the Countess of Oldi, arrived. She spoke 'very vulgar Italian' and no French, while Caroline spoke little Italian. An Englishman, Mr William Burrell, had joined the group for about a month and when he left 'there was more freedom in the house, more liberty'. Every evening the servants indulged in games and frolics and played blind man's buff. Caroline, she said, sometimes joined in.

When the party finally settled at the Villa d'Este the familiarity continued. When Caroline and Pergami parted she would often call him *mon coeur* or say *adieu, mon coeur; prenez garde* or 'take care'. They sometimes embraced, she said: 'I heard them kiss each other behind me.' On one occasion she had seen Caroline emerge from Pergami's bedroom wearing only her nightdress and carrying a pillow. By this time, little Victorine was calling Caroline 'Mama'.

When Caroline visited Sicily, said Demont, she had commissioned a portrait of herself in the character of a penitent Magdalen:

> *How much of the person of her Royal Highness did that picture present;*
> *the head or more than the head?*
> As far as the waist.
> *How was the upper part of the person, covered or uncovered, in the picture?*
> Uncovered.
> *Were the breasts covered or uncovered?*
> It was uncovered as far as here, about the middle of it.

Demont corroborated Majocchi's evidence regarding the sleeping arrangements on the polacca voyage across the Mediterranean from Jaffa to Italy. Caroline and Pergami had shared the tent on deck and the Queen had twice taken a bath, both times being assisted by Pergami. Countess Oldi had spent some of her time on the ship making shirts for her brother. 'Her Royal Highness said to Pergami that she wished to make those shirts herself,' and he had answered her with a smile. Later, back in Italy, Pergami had constantly called Caroline 'Princess', while everybody else addressed her as 'Your Royal Highness'. Pergami, Demont continued, had worn earrings that she later saw being worn by the Queen. At Pesaro the Queen had worn pantaloons, with an upper garment which left her neck and breasts uncovered. Pergami had complemented her on her appearance, saying: 'How pretty you are, I like you much better so.'

The cross-examination of Demont was conducted by John Williams – a short man who magnified his presence in the House by taking on a severe attitude quite contrary to his usual mild manner. His bold performance was to make his name as a barrister. He suggested that Demont had been living in England for more than a year under the assumed name Countess Colombier, his assertion sending her into a state of confusion in which she professed not to remember whether she had ever been called by that name. He revealed that she had been sacked by Caroline for telling lies, and read out sections of a letter which Demont had sent to her sister, praising the Queen in the highest terms for her patience, charity and 'all the perfections which she possesses'. These sentiments were also expressed in a journal which Demont had kept and shown to various English people who were eager to see it. However, Demont refused to swear to having written such things on the grounds she did 'not recollect it'. Her responses, in fact, assumed a similarity in character to Majocchi's *non mi ricordo*.

Williams asked whether Demont remembered representing that her money had begun to run out. 'I know nothing of that,' she replied, 'but I have never been in want of money.' Williams then produced the full text of the letter written by Demont to her sister, which was read out in court, and made clear that she did indeed have financial worries after her dismissal. Moreover, she wrote of receiving a letter, personally delivered to her in January 1818:

> Judge of my astonishment when I broke the seal; a proposal was made to me to set off for London, under the false pretence of being a governess. I was promised a high protection and a most brilliant future in a short time. The letter was without signature; but, to assure me of the truth of it, I was informed I might draw at the banker's for as much money as I wished. Can you conceive of any thing so singular!

She followed this revelation by telling her sister, unconvincingly, that money would never tempt her, after all, 'a good reputation is better than a golden girdle'. It was, by now, clear that the defence team were being supplied with information that damaged Demont by her sister, Mariette, who remained in Caroline's service as a maid.

Soon after, the Lords examined Demont and she was asked more about the state of Caroline's bed after her supposed 'first night' with

Pergami – their second night in Naples. The maid was unwilling to give details 'because I might have to make use of terms which are not decent'. When pressed, she said that the bed cover was 'extremely pressed down in the middle' and 'there were things upon the bed which I had never seen before'. What were those things? 'Large stains,' she replied. Were those on the outside cover of the bed or the inside? 'Upon the cover.'

Her interrogation ended with a couple of questions from undistinguished Lords who fancied they could now cause a stir in the House – only to make a hash of it. The Earl of Darnley pressed Demont on the colour of the bed cover, but not the nature of the stains, while the Earl of Morton, for no apparent reason, wished to establish whether the Queen bathed in salt water or fresh water. Bumbling contributions such as these did nothing for the authority of the Lords in the public mind, and they were regularly parodied in the prints. Demont's testimony now became the subject of a popular shilling squib by Thomas Dolby, a competitor of Hone's, which was sold under the title *Doll Tear-Sheet*; it portrayed the less able Lords as doddery 'Piers in the scullery'. The cross-examination of the Swiss maid was ridiculed thus:

Do you . . . recollect whether your mistress went to the *uproar* near Mount Vesuvius the night after her arrival? – On the second night she told me she was going to the uproar.

Here a Pier from the scullery wished to ask the Witness what she meant by an uproar.

The Interpreter said that it was an ambiguous term; that it might be construed either into an irruption of Mount Vesuvius, or a multitude of cats squalling. This explanation seemed to satisfy the Pier in the scullery.[18]

With the extent of her treachery, Louise Demont had gratified all those who had denounced her already, but had not yet sated their appetite for loathing. 'Oh, Demont! Demont!' wailed Dolby. 'Thou has sworn falsely in thy disgusting details regarding thy royal mistress . . . Go forth, wretched woman! Like the fratricide Cain – there is mark upon thee! – Thou has confessed – to treachery – to falsehood – to ingratitude – crimes of the very darkest dye, in the black catalogue of human turpitude.' He published such thoughts under the title *A Letter to the People of England upon Passing Events*, and sold them on the Strand for sixpence.

While female witnesses took centre stage in the House of Lords, the street theatre outside continued to be largely feminine in character. Women in their thousands made their way to Caroline's home at Hammersmith to present Addresses. The Married Females of the Parish of Marylebone processed 'covered with feathers and white cockades, escorted by the mob', and presented a petition expressing their conviction that Princess Charlotte and George III were in heaven, pleading to a merciful Father to protect Caroline from 'the pelting and pitiless storm raised by the wickedness of her enemies'. Her husband had failed her, despite being 'a man with a splendid income, derived from the purses of the people'. Caroline's speech-writers responded in kind, commenting on the heroism of women who were 'meek in sorrow and not querulous in suffering'. The female sex, they said, drew its happiness and satisfaction from con-tributing to 'the gratification of others and to the general stock of human felicity'. They appealed to the chivalry due to females every-where, and her response, according to *The Times* 'moved many of the ladies to tears'.[19]

At the same time Caroline received an Address from the men of Marylebone. To them, her answer was boldly radical. The question is, she said, 'whether the destruction of the Queen shall pave the way for the destruction of public liberty'. The House of Lords, she said, had become an armed fortress, raising the image of 'the bayonets of the troops glittering on the walls of Parliament'. She also brought up the sensitive subject of whether the government could rely on the military. She stated that English men and women were living in times in which 'it is well understood that the interests of the army can never be really distinct from the other interests of the community'.

The impression given in the Queen's responses was that women should demand the right of protection from men, while the men should demand liberty for the nation. It went beyond the boundaries of conventional radical talk, though, for women to demand liberty directly; and there was no call for equal rights. There was no resurgence of interest in Mary Wollstonecraft's famous *Vindication of the Rights of Woman*, which had been a best-seller on publication in 1792. As a popular song published by Thomas Dolby put it:

> Let England and Ireland and Scotland aloud,
> For the RIGHTS of the WOMEN declare;
> May the Man who would wrong them be branded and shunn'd,
> As unworthy the smiles of the Fair![20]

Another cheap publication entitled *Glorious Deeds of Women!* began: 'Woe be to the age wherein WOMEN lose their influence, and their judgements are disregarded.'[21]

Through her writers Caroline was expressing herself in male as well as female language. Male Addresses received manly responses setting out the struggle for liberty and reform, while women received recognition of their role as custodians of the nation's morals. So it was appropriate that portrayals of Caroline by her supporters endowed her with the qualities of both sexes – she was at once (and primarily) a *defenceless* and vulnerable woman who was right 'bravely to fling herself upon the wave of the people'. But she was also portrayed as a fighter as manly as five men. On one occasion she was likened to a fighting ship. 'Britain's red cross is her flag and Brunswick's spirit is her pilot,' according to the pamphleteer Charles Phillips. 'May the Almighty send the royal vessel triumphant into harbour!'[22] Walter Scott was among those who, in private, ridiculed Caroline for 'manly' behaviour. 'I should not be surprised to see her fat bottom in a pair of buckskins,' he wrote, 'and at the head of an army'.[23]

Although the majority view amongst non-aristocratic women appeared to be pro-Caroline, there were undoubtedly dissenters – including a 'widowed wife' who took the view that the Queen had not done enough to save her marriage. She published a letter to Caroline asking: 'Did you studiously endeavour to conform to his taste, to model your character by his ideas; did you oppose submission to his will, gentleness to his impetuosity, and tenderness to his coldness?' This was one of a number of tracts written and published by the 'loyal voices of Suffolk in the years of Caroline's follies'.

Cobbett took much the same view as other Queenites – although, being Cobbett, he expressed it with twice the amount of twists and turns of argument, and ten times as much verve. Women's power in the land, he argued, came from their cohesion as a sisterhood. Men, he said, are 'so many detached individuals' while women are 'a body corporate. Touch one and you touch the whole.' And the 'whole weight of this corporation was thrown into the Queen's scale the moment she quitted Carlton House without any offence even alleged against her'.

Man, meanwhile, was the protector of woman. According to Holy Scripture, he said, wives could not be punished for any cause except for adultery. And 'he who putteth away his wife without this provocation, *causeth her to commit fornication*'. Thus, even if Caroline had taken lovers, then the guilt lay with George. With rules of behaviour in marriage so much favouring the woman, he argued, there was no need to change laws (of marriage and property) which gave all the rights and power to men.[24]

Some men thought the Caroline affair was corrupting of women, and would encourage them to act in the independent and vulgar manner of the Queen. A Mr J. Hatsell wrote to Lord Colchester:

> Sir Thomas Acland told me at Brighton, the ladies said, 'Well, if my husband had used me as hers has done, I should have thought myself entitled to act as she has done.' The mischief introduced into private families (where the father has not been cautious, like Lord Sidmouth and Lord Lilford, to prevent the newspapers from being read by his daughters) will be very great in corrupting the imaginations of the young ladies and encouraging them to take part in every conversation, however indecent . . . In short it appears as if all the world was run mad.[25]

At home Cobbett's daughter Anne considered it a great credit to the female sex that the system was being shaken up 'by a *woman*!' – Caroline achieving the political change which 'all the reformers, radicals [and] jacobins' had tried to secure, and failed. 'An *Old Woman* will not now be thought so foolish a thing,' she thought, and she told her friend Miss Boxall that 'Papa says that for the future husbands must be content to be henpecked, and he has given Mama notice that she may begin to exert her Sovereign authority forthwith.'[26] Cobbett's view of women may have been, in modern terms, conservative. But he was radical by the standards of the times. He told women their '*sisterhood*' had 'immense weight' in influencing the ministry. But, more important, he urged women to move out of the domestic sphere into the public one in supporting the Queen. Influenced by him, or not, they did so in their tens of thousands, processing in the streets and putting their names to Addresses. During 1820, for the first time in British history, great numbers of women stood together in public; not merely taking part in the political world, but making demands of the King and his government.

15

INVESTIGATION

Thou who cast the first stone at thy wife,
Art thou without sin, and is spotless *thy* life?
Ah! what if *thy* faults should 'outrival the sloe',
And thy wife's, beside thine, should look 'whiter than snow'!
Bethink thee! The old British Lion awoke,
Turns indignant, and treads out thy bag-full of smoke.

The Queen's Matrimonial Ladder

The Queen's behaviour continued to intrigue Countess Lieven, who wrote to Metternich on 2 September: 'Do you know, *mon Prince*, what the Queen does in Parliament? You will never guess. She plays – at backgammon. Since she announced at the start that she would be at the House of Lords every day in order to confound the witnesses by her presence, she does not like to go back on her word.

So she goes; sometimes she goes into the hearing, sometimes not; generally, she stays in the next room and plays with Alderman Wood.'[1]
The Queen's decision to absent herself from the chamber was not,
however, entirely frivolous. Much of the evidence was simply too
demeaning for her to listen to. From her point of view, it was more
dignified to stay hidden in a room nearby.

The evidence of the prosecution witnesses in those first days of
September was damaging for Caroline. Luigi Galdini, a mason, told
the Lords that he had opened a wrong door at the Villa d'Este and
found Pergami sitting with his arm round Caroline and his hand on
her bare breast. A second mason, Domenico Brusa, had seen the
couple caressing each other's faces. Giuseppe Restelli, the head superintendent of the Queen's stables, had seen Caroline and Pergami in an
open carriage together. Her hand, he said, was 'in the small-clothes of
Mr Pergami . . . I saw it distinctly'. The trial shifted slightly back in
the Queen's favour, though, when Restelli was cross-examined by
Thomas Denman. He admitted that he had been dismissed from
Caroline's suite, and soon afterwards began working for the Milan
Commission, in the role of courier. But he rejected the suggestion that
he had been bribed to give evidence against the Queen.

The next witness, Giuseppe Sacchi, appeared on 5 September and
said that during his travels with Caroline in 1816 it had been the
custom, at night, for him to ride close to Caroline's carriage. From
time to time he would draw up alongside and pull back the curtains
to enquire whether she wanted anything. 'It has happened to me
two or three times,' he said, 'to have found them both asleep, and
having their respective hands one upon another.' The Attorney
General responded:

Describe in what way, one upon another?
Her Royal Highness held her hand upon a particular part of Mr
Pergami and Pergami held his own upon that of Her Royal Highness.
Did you observe on any of these occasions the state of Pergami's breeches?
Once I saw that Pergami had his breeches loosened from the braces,
that he had the front part half unbuttoned.

Upon that occasion did you observe where the Princess's hand was?
One hand was upon that part.
. . . Did you say that they were asleep at the time?
I did.

Such testimony did nothing to convince the public that Caroline had, in reality, indulged in such disgraceful acts. The *Times* editor, Thomas Barnes, found that the best way to increase sales was to remain faithful to the Queen and to deride her accusers. On 6 September the paper published its opinion of Sacchi's evidence:

> the thing is monstrous. Signor Giuseppe Sacchi has sworn directly against the laws of gravitation, as they have hitherto been thought to exist in the universe. He has done more than upset the Newtonic philosophy by his evidence; he has actually proved that an unsupported heavy body will remain in its position . . . Sacchi swore . . . that he saw the hand of Pergami in a most indecent position with respect to the Queen, and that of the Queen similarly placed with respect to Pergami; the parties – (observe this) – *the parties being asleep*. Such a position in a carriage, where the bodies are themselves upright, or nearly so, is beyond all question absolutely and physically impossible. That the hands might be respectively there *placed*, with regard to the persons of each other, no one can deny; but that they could *remain* there, in a rattling carriage, or even in a still one, when volition had ceased and was absorbed in sleep (except they were tied or glued) is as impossible as that lead should ascend, or smoke sink.

The prosecution case was now concluded, and John Copley, the Solicitor General, in his summing up, relied on the collective weight of the evidence to convince the Lords of the Queen's guilt. Indeed, he had little choice but to do so, since he had no single, conclusive piece of proof to present. But, he observed, it was normal in adultery cases to rely on the overall picture and he could not remember a single case where the 'actual fact' was fully proved in evidence. 'The crime is always to be inferred from accompanying circumstances, which leaves no doubt of the fact upon the mind of a rational and intelligent man.' And, he thought, there could be no doubt in this case since Caroline and Pergami were 'constantly conducting themselves like lovers, or like man and wife during the day, while every preparation was made to prevent the interruption of their intercourse at night'.

This marked the end of the first phase of the trial. *The Times* concluded that it was, in effect, over. There had not been one witness, according to the leader writer, whose character had borne the test of a cross-examination. And the paper was quick to infer infamy from the fact that it had just emerged that the loathed Majocchi had arrived in England on the day of George III's funeral. Even as the much loved old King was dying, it concluded, his 'near kindred' had been planning to bring the Queen to trial. The paper urged 'some noble Lord' to 'move that there is no cause for proceeding further with this bill'.

On the King's side there was great anxiety. Before Copley's final summing-up, the Prime Minister, Lord Liverpool, had written to George warning him that success for the government was far from guaranteed. Some parts of the prosecution evidence had, he wrote, 'made a considerable impression upon the minds of the Peers against the Queen'. But he told the King that the two most material witnesses – Majocchi and Demont – had 'been shaken in their credit and character'. The Prime Minister was now fearful that Caroline would produce defence witnesses with greater credibility, whose evidence would damage the prosecution's case still further. He was particularly worried about Brougham calling Louise Demont's sister, Mariette Brun, to testify, along with two officers of the British navy, Lieutenant Flynn and Lieutenant Hownam.

In the boldest terms and leaving no room for doubt, Liverpool warned George that the divorce clause in the Bill was in jeopardy. He had spoken extensively to the Lords, both ecclesiastical and lay, about the matter, he said, and considered that 'there is scarcely a chance of this part of the Bill passing the House of Lords, and that it is quite impossible it should pass the House of Commons'. He informed the King that no person acquainted with public opinion disagreed with him. Then, to make matters even more disagreeable, he brought up the subject of witnesses being produced to testify to George's own adultery. 'Your Majesty will be graciously pleased to reflect,' he wrote, that we are now approaching that stage of the proceedings when all the delicate and difficult questions connected with recrimination will arise.' He did not include the latest gossip – that the King's current mistress, Lady Conyngham, would be summoned to give evidence. Indeed, at a dinner party Brougham confided to Countess Lieven that he was planning to do just that.[2]

The Prime Minister stressed that the likelihood of recrimination being used to defend the Queen would be reduced if the government volunteered to give up the divorce part of the Bill at this stage of the proceedings; 'The House of Lords would [then] be greatly conciliated and Mr Brougham would be precluded from all pretence for entering upon the distressing subject of recrimination. Lord Liverpool is most anxious that your Majesty should have the grace of such a concession rather than that it should be extorted from you.'[3]

George had been spending much of the time at his cottage in Windsor Great Park, so avoiding the turbulence in central London. He replied to Liverpool's blunt letter in his usual emotive manner: 'The King must not suffer himself to be brought, either hastily or *timidly* into any considerate, sudden or premature, possibly degrading and disgraceful (even if not fatal) compromise and decision,' he wrote.[4] According to Countess Lieven, when Liverpool and his ministers visited George at Windsor in an effort to persuade him to abandon the divorce clause, he listened to them and said, 'Do as you please,' and then showed them the door. They were not even given anything to eat and came back famished, she told Metternich, adding in her customary sardonic tone: 'That's friendly and promises well.'[5] The matter remained unresolved.

A three-week break in the trial allowed Henry Brougham and Thomas Denman to go off to the country to recover their energy and prepare themselves for the defence case. Denman was, by this point, exhausted, and suffering from jaundice, which he decided to 'wash away' at the spa town of Cheltenham. When he arrived his identity was quickly discovered by the townspeople who surrounded the house with loud shouts of 'Queen! Queen!' 'Ill as I was,' Denman noted in his memoirs, 'I had serious thought of leaving the place again on the instant but at length resolved to muster up voice and spirits for a speech at the window, and finding myself opposite to a brilliant star I told the multitude that the Queen could no more be plucked from the throne than that beautiful star from the heavens.' The crowds were, according to Denman, then in 'great good humour'. Nonetheless they started smashing the windows of the houses around, 'particularly the parson's who had very imprudently refused them permission to ring the bells on my arrival'. A magistrate was called and Denman was persuaded to go among the mob asking them to disperse and to spare the few of the parson's windows that remained in one piece.

Denman confessed to a friend that he was surprised at the strength of pro-Caroline public opinion in Cheltenham given the scandalous evidence against her that had so far been heard. He was welcomed wherever he went, finding that 'respectable persons', although strangers, pressed his hand, wished him success and 'called for blessings on her Majesty'. On one occasion a German man who worked as a servant came to see him pleading for a certificate guaranteeing that he was not Majocchi, the mere fact of his being foreign evidently having put him in danger, never mind that he was not Italian. He had been 'grossly ill-used and insulted' by the suspicious mob and 'his wife driven from her lodgings by reason of the suspicion that he was that detestable traitor'. Despite such inconveniences, Denman enjoyed his Cheltenham stay. He found the waters beneficial, went riding every day, and to concerts in the evening. Before he left the town his jaundice had 'worn itself from pure gold to counterfeit silver', and he now endeavoured 'to wash away the last remains of gilt'.[6]

Henry Brougham's team was now hyperactive, and determined to get together every morsel of evidence that might be of any use before the defence case opened on 3 October. Brougham favoured an approach that he called the '*battering* plan', based on demolishing the prosecution's evidence. As he put it in a note written on 22 September: 'The more I have examined the case the less I think our answer to it will depend on any evidence we can hope to have even if we had a year, but it is very strong on *theirs*.'[7]

The Queen's solicitor, William Vizard, was in charge of coordinating and directing the activity. At forty-six, Vizard was four years older than Brougham, but was his protégé nonetheless. Brougham had put him in contact with Caroline in 1811, when she appointed him her solicitor, and had also introduced him to the movers and shakers in Whig politics – many of whom became his clients. To show his appreciation William Vizard named one of his two sons Henry Brougham, and one of his three daughters Caroline. He was, according to an obituarist, known for his 'great zeal, promptitude and ability', and these qualities are evident in the vast amount of correspondence that he sent around the country and across Europe during Caroline's trial. His missives are filled with a sense of urgency as he tries to bludgeon the Queen's agents into sending him precise and supportable evidence about the movements of Adam and Eve, as he occasionally described Caroline and Pergami, instead of the hearsay and gossip that was widely on offer, especially in Italy and often for a price.[8]

Vizard was also in charge of the money, which proved an unending source of frustration and misery for him. Ten thousand pounds had been earmarked by the Treasury for the cost of the Queen's case. But one of the Queen's most senior agents on the continent, Jabez Henry, appeared to be spending far too much on Italian witnesses who were likely to be of little or no use – and a serious danger was arising that the defence evidence might be as open as the prosecution's had been to being tainted by charges of bribery.

Vizard was also the recipient of a great many 'leads' and 'interesting observations' that correspondents felt might be of use to the Queen. At his rooms at 50 Lincoln's Inn he sifted through these, sorting out the nonsense from the substantial, and commissioning follow-up research. William Gell sent a note urging Vizard to start an enquiry into the relationship between the Milan Commissioner James Brown and Sir John Douglas, husband of the infamous Lady Douglas. Sir John, he had heard, was the nephew of Brown. Also, he had been assured by a Mrs Serres (who claimed to be the daughter of

George III's brother the Duke of Cumberland), that Colonel Brown
had said that if well paid he would 'get up a plot which would ruin the
Queen . . . The lady offers to appear and swear this herself.'
Brougham meanwhile passed Vizard a letter from Archdeacon
Bathurst, who had heard that the prosecution witness Sacchi, while
staying in Norfolk, had committed a forgery on a bank in Yarmouth.[9]
A further lead was supplied by Matthew Wood who had received
information from a man in Ireland claiming to possess two letters that
would be helpful to the Queen's cause. Others wrote to offer their
services as investigators in Europe, witnesses, translators and informers. Vizard found that in order to manage the vast amount of
correspondence, he regularly needed to work late into the night.

The team established that nobody who had worked for Caroline
during the previous three years, and nobody from Pesaro, had been
prepared to testify against her, despite the strenuous efforts of
George's agents. Indeed, several were anxious to come to her aid.
Colonel Alessandro Olivieri stated that he was ready to rush to
London if necessary, 'for I will never allow our good Queen to be
calumniated, without detecting the imposture'.[10] Colonel Charles
Vassalli, who had worked as an equerry for Caroline, told her lawyers
that he had never seen 'any act either indecent or improperly familiar
between the Queen and Pergami nor ever heard the Queen use expressions to Pergami other than she has used to himself'.[11] He had taken
coffee to Caroline in the mornings and found that, unless she was ill,
she slept with Pergami's little girl, Victorine, in her bed, and not with
Pergami. Caroline would give Vassalli his instructions for the day
from bed, often with Pergami present. He had seen Caroline and
Pergami walking together, she leaning on his arm, but said that the
Queen had often walked in such a manner with other gentlemen,
including himself.[12]

A letter from Captain Joseph Hownam to Vizard stated that 'I feel
my duty towards her Majesty and you may depend that I will keep my
promise'.[13] Hownam had been with Caroline when she rode into
Jerusalem on a donkey, and had challenged the spy Ompteda – who
had since died – to a duel. He had quit her service because he had

fallen out with Pergami, but now wished to join her supporters. Unfortunately, though, he was experiencing 'violent rheumatic spasms' in his head which were being treated with the application of leeches.[14] Consequently, he feared he might be prevented by illness from appearing.

Lady Charlotte Lindsay, to everyone's relief, was prepared to testify. In August, Vizard had informed Caroline's lady-in-waiting, Anne Hamilton, that Lady Charlotte had given him a 'very favourable statement of the evidence she is prepared to give for H.M . . . and [she also] spoke in the strongest terms of her desire to make herself useful to the Queen'.[15] Lady Elisabeth Forbes, another former lady-in-waiting to the Queen, was also ready to lend help, and her testimony was 'important on some points and satisfactory altogether'.[16] However, Caroline's advisers felt that, due to a certain instability of mind, Lady Elisabeth would do more harm than good in the witness box. We do not know the exact nature of her unreliability, and can only make inferences from letters such as that from William Gell to Henry Brougham: 'Lady Elisabeth can do no good – she will do infinite mischief. She is now in our house in 17 Lower Brook St in a most dangerous way . . . There is no minimising matters – if you don't believe it come and see.'[17] Lady Elisabeth was soon afterwards dispatched to the country.

Huge effort went into finding nuggets of information that would contradict the prosecution's evidence. One of the Queen's men in Europe was charged with checking the testimony of the innkeeper, Pietro Cuchi, who had spied on her through the hole in the canvas. He was told to set off without the delay of an hour to the Black Eagle inn in Trieste 'and to make the most particular inquiries there and in the town as to the evidence given by this man . . . you will see particularly what was the situation of the doors in the Queen's room'. He was instructed to search for the canvas and the hole, and to look through the keyhole in the nearby door to check whether the door to Pergami's room was, in fact, visible.[18] At Carlsruhe the local agent was instructed by William Vizard to be 'most zealous in your inquiries about [Barbara] Kress . . . Let no part of the statement she has made about either her past or her present situation in life pass without your thorough inquiry into the truth of every part – Inquire whether there is or was a lock or bolt to the door of the Chamber which she says was bolted.'[19] Kress herself was subjected to as much scrutiny as her evidence, and a note was sent to Thomas Denman stating that Caroline's equerry, Charles Vassalli, 'can prove a perfect readiness on the part of Kress to submit to his embraces, but he quitted her on observing by her fingers that she had the itch'.[20] An anonymous letter arrived claiming that 'this Mrs Barbara undoubtedly knows the wüst with which she intended to pollute the Queen . . . more from her own manner of living than from any observation made on her Majesty'.[21]

Kress might be diseased, but Demont was to be despised as the ultimate whore. She had slept with another witness, Giuseppe Sacchi, and her relationship with him had been exposed in the Lords, along with the fact that their liaison had been a contributing factor in the Queen's decision to dismiss her maid. Now Vizard and his agents set about questioning other men with whom Demont had been acquainted, in a quest to find more lovers. Caroline's chamberlain, Keppel Craven, it turned out, employed a manservant by the name of John Whitcomb who 'used to go continually to the bed room of Demont where he was received without restraint . . . and he was allowed to take every, even the last liberty'.[22] Moreover, Whitcomb told the defence lawyers that 'she used to caution him not to let the Princess see him or find this out, [and] amidst all this intricate intercourse Demont never insinuated even in the slightest manner that there was any improper intercourse between Pergami and the Princess'.[23]

All the time that Vizard was commissioning new investigations, he was also receiving letters from members of the public who wished to offer up their own revelations and opinions. One correspondent claimed to know of someone who was at Pesaro who would testify to the Queen's good name, another professed that the allegations against the Queen arose from the difference in customs between Britain and Europe. In France and Germany, he wrote, '*men* unconnected by parentage . . . kiss each other on the lips; their mouths remain pressed one upon the other for several seconds, and they repeat such a kiss

three or four times. What could be more indelicate in *this* country! . . .
As to Ladies' bathing – I have seen in France many times the male servant go into his Mistress's bathing room to carry more water or a
message to her whilst she was lying in her bath and nobody with her
(the bath covers the lady as far as to her neck).'[24]

A Mr Edmunds wrote to Brougham to say that the poet William
Wordsworth, his wife and his sister Dorothy were on a trip, 'it was
said to *France*', but he had learned that they had taken in 'Milan,
Carlsruhe, Como and, in short, all the other places which our gracious
but persecuted Queen visited in her travels'. 'We know the state of his
finances will not permit his single purse to bear the expenses of such
a long journey for pleasure,' he continued, 'and that he has been hired
to do some dirty work there is little doubt – Your brother [James] will
I hope have heard and kept an eye on him.' Other correspondents
were less specific, simply asking Vizard to meet at this or that coffee
house where vital information would be handed over.

Brougham had not yet decided on whether to bring Pergami's
family and particularly his sister, the Countess of Oldi, to the House
of Lords to testify. Intelligence arrived to the effect that Count Oldi
was indeed from a 'most ancient family' which had once fallen on hard
times but was 'now again in good circumstances'.[25] The Countess herself had been ordered to Boulogne where she was waiting to cross the
channel.

As for Pergami himself, Brougham's brother and others were in
constant communication with him. The defence's agent Jabez Henry
was stationed for some of the time in Pesaro where he quizzed
Pergami on his version of events, then reported back to Vizard.
According to Henry's letters, Pergami was 'very docile and perfectly
ready to act according to our directions . . . So far as I can judge of P,
and I have seen a good deal of him and our communication has been
without reserve, I think he would stand a cross-examination and if so
he could be a most important witness.'[26]

It seemed that Pergami, if produced in the House of Lords, would
be able to offer innocent explanations of seemingly indecent occur-
rences. Caroline had, for instance, been accused of behaving in an

intimate way with Pergami when dining with him in the kitchen. 'P
says it is true,' wrote Jabez Henry, 'that the Q gave him a spoonful of
the polenta to see if it was bad and the complaints against the cook
were well-founded.' This account, thought Henry, put the incident 'in
a good light'.[27] As for Louise Demont having testified to Pergami's
bed appearing not to have been slept in or 'tumbled', 'he will swear as
the reason that he slept with her' – meaning that Pergami was sleeping not with Caroline but with her chambermaid. This would,
according to Pergami, be 'a thing of very easy belief after her amours
with Sacchi'. Moreover, Demont 'amused herself with looking over a
collection of very obscene drawings'.[28]

Pergami claimed that he had been offered large sums of money by
a government agent to 'destroy the Queen'. But instead of getting
proof he 'threatened the man, who immediately disappeared'. Most
significantly for the defence case, though, he assured Henry 'privately
and in the most solemn manner that he could take his oath that he
never had had an intercourse with the Queen'.[29] The question for
Brougham was whether he thought Pergami a trustworthy witness,
and capable of withstanding a cross-examination. He also needed to
consider the effect on public opinion of the arrival in London of the
fine-looking man alleged to be the Queen's lover, but cast by many as
her protector against George, his spies and assassins. The climate in
the streets of London was frenzied enough without Pergami riding in.

16

CONVULSION

The Br[and]enb[ur]ghian jollity!
Come, join the million (*Folly's bands!*)
Present Addresses, and kiss Hands;
No longer mind your Occupation,
For staring mad is all the nation;
And those who liv'd by mending *Shoes*
Now mend the *State!* and read the *News!*

More loyal Addresses!!!, or
All the World at Hammersmith!!! (1820)

The three week recess marked the height of Queenite protest. 'Nobody seems to *think* of anything but the Queen,' Anne Cobbett wrote to her brother James, and 'nobody seems to *expect* anything but a revolution'.[1] Her father, she said, 'feels every cheer given to the Queen

as so much vengeance upon the Boroughmongers'. And she was thrilled
to report that the veteran reformer, Major John Cartwright, had joined
the thousands of visitors flocking to Brandenburgh House. He 'carried
up an Address from some place or other, and the Queen invited him to
stay and dine with her. So here is a pretty confusion, a man convicted of
sedition and expecting to go into prison, dining at the Queen's table!' The
Major, Anne believed, meant nothing to Caroline personally, and the
Queen's hospitality was 'shewing what she thought of the *cause*'.[2] The
Cobbetts, in the grip of euphoria, were overestimating Caroline's commitment to political change. But in doing so, they were joined by many
thousands of like-minded reformers.

The Queen was, indeed, allowing the most extraordinary proclamations about the tide of history to be made in her name. 'A government
cannot stop the march of intellect any more than they can arrest the
motion of the tides or the course of the planets,' was her response to one
group. And the ministers should give in to the 'force of public opinion
which must be finally irresistible'. She informed the world that 'the
captive has burst his intellectual chains . . . And a spirit has arisen which
will not endure servitude under any of its imposing forms.' On one
occasion, 160 gentlemen from Cripplegate, dressed in black with white
favours on their breasts, arrived at Brandenburgh House in 28 landaus,
and presented her with an Address. Her response proclaimed that any
King and government which 'capriciously changed' its laws was
arbitrary, and destitute of legitimacy. Even if the Bill of Pains and
Penalties was passed, she said, 'consider how far it ought to be obeyed'.
In a limited monarchy the King and his government are answerable to
'a higher authority . . . that of God and of the People'.[3]

Government loyalists were duly outraged by the subversive nature
of the Queen's pronouncements. 'The framing of these answers has
invariably been to excite, to irritate and to inflame the feelings of the
mob,' wrote Thomas Harral. Their purpose was to 'contaminate our
morals, to sap our religion – to subvert the constitution of the state
and, if possible, to destroy that monarchy which has so long been the
envy, the pride, and the glory of the earth'.[4] The language of the
declamations attempted to split the country in two. You could be for

the Queen and against the corrupted political system, or against the Queen and a defender of the political status quo. Both sides claimed to be the true champions of the constitution. The Queenites portrayed the establishment as traitor to Magna Carta and the Glorious Revolution of 1688, while loyalists saw the protestors as the would-be destroyers of Britain's magnificent constitutional legacy. Right now, though, the loyalists were in the shadows and the Queenites centre stage, dominating public space, whether it be on the road to Hammersmith or in the pages of the newspapers and popular prints.

The Addresses were now arriving not just daily, but by the hour – and they demonstrated that there was strong support for Caroline in every part of the kingdom. The petition from inhabitants of the City of Bristol had more than 24,000 signatures; that from the female inhabitants of Nottingham 7,000, Newcastle upon Tyne 3,800; the married females of Marylebone, 8,700; the inhabitants of Birmingham 11,800; the ladies of Edinburgh 8,300 or so; the 'industrious classes' in and about London nearly 29,400; the inhabitants of Paisley 6,000; the females of Manchester 20,241; inhabitants of Glasgow 35,718; the married females of Bristol 2,102; the young men of Monmouth 330; the inhabitants of Portsmouth 11,500 and so it went on. In total more than 800 petitions were received with close to a million signatures. William Cobbett would soon be, at last, received in person by the Queen, bearing Addresses from the people of Warwick and from Bury St Edmunds.

Countess Lieven witnessed a procession carrying eleven Addresses 'accompanied in each case by a deputation of several thousand people carrying banners with the most subversive inscriptions'. And as she passed by stables of her home she saw, written in large letters on the wall: 'The Queen for ever, the King in the river.' All the walls in London, she wrote, 'are scrawled over with nice things of this kind'. And, worse still, 'I can't tell you what horrible faces one sees nowadays in the streets and the main roads, and how insolently they come up and bawl in one's ears.'[5] Shortly afterwards, one of the Queen's most ardent supporters, the reformer John Cam Hobhouse, wrote that he was 'almost cheer'd off my horse' as he rode to Hammersmith with an

Address from Kensington. At the Queen's house, he wrote in his diary, 'one man said that he hoped to see Castlereagh punished capitally – I never heard this kind of language before – the feeling gone abroad is most intense'.[6] The *Manchester Observer* professed that political upheaval was imminent. The Queen's trial, it stated, 'has enabled all who dislike the present system, to league together for its destruction.'

During the recess the Home Secretary, according to his son-in-law George Pellew, 'found it impossible to leave his post for a single day'.[7] Sidmouth was, unsurprisingly, still receiving his daily anonymous threats to life and limb. '*The whole country hates you, all of you*,' wrote a man who had 'travailed a great part of the country over'. They hate 'your master into the bargain', he continued. 'PS. The soldiers all *hate* you.'[8] Similar letters threatened the assassination of Sidmouth and Castlereagh, and asserted that 'we will have no King if there is no Queen'.[9] Others wrote to offer their support to the King and his government in the event of unrest, revolution or civil war. Agnes Barber of Exeter was particularly anxious. The public feeling, she thought, was so strong that 'every one who has witnessed the horrors of the French Revolution looks with the most fearful apprehension at the gathering storm which may pour destruction on this once happy country'. But the government should be sure, she said, that only the 'rabble' were disloyal to the King and the constitution. She recommended that the King come to the south-west where the people would protect him. 'The storm is ready to burst,' she wrote, 'trust not the military – let the King come to Exeter, immediately. Here he would be safe.'[10] George did, throughout the crisis, hide from the people – primarily at his cottage at Windsor. The hated Lords Sidmouth and Castlereagh, however, showed no cowardice. On one occasion the two men were walking together in London and encountered a mob who began 'hissing and groaning'. 'Here we go,' observed Lord Sidmouth, 'the two most popular men in England.' 'Yes,' Lord Castlereagh replied, 'through a grateful and admiring multitude.'[11]

The extraordinary reach of the protests to every part and every class of the population was partly due to the organisation of the radicals. The republican Francis Place was one of those who had seized Caroline's cause and used it to stir up public feeling, although his role was a minor one. He later wrote of his activity, and his objectives:

> I cared nothing for the Queen as the Queen . . . but I saw very plainly that if a public meeting was held, it would be followed by many others, and thus nearly the whole of the unprivileged unfrocked unpensioned unofficered part of the people would meet and Address the Queen and go to the Queen in thousands. I knew very well that the consequence would be a familiarity with the Royalty highly injurious to its state . . . and that many thousands of people would lose their reverence both for Royalty and Aristocracy . . . I was now sure that the excitement would be general and that the consequence would be such a falling off of respect for Royalty and Aristocracy as had never before existed amongst the people in this country. I saw that to [an] immense extent this falling off would be followed by contempt.[12]

Radicals such as John Gast, Samuel Waddington and the editor of the *Black Dwarf*, Thomas Wooler – all men with republican leanings – were joined by 'softer' democrats such as John Cam Hobhouse, Joseph Hume and Matthew Wood, to organise meetings and demonstrations through trade societies. Thanks to their efforts, many of the processions to reach Caroline were organised on trade lines – which lent an extra air of defiance to the protests, since two loathed Combination Acts, passed in 1799 and 1800, banned trade unions. In September and October the coachmakers came to Hammersmith along with the glassblowers, the bakers, Spitalfields weavers, carpenters and joiners, coopers, sawyers, corset makers, printers, cabinetmakers, chair makers, carvers, musical instrument makers, upholsterers, leather workers, silversmiths, paper hangers, bricklayers and brass founders. The benefit societies en masse provided a particularly magnificent display – with 54 flags flying, each of them representing 25,000 members.[13] A progovernment pamphlet called *All the World at Hammersmith* and published by Robins and Sons of Tooley Street was designed to make the dazzling variety of trade representatives sound absurd. It suggested that Caroline's crowds included cobblers, cook-maids, barbers, tailors, shipwrights, churchwardens, seamen, publicans, cheesemongers, carpenters, doctors, pawnbrokers, overseers, tallow chandlers, dustmen, weavers, butchers – that is, anyone and everyone, many of them 'wheedl'd by their *loving* wives'. The *Traveller* newspaper recorded that the Queenite sentiment 'is moving bodies which never before felt political agitation . . . the whole mass of the people is excited.'

For three or four days every week the 'whole population of London' would turn out to see the Addresses being taken to Hammersmith. One of the great spectacles was that of the British seamen being received by the Queen on 13 September. These were men who had fought Britain's great sea battles against the French; and the navy, even more than the army, embodied British ideals of heroism, manliness and chivalry. According to a popular rhyme, the sailors passed by William Hone's house on Ludgate Hill:

> At HONE's – who has not heard of HONE
> Of *Satire* he the nerve and bone . . .
> At HONE's a cheer of three times three
> Re-echoed from the *Sons of Sea*

The Queen's response paid tribute to their status. 'A British seaman is another name for downright sincerity and plain-spoken truth,' it began. 'A British seaman never deserts his flag and never abandons his companion in distress . . . the British sailor is brave even to a fault' and would always prefer 'death to disgrace'. She ended by stating that 'insulted greatness or depressed rank can nowhere find a surer refuge or more steady protection than in the sailors and soldiers of this country'. She would benefit the military community as best she could – 'all classes will ever find in me a sincere friend to their liberties, and a zealous advocate of their rights'. On the same day a response to the people of Ipswich championed the principles of liberty which 'have still too firm a hold on the hearts of Englishmen to be readily shaken by the menaces of tyranny'. On this day in September it seemed that the Queen had allied herself with the armed forces of Britain against the British government. And she had used the familiar rhetoric of patriotism as protest.

Brandenburgh House was the ultimate focus of the activity, but there were other Queenite dramas being played out around the country. In Newcastle upon Tyne, a Mr Marshall who was a printer and bookseller with premises in the Old Flesh Market made posters for display around the city stating that an Address to the Queen would lie 'for a few days only' at his printing office, as well as at the premises of the hatter, Mr Francis, the grocer, Mr Cook, the shoemaker, Mr Lister, and so on. The Address was organised by a Mr Eneas Mackenzie, who according to a local commentator 'was chairman of the great Radical Meeting on the Town Moor, here, on 11th of October last, when upwards of 7,000 men marched through the streets in military array'. Mackenzie was described by a correspondent to a local newspaper as 'this secretary of state for the northern radical department'.[14] In the same region the people of Hexham organised an Address, as did the citizens of Sunderland, all of them fervently hoping that 'your Majesty's persecutors will be ultimately covered with shame and confusion'.[15]

Mr Marshall of Newcastle had also copied the seditious *Queen's Letter to the King* composed by Cobbett, on a single sheet of paper, and sold it in the city, and published a political broadside called *The Queen in Danger*. Another Newcastle pressman, a Mr Hodgson, offered the most exciting days of trial evidence for sale on single sheets, as did Edward Walker, a printer of Pilgrim Street who earlier in the year had sold reports of the trial of the Cato Street conspirators. Meanwhile, the northern rebel Eneas Mackenzie had organised a public meeting at the White Hart inn at which pro-Caroline sentiment was whipped up and twelve 'declarations' made in her favour. A particular issue was that of the 'royal plate'. George had asked his wife to return to the Crown the full set of china that she had received from George III as Princess of Wales – and the Newcastle Queenites, like thousands elsewhere, were aggrieved. The plate issue, according to the Newcastle declaration, was 'derogatory to the dignity of royalty – a petty and unmanly insult to an oppressed and persecuted woman, and exhibits an unwarrantable contempt of public feeling'.[16]

Everywhere it was recognised that while the radicals were stirring up trouble, the press was more effective still – partly because its message was usually anti-government but not 'extremist'. *The Printers' Address to Caroline* was written by the masterful William Hone – and it raised the press to great heights, claiming it as the true means by which the people were exercising their power:

> In future times, should the page of history record the present era as one in which overwhelming power combined with senatorial venality to crush an unprotected female, we trust it will also preserve the gratifying remembrance that the base conspiracy was defeated by the irresistible force of Public Opinion, directed and displayed through the powerful medium of a Free, Uncorrupted, and Uncorruptible British Press.[17]

Caroline's reply was equally exultant, proclaiming: 'The press is at present the only stronghold that Liberty has left. If we lose this we lose all. We have no other rampart against an implacable foe.'[18]

At the forefront of press influence was *The Times*. Its circulation had doubled as a result of its support for the Queen, to around 20,000 copies – and it was highly profitable, earning more than £18,000 a year for its proprietor, John Walters. But the paper was not bought by the mass of people who were demonstrating for the Queen – at seven pence a copy, they could not afford it. The Tory government levied a tax on each newspaper to keep the sales price high, with the aim of preventing the lower classes from reading unsettling, 'licentious' or 'seditious' writings. But, in a sense, the tax, a stamp duty, failed because even if the general population could not buy the main newspapers, they could still read them, or listen to them being read aloud. A treatise on the British press published anonymously in 1824 describes the situation eloquently. 'The people of these Kingdoms have been an inquisitive, prying, doubting and reading people,' it states, particularly since the French Revolution. The great mass of the population were '*readers* not buyers' of the papers, reading in 'club rooms, taverns and coffee houses, and in subscription companies of from twenty to a hundred or even two hundred members. From these sources alone did the tradesmen and mechanics and labourers of England and Scotland derive their news.'[19] Other writers suggest that if a man were literate, then he would be expected to read the paper aloud to those who were not – especially if all were congregated at the congenial premises of the local tavern.[20]

Richard Rush, the American envoy in London, observed that 'sub-division' made the cost of reading a newspaper cheap. 'They are circulated by agents at a penny an hour in London,' he wrote. 'When a few days old they are sent to the provincial towns and through the country at reduced prices . . . In three days a London newspaper reaches every part of the kingdom, and in three months every part of the globe.'[21] Whilst the latter claim is doubtless exaggerated, the impression was right – despite the theoretically high price of news, in reality it travelled everywhere. It is likely that by 1820 a majority of adults in London were reading, or hearing news read, about the trial. One analyst of the London press, writing in the *Westminster Review* in 1829, estimated that every London paper was read by thirty people, and put the average for Great Britain as a whole at twenty-five. Even if the true figure were half this, the nation was evidently a greedy consumer of news.

In the streets news was a noisy affair. A writer in 1807 described how newspapers were advertised in London:

> Besides the gross indecency of announcing them by the blowing of horns whenever they contain any extraordinary news, greengrocers, hair-dressers and pastry cooks throughout the metropolis and its vicinity are furnished with signboards intimating that particular papers are to be sold at their respective shops, and they are copiously supplied with copies, of which the number unsold are returned on the Monday morning. These papers are diffusely circulated, by means of the stage coaches, throughout the country.[22]

By 1820 regional papers were established in every major town in the country, all of them carrying reports of Caroline's trial. It was common for an editor to await the arrival of the morning papers by coach from London, then to copy out the news as fast as possible in the local paper. Bristol had 5 newspapers, Bath 4, Canterbury 3 and Chelmsford 2. Liverpool had 6 newspapers, Manchester 7, Glasgow 4 and Edinburgh 9. And, despite the stamp duty, the number of new newspapers and periodicals had been rising rapidly from around 75 in England alone in 1734, to more than 260 in 1800. On one Sunday at the height of the Caroline affair William Wilberforce was able to buy 19 different London papers.[23]

When the writer of Caroline's response to the printers recognised the power of the press, though, he was referring to a much wider community than that of newspapers alone. There was, in 1820, a media network, as there is now, or a sort of news chain – the news in the papers would radiate out into publications of all types, many of which were able to evade the stamp duty. William Hone would read *The Times* and produce a satire as a result which might sell 100,000 copies or more at sixpence, while Hone's works would have their own effect on another type of printer – those men who produced the one-penny broadsides, and penny-a-yard ballads that were often cheap and sentimentalised comments on the news, and which were sold on the streets in even larger numbers than Hone's works. These have been largely forgotten by historians of the British press.

Chief amongst the broadside men was James Catnach, a young entrepreneur from Newcastle – he was still in his twenties in 1820 – who had come to London to set himself up in business as a printer. He moved an old wooden printing press into cramped rooms at Monmouth Court in the heart of the Seven Dials district of London, a slum area in which printers operated alongside street traders, gin sellers, beggars and criminals. Catnach was soon making money selling ballads, lurid tales of crime and repentance to be sold at executions, and news broadsides – all printed on cheap paper and often sold by 'patterers' who would call out the news or sing out the ballads. The nineteenth-century social historian Henry Mayhew later interviewed a 'patterer' who said that, in his announcement of a murder story he would talk so that 'the words *Murder*, *Horrible*, *Barbarous*, *Love*, *Mysterious*, *Former Crimes* and the like' were all that could be heard.[24] The words stressed in selling a story about the Queen's trial can only be imagined.

When Catnach arrived in Seven Dials in 1813 he quickly established himself as more topical and more outrageous than rival printers. He packed more printing presses into his premises and stole business from his neighbour John Pitts, who since 1812 had been selling stories of sea battles, romantic ballads and morality tales. With his staff working day and night, the newcomer, Catnach, claimed he could print more than 100,000 broadsides in 24 hours.

If he came across a news story that looked as though it would sell, Catnach would often close an eye to the truth of the matter. He printed a fabulous broadside declaring that Napoleon Bonaparte had escaped from St Helena in a balloon, not caring that it was entirely fabricated.[25] And in 1818 he made money selling a story suggesting that a local butcher by the name of Mr Pizzey filled his sausages with human flesh. The butcher was besieged by a mob and Catnach was, for once, sued for libel and was sentenced to six months' imprisonment in the House of Correction at Clerkenwell.[26] His reputation was established as a hard-drinking maverick – ignorant, dirty, but despite his incarceration, successful. And Queen Caroline's trial was the most lucrative story of his career thus far. Throughout 1820 he published whatever he could, including reports from the trial itself, Addresses from the Queen's supporters and, most often, ballads in favour of the Queen.

These were adorned with titles such as 'The Rose of Albion', 'Britons Claim her as your Queen!', 'Brave Alderman Wood', 'The British Seamen and their Beloved Queen' and 'The Green Bag'. Numerous versions of 'God Save the Queen' were sold. The street literature was, in the main, populist rather than overtly political. But it was, nonetheless, anti-government and anti-King. George was generally portrayed in verse as despicable. An attack on Lord Castlereagh was more than once set beneath a woodcut of a hanged man. Sidmouth and the rest of the ministers were seen as part of the filthy crowd who had brought the Queen and Britons low. One verse, entitled 'England's Lamentation', stated that the country had:

> now become a bed of foul disease,
> Where naught but immorality can please;
> Not long ago thy better taste had spurn'd
> Filth, to which now e'en Woman's eyes are turned;
> Thy throne, till now, from Slander's voice exempt,
> Is made the theme of laughter and contempt . . . [27]

The worst insults were aimed at John Leach (generally, for effect, spelt Leech), who had set up the Milan Commission, and, of course, at the poor Italian witnesses and Louise Demont. The rhymes assumed that the people who purchased them had some knowledge of the trial proceedings. A rhyme about Demont, for instance, referred to her evidence that Pergami's bed was 'tumbled', and was published alongside jokes about Caroline's journey to Jerusalem. It was not surprising that Richard Rush felt moved to write of 'the boundless range of the press and liberty of speech'. Every day during the trial, he wrote, 'produced its thousand fiery libels against the King and his adherents, and as many caricatures, under the worst forms, [that] were hawked about all the streets'.[28] And in the process, Sidmouth's Six Acts were being not just ignored, but scorned. In September 1820 the government made an attempt to imprison the radical Samuel Waddington for having published a libel intended to excite sedition amongst the soldiers. Waddington conducted his own defence, and won the case. For the most part, Sidmouth simply stood back, not daring to bring court actions for 'seditious' articles that three years earlier would have earned their publishers a term in Newgate.

The Duke of Wellington thought the combination of press activity and army discontent would result in convulsion. His close friend Harriet Arbuthnot wrote: 'He is decidedly of opinion that the Radicals and ill-disposed people will never be quiet till force has been had recourse to, and he is perfectly convinced that if the press is allowed to go on in its present latitude, it will be the destruction of every thing'.[29] Nerves, generally, were still jittery. Henry Brougham's mother informed him 'with some alarm' of a regiment of cavalry in Penrith that had vowed 'they would fight up to their knees in blood for the Queen', and Brougham later wrote that all the intelligence he received indicated that the soldiers were allied 'with the multitude in their cheers and yells'.[30] With this explosive state of affairs at his back, Henry Brougham now prepared to face the Lords once more, opening the case for the defence of the Queen.

17

DEFENCE

The whole GANG are completely entangled,
And the more they shall struggle, the more they'll be mangled;

Derry Down Triangle (1820)

On 3 October Brougham commenced his oration, speaking in a low voice and telling the Lords that he felt oppressed by the millions of eyes upon him. Other lawyers may have trembled at the august presence of the peers, or for a client they knew to be guilty, he said. But *he* was awed by his knowledge of the Queen's innocence. Brougham professed to have the facts at his disposal to make a charge of recrimination against George, adding that he would produce this material only if the case began to go against him. In the final analysis, his duty must be to his client, whatever the consequences. The highest duty of an advocate, he told the Lords, is to promote his client 'at all hazards': 'I must not regard the alarm, or the suffering, the torment, or even the destruction I may bring upon another – nay, separating the duties of a patriot from those of an advocate, I must go on, reckless of the consequences, though my fate should be to involve his country in confusion and conflict.' This was to become known as the 'hired-hand' principle of advocacy, and is still cited in British law.

Brougham then ran through the arguments which their Lordships had heard already – though not expressed with such eloquence. The charge against Caroline was 'foul, false and scandalous'. Her only crime had been to associate with Italians, some of them nobles, others of the 'commonality'. But it was 'you . . . your Lordships' who put her in the position of having to choose between solitude and of mixing with those 'beneath her' by refusing to befriend her – 'it pleased you to reduce her to a state of humiliation'. She had been persecuted relentlessly, had been left to learn of the marriage and then the death of her daughter by chance. Fruitless investigations into her conduct had been followed only by more persecution. Her defenders – William Pitt, Spencer Perceval, Princess Charlotte, Samuel Whitbread and King George III – had all died, leaving her vulnerable to 'the whole weight of accusation' which 'burst upon her head'.

The Attorney General's witnesses, he said, had failed to prove the prosecution's case. Although they were the people most intimate with Caroline, her servants, who were at her side day after day, their testimonies did not demonstrate that she had committed adultery. Moreover, they were predominantly Italians. 'All foreigners are not made of the same materials,' but if any nation is marked by its tendency to perjury, 'it is Italy; the country of Borghia'. Italians were used by Henry VIII to give evidence when that King divorced Catherine of Aragon, and they were unreliable witnesses then. These days, he continued, they are no better. Let me read you the testimony of a native of Italy, of distinguished character. He says, 'To the dishonour of human nature, there is nothing at Naples so notorious as the free and public sale of false evidence. Their ordinary tariff is three or four ducats . . . the shop of perjury is ever open.'

Note, said Brougham, that the Attorney General had failed to call upon those English gentlewomen who, according to rumour, were so appalled by Caroline's conduct that they left her service. 'Where were these ladies, women of high rank and great station in society, well known in their own country; loved, esteemed and respected . . . women of talent as well as character, the very persons to have brought forward, if he had durst bring them forward?' As for the witnesses who were called – they were discredited. Majocchi was damned by his highly selective memory. Demont, the only other witness of substance, gave evidence that was self-evidently a concoction of 'falsehood and lies'.

Brougham retired after a day on his feet, and resumed his speech the following morning when he made further attacks on the prosecution's witnesses, in particular the unfortunate Pietro Cuchi: 'Can you forget those ardent eyes – that nose, that mouth, that lecherous mouth with which the wretch detailed such scenes of filthiness before you?' he asked. 'That hoary wretch, that profligate pander – who eyed your lordships as the old tailor did in hell through the eye of his worn needle?'

He told the Lords that if they believed the prosecution witnesses then 'there is proof positive of adultery'. The accounts of Majocchi, Demont and Sacchi all pointed to 'alleged intimacy'. Indeed, if they believed these witnesses 'she is not only guilty of the crime alleged against her in the bill but she is as bad even as Messalina'. If, however, the witnesses had perjured themselves, 'we must conclude them to be more vile than those Jacobins who, in the progress of the French revolution, attempted to affix so unnatural a charge upon Marie Antoinette' – a reference to the allegation made at the trial of the French Queen that she had sexually abused her son.

Note, railed Brougham, that on every vital piece of evidence there was never more than one witness testifying to one single fact. The thing would have been different if any two witnesses had concurred – 'this is what forms the safeguard of every man, and without it no person can be protected from the machinations of a conspirator'. Add to that the defence's ability to show that falsehoods have been told by the witnesses and the evidence, he claimed, falls away to nothing. Evidence, he argued, should be robust: 'I ask only this protection for her Majesty, a protection which justice and innocence demand.'

Brougham next read out two letters. The first was from George III to Caroline, written in 1804, offering her his affection and support. The second was from her husband – the infamous 'letter of licence'. The familiar words echoed around the chamber: 'Our inclinations are not in our power; nor should either of us be held answerable for the other, because nature has not made us suitable to each other.' Brougham expressed his wonder that the recipient of such a letter had been subjected to such 'rigour of observation', had been 'haunted' by a 'secret agency' and was now 'dragged to your bar'.

After more than six hours, he was now approaching the end of his speech and he urged the peers to beware of bringing about a cataclysm in the country on the basis of flimsy evidence.

> Can you, I say, upon such scandalous and barefaced perjury, in this, the highest court which is known to the law of the land, entertain a charge so monstrous as that which has for its object the ruin of the honour of an English Queen? What would be said by the people of England – what would be said by the world at large – if upon this species of proof, acting as you do as judges and legislators, you were to pass a bill, which must for ever debase and degrade an injured, an innocent woman?

He believed that the nation would be far from peaceful. 'Save the country, my Lords, from the horrors of such an occurrence; save yourselves' – and also, by favouring the Queen, spare the Church and the Crown. 'Spare the altar, which must stagger with the shock that rends its kindred throne.' And, finally, he implored the Lords 'that your hearts may be turned towards justice'.

Thomas Denman thought Brougham's speech 'one of the most powerful orations that ever proceeded from human lips', and was in awe of his 'arguments, his observations, his tones, his attitude, his eye', while Charles Greville considered it the 'most magnificent display of argument and oratory that has been heard in years'.[1] The impression made on the House of Lords, he wrote, 'was immense' and 'even his most violent opponents were struck with admiration and astonishment'. Lord Erskine was so affected that he rushed from the chamber in tears,[2] while William Vizard wrote to James Brougham, who was still in Milan, 'your brother has today concluded one of the most magnificent speeches ever made in this or any other country . . . we are in high spirits and full of confidence'.[3]

Harriet, Lady Granville, was still dissecting every aspect of the trial and told her sister, Georgiana, that her male friends judged Brougham's speech 'in eloquence, ability and judicious management beyond almost anything they ever heard'(although her husband disagreed), and reported that high bets were being taken at Brooks's club that the Bill would be thrown out. One friend, she wrote, had encountered Brougham immediately after his speech and found him 'looking quite exhausted, but talking and cutting his jokes just as if he had been the only person there who had not been exerting himself'. The Whig cynic Thomas Creevey was unsettled, and wrote to his friend Miss Ord: 'If he can prove what he has stated in his speech, I for one believe she is innocent, and the whole case a conspiracy.' The speech had 'not only astonished but has shaken the aristocracy', he wrote, 'though Lord Granville did tell me at parting not to be too confident of that, for that the H. of Lords was by far the stupidest and the most obstinate collection of men that could be selected from all England'.[4]

The time had now come to call the defence witnesses, who, the public confidently expected, would be a cut above those for the prosecution. The first to give evidence of any substance was Frederick North, Lord Guilford, the brother of Lady Charlotte Lindsay. Guilford was an amiable eccentric, an odd-looking man, and an enthusiast about all things Greek. As he took the stand to testify for the Queen he appeared, to Thomas Creevey at least, as 'the most ramshackle fellow you ever saw'. Under cross-examination it became clear that he had advised his sister to quit Caroline's entourage, but his reasons for doing so were not established. He testified to the Queen having behaved properly whenever he had seen her, although he did once see her in a boat on Lake Como, being rowed by Pergami.

Guilford's evidence overall was bland and neither incriminating nor tremendously helpful for Caroline. Harriet Arbuthnot, for one, was not ready to believe his testimony anyway. She wrote in her diary that she had heard that Guilford had told William Huskisson that 'the Queen was so infamous a character that he could not account for it otherwise than to suppose it was *a disease*'. According to the whispers, Guilford had gossiped that when he was at Como Caroline had sent him off on a ride and 'that she did so in order to spend the time of his absence with a very handsome Greek servant of his, who she took to a grotto or summerhouse in the grounds and remained with for three quarters of an hour'. But when questioned by the Lords, Guilford was unable to remember anything about the Greek servant incident.[5]

An old friend of Caroline's, Lord Glenbervie, followed and, in a short appearance, testified that the Queen had, whilst living abroad, received many British visitors of high social standing, and that his own wife, Lady Glenbervie had *volunteered* to be her Lady of the Bedchamber. But he soon made way for the defence's star witness, Lady Charlotte Lindsay. She was led to the bar by Henry Brougham, who had earlier sent her a dose of lavender drops for her nerves, and who asked the Lords that she might be accommodated with a chair. The request was granted, after which she was sworn in and examined by Brougham's colleague, Stephen Lushington, an up-and-coming lawyer still in this thirties. Like Brougham he was a Whig member of the House of Commons with crusading tendencies – he favoured parliamentary reform, an end to slavery, Catholic emancipation and full civil rights for Jews and dissenters. Unlike Brougham, he was building a genuine friendship with the Queen.

Charlotte Lindsay confirmed that when in Naples her mistress had received visitors 'of distinction', both English and Neapolitan; these had included the leaders of Whig society, Lord and Lady Holland, the (promiscuous) Lady Oxford and her husband, as well as Caroline's on-off chamberlain, Sir William Gell. When Charlotte Lindsay had accompanied Caroline on board a ship named the *Clorinde* there had been, she said, nothing unusual in the cabin arrangements. Then Lushington asked:

Do you remember a person of the name of Pergami being in the service of her Royal Highness?

I was often in company with the Queen when Pergami attended.

How did Pergami conduct himself?

In the common way in which a servant would.

How did her Royal Highness conduct herself?

In the manner that a mistress would conduct herself.

Did you ever observe any impropriety of conduct between the Princess and Pergami?

Never.

The Solicitor General, John Copley, now stepped forward for the cross-examination, which he conducted, thought Charlotte Lindsay, 'in as harsh a manner as if he had been endeavouring to bring out the confession of a murderer at the Old Bailey'.[6] However, the witness stood firm. She said she could remember no occasion upon which Caroline and Pergami had walked arm-in-arm, and reiterated that she had seen no improper conduct. She explained that the Queen's attitude to servants in general was one of affability. 'I think the higher classes in this country are more apt to be condescending and kind in their conduct towards their servants than persons in the ranks beneath them towards their servants,' she said. In addition, Caroline was a foreigner, and 'I have observed that [foreigners] . . . are more apt to converse familiarly with their servants than English people.'

At one stage she was asked about her personal circumstances, including her situation in 1817 when her brother and sister had died within a fortnight of each other. 'These questions, asked me in such a place, and when my spirits were so much harassed,' she wrote, 'quite overwhelmed me for a moment and I burst into tears; but these tears, together with a glass of water that was brought me, relieved me immediately.'[7]

She confirmed that a letter had been received from Lord Guilford urging her to leave Caroline's suite. The contents of the letter became an issue. Had the lady left because her brother had evidence of Caroline's adultery, or rumours of that adultery? The Lords decided that it would contravene the rules of evidence for Lady Charlotte to try to remember the contents of the letter – and Brougham advised the Lords that she would search for it. Lady Charlotte confirmed, meanwhile, that the main reason for her leaving Caroline's service was that she was 'influenced by the degrading reports that had reached me, although I had myself never seen any improprieties in her Majesty's conduct while I was with her in Italy'.

Charlotte Lindsay was happy with her performance and recorded in her journal that it seemed to give 'universal satisfaction'. She wrote that the Lords, including those in the government, were remarkably gentlemanly during her interrogation, while the defence team thought her evidence strengthened the impression that a conspiracy had been hatched to drive away all Caroline's respectable servants. At one stage, Denman was heard to whisper to Brougham, 'That was well answered,' while Brougham replied, 'Perfect! perfect!'[8] Less satisfactory, though, was her admission under cross-examination that she had spent only twenty-four days in Caroline's employ. And her promise to look for Lord Glenbervie's letter led to nothing.

Lady Granville wrote to her sister: 'Lady Charlotte Lindsay did it well. The Attorney General very offensive in his manner to her. Today for the Queen, as far as it goes.'[9] The King was more vituperative. 'I never thought that I should have lived to witness so much prevarication, so much lying, and so much wilful and convenient forgetfulness as, I am sorry to say, both Lord Guilford and Lady Charlotte Lindsay have display'd in their late examinations,' he wrote to his brother the Duke of York. 'For certain,' he thought, 'it is a very strange world that we do now live in, where everyone now thinks that he has a right to say [whatever] he pleases, and in defiance of all truth and reason, that black is white and white is black.'[10] The *Courier*, as usual, did its work for the King, protesting that Charlotte Lindsay had on occasion said 'I do not recollect' without the slightest imputation on the truth of her testimony, while Majocchi's *non mi ricordo* had been paraded as evidence of his mendacity.[11]

An Irish peer, Lord Landaff, next testified that it was an ordinary practice in Italy for men to see ladies in their bed in the morning when they called, and said that he had himself seen 'many ladies in bed in a morning'. Then Caroline's former chamberlain, Keppel Craven, was brought forward, attired in full court dress. He stated that it was he who had appointed Pergami as Caroline's courier, on the recommendation of the Lord Chamberlain to the Emperor of Austria. On the question of the arrangement of the bedrooms at Naples, he 'did not recollect exactly' where they all were. He remembered Caroline dressed up for a masquerade ball at Naples both in her Turkish peasant costume, and her Genius (or Muse) of History outfit, which 'did not appear to me in the slightest degree indecent or improper', and thought that she might have been able to change into her Genius of History clothes without taking off all of the Turkish peasant costume – thus making it not impossible for Pergami to have been present during the manoeuvre without committing a grave impropriety. He had not seen any 'degrading familiarity' between the Queen and Pergami, and testified that the Countess of Oldi 'was not a person of vulgar manners'. As for Pergami himself, he did not appear to have 'the fawning and sycophantic manner of an ordinary Italian servant; but had rather the manner of a superior person'.

Craven said that it was he who had suggested that William Austin should no longer sleep in the Queen's bed, as he had done for years. Austin, he stated, was by then about thirteen or fourteen and he had thought 'the people of Italy might make observations on it'. He confirmed that he had cautioned the Queen to be on her guard and to check 'against any appearance that might be misconstrued', since he had heard 'by letter from England that there was a spy near her'.

Craven's close companion and fellow chamberlain Sir William Gell was next to testify. Gell was, like Craven, a bachelor and the strong bond between the two men would, these days, suggest that they were gay. Certainly, in the context of Caroline's life, they functioned as a couple, with Gell the older and senior of the two. He was a well-respected expert on the history and geography of the eastern Mediterranean, had published extensively on these subjects and, in 1814, was knighted for his scholarly works. Partly because of his poor health, Gell preferred living in Europe, especially Italy, to Britain; but he did not let his physical discomfort affect his good temper, and was known for his hospitality, conversation and wit. When he came into the chamber of the House of Lords he was 'in consequence of having the gout . . . indulged with a chair'.

Sir William testified that the Lord Chamberlain to the Emperor of Austria had recommended Pergami in 'the strongest manner', saying that his family was respectable but had lost its fortune during the French Revolution. The Lord Chamberlain had thought Pergami a 'perfectly honest, honourable and trustworthy man' and had believed that he would be promoted by the Queen. Gell also remembered that the Lord Chamberlain in his full Austrian uniform and in the public streets had 'embraced Pergami before the people and kissed each of his cheeks. This was the common customary salutation in Italy not from a superior to an inferior but among equals.' He had observed Caroline on the night that the affair with Pergami was said to have begun and, contrary to the prosecution evidence, she had not rushed home from the opera and did not appear at all agitated. Gell had also seen Mahomet's dance and thought it something like the Spanish bolero that 'everybody in London' had seen in the theatre.

Lady Granville, despite the 'agony and bustle of a London morn-ing', managed to find time to write to her sister, Lady Morpeth, on 7 October. 'Yesterday was . . . triumphant for the Queen, "Vivat Regina", with accompaniment and a full band,' she wrote. 'Sir William and Keppel Craven, God help their souls, giving the most entire and cordial testimony in her favour, confuting much of the pre-vious evidence against her.' The Queen's principal fan, Lady Jersey, was now 'in a phrenzy of delight' and Lady Harrowby 'more moved than I ever before saw her'. Lady Granville felt that, all in all, 'the morals and decency of the age are at a low pitch'.[12]

The testimony of two gentlemen's gentlemen was next presented to the Lords. John Whitcomb, valet to Keppel Craven, confirmed that Louise Demont had 'very frequently' invited him to spend the night with her, and he had done so with the door to the room being 'locked and bolted' – thus grinding the Swiss maid's reputation deeper still into the mud. He also insisted that there had been no untoward familiarity between Pergami and the Queen. Sir William Gell's valet, William Carrington, also testified, and was well received by both the Lords and the country, being a navy man who had been the victim of a press gang. He stated that in Naples Pergami's bedroom had been moved, not so that he could be intimate with the Queen, but because the ceiling in the one first given him was so low, and he was so tall, that he could not stand up. Carrington then testified that the reviled Majocchi had earlier been entirely convinced of the Queen's innocence. At least that was the implication of his actions. Majocchi had been so angry at the activities of the spy Ompteda, said Carrington, that he had threatened to thrash Ompteda in the street 'like a dog' and kill him. The next witness, John Sicard, was born a foreigner – in Ansbach – but told the Lords that he was now a naturalised Englishman. He had worked for Caroline as her *maître d'hôtel*, and insisted that he had never seen any impropriety or familiarity between Caroline and Pergami.

Lady Granville noted in a letter to her sister that Lord Grey, the pre-eminent Whig peer (and future prime minister), had visited Caroline and left the cards of two other men and of his daughter Louisa. 'Her Majesty begged them to come in,' she wrote. 'The men obeyed, leaving Lady Louisa in the carriage, a proof of the wish these noble Whigs have that their wives and daughters should cultivate the acquaintance.'[13] This was an indication that, at this point, high society felt that events were to some degree moving in the Queen's favour. Until Lord Grey's visit most of the aristocratic Whigs, unlike those in the reforming wing of the party, had kept a safe distance from the Queen, and the only ladies to leave their cards were – still – mavericks such as Lady Jersey and Anne Damer. At this point, however, Lady Jersey suddenly became popular, hosting soirées attended by 'all the political grandees', including Brougham.[14]

The Queen's witnesses, it was generally thought, had performed brilliantly. Thomas Creevey thought that William Gell had been so effective that several 'bishops are gone home to cut their throats'. He wrote to his stepdaughter Elizabeth Ord saying 'Lord Enniskillen has just said in my hearing that the Ministers ought to be damned for coming out with such a case,' and on the morning of 9 October

Creevey observed that 'the town is literally drunk with joy at this
unparalleled triumph of the Queen'. He claimed that Lord Lauderdale
was the only peer remaining who had any doubt 'that the whole thing
has been a conspiracy for money'.[15] On the same day Lady Granville
wrote to her sister, Lady Morpeth: 'It is said that there is much squab-
bling in the Cabinet,' she added. 'Five times a day I listen to the same
discussion, whether or not the ministers should resign.'[16]

Dr Henry Holland now took the stand. He said that he had attended
Pergami for an illness and, as far as he had seen, the Queen had not
once come to visit him. He had never noticed anything in the conduct
of either the Queen or Pergami that was 'in the slightest degree
derogatory to the honour of the English empire, or likely to wound the
moral feelings of this country'. Indeed, Pergami had always behaved
with 'utmost respect'. The Countess Oldi, he said, had manners that
were 'unobtrusive and natural', and although she spoke Italian with a
Lombardy accent, this was not indicative of vulgarity.

Later the same day Carlo Forti, a courier, stepped up to give evidence. Forti was the nephew of the Duchess of Torlonia, so more
respectable than most of the Italian witnesses for the prosecution; and
he had been a rider accompanying Caroline's coaches for a journey
from Milan to Rome. This, significantly, was the journey referred to
by Giuseppe Sacchi, during which, he said, he had opened the curtain
of her carriage to find Caroline and Pergami asleep with their hands
on the 'particular parts' of the other.

Forti, however, asserted that Caroline's carriage had no such curtains. Instead it had a system of blinds that were drawn up and down
with a spring. Furthermore, Forti said that Sacchi rode with the carriages only for the first small part of their journey as he was 'chafed'
and riding was uncomfortable for him. For the most part Sacchi had
ridden ahead in a 'caratella' or calash to order and pay for the horses
for the next stage. It was he, Carlo Forti, and not Sacchi, who had
ridden with Caroline's carriage – and he had noted that inside the carriage the Countess of Oldi had been seated between the Queen and
Pergami, while the child Victorine sometimes sat on Caroline's lap,
and sometimes on the lap of the Countess.

Henry Brougham was conducting the examination and having demolished the main part of Sacchi's evidence, he now attempted to undermine Majocchi's claim that on parting with Caroline, Pergami had kissed her on the lips. Throughout his examination of Forti, Brougham referred to Pergami as 'the Baron':

Did you ever see the Baron kiss the Princess at any time upon taking leave of her, or at any other time?
I never saw him kiss the Princess.
Did you ever see the Baron take leave of her Royal Highness upon any occasion?
Yes I have.
What did the Baron do in taking leave of her Royal Highness when you saw him?
He kissed her hand and nothing else, with much respect.

Forti's evidence was, like that of his predecessors, judged to be beneficial to the Queen, although the *Courier* could not resist pointing out that he was Italian. 'Remember . . . the frantic and fiend-like abuse which was heaped upon the witnesses on the other side, merely *because they were Italians*,' urged the leader writer. 'Yet *Carlo Forti*, the courier, who swears to the contrary of some points of *Sacchi's* evidence, is an Italian too. What is it then that makes his testimony a whit more credible than *Sacchi's?*'[17]

The next witness was a disaster. Lieutenant John Flynn of the Royal Navy was sworn in, and in the early stages of his examination by Denman, he seemed reasonably competent. He testified that when on board the (by now famous) polacca he had, on the return from Jaffa, slept on deck, less than five feet from Caroline's tent. He said that, despite his proximity, he had heard no conversation from the tent, and did not know where Pergami had slept. On the deck, he said, there was a gun. But he had never seen Caroline sitting on it, or sitting in the lap of any person on board. Thomas Denman asked:

Did you ever see her with her arms round the neck of any person?
No.
Or kissing any person, except perhaps the child Victorine?
No.
During the whole time that you had the management of this vessel, and that her Royal Highness was on board, did you see the slightest impropriety or indecency in her behaviour towards Pergami or towards any other person?
No.

John Copley rose for the cross-examination, once again conducting himself in an aggressive manner. After much questioning on the minutiae of Flynn's management of his ship the naval officer started to appear anxious. Copley turned his questioning to the seemingly innocuous question of the nationality of the clerk who took dictation from Flynn for his log. The sea captain seemed flustered, and kept muddling his answers. Then, quite suddenly, on the witness stand, he fainted. He was immediately removed from the bar. While he was away several peers complained of the oppressive state of the air in the House, and desired that all the windows be thrown open.

Flynn was eventually brought back and throughout the rest of his examination, appeared nervous and unsure. He had mysteriously left his full log book – which had acted as a sort of personal journal – in Italy, bringing only copied excerpts with him, creating a suspicion that he had spent time doctoring any notes that might have potential to harm the Queen. And he seemed to have a much better memory for the first part of the journey, during which Caroline slept in her cabin, than for the later part when she had slept in the tent. He knew that Pergami had slept on a bed in the dining room on the outward journey, but could not say where he had slept on the homeward voyage.

Creevey wrote to Miss Ord, and told her that in trying to 'do too much' for the Queen, Flynn had done harm. 'He has perjured himself three or four times over, and his evidence and himself are gone to the devil. He is evidently a crack-brained sailor.'[18] Countess Lieven wrote to Metternich telling him that once Flynn had fainted 'the impression against' Caroline was 'unmistakable'. 'Perhaps,' thought the Countess, 'the fate of the trial rested with the lieutenant.'[19]

The Queen's hopes now rested on another navy man, and a former protégé, Joseph Hownam. Hownam's father had worked for both Caroline and Princess Charlotte, and Joseph owed his education and his naval rank to Caroline's interventions. Furthermore, at Jerusalem, she had made him a 'Knight of the Order of St Caroline'. He had lived with her from April 1815 to April 1818 and his knowledge of her lifestyle was extensive. He had often found the Queen's manner exasperating, and he loathed Pergami; nevertheless, he was fond of her, was loyal and, despite recent illness, was anxious to be of service in her hour of need.

He began well enough, asserting that at various locations, including the Villa d'Este, the bedrooms of the Queen and Pergami were not near to each other. He described Caroline's informal way of interacting with her servants when travelling, recalling that at Ephesus she had slept under a makeshift wooden roof with members of her entourage, including himself, sleeping all around. He confirmed that on her celebrated journey to Jerusalem Caroline had ridden by night on an ass and rested under a tent during the day. To travel by mule or ass was perfectly usual in that part of the world, he said, and after a long night's journey the Queen had become so fatigued that, more than once, she fell off.

He had been on board the polacca and said that during the return journey from Jaffa to Italy at the height of summer, the weather had been excessively hot. Conditions on board were made more uncomfortable still by the smell and noise of the horses and asses that were kept in the hold. He confirmed that Caroline had slept under a tent on deck, and said that a sofa and a travelling bed were placed inside the tent. He knew that the Queen had slept on the sofa but did not know who, if anyone, had slept on the travelling bed.

He believed that the Queen had slept in her clothes, because he had never seen any bedclothes upon the sofa. On one occasion a squall had caused the sea to spill over the side of the ship, and Caroline had decided to move from her tent to a cabin to sleep. When she was escorted down below by Pergami and Mr Flynn, he had seen that the

Queen and Pergami were both dressed. He had never seen her sitting upon a gun with Pergami, and had never seen any 'impropriety or indecency of behaviour of the one towards the other'. As for Mahomet's dance, it was no more improper than 'the Spanish bolero or the Negro dance'.

Hownam was then cross-examined by Robert Gifford. The interrogation turned to the polacca, and the subject of the tent:

Do you know who was under the tent . . . ?
Her Royal Highness the Princess.
Any other person?
I do not know, for I did not see anybody.
Was it dark?
It was dark.
Did you see the Princess?
I did not.
Did you see Pergami anywhere?
I did not.
. . . You have said that you do not know where Pergami slept; upon your oath, do not you believe he slept under the tent?
I have heard he did sleep under the tent.
I do not wish to know what you have heard.
And I believe he did sleep under the tent.
. . . Believing that, do you think that degrading or not to her Royal Highness?
No, I think it was necessary that somebody should sleep near her Royal Highness on deck on that occasion; I have heard that [other] people have slept there too.
You are not asked as to hearing what other people have done, but whether your belief that Pergami slept under the tent with her Royal Highness was or was not a matter degrading to her Royal Highness's station?
No, I do not think it was.

Caroline, he said, had wanted a male servant to sleep in the tent with her for safety reasons. Pirate ships had been spotted during the voyage, but Hownam admitted that he knew of no immediate danger.

Hownam's admission that Caroline and Pergami had both slept under the tent marked the climax of the trial so far. As an Englishman and a defence witness his words held a thousand times more weight than the allegations of foreigners speaking for the prosecution. 'By Jove, my dear,' Creevey wrote to Miss Ord, 'we are coming to critical times such as no man can tell the consequences of.' All society, he observed, judged that the Lords would pass the Bill 'upon the sole point of the Queen being admitted to have slept under the tent on board the polacca, while Pergami slept there likewise . . . I predict with the most perfect confidence that commotion and bloodshed must follow this enormous act of injustice'. His personal view was that the Lords would not be so bold, but he acknowledged that his was a minority voice.[20]

Henry Brougham, he reported, was making all sorts of threats to ensure that the Queen would win the case, despite the incriminating testimonies of Flynn and Hownam. He threatened to call to the witness stand such great names as the Duchess of Beaufort, Lady Harrowby and Lady Bathurst, as well as their husbands, to show that they were all great friends with the Queen '*till the Regency*'. That is, until her husband's dominance in society was too great to be resisted.

'He means too that the Queen shall bring down a statement of all her sufferings,' wrote Creevey, 'and of everything relating to the royal family, from her arrival in England.' That, presumably, would include details of all George's affairs from Lady Jersey onwards, and of his earlier illicit marriage to Maria Fitzherbert. At one o'clock on Thursday 12 October, Creevey wrote to inform Miss Ord that Brougham was now copying out the Queen's statement 'and she is to come down and deliver it to the Chancellor to be read before the Bill passes. Brougham says everything that has happened yet is absolutely nothing in effect compared with what this statement will do'.[21]

While the drama being played out in the Lords during the Queen's defence was sensational, it was matched by events in the kingdom, and particularly in the capital. On Wednesday 11 October, a mass procession of the people bearing Addresses to the Queen took place, packing the road all the way from Hyde Park Corner to Hammersmith. The Addresses came from Holborn, Croydon, Wandsworth, Limehouse, Farringdon, and Christchurch in Surrey. They also came from further afield – from Winchester, Oxford, St Ives, Hereford, Stockton-on-Tees, Cardiff, Leicester, Taunton, Truro, Sedgeley, Kendal, Ambleside, Leeds, Glasgow, Perth and many other towns.

The first Address to arrive at Brandenburgh House was from the inhabitants of the parish of St Abbot's in Kensington. The procession for this one Address consisted of forty-two carriages, chiefly filled with 'ladies of the first respectability'. Caroline's early biographer, Robert Huish, wrote in memoirs published in the year after the trial: 'They [the ladies] were elegantly dressed in white, and wore her Majesty's medals suspended from their necklaces. The Queen was in excellent health, and received the deputation in her usual gracious and condescending manner. Her Majesty wore a dress of black silk and spangled velvet, trimmed with roses, under a dress of crape.'[22]

The radical MP Joseph Hume presented the addresses from Scotland (the Glasgow address alone bore around 37,000 signatures). Major John Cartwright, provocatively dressed in the full regimental uniform of the Nottingham militia, was also prominent that day, and presented Addresses from the ladies of Manchester, and from the inhabitants of Leeds and Hinckley in Leicestershire. At half past two the deputation from the ward of Portsoken arrived. 'The gentlemen who composed it filled 35 coaches and four,' wrote Huish. 'The postilions were in new pink dresses with white hats and cockades.' Other deputations were equally colourful. The ladies and gentlemen of St Ann's in Limehouse arrived 'in open landaus and four' wearing white favours, while the postilions were dressed in crimson jackets. The crowds were so great that, according to the Queenite Huish, there was never a moment when fewer than 10,000 people were crammed into the avenue of Brandenburgh House.[23] The Queen stood to receive her followers throughout the day, with Lady Anne Hamilton and Anne Damer in attendance.

The public theatre of the Queen's trial was, appropriately enough, also being played out at Covent Garden, where Shakespeare's

Cymbeline was being staged. In the second act Iachimo tries to convince Posthumus of Imogen's infidelity by producing one of her bracelets. The husband is staggered, but is reassured by a friend:

> Have patience, Sir;
> It may be probable she lost it; or
> Who knows if one of her women, being corrupted,
> Hath not stolen it from her?

The audience let out 'the most vehement applause' at the clear parallel with Caroline and Demont, and did so again in the following act with the reference to a 'false Italian, as poisonous tongued as handed' who had betrayed Imogen. But the greatest and longest cheers came in the final act, as the lying Italian is penitent and proclaims:

> The heaviness of guilt within my bosom
> Takes off my manhood: I have belied a lady,
> The princess of this country.[24]

Perhaps encouraged by the public mood, or perhaps as a desperate measure, Henry Brougham now joined the country in attacking the King and ministers as never before. From here on, the defence case was based on crying foul about the prosecution's methods of obtaining evidence, rather than defending Caroline against the charges. Countess Lieven, as astute as ever, wrote to Metternich: 'The Queen's counsel is now hoping to carry the war into the enemy's camp; and instead of trying her, they are hoping to try the Commission of Milan. If Brougham succeeds in bringing it off, it will be a smart move.'[25]

The Queen did not deliver the statement that Brougham had threatened. Perhaps this was because the events in the House of Lords once again took a dramatic turn. Under examination a defence witness, the Italian artisan Giuseppe Giaroline, said that he had done building work on the Villa d'Este and had been owed a considerable amount of money by Caroline. He had gone to see Giuseppe Restelli, the head superintendent of the stables, about payment, and Restelli had told

Giaroline to send the account to him 'and he would contrive to see me paid'.

The amount in question was 455,000 livres (or lira). Giaroline was asked:

What did Restelli say you were to do for that?
He told me that if I had anything to say against her Royal Highness (for I had been a long time in her service) to tell him, and he would endeavour to make me be paid.

This was the clearest testimony thus far that attempts had been made to bribe the prosecution witnesses. The Whig Lords now weighed in behind the Queen, making it clear for the first time that their disgust with the Bill was unequivocal. The Earl of Caernarvon began with one of the strongest speeches of the entire trial, urging the peers not to proceed one step further in this 'odious, detested, and infamous proceeding, without inquiring whether the agency which procured evidence was or was not an active subornation of perjury'. If the Milan Commission had bribed witnesses to lie, he said, then not a moment should be lost 'in rescuing this country from the greatest curse which either the folly or the wickedness of men had ever inflicted on a nation'.

Caernarvon was sure the Bill had excited feelings that could never be excited in England, or indeed in any other country, 'without the utmost danger'. Public feeling was so powerful, and so much was at risk including 'the foundations of all our institutions, the venerable bulwarks of order, justice and religion'. If the prosecution witnesses had been tampered with, then this Bill would 'like a mill-stone, drag them [the Lords] down to destruction and with them every sacred and valuable institution in the country'.

Thomas Creevey thought this a 'most capital speech'. But it did not stop their Lordships from proceeding further. Under further examination Giaroline gave more damning revelations about Restelli's activities. He said Restelli had gone about Italy looking for witnesses, and when he found any he would ask them if they knew others. Once he had rounded the witnesses up, he had taken them to Milan, put them up at an inn where they were to be given 'everything they wanted for their victuals' and, most damningly, paid them forty francs each.

The defence team realised that at last it had found firm evidence of corruption. Finally, to use a modern term, there was a smoking gun. Henry Brougham rose to ask whether Restelli could be brought before the Lords for further interrogation. No answer came, and Brougham asked, 'Is he here? Is he in this country?' But, again there was no answer. So Brougham said, 'My Lords, I wish Restelli to be called.' The Attorney General this time responded with, 'If my learned friend wishes to call Restelli, he certainly can call him.'

'I wish to know,' Brougham came back, 'if Restelli is in the country, and if in the country where he is?'

'Whether Restelli is in the country or not,' answered Robert Gifford, 'my learned friend must take the ordinary means to procure his attendance.'

The Lord Chancellor intervened: 'Mr Attorney, is Restelli here?'

'No!' came the reply 'He is sent to Milan.'

'I wish to know,' said Brougham, 'whether under these circumstances, after it is made known to your Lordships that this individual whose conduct has been so strongly implicated, has been sent out to Milan – I say, my Lords, I wish to know whether I am to be obliged to go on with this Bill?'

Gifford said that if Brougham had intended to cross-examine Restelli in the course of the defence it was 'his duty to have communicated the fact', or to have obtained from the Lords an order requiring his attendance. If Restelli was his learned friend's witness 'he must procure his attendance as he could'.

Brougham's thundering response was that his learned friend or his instructors (but who those instructors were nobody knew, though everybody saw that they were very active) must have seen that he had laid a foundation for contradicting the whole of Restelli's evidence. It was their duty to have kept Restelli in this country. But if there was anything which they ought not to have done, it was to 'send Restelli out as the agent of this . . . Milan Commission'.

Gifford argued back, claiming that Restelli had been sent to Milan to calm the anxieties of the relatives of the Italian witnesses, who feared for their safety because of the earlier ructions at Dover. Brougham retaliated. If the witnesses could leave England at will, he argued, then perjury might be committed in the Lords 'with impunity'. Again he asked whether he was obliged to go on with the case.

Lord Holland now rose and asked that counsel withdraw. The sending away of Restelli, he thought, was abominable, and the proceedings had become 'a mockery and a burlesque'. The institutions of the country, he said, could be in 'the utmost jeopardy and danger'. Right now, he thought, there was a prima facie case for conspiracy to pervert the course of justice and the peers would 'do well to get rid of the disgust and fatigue of this infamous proceeding'.

Earl Grey, the leader of the Whigs in the Lords, had until this moment stayed virtually silent. But now he informed the House that it was essential for the defence's case that it recall Restelli, to establish that witnesses had been bribed. And yet it could not, as Restelli was in Italy. In what situation was the Queen placed? Her Majesty's counsel had trusted in Lord Liverpool's assurance that witnesses would be kept in the country – but now it was impossible that she could receive justice. The Bill, he concluded, should be abandoned.

Lord Liverpool rose. Even if the Milan Commission had acted improperly, he said, there was still plenty of evidence before the Lords upon which her Majesty might be found guilty – evidence that did not come from Milan, and not from any of the witnesses who had been secured by Restelli. (Thomas Creevey took this to mean that *all the Italian evidence* is to be flung overboard – so much for the Milan Commission!')[26] There was no question whether substantial justice could be done, Liverpool continued. It was quite clear that it could.

The House was divided and the Milan Commissioner John Powell was called to give evidence. He said that he had told Restelli to return to England by 3 October (it was now the 13th), but claimed that the Italian courier had been too ill to travel. The Lord Chancellor then asked the defence counsel whether they had any questions for Powell.

Brougham replied: 'My Lords, I wish to ask the question "Who is your client or employer in this case?"' Cries went up of 'Order! Order!' and the witness was instructed to withdraw.

But Brougham ploughed on. He was, he claimed, disadvantaged by lack of knowledge of the identity of the person bringing the case against the Queen. If only he knew who that person was, he argued disingenuously: 'I [could] bring forwards a mass of evidence furnished by himself – namely, speeches, declarations, and acts of that opposite party.' As things stand he could not fix 'this interesting unknown', this 'undiscovered being' with any character. 'I know nothing about this shrouded, this mysterious being,' he continued, 'this retiring phantom – this uncertain shape . . . I am to be met at every turn . . . by not being able to put a single question to this visionary personage. I am to pursue this shape.' The King was never to forgive Brougham for the 'uncertain shape' image, taking it as a reference to his size.

The Lord Chancellor interjected to tell Brougham that his question was inadmissible. It now fell upon Brougham to decide whether he was prepared to go on with the defence case while Restelli was out of the country, or to accept that the trial should be delayed until he was brought back. Brougham decided to continue and summoned Filippo Pomi, a carpenter, who stated that Restelli had given him a 'present' of forty francs and had 'told me that if I had anything to say against her Royal Highness I should receive a great present'. However, 'I said that I had nothing to depose against her Royal Highness, and that I had nothing to speak but well of her.'

At this point of the trial the defence lawyers began, in earnest, to try to establish the existence of a conspiracy against the Queen. They put questions to Pomi about the activities of a man named Riganti who, they asserted, was a friend of Restelli and who, like him, had scoured northern Italy for witnesses who could be bribed to give damning evidence. However, each time a question was put the prosecution lawyers objected – and the proceedings became bogged down in hours of legal argument. Brougham, Denman and Lushington asserted their right to go on the offensive and to interrogate the means by which the evidence had reached the Lords, while Gifford and Copley argued that the defence strategy was a digression and not admissible. The defence's approach, argued Copley, would lead 'to endless collateral inquiries and irrelevant charges'.

On 18 October, Lord Grey once again entered the debate. The Queen's case, he said, should not be governed by the rules of evidence in civil cases, as the prosecution was arguing. This was a criminal case 'of the highest kind' and the Queen should have the benefit of the high degree of proof required in a capital case. Their Lordships should not 'shut their eyes' to evidence of 'a foul and wicked conspiracy'.

The Prime Minister, Lord Liverpool, responded. The problem, he said, did not arise from the suggestion that witnesses had been bribed, but from the accusation that a wider level of corruption had taken place, a conspiracy involving people not appearing before their Lordships, including Riganti. To become entangled in such an investigation would mean calling more witnesses, including members of the Milan Commission, who had a right to defend themselves of such charges. This would lead the House 'into an inquiry that he could not regard as relevant to the matter now at issue'.

Lord Erskine, now rose. Erskine's contribution to the debate carried great weight, not just because of his seniority, but also because this former Lord Chancellor was attending the trial when he might have been excused on account of his age. He now disagreed with Liverpool and supported Grey, and in doing so made himself a people's hero. Erskine thought it strange that the House had decided that it was bound by no technical rules, and yet was contemplating the exclusion of particular testimonies favourable to the defence. 'All the disadvantages' of the proceedings, he thought, were unjustly 'thrust upon the Queen'. If there had been a conspiracy, he continued, it was the duty of the Lords to get to the bottom of it; to trace it to its source. Restelli's attempt to corrupt witnesses, he added, was 'unexampled in the history of jurisprudence'. He felt perfectly sure that if the Prime Minister had known at the beginning of the trial 'what he knows now' he would never have gone ahead with the prosecution.

The debate exhausted itself without coming to a conclusion, and the trial continued. The next witness of substance was Caroline's friend Colonel Alessandro Oliveri, a revolutionary and democrat who had fought in Napoleon's army before becoming her co-Chamberlain in November 1818. He had worked alongside Pergami for a year. Oliveri said he had never seen anything improper or indecorous in Pergami's conduct towards the Queen. Carlo Vassalli, Caroline's equerry, and another soldier, supported Oliveri's evidence. The two men, like others before them, testified that the Queen's modesty had on many occasions been served by the presence of the Countess Oldi. Vassalli also told the peers that he had recently met the Countess Oldi, and that she was now in England.

On 23 October Louise Demont was brought back into the picture. A French milliner by the name of Fanchette Martigner testified that she had known Demont since she was a young girl, and that the Swiss maid had later been her customer. In April 1818, Martigner had spoken with Demont about Caroline's conduct. 'I observed to Madamoiselle Demont that the Princess of Wales was a *femme libertine et galante*,' Martigner said, 'and I said so frankly, for such was my opinion.' But, in replying Demont had 'put herself in a great passion', and said the rumours against the Queen 'were nothing but calumnies invented by her enemies in order to ruin her'.

The defence case was now at its end, and the time had come for the lawyers to sum up. Society plainly felt that the balance of evidence was in the Queen's favour, and many Whig ladies and gentlemen now visited Caroline for the first time since her return to England. The Duke and Duchess of Leinster called on her, as did the Duke and Duchess of Bedford, who lent her their boxes at Covent Garden and Drury Lane. The Duchess of Somerset, the Duke of Norfolk, the Jerseys, Tavistocks, Fitzwilliams and many others also visited. The Whigs were, at last, betting that the Queen would win the case.[27] The Tories, however, were still convinced that she would not.

18

RESOLUTION

'Ten thousand bright swords from their scabbards shall fly
To avenge her foul wrongs,' you would instantly cry;
But hold, pray, good sir, there is no want of swords;
And, thou YOU are not living, no lack of big words.

To 'chivalrous Burke' in *Derry Down Triangle*

I t fell to Thomas Denman to sum up the defence case. The evidence, he said boldly, had satisfied his mind, his colleagues' minds and the 'minds of all the people of England and those too of all the civilised nations in the world' that his illustrious client deserved 'a most complete acquittal' of all the charges which had been made against her.

He drew the Lords' attention to the night at Naples when, according to the Attorney General, the first overt act of 'high treason' had occurred. Gifford had alleged that the Queen had removed William Austin from her bedroom so that the 'act' could take place. But the defence evidence contradicted this, demonstrating that the boy had been dismissed much earlier — and this was 'most properly done', on the advice of Caroline's chamberlain, Keppel Craven. Her second chamberlain, Sir William Gell, had testified that 'no agitation was observed . . . in the Princess's manner, nothing unusual or particular seen in her conduct that night, no oversleeping the following morning'. The evidence against Caroline on these points came from Louise Demont alone, and whenever any other person had been present, her statements had been contradicted. He referred the Lords to the relevant places in the minutes, which now ran to more than 500 pages, so that they could check the facts for themselves.

Louise Demont had also said she had seen 'remarkable appearances on the counterpane' but was it not strange that she revealed such 'unquestionable proofs of the criminality' on the part of the Queen only on the third or fourth day of giving evidence and under cross-examination by the defence? If the Attorney General had known his witness had seen such 'proof', why had he not asked her about it in the opening examination? And if Demont had seen stains on the bed, surely Caroline's other chambermaid, Annette Preising, would also have seen stains? But this chambermaid was never produced by the prosecution. Why not? Would the agents of the prosecution who had 'ransacked filthy clothes-bags, who had raked into every sewer, pried into every water-closet, who attempted to destroy all the secrecies of private life'; would these people have 'stopped short at producing such a witness as Annette Preising if they thought she would have borne out the testimony of Demont?' No. Of course not.

He turned to the 'ball scene' at which Caroline was alleged to have disappeared to an inner room, with Pergami, to change into an indecent costume. But Demont was, again, the 'sole inventor' of the event; with Keppel Craven and William Gell both testifying as to the falsehood of her account. Demont had said she had seen Pergami in the passage leading to Caroline's bedroom. Pergami was seen out of his room. So what? Surely the Queen could not be plucked from the throne merely because she could not account for Pergami being out of his room at a particular hour. 'The proposition is monstrous.'

Moreover, the testimony of William Carrington and John Whitcomb had *proved* that the whole story of the illicit connection at Naples was the fabrication of Demont. Denman noted that Carrington had embodied 'what foreign writers had said of the English nation – that you might find gentlemen, in the general sense of the word, amongst the lowest classes in it'. He would say of William Carrington that, 'in whatever rank in life he had been placed, nature had made him a gentleman, and that his evidence was placed far out of the reach of all dispute'. Louise Demont's evidence, by contrast, was 'nothing but invention'.

As for the evidence of the 'wretched, discarded servant' Majocchi. Good God! 'If such an account were to be credited, what safety was there for the life or character of the most innocent individual?' The Attorney General in his opening speech had said that *kissing* had been heard after the Queen had passed through this servant's room in search of Pergami. But under examination the witness heard only *whispering*. It was sworn by Majocchi that Pergami had dined with Caroline at Genoa, and every day after. But this evidence had been contradicted by 'three most respectable witnesses' – Dr Holland, Lieutenant Hownam and by Lord Glenbervie. It seemed, then, that Majocchi's evidence was 'palpable perjury'. And his memory proved to be an astonishing thing – so acute on specific times and places and entirely inadequate under cross-examination, when the *non mi ricordos* had been so frequently proffered.

The polacca scene was devoid of any proof of criminal adultery. The Captain of the polacca, Garguilo, had testified for the prosecution. 'Kisses and caresses were spoken to, and really such evidence deserved the pay which had been received for it'. The captain's mate had supported him. But how was it that these two alone should be called to speak to the indecent acts mentioned? The crew was composed of twenty-two persons, and not one of them was produced to confirm the story. He would contend before their Lordships that 'the absence of all that crew was in itself proof of criminality on the part of the prosecution; and was in itself an acquittal of her Majesty'. Moreover, if the Queen really had a passion for Pergami would she have chosen to sleep in a tent on deck rather than in the privacy of a cabin? Remember too, that the whole time that Caroline reposed there she had her clothes on; 'no time was found when the parties were not clothed'.

There had, said Denman, been a 'triumphant echo from all parts of the town' when Lieutenant Hownam had said he believed both Caroline and Pergami had slept under the tent. But the Lieutenant was relying on hearsay. He had only stated what he heard from other persons. 'It was therefore natural to suppose that when the weather was fair her Majesty had her female attendants with her in the tent; but that when any alarm arose in consequence of squally weather or when danger was apprehended from the crew . . . it was likely that she would then be attended by some of the male part of her suite, and more particularly by her chamberlain, whose duty it was to assist and protect her in danger.'

Other parts of the evidence were equally weak. Barbara Kress had seen stains on the bed that were 'wet and white,' but 'this part of her account was left isolated'. The Lords had not been told when these stains had been seen, and other parts of Kress's evidence had been entirely contradicted by Hownam and Vassalli, casting doubt on her entire testimony. Barbara Kress had blushed at giving evidence, but these 'were not the blushes of expiring modesty; no, they were the blushes of expiring truth'. Pietro Cuchi, the innkeeper at Trieste who had spied on Caroline through a hole in the tapestry, had sworn that Caroline stayed at his inn for six days. This was 'most satisfactorily' refuted by Lieutenant Hownam and Count Vassalli, who both testified that the Queen had remained at Trieste for one night only. This amounted to 'downright proof' of Cuchi's perjury. Again, said Denman, there were too few prosecution witnesses. Caroline, in her travels, had stayed at more than fifty inns – but only Cuchi and Kress could be found amongst their staff to testify to 'anything criminal' in the Queen's behaviour.

Sacchi's evidence regarding the touching of each other's private parts inside a moving carriage was no better. Their Lordships could not fail to remember the 'unfeeling coldness with which Sacchi had recited his obscene and filthy tale'. There were four witnesses – Hownam, Vassalli, Olivieri and Forti – who testified that Sacchi could not have ridden alongside Caroline's coach and seen what he professed to have seen. The only witness to support Sacchi was the controversially absent Restelli, who was first engaged as a witness for the prosecution, and then as the prosecutors' courier and agent.

The object of the prosecution, maintained Denman, was to fix a stigma to the Queen. The Attorney General had likened the Barona Pergami to a brothel, but the only witnesses to see any impropriety there were Majocchi and Demont. Their Lordships could not forget the failed attempt to turn Mahomet's antics into a serious charge against the Queen. The 'bloodhounds of scandal' in Milan, he said, had allowed rumours and reports to ripen into 'the most malignant charges'.

He thought that 'no husband of the slightest feeling' would have allowed evidence such as this to be given against his wife 'even if she had deserted his fond and affectionate embraces, much less if he had driven her into guilt by thrusting her from his dwelling'. And he knew of no example in history of a *Christian* king who had thought himself free to divorce his wife when 'his own misconduct in the first instance was the occasion of her fall'.

Denman had, however, found an example in the history of *Imperial Rome* which bore a resemblance to the current proceeding – and that was the case of Nero, who had banished his wife Octavia and put a mistress in her place. Nero had then contrived a conspiracy against Octavia's honour. But the people were 'convinced of her purity' and her return to Rome was 'like a flood. The generous people received her with those feelings which ought to have existed in the heart of her husband.' A second conspiracy was set up against Octavia, and as a result she was convicted and condemned. The only mercy shown her was 'putting an end to her sufferings by poison or the dagger'.

Caroline's experience had been just as terrible. In November 1817, when Charlotte had died, it so happened that every one of the material witnesses for the prosecution was discharged from the services of the Queen. Demont, Majocchi, Sacchi and Restelli had all had their contracts terminated. Now these witnesses were making the Queen the victim of perjury and conspiracy. It was not part of his case to prove a conspiracy, and perhaps he could not prove one. But all that had occurred – 'all the results that arose from the Milan Commission' – amounted to strong grounds for reasoning that a conspiracy existed. And it was certain that efforts had been made to spy on the Queen and to pursue her with fresh calumnies. Baron Ompteda had sat at her table 'at once her guest and her betrayer'.

Their Lordships were now trying 'the highest subject of the realm for the highest crime a subject could commit'. They must not accept 'light evidence' under the supposition that the punishment was light – it was the heaviest that could be inflicted on a Queen. For his part, Denman would rather have seen Caroline tried in a conventional court of law, as Anne Boleyn had been, than under this bizarre act of Parliament. He would much rather have to 'hand her to the scaffold, where she would have to lay her august head upon the block . . . than witness her condemnation under the present charges, which would render her an object indeed of general pity, but of more general scorn', a most 'deplorable instance of degraded rank and ruined character'.

In his concluding remarks Denman dismissed the divorce clause in the Bill out of hand. The mere fact that the crime was supposed to have been committed six years ago ruled out divorce, as did the letter of licence that was written so soon after the marriage. But, he continued, this is a Bill of Pains and Penalties – 'a bill of degradation, dethronement and disgrace'. He was sure that the honour of those present – as peers, as judges and as men – would compel them to take part with 'the oppressed instead of giving the victory to the oppressor!'

Denman had been speaking for ten hours over two days, and he now turned to Shakespeare and Henry V to acknowledge his debt to Henry Brougham: 'We have fought the battles of morality,

Christianity and civilised society throughout the world; and in the language of the dying warrior I may say:

> In this glorious and well-foughten field
> We kept together in our chivalry.'

His final words summoned the spirit of God, and he asked the peers to imitate the wisdom of 'that benignant Being who, in a case like this where innocence is manifest, but when guilt was detected and vice revealed said – "If no accuser can come forward to condemn thee, neither do I condemn thee: go, and sin no more"'.

Thomas Creevey heard the speech and then went to Brooks's club in St James's. 'Denman's last two hours have been *brilliant*,' he wrote to Miss Ord. 'His parallel case of Nero and his wife Octavia was perfect in all its parts . . . I am just going to dinner . . . and then to go and see Cymbeline with him and Brougham.'[1] Lady Cowper thought that 'Denman's speech was very fine', and reported that 'everybody agrees'.[2] Wellington's dear friend, Mrs Arbuthnot, though, was a rare dissenter. She did not approve of the way in which Denman was 'violently abusive' of the King, nor of his Nero comparison. As for his final quotation from scripture, using the words 'of Our Saviour to the woman taken in adultery – Go thou and sin no more, was certainly strangely indiscreet'.[3] This was, indeed, widely seen as comical and made its way on to the streets via the press in the form of a verse:

> Most Gracious Queen, we thee implore
> To go away, and sin no more;
> But if the effort prove too great,
> To go away at any rate.[4]

Stephen Lushington next made a speech which put more emphasis than Denman's on the unreasonable expectation of George that Parliament would grant him a divorce. He could find no precedent in modern times where a husband had accused a wife of fifty years of age of committing adultery. Indeed, he could not find an instance in which the wife was forty-five. 'But whoever imagined a case like the present?' Here were a husband and wife who had been separated for twenty-four years by *his* own act and choice. As a husband, the King had no right to seek redress. Lushington told the peers that (contrary to the private briefings given by Brougham) the defence would not 'say one word by way of recrimination'. Thus, he said, he would save the House and the country from 'all its consequences'. Instead he would rely on the 'perfect innocence' of the Queen, and observed that 'the laws of God and of the country are on her side'.

He listed twelve witnesses who had seen no impropriety by the Queen or Pergami, including Lord Guilford, Lord Glenbervie, Keppel Craven, William Gell, Dr Holland and John Sicard. William Gell in his three months with Caroline had only ever seen her talk to Pergami on matters of business. John Sicard, meanwhile, had been asked about the Queen's manner towards her servants, and had replied 'uncommon kind, almost to a fault'. How sad it was that the Queen's kindness was 'at last charged against her in order to destroy her'.

The defence, he said, would be criticised for not producing witnesses such as William Austin, the Countess of Oldi and Mariette, the sister of Demont (he did not mention Pergami himself). But, he argued, there was no need to subject these people to the 'merciless fangs of such a cross-examination as Carlo Forti and some of the Queen's witnesses had undergone', as the prosecution case had fallen apart anyway – both Lushington and Denman repeatedly portrayed the Solicitor General, John Copley, as mean and bloodthirsty in attack. Instead, a 'false, foul, dark and malignant conspiracy' had been exposed; and the Milan Commission had been shown not to be investigating the guilt or innocence of the Queen but only to be amassing testimony against her.

The Attorney General, Robert Gifford, now had his chance to respond. Unlimited funds had been granted for the Queen's defence, he said, and he noted the 'extraordinary talents' of the defence lawyers who had argued her case (this was directed mainly at Brougham – who had been at the peak of his powers throughout). However, if their Lordships believed the witnesses, then they must accept that the prosecution had made its case. The defence team had merely put undue focus on contradictions in minor facts, to divert the gaze from major ones.

On William Austin being sent out of Caroline's room in Naples, John Sicard — a *defence* witness — had in effect corroborated Louise Demont, by acknowledging that Austin *was* sent away. There was no other witness who could say why Austin was dismissed from the Queen's bedroom, or exactly when. The defence could have called one of Caroline's closest and most faithful servants, Hieronymous, but did not. Why? Perhaps because Hieronymous took the instruction about Austin's sleeping arrangements directly from his mistress, and would have been compromised if he had taken the witness stand. Also, despite the defence team's belittling of Louise Demont's sighting of Pergami in the passage at night, 'in a state of undress' and 'approaching the chamber of her Royal Highness' — this was 'an undeniable proof of her Majesty's guilt'.

Majocchi, it will be remembered, had seen Caroline passing through his own sleeping 'cabinet' on her way to Pergami's room and 'whether adultery took place that night or not, I care not', said Gifford, '[as] this is satisfactory proof that adultery, if not committed on that night, had previously taken place, because no woman who had not had a previous illicit intercourse with that man would have ventured . . . to go into his room while he was in bed'. Demont and Majocchi had both testified that at Genoa Caroline and Pergami breakfasted together. The defence could have challenged this evidence by calling Bartolomeo Pergami's brother Louis to give evidence — but they had declined to do so. He urged their Lordships to vote for the Bill.

The peers were now collecting their thoughts for the great decision ahead and according to Countess Lieven: 'Among other methods of arriving at the requisite frame of mind, a large party of them have just gone gadding off to Newmarket.' Others were putting money not on horses, but on the outcome of the trial. 'Today the English have a grand opportunity to gratify their passion for betting,' Countess Lieven wrote to Metternich. 'The odds are that the Bill will not pass.

It will be decided in a few days; the first debate . . . will give one an idea of what is going to happen to the Bill. I am as anxious about it as any Englishwoman. They say that the Queen is in a pitiful state of nerves. Really, I am soft-hearted enough to feel sorry for the woman.'[5]

The moment had now come for Charles, Earl Grey to speak for the Whigs. The Bill of Pains and Penalties was so 'remote from ordinary practice' of law, he said, that it could be justified only by a 'great, paramount and pressing public interest'. But there was none. On the contrary, the whole force of the government was 'drawn out in array against the accused'. And if the Bill was passed in the House of Lords, then she would be tried all over again in the House of Commons, with the government having the opportunity of 'mending the case against her' in the meantime by amassing new evidence to fill any holes. If the Commons came to a different conclusion from the Lords, the result could be catastrophic. 'In the present temper and situation of the country,' he continued, 'I could hardly imagine anything more dreadful.'

However, he would not vote against the Bill on those grounds – but on the evidence alone. The choice, though he did not like it, was 'either to affix a punishing on the Queen, or to suffer her to sit upon the throne, tainted and blasted by the odious charges'. He interpreted those charges to go beyond simple adultery. To be consistent with the wording of the Bill, the Queen's acts must have amounted to 'gross, scandalous and licentious conduct' which had brought dishonour to the country, and threatened the dignity of the Crown. And to support these charges there had to be 'clear, unequivocal and irresistible proof'.

Grey told the Lords that, given the problems with the rest of the evidence, the prosecution's case was 'reduced to the simple polacca scene'. If the Prime Minister had foreseen this, would he really have gone ahead with the Bill? And were the Lords really 'to consign the Queen of England to infamy and ruin, upon the mere case of what occurred on board the polacca?' It had been argued that such scenes were to be assessed in accordance with the combined (and allegedly damning) weight of the evidence as a whole – taking into account the advancement of Pergami, and the Queen's general informality. He agreed that the 'great favour' Caroline showed Pergami and her 'intimacy' with him were 'deviations from her Royal Highness's rank' — but impropriety was no proof of guilt, especially when it was remembered that 'sovereigns are in situation as much above the rest of mankind as a person on a lofty mountain is above the passenger on the plain beneath him'. It was not surprising, he argued, if they sometimes seemed to lose sight of the gulf that existed between themselves and others of lower rank. Besides, sovereigns had the right to raise individuals from the lowest part of society to 'the most distinguished rank and the finest honour'. Indeed, it was one of the 'noblest points of the British constitution that it placed no bar in the road to promotion before any individual'.

Consider, too, that when Caroline was in Italy she was surrounded by war and convulsions that had 'shaken society from its very basis'. Every day she had seen individuals who had 'been reduced from affluence to poverty' alongside those who had been 'exalted from obscurity to distinction by the appalling events of the French revolution'. She was in a country 'whose very sovereign [Murat] had risen from a situation in life as humble and obscure as that of Pergami'. He thought that the elevation of Pergami was suspicious — but suspicions were not enough to convict the Queen.

The evidence itself was riddled with difficulties. Lord Grey had found six or seven contradictions in Majocchi's testimony, and said that in his view the man was disqualified as a witness. He had noted the 'glee' shown by Majocchi when recounting parts of his evidence and considered him to have a 'malignant spirit' about him. As for Demont, she had been dismissed by Caroline for lying and for the 'improper connexion' between Sacchi and herself. When he considered the combined role of Sacchi and Demont, 'he felt perfectly convinced that those two wretches were at the foot and foundation of the conspiracy which had been unfortunately got up against her Majesty'.

Demont had deposed to the 'gross indecency' of Caroline's dress at Naples, but had been contradicted by both Sir William Gell and

Keppel Craven. Indeed, Gell had shown that her dress was 'quite the reverse of nakedness and indecency'. 'Their Lordships,' he continued, 'if they looked to the dress of some of their own wives and daughters, would find that their dresses, in the vagaries of modern fashions, had often led to much more shameful and indelicate exhibitions than that upon which, as a foundation, the whole fabric of this abominable conspiracy has been built.'

Thomas Creevey thought that Lord Grey's speech was 'quite of the highest order – beautiful – magnificent – all honor and right feeling, with the most powerful argument into the bargain. There is nothing approaching this damned fellow in the kingdom, when he mounts his best horse.'[6]

The time was now approaching for the Lords to vote – and the feverish atmosphere 'out of doors' was unabated. John Cam Hobhouse took part in a procession of fifty carriages of Addresses to the Queen which rode out to Brandenburgh House on 25 October. The following day Creevey expressed his anxiety at the great demonstrations. 'Every Wednesday the scene which caused such alarm at Manchester [Peterloo] is repeated under the very nose of Parliament,' he wrote, 'and in a tenfold degree more alarming. A certain number of regiments of the efficient population of the town march on each of these days in a regular lock step, four or five abreast – banners flying – music playing . . . I should like anyone to tell me what is to come next if this organised army loses its temper.'[7]

It is possible that Caroline herself was having similar concerns. John Cam Hobhouse recorded in his diary a conversation that he had with the Queen on the twenty-fifth. He told her that he wondered about the propriety of her receiving any more Addresses in person. '"You think so," said she – "so do I. We had better leave off whilst we are well – we must not keep squeezing the orange till all the juice is out – do pray speak to Mr Wood about this."' 'I told the Queen,' wrote Hobhouse, 'that it would be necessary to keep her counsel on this subject, that there were a certain set of men who thought they never could have enough of a good thing and who were very jealous of any prudent advice given to her Majesty.' I said this pointing to

Cartwright. '"Oh – I understand you," she said. "Yes, he would go on to the day of judgement."'

He told the Queen that he had heard that the Bill would not pass in the Lords – but that there would be a censure of her. 'She snapped her fingers and said – *that for their answer*.' She then asked Hobhouse for his opinion on what the Commons would do. His answer was, 'Any dirty thing they were desired by Castlereagh.' 'I quite agree with you,' she replied. 'Some about me tell me otherwise, but I think as you do.'[8]

As a radical, Hobhouse was worried that the constant displays of support for the Queen would play themselves out and that 'after a certain time all exhibition became futile and ridiculous'. After speaking with Caroline he was approached by her speech-writer Robert Fellowes, who said that he 'very much wished to speak to me as to the manner in which some use might be made of public feeling'. Hobhouse replied that 'the great thing now was to take care not to exhaust it'. Fellowes agreed, and said he 'had often told *Wood so*, but that he was a vain man and liked the continuation of the shows'.[9]

If political activists wished for the hysteria to subside while they marshalled the forces of radicalism, the pressmen had a different idea. On the morning of 6 November – the day that the Lords were to vote – *The Times* put the Queen's affairs on the front page, which usually held nothing but advertisements, and inside carried a long and emotive editorial – the first sentence of which reminded readers that this was the third anniversary of the death of the lamented Princess Charlotte, the daughter of our 'ill-fated' Queen, and the rest of which was a eulogy to the public and public opinion. At first, proclaimed *The Times*, the prosecutors of the Queen had denied that the people were with her: 'the myriads upon myriads, we may say the accumulated millions, who addressed her, were called the mob, the rabble, a "herd of rude mechanicals"'. But now it was acknowledged that 'all the world' – the minds of Britain, Europe and America – had decided that the Queen was innocent. It was with 'infinite pleasure' that *The Times* had heard the part of Lord Grey's speech which 'deprecated the practice of drawing an odious line of distinction between the different gradations in society' and the habit of calling the lower classes by insulting names. The newspaper was not radical, but it believed that in 'moments of effervescence' it was vital that Britain's rulers kept their 'hold upon the public sentiment'. If they lost it they must be 'ready to regain it, for their own good, and the good of the state, by acts of condescension and expressions of sympathy'. The language of *The Times* was self-confident and imbued with a sense of its own power. In short, it was informing the Lords that if they did not follow public opinion and the press, the forces of hell would rain down on them.

The vote on the Bill of Pains and Penalties in its entirety, with the divorce clause intact, was taken at three o'clock that afternoon. Each peer said aloud 'content' or 'not content'. One hundred and twenty-three of the Lords voted for the Bill and ninety-five against – giving a majority of only twenty-eight, too slight to give the government any confidence in the Bill being passed in the Commons. Thomas Creevey noted: 'This is fatal. Eleven bishops voted for it, and the Archbishop of York alone against it.'[10] The majority of the clergymen had apparently decided that the Bill must succeed for the sake of the morals of the country, while those peers who voted *against* the Bill, according to Countess Lieven, included 'all the greatest, richest and most respectable members', the Whigs and others who opposed the Whigs, alongside 'others whose positions and fortunes are dependent on the goodwill of the Government'. En masse, she thought, this was 'an imposing and alarming body for the Ministry to have to face'.[11]

As the majority was so slim, the House of Lords next debated dropping the divorce clause – but not before a statement from the Queen was read out. If the Bill did not reach the House of Commons, she stated, she would 'make no reference whatever to the treatment experienced by her during the last twenty-five years'. Thus she raised one more time the familiar threat of recrimination, and fed the constant rumours that she was about to make public devastating and intimate revelations about George.

On 7 November the divorce clause debate began, and the Archbishop of York declared himself in favour of dropping it: 'I must look on the word of God, and on that only, as the guide of my conduct.' In his speech he also revealed that the previous day he had voted against the Bill only as a legislator; had he been deciding in a 'purely judicial character' he would have declared the Queen guilty. The Bishop of Chester, by contrast, had voted for the Bill although he thought the Queen not guilty of adultery – and had done so because he had understood that the divorce clause would be dropped. The Archbishop of Canterbury took a third line, and spoke against drop- ping the divorce clause, since adultery, in his view, *had* been established. The Bishop of London agreed that the divorce clause should be retained 'on religious, moral and constitutional grounds'.

Lord King, who disliked the Church, now observed that its opinions were not convincing nor enlightened and went on to tell the House that many years ago when the Queen had lived at Blackheath she was appar- ently guilty of indecorum not with Pergami but with the Prime Minister, Lord Liverpool, and had also played blind man's buff with the Chancellor of the Exchequer. These were, he said, 'extraordinary and indecent proceedings'. Lord Liverpool barked: 'They never took place!' And Lord King replied that while he could not remember the exact dates of the incidents, it must have been before the Regency when the noble Lord was 'out of place and looking for means to get into office'.

Lord Grey raised the tone. He would vote for the retention of the divorce clause, he said, as the Bill must either stand as a whole or not at all. Lord Holland consolidated the Whig view, saying that he too would vote for the inclusion of the clause in order to make it more likely that the Bill, as a whole, would fail. This tactical position of the Whigs produced an unholy alliance of Whigs and bishops, who were able to ensure that the divorce clause remained. On 10 November the Bill of Pains and Penalties was read again. Thomas Creevey reported that this time the King's brother, the Duke of Clarence, when his name was called, 'leaned over the rail of the gallery as far into the House as he could, and then halloed "Content," with a yell that would quite have become a savage. The Duke of York then followed with his "Content" delivered with singular propriety.'[12] The vote, in the end, was carried by 108 votes to 99 – a majority of only 9.

Lord Liverpool rose. According to Mrs Arbuthnot the Prime

Minister had endured a terrible night arguing with the rest of the Cabinet, three-quarters of whom now wished the Bill to be withdrawn. He 'was in a phrenzy', she wrote, 'and his rage got so high that for a time it stopped all deliberation'. He lashed out at his colleagues, and 'ended by crying'.[13] Now Liverpool solemnly declared before the peers that in the present state of the country, and with the votes so close, the government had decided not to proceed with the Bill. As Cobbett put it: 'Though they voted her guilty three times, they flinched when they came to the point which must have brought them to an open contest with the people.'[14]

At the time of the announcement Caroline was in a private room at the House of Lords awaiting the result. She is said to have wept when Brougham arrived with the news of her 'acquittal' and to have proclaimed herself 'Regina still, in spite of them!'[15] She was then hurried out of the building, and driven away to the huzzahs of an immense crowd that followed her, and which quickly filled the whole of central London. The abandonment of the Bill was seen by the mass of the people as the Queen's triumph over the government and, more thrilling still, the victory of the people. 'The state of the town is beyond everything,' wrote Creevey. There was no business that day in the City, and everywhere people called out 'God save the Queen!' and 'Long live Queen Caroline!' and paraded banners insulting to Liverpool, John Leach, Demont and Majocchi. Others were embroidered with the words: 'The Queen's guards are the people', 'Vindicated Innocence', and '*Non mi ricordo*'. The Green Bag was the preferred symbol of government corruption.[16]

Lords Liverpool and Sidmouth took the news to the King. Liverpool then left, but George asked Sidmouth, the only Cabinet member whom he regarded as a friend, to stay behind. The King confided that 'his body, his nerves and his spirits' were 'so shattered that he was unfit to cope with the difficulties of his station', and told his Home Secretary of his 'serious thoughts' of retiring to Hanover. He would, he said, leave the kingdom of Great Britain to his brother the Duke of York.[17] George did not act on his melancholy musings, but remained in poor spirits.

Neither George nor the Tory government realised that the abandonment of the Bill amounted to an escape for them from the fearless intentions of Henry Brougham. His constant threats of 'recrimination' which might plunge the country into 'confusion and conflict' were based on a battle plan that was more aggressive than that supposed by supporters of both the King and Queen; at least this was the claim he made in his memoirs, published fifty years after the trial. Brougham wrote that he had been astonished that everybody had conceived recrimination to be '*all*' that he had intended, should the trial not favour the Queen. If forced, he said, he would have endeavoured to remove the crown from the King, through impeachment. He would have *proved* that George had married Mrs Fitzherbert, and claims that, in law, he would have shown that, since Maria Fitzherbert was a Roman Catholic, George had forfeited his title. He had in his possession, he asserts, a copy of George's will in which he referred to Mrs Fitzherbert as his wife, and he was ready to bring to the witness stand her uncle, Henry Errington, who was present at the marriage. In short, he would have established that 'the King had ceased to be King'. Brougham expresses his customary confidence in his opinion that the law was on his side.[18] In truth, had he ventured this far, the government would have retaliated, arguing that, contrary to Brougham's assertions, George's marriage to Maria Fitzherbert was invalid because it contravened the Royal Settlements Act – a position that Brougham anticipated and was ready to counter.

Whether or not Brougham was right in his legal opinion, his political judgement was acute. Merely to raise the subject of impeachment of the King would have amounted to the release of an incendiary device in the midst of a frenzied political atmosphere. The Caroline crowds might easily have been persuaded to raise their demands from salvation of the Queen to destruction of the King, their position legitimised by the fact that the attack on George came not from the mob but from within the establishment, its origin not on the streets, but within Parliament. Most established politicians of the period were not sufficiently independent from the forces of tradition to initiate such a bomb blast of a proceeding, but Henry Brougham was. His self-belief outweighed his susceptibility to outside political pressure; and when in the grip of a cause, his determination was legendary, as was the manic energy with which he pursued his goals. George and his government would probably have buckled, rather than face Brougham's attack.

On 10 November 1820, though, the nation was focused not on what might have been, but on the reality of the Queen's triumph. That night London was filled with illuminations which outshone those on any other occasion, including Wellington's victory at Waterloo. Cannons and muskets were fired – William Cobbett (who was prone to hyperbole) put the number at 50,000 guns – and the people went 'mad with enthusiasm for the Queen', here and there indulging in 'looting and all kinds of brutality'.[19] Countess Lieven told her servants that they could take off their hats to the Queen as much as they liked, as 'when it is a question of being shot, I submit to the law of force'. Without a military escort, she said, 'the mob is my master'.[20] In several streets witnesses against Caroline, in particular Majocchi and Demont, were burned in effigy and a pub at the corner of Half Moon Street displayed a flag bearing a picture of a gallows with the inscription:

Q. What's that for?
A. *Non mi ricordo.*

A house in Colman Street was adorned with 'a splendid crown of variegated lamps, supported by C. R. under which was a star, then a profusion of lamps and under them the letters B, D, L, the initials of . . . her Majesty's counsel, Brougham, Denman and Lushington'.[21] The club houses of St James's were brilliantly decorated with lamps, but the Guard's mess room was not illuminated. Caroline's son-in-law Prince Leopold had ordered Marlborough House to be lit up with flambeaux. Amongst the displays in Holborn was a transparency bearing the words: 'May the Queen stand like an oak, and may her enemies fall like the leaves.' In Bernard Street a sign was displayed, with the rhyme:

Thus truth will prevail
Where Justice presides,
In spite of Old Bags,
And Green Bags besides.[22]

A party of Horse Guards was paraded in front of Lord Castlereagh's house, and the military was called upon to drive a rampaging mob from the Strand, while another mob of about 600 people went about the Aldgate area smashing the windows of any house that was not illuminated for the Queen.[23] The soldiers attempted to enter the City at Temple Bar, but were prevented from doing so by the gates being shut against them.[24]

Anne Cobbett wrote to her brother James in New York: 'The greatest triumph has been gained by the People of England that ever was gained in this world.' The result of the vote was known at about four o'clock in the afternoon, she told him, and 'in less than half an hour afterwards guns were firing in all directions' and 'the church bells ringing in all parts of the town . . . All the gentlemen's carriages are stopped and abused, unless their servants have white bows in their hats or laurel leaves.' At night the government paraded the military through the streets, 'though they knew they could not trust them', and the soldiers 'actually *cheered* and *waved their caps*' as they passed the house of William Benbow, which was 'one mass of blaze' in celebration of the Queen's victory. 'Papa got a coach,' she wrote:

and took us all through the town . . . to see the illuminations, and the spectacle was fine beyond anything you can imagine. All the ships in the river lighted to the mast-heads, processions marching with bands of music, carrying busts of the Queen with the crown on her head, covered with laurels, playing God save the Queen and bearing torches; altogether the sight was such to overcome one, at the same time that it was most particularly gratifying to *us*.[25]

Over the next five days the offices of those London papers that had supported the ministry against the Queen were torched by the mob, with particular vengeance directed at the *Courier*, where the riot act was read, and the *New Times*, which suffered most by virtue of being in Fleet Street, which was part of the City of London and protected by municipal police rather than the military. (The *Courier* was not cowed by the attack; it still insisted that the Queen had assumed 'the office of first revolutionary leader'.) *The Times*, by contrast, was feted, while bonfires were lit and fireworks set off in St Giles, the location of the fiercely Queenite Catnach and Pitts' presses. William Hone's office was a centre for celebrations, and was decorated with the words 'Triumph of the Press' in lights displayed above a transparency by Cruikshank on the same theme.[26]

Sir Francis Burdett, who had just been released from prison, now proclaimed to his supporters that the ministers 'all deserved to be hanged!' – a view that he also arranged to be published in the newspapers.[27] William Cobbett's son John, meanwhile, wrote that the events amounted to 'almost a Revolution; for the Queen is a Radical, and has consequently joined all together against the Government'. The administration had, he thought, become 'one universally hated monster!' He believed the ministers would resign and be replaced by politicians who would listen to the voice of the people. The masses, he believed, would call first 'for the Trial of the Ministers as Criminals and secondly for Parliamentary Reform'. His sister Anne agreed, adding that 'everybody' credited her father 'the Governor' with the Queen's victory 'solely and undividedly' (this was not true – Matthew Wood, Henry Brougham, Thomas Denman, Lord Grey and others were also heroes of the hour). He would at last, she noted, have his place in Parliament as part of a reforming House of Commons. For the Cobbetts 'the state of things' was 'delightful'.[28]

The euphoria was not limited to London. William Cobbett, with customary aplomb, proclaimed that the celebrations reached 'every cottage in the kingdom, and every little obscure hole or shed in and about great towns'.[29] Manchester, Liverpool, Dublin and Glasgow hosted scenes of great jubilation, and the painter Benjamin Haydon reported that 'Edinburgh was in an uproar'. He had been awakened in the night by a thumping at his door and an instruction 'to light up'.

'I got up, scarce awake,' he noted in his memoirs, 'when bump came a stone against my bedroom window, and tinkle went the falling glass. The shout of the crowd was savage . . . and they battered till there was not a pane left . . . After smashing all the glass right and left of us, the drum beat, and away roared the mob into St Andrew's Square – certainly a more ferocious crowd than a London one.'[30]

The twenty-year-old Thomas Babington Macaulay, who was in Cambridge, wrote to his father on 13 November saying that the 'symptoms of popular violence' had been terrific on the 10th – when a battle broke out between the townspeople and university students who had decided to support the King. Macaulay saw about 'four hundred gownsmen at the scene of the main battle'. But within days the mood, he thought, was benign with '"Thank God the Country is saved!" written in every face and echoed by every voice'.[31] At Gridlington the Tory Lord Kenyon was mistaken for one of the Queen's supporters and the mob attempted to 'draw him through the town' with banners proclaiming 'the Queen and Kenyon for ever!' Nothing, however, could have annoyed him more and 'he was forced to run for it through the town and escape'.[32]

In Royton the Queen's victory was celebrated together with the revolutions in Spain, Portugal and Naples, and toasts were made to more revolutions 'till the whole civilised world has adopted representative governments on the principle of Universal Suffrage', along with toasts to George Washington, Thomas Paine, the navy, the army, the King (that he might 'wrest his prerogative from the grasp of the aristocracy') and the Queen (that she might live to see her persecutors brought to justice).[33] Leeds was illuminated, despite the best efforts of the authorities, as were York, Sheffield, Barnsley, Wakefield, Huddersfield, Skipton, Birmingham, Wigan, Oldham and many other towns.

In Glasgow there was rioting when, according to the pro-government *Glasgow Herald*, the populace 'broke out into acts of outrage, by firing guns and pistols, and carrying along the streets burning tar barrels, at the same time throwing stones and brick-bats against the windows of the principal houses in the different streets'. Similar scenes occurred at Paisley and there were illuminations in Falkirk, Rutherglen, Stewarton and the Glasgow suburbs. Illuminations were also reported at Kilmarnock, Girvan, Kilwinning and Perth. In all, the Scottish press recorded celebrations in more than eighty districts.[34]

The Queenite *Norwich, Yarmouth and Lynn Courier,* meanwhile, reported that illuminations were to be seen all over Norfolk: 'Not a lane, however insignificant and scarcely a court however inaccessible could be found in which the inhabitants did not vie with each other to shew their loyalty . . . and their joy that anarchy, civil war and perhaps even revolution had been averted by the glorious event.'[35] Throughout the celebrations, Addresses continued to arrive at Brandenburgh House from towns including Glastonbury, Colyton, Ramsgate, Truro, Buckland, Wigan, Wokingham, Leigh, Hereford, Monmouth and Irvine. According to the *Traveller* an address was also received from the East Kent Militia.[36]

Throughout the country mobs torched the offices of pro-government newspapers, including the *Macclesfield Courier*, the *Stamford Mercury*, and *Harrop's Manchester Journal*. The editor of the *Chester Courier* was burned in effigy, with his newspaper pinned to his chest.[37] The Queenite press, meanwhile, rejoiced in the triumph of the people over the King and government. The *Traveller* lampooned the ministers for proclaiming that the Caroline demonstrations were merely the work of the 'ruffian mob', and restricted to rare radicalised parts of the population:

> There was scarcely a pretence of any disturbance south of Trent; and it was generally affirmed with joy that, with the exception of Lancashire, part of Yorkshire, the armed population between Tyne and Wear, and the valley of the Clyde, the labouring population of the kingdom, were sound – quite sound; that is to say, perfectly ignorant and perfectly careless about politics. But now we find all the South and West of England under 'the domination of the ruffian mob.' Buckinghamshire, which was always considered as 'sound' as if it had been one great rotten borough, the people are flagitiously joyful at the triumph of the Queen . . . Oxford does not escape the contagion.[38]

The Times, which, through its support of Caroline, was now established as the country's premier newspaper, took the line that was to sustain its position at the heart of British politics for the next two centuries. This was, it proclaimed, the triumph of *public opinion*. 'It is the people who bestow and take away crowns,' it declared, 'not pampered courtiers and factious Ministers of State.' Once again comparing Caroline with Marie Antoinette, the paper boasted that she, unlike the French Queen, had been 'saved by the people'. 'In France . . . the people and the privileged orders were alike corrupt: in England, the people are more pure, more humane, more just, more prudent than their rulers; and those who ought to take the lead in society, are the lowest in intellect or virtue . . . The Revolution had actually begun in England under the auspices of the King's ministers,' it argued, '*and has been stopped by the people!*'[39]

The Times was right. By dropping the Bill the government defused the revolutionary sentiments that had seemed so sinister at the outset of the trial. The Home Secretary, Lord Sidmouth, had believed that convulsion was imminent, and later described Caroline's trial as 'the most formidable crisis' that the country had faced since the Napoleonic wars.[40] But any possibility of bloody revolution had been prevented by the government's defeat and its surrender to the people. For the most part, the mood was one of great celebration, not angry rebellion; and the trial had left much of the populace with a sense of empowerment. Those who did not have the vote had nonetheless compelled the ministers to submit to their will. As the *Traveller* put it, the voice of the people was triumphant: 'The untitled, the unrepresented or inadequately represented people of England, that best security for public liberty operating on the fear of a minister.'[41] This, of course, carried its own implications – the general public had entered the soul of politics as never before. And it was there for good.

Caroline, meanwhile, issued a message to the nation in which she proclaimed that she was 'wholly guiltless of the foul crimes' that had been charged against her by those who had now abandoned them 'in confessed compliance with Public Opinion expressed in the most unequivocal manner'. In private, though, she was feeling exhausted and used by those with political agendas (albeit that she had gone along with them with enthusiasm). 'This business has been more cared for as a political affair, than as the cause of a poor forlorn woman,' she wrote to Charlotte Lindsay. '*Mais n'importe!* I ought to be grateful; and I reflect on these proceedings with astonishment . . . That I should have been saved out of the Philistines' hands is truly a miracle considering the power of my enemies and their chiefs.' She added, somewhat enigmatically, that her foes had 'left undone' some acts that 'could be done to destroy my character for evermore. I could tell you someting – oh! *mein Gott!* Some day I will – but I cannot write them.' She also confessed to feeling 'very unwell, fatigued, and *ebaye*'.[42]

This tiredness was at odds with the public perception of her as a new political force. 'If the Queen has political courage, and will stand her ground, the trouble is only beginning,' Croker wrote in his diary on 13 November. On the following day he learned that Caroline had promised her friends that she would not leave the country. 'If she has strength and courage to push her advantage,' he continued, 'she must turn out the Ministers and may overturn the country, but then she must have a Whig ministry to assist her.'[43] The assessment of whether he was right was to be deferred to 29 November when, it soon became known, the Queen would attend a service of thanksgiving for her deliverance at St Paul's Cathedral – located, by no coincidence, in the City, where her followers were both ardent and powerful, and were led by the former mayor, Matthew Wood.

The Dean of St Paul's was distressed at the foul business of politics being brought into his church and wrote to Sidmouth asking him to prevent the Queen from coming. The reply informed him that such action was 'wholly out of the power of the government'. A further letter from Sidmouth told him that arrangements had been made for 'the most effectual military support to the civil power' to be in place for the occasion. 'Barriers will be erected,' wrote the Home Secretary, and 'other measures of precaution taken to regulate and control the description and number of persons to be admitted into the church and churchyard'. He assured the nervous Dean that both he and his cathedral would be safe.[44]

On the 29th, a great procession made its way from Hammersmith to St Paul's attended by vast crowds. Caroline rode in a state carriage drawn by six chestnut horses and attended by 150 men on horseback and was followed by an 'immense number of carriages of every description, from the barouch to the taxed cart' – many of which became stranded at Hyde Park Corner because of the congestion in Piccadilly. Countess Lieven put the size of the crowds at 50,000 people. Sir Robert Wilson, who rode at the front of the procession, thought almost half a million people had come, and *The Times* thought 'that so numerous a concourse of human beings was never before seen on the face of the earth'.[45] 'It was beautiful, absurd, frightening all at once,' Dorothea Lieven wrote to Metternich. 'Perfect order, enthusiasm and good humour. On the first banner in the procession was written: "The Queen's Guard – the People". You could see nothing but laurels and white ribbons.'[46] The windows of houses along the route were 'thronged with well-dressed females' while the streets were filled with 'spectators of every class'. Hyde Park was packed and the 'shouts, cheers and loud huzzahs which rent the air on every side . . . might have been heard for more than a mile around'. At Ludgate Hill, William Hone displayed a large blue silk flag from his upper windows bearing the words: 'The People'. He and Mrs Hone gave a party that night at which some of the dances and music were specially arranged to celebrate Caroline's 'victory'.[47]

At Temple Bar the Queen was met by the Lord Mayor of London, Sheriffs of London, members of the Common Council and Matthew Wood. Before Caroline arrived at St Paul's a committee of sixty women entered the cathedral, all of them, with two exceptions, dressed in white, 'their hair decorated with white ribands, and white veils hanging gracefully on their shoulders and bosoms'. According to the *Times*' reporter at the scene, 'the effect produced by seeing so many beautiful and elegant females uniformly dressed and seated together was peculiarly striking and pleasing'. As Caroline's carriage drew up, the west centre doors of the cathedral were thrown open and the cheers of the multitude were heard by those inside. Soon after, 'Her Majesty entered the cathedral amidst loud shouts. The west door was then closed and her Majesty advanced.' She had with her Sir Robert Wilson, Joseph Hume, John Cam Hobhouse and Keppel Craven. The aristocracy, however, stayed away. The service proceeded without incident, although the Dean held the view that 'it has been a mockery of religious solemnity at which every serious Christian must shudder'.[48] The chosen psalm was: 'Deliver me, O Jehovah, from the evil man: Preserve me from the violent man'.

The triumphant Queenites were unaware of an encounter in Italy on 16 November, which might have altered the course of the Queen's trial dramatically had it happened a few weeks earlier. A Sicilian cook by the name of Iacinto Greco on that day gave the following statement to the King's agent:

> I was taken into the service of the Princess of Wales on her arrival at Syracuse as Cook. A few days after entering the family, I was, one evening after dinner, passing from the kitchen to the saloon for the purpose of going down the principal staircase to the wood house, when on opening the door which led into the saloon I saw the Princess on the sofa at the further end of the saloon – Pergami was standing between her legs, which were in his arms – his breeches were down and his back towards the door – at which I was. I saw the Princess's thighs quite naked – Pergami was moving backwards and forwards and in the very act with the Princess. Pergami turned round his head – I shut the door and instantly retired – The next day after dinner I was discharged.[49]

This was the evidence of the 'very act' that had been so conspicuously missing from the prosecution evidence. Perhaps Greco, like many of the other witnesses, would have been discredited had he faced Brougham and his team. But perhaps not.

British radical activists, meanwhile, continued to glorify the Queen in order to further their cause. In Newcastle, J. Marshall rushed out a two-sided broadside entitled *The Queen in Danger*, stressing that the people's victory should not give rise to complacency. 'The people or the Radicals . . . have flocked in their millions around their injured, oppressed and insulted Queen,' it declared. But she had been visited by the enemies of reform, who were trying to 'neutralise' her. 'Yes,' it concluded, 'the Queen is still surrounded by perils . . . and nothing can save her from final ruin but the unanimous and zealous exertions of the people.'[50]

And Thomas Wooler, editor of the *Black Dwarf*, published a plea to Caroline to tour the country, taking in Edinburgh, Dublin, York, Manchester, Birmingham and Glasgow. 'Every place would rival London,' he wrote, 'in its affection for a Princess who appeals to the people to vindicate her rights, that they may secure their own!'[51] He, like other radicals, was anxious not to let the Queenite agitation die away. If it was to produce hard results, if the goal of political reform was to be achieved, the momentum had somehow to be maintained.

19

BACKLASH

Every stratagem is used to delude the common and unthinking part of the people into a belief that their only way of displaying loyalty is to display a most servile obsequiousness to the throne, and to oppose every popular measure.

The Spirit of Despotism, ed. William Hone (1821)

The radicals' dreams were not to be realised. Queen Caroline did not go on a nationwide tour but retreated from the political stage, exhausted by her ordeal. During the final stages of the trial she had become weary of the radical cause; and the pronouncements made in her name were less confrontational, less angry at the establishment: 'Let us endeavour,' she implored the artisans of Manchester, 'to calm the perturbed passions and to heal the bleeding wounds of our

distracted and lacerated country.'[1] On 30 October, following her conversation on the subject with John Cam Hobhouse, she declared that
she would receive no more Addresses in person.

And now that she had triumphed over her husband, there was no
further need to ally herself with all the 'oppressed nation'. She had
achieved her ends, and her enthusiasm had gone. Henry Brougham
wrote in his memoirs that 'it was with great difficulty that we could
get her to St Paul's on 29 November'.[2] Cobbett, with his keen nose for
such things, sniffed conspiracy:

> In the month of October the courtiers got about her. Some of the
> peers had defended her with great zeal; these, seeing that she was again
> in the hands of the reformers; knowing the use that they would make
> of her, if she remained in this country, set to work to get her out of the
> hands of the reformers; and they did it very artfully. They knew that
> a very sore place was, with her, *neglect* which she had received at the
> hands of the nobility; and they imagined, and rightly imagined, that
> they could soon bring her back again, by showing her marks of friend-
> ship and respect. The first step was (*when they saw how the trial would
> end!*) to persuade her to soften the asperity of her language *in her
> answers to Addresses*; the next step to place about her, as Chamberlains,
> Craven and Gell, who had been with her on the Continent; the next
> step to induce her to *affront the people*; and lastly, to get her, if possi-
> ble, *out of the country quietly*.[3]

Her victory and her withdrawal left the radicals without the language
of the 'injured wife' and the quest for justice which had been so useful
to them. Their cause was stripped of the rhetorical trappings that the
trial had provided, and denied the urgency and anger that had arisen
from the possibility that the Lords would defy the people and pass the
Bill of Pains and Penalties. Above all, the radicals had lost the imagery
that Caroline had supplied when she paraded herself about London as
the symbol of oppression.

It was as if the ever present chorus in this garish drama was suddenly naked. The radicals were once again the diverse and

quarrelsome band of agitators with a range of political demands, united only in their loathing of the corrupt system. In a sense, this was the showdown. They now had to demonstrate that the extraordinary swell of support shown throughout the summer could be sustained without the Queen, without the trial. The Home Secretary, Lord Sidmouth, thought they would succeed. In December he wrote: 'Should the loyal remain inactive, they will be borne away by the Disaffected.' All depended, he thought, on 'the country gentlemen of England' remaining 'what they are'.[4]

However, the loyalist voice that had been drowned out by the noise of the trial was now, with the encouragement of the ministry, starting to reassert itself. In December a new Sunday paper was launched called *John Bull*, which orchestrated a backlash against the Queen and radicalism. It was founded and edited, anonymously, by a clever and engaging young man of Tory leanings named Theodore Hook. Hook made it his goal to attack the Queen with more wit, and more venom, than any of the pro-government press had so far managed. *John Bull*, he wrote, stood for 'the Truth, and King and Constitution'. It would redress the 'shameful licentiousness of a prostituted Press, the infamous tendency of the caricatures which issue from every sink of vice and infamy in or near the Metropolis . . . the absurd unmeaning addresses to the Queen and the libellous and treasonable answers given to them'.[5]

The first issue, published on 17 December, claimed that the merchant seamen who had that week turned out for the Queen, had 'mustered very scantily, and the thousands expected proved a few hundreds'. Further editions, informed by the King's friends, made a particular point of printing scandal about the ladies who visited Caroline. Of Mrs Brougham, Hook wrote that the newspaper notice of 'her marriage and that of the birth of her child followed one another much more closely than has been usual in *well regulated families*'. Mrs Damer 'has always been strangely susceptible to *the charms of her own sex*'. Lady Jersey came under attack, as, of course, did Caroline – whom Hook accused of having a drink problem. In the pages of *John Bull* the Queen lived at 'Brandyburg House'. Anne Damer and Lady Jersey continued to visit Caroline, but many other aristocratic women did not.[6]

John Bull fared better than any observer of the public mood at the height of the summer of 1820 might have predicted. It, of course, amused those in high society who had, all along, found the Queen a low and vulgar woman. But the note it sounded, so at odds with the great blast of Queenite propaganda, must have had a wider appeal, as the paper's circulation soon reached 9,000–10,000 copies a week, and Hook was delivered from pressing financial difficulties. The King reckoned that 'neither he nor his ministers nor his parliament nor his courts of justice all together had done so much good as *John Bull*'.[7]

At the same time, George's ally, John Wilson Croker, authored a long pamphlet entitled *A Letter from the King to his People*, which set out George's version of the story of his marriage. It was an eloquent, authoritative work professing to put the record straight. The Princess of Wales, it stated, could always have demanded a restitution of her conjugal rights, and in that sense her separation from her husband had never been forced upon her. It was *she* who had turned 'an unhappy but unavoidable domestic occurrence' into a political affair by publishing her letter to the Prince Regent (written by Brougham) of 1813. Her return to Britain in 1820 was, in the wake of the Cato Street conspiracy, calculated to revive 'internal agitation' in the country. And the Queen had then become a 'tool of party'.[8] The letter ran to twenty-three editions or more – and was accompanied by a stream of further loyalist newspapers and pamphlets which attempted to reclaim the language of patriotism for the King and the Tory status quo. The mood was changing. The political landscape was not so dominated by the call for reform, but was now split between reformists and loyalists. The loyalists, doubtless, had always been there. But throughout the trial they had been less vocal and less strident than the Queenites. For the most part, they had remained indoors, while Caroline and the radicals were out of doors, on the streets and in the newspapers, dominating the public space.

Meanwhile, the intense private battle between the King and Queen continued. Caroline demanded a palace and received a rude answer from Lord Liverpool stating that it was not possible for the King to assign her any of the royal residences. He added that Parliament would decide on the amount of future provision she would receive when it next met. Keppel Craven replied on Caroline's behalf complaining that the government's behaviour on these matters was contemptuous towards both Parliament and the nation. He threatened that the Queen would once more use 'the people' to secure her rights. Caroline, he said, 'has the firmest reliance upon their support so long as she is the victim of oppression; and to herself she deems it due to add, that no harassing treatment on the part of the King's Ministers will ever shake the duty she owes to this generous people'.[9]

But, in practice, she had no inclination to reclaim her position as the country's leading radical. Cobbett was probably right – she had decided to negotiate her situation privately, influenced by those who promised her rehabilitation into society. Anne Cobbett described the situation to her brother James. Their father, she said, had become a regular visitor at Brandenburgh House, presenting himself in 'a claret-coloured coat, white waistcoat and silk stockings, dancing pumps and powdered head'. But Caroline was not interested in talking politics. 'The country need not expect much assistance from her,' she told James. 'She likes a game of blind man's buff much better . . . She loves fun to her heart.' The Cobbett family could no longer believe that Caroline's motivation was political. Nonetheless, they were still clinging to the idea that she might be an instrument of power. 'I think the Governor [William Cobbett] is the man of all men to be her Prime Minister,' Anne felt able to write in January 1821.[10]

Her dream might have seemed realistic. After all, the country's politics were still chaotic, and nobody was more acutely aware of this than the King. He had spent the final days of the trial hiding at his cottage at Windsor and fuming at the way in which his ministers were giving up the fight. He threatened to throw them out of office, claiming that they had tried to drop the divorce clause without his knowledge – which was not true – and accusing them of 'insincerity to their Sovereign' and of 'rank Cowardice'. He was particularly angry with Liverpool, whom he disliked anyway, and was incensed by George Canning's return to Parliament once the trial was over. Canning had almost openly admitted his criminal intercourse with 'the

Princess', he railed. 'And then whilst he half acknowledged his treason on the one hand, he added insult and injustice to his sovereign on
the other.' It seemed impossible that the King could continue to work
with this government.[11]

George did not know what to do. First, he had to consider whether to
prorogue Parliament, which was the obvious next step. But if
Parliament was not sitting, he worried, the country would go mad.
'Would not the Radicals work double . . . to keep treason and tumult
alive?' he asked Lord Eldon rhetorically. Would they not use the
'medium of the press and all the collateral engines which we know are
resorted to for the most wicked purposes? . . . Addresses both to myself
and the Queen will flow in from every part of the country.' He seemed
almost to be summoning the spectre of a civil war. If, however,
Parliament were to sit for the remainder of the year, a deal might quickly
be achieved with the Queen and, he believed, she would then leave the
country. But if the negotiations were prolonged, 'rely upon it every effort
will be used to keep her where she is. Hence no tranquillity.'[12]

If the Tories were expelled and the Whigs brought in, he suggested
to his confidante William Knighton, the Queen's power would be
defused and the 'publick mind would probably be diverted'[13] – and he
attempted to sound out the Whig leaders, Lord Grey and George
Tierney, on whether the opposition would, given its political leanings,
have a 'plan of conduct' which was consistent 'with my honour and
character, considering the exulted station which I hold as Sovereign of
this Kingdom'. The opposition, it turned out, had no such plan. The
Whigs were split on the central issue of political reform, and contained in their ranks out-and-out radicals who were entirely at odds
with the aristocratic Whig elite. In any case, George quickly decided
that the Whigs would not do at all, since the majority wanted Catholic
emancipation, which was 'entirely opposite to my own conscientious
feelings' and the party would also demand cuts in government spending, and a reduction in the army – both of which George opposed. In
the end he decided that although Liverpool and the Tories 'might have
consulted my feelings more, and added to my happiness', they had
been 'a good government for the country'.[14]

The fragile equilibrium of his emotions was soothed when on 12 December George Canning resigned – a reflection of the difficulty of his own position in relation not just to the King but also to his fellow ministers, who had all voted for the Bill and against the Queen. The King accepted his resignation 'with regret but not with surprise'.[15] By the end of the year the general tumult had so died down that the Tories started to believe that they had endured the worst of the country's discontent, and that they could, despite everything, remain in power. Sidmouth finally felt confident enough to write that 'the disaffected [of England] will never succeed in exciting rebellion, or in effecting a revolution . . . Thank God Great Britain is a good sea boat and there never yet was a storm which she was unable to weather'.[16] And Mrs Arbuthnot noted that when George opened Parliament on 23 January 1821 he was 'better received than we expected. The crowd was immense, but they were perfectly orderly.'[17]

Three days later the Whigs' strength in Parliament was tested when Sir Archibald Hamilton put forward in the Commons the motion that the Queen's name be restored to the liturgy. It was defeated by 310 to 209 votes – confirming the Tory belief that the government was out of danger. The fact was that most of the Commons did not want a change of government, and Parliament was now able to resist public opinion. Nonetheless, the Queen's business, as it was known, had not gone away entirely. On 31 January Caroline delivered a message to the House of Commons stating that she would not accept any financial arrangement from the government whilst excluded from Sunday prayers. Brougham read the message aloud and spoke of the impossibility of any settlement while the government acted as though she had not been acquitted at her trial. The Prime Minister ignored her message, and ensured that she was offered a pension of £50,000 a year. Against the advice of Brougham, and also of William Cobbett, the Queen replied to Lord Liverpool on 3 March 1821 accepting the money and stating that she:

is only anxious to show to the King that she wishes to Receive from him, and not from a mere party spirit. The Queen at the same time

thinks herself authorised to look upon this messure as the first act of
Justice of his Majesty towards the Queen. She also add that she most
entertains the flattering expectation that the same sentimens of Justice
which has prevailed in her favour will also effect upon the heart of the
King, by placing her name in the Liturgi as Queen, as such having
been the Rights and custum of her Predecessors . . . [18]

Brougham was furious at her action and blamed it on bad advice from
Matthew Wood. Cobbett was also dismayed, as was Thomas Barnes,
the editor of *The Times*. Caroline had deluded herself into thinking
that an appeal to George directly would soften his attitude. She
appeared to have no realisation, even after all that had passed, that his
revulsion for her was great and immovable, and would only be exacerbated by her appalling spelling and grammar. Her name was not
restored to the liturgy, while in accepting the £50,000 pension, she
gave up her political power. In becoming an immensely wealthy
woman she had destroyed her image as the victim of oppression, at
one with the people.

Addresses to her had continued to arrive, and were still linked to
political reform. But now they were matched by Addresses to the King
and his government, got up with Tory support. The Universities of
Oxford and Cambridge declared their loyalty in December, and were
followed by several hundred Addresses from around the country in
the early months of 1821. George decided that he could risk going out
in public and although he was still hissed, his reception was often
'warm and cordial', although – as the Queenite writer Joseph
Nightingale observed, he might have turned up 'with somewhat less of
a military parade'.[19] The Duke of Wellington, who had become so
unpopular with the masses, visited Covent Garden on 8 February and
'was most loudly cheered by the whole house . . . standing up and
waving their hats and handkerchiefs for near a quarter of an hour'.[20]
This was, perhaps, an indication of relief in Tory high society that it
was now safe to express antipathy to the Queen without being shouted
down.

Caroline's behaviour suggests that she was no longer accepting advice from Brougham, Cobbett or even Matthew Wood. She continued to see all these men, as well as the radicals John Cam Hobhouse and Joseph Hume, so she was surrounded by intelligent and canny political operators. Nonetheless, she acted rashly. In March she wrote to Lord Liverpool saying that she would turn up at the King's next Drawing Room to present him with a petition demanding 'that the Queen's name should be restored to the Liturge as her Predecessoreries'.[21] She did not carry out her plan, her name was still excluded from the liturgy, and she felt wounded. It was 'terrible, shocking, too much to bear,' she told her steward Hieronymus. 'I see they wish to get me gone.'[22]

At home in Hammersmith she was spied upon by George's agents. It was noted in a 'secret intelligence' report made in March that a man named Bisquetti had often visited the Queen, and that some of her servants referred to him as 'Baron Bisquetti'. It is not at all likely that the man was Pergami, as it would have been an extraordinary achievement to smuggle him into the country and keep him there undetected. However, it is not entirely impossible. The Countess of Oldi was at that time 'much more with the Queen than before' despite falling out with Lady Anne Hamilton. Either way, the man Bisquetti seems to have soon disappeared and in the next few months Caroline was certainly writing to Pergami in Milan. Her letters were intercepted by spies, and have since disappeared. Caroline continued to surround herself with foreign servants, including Italians; and Alderman Wood, according to the King's agent, advised her to dismiss some of them. But 'the Queen said those that she had with Her were well known for their fidelity . . . and that she could place her life in their hands'.[23]

At about this time the subject of George's Coronation, which had been so long postponed, came to the fore. The trial over, the Coronation was to go ahead and preparations were underway for the King to be crowned, without his wife, in the greatest splendour on 19 July. In April, Caroline wrote to Liverpool to inform him that she would attend anyway. She also wrote to George 'most earnestly' entreating him 'to inform the Queen in what Dresse the King wish's the Queen to appear on that day of the Coronation'.[24] George, of course, would not open her letter 'in conformity to a resolution adopted more than twenty years ago'.[25] Lord Liverpool was inclined to think that Caroline's threat could be ignored. But George was less sanguine and instructed the Prime Minister to write to the Queen informing her that she could 'form no part' of the ceremonial. He added that 'the King has dispensed with the attendance of all Ladies upon His Coronation'. The following day Caroline replied, insisting that 'the Queen is much surprised at Lord Liverpool's answer: and assure the Earl that her Majesty is determined to attend at the Coronation; the Queen considering it as one of her Rights and Privileges, which her Majesty is resolved ever to maintain'. Liverpool, on George's insistence, once more wrote to Caroline informing her that it was the King's 'Royal Pleasure that the Queen shall not attend'.[26]

Matthew Wood had, according to a secret report on Caroline's activities, taken the view that 'the people will never suffer the ceremony to take place without the Queen', and predicted 'violent riots' if the King succeeded in excluding her.[27] He was not the only one. Lord Temple reported that fear of violence was making it difficult to sell seats to view the coronation procession to Westminster Abbey, and Sarah Lyttelton thought the 'mob are rather too cross' for the Coronation to be peaceful. 'We are all in a fright about it,' she wrote.[28] On 19 June, a month before the big event, an intelligence report informed the King that the Queen would 'certainly' attend – and that she would also be honoured separately, by the City of London. The information, gleaned from a Mrs Brown who was the porter's wife at Brandenburgh House, indicated that 'the Queen was to have a Crown from the City, that she was to be Queen of the City and having all the People for Her she would then have as much power there as the King himself, that the Bank of England and other Public Buildings in the city would be under her Majesty's control'.[29]

That same day Caroline hosted a grand dinner at Cambridge House, her residence in central London, which was attended by the grandest people whom she could muster to brave the barbed words of *John Bull*. The guests included the Duke of Bedford, the Marchioness of Tavistock, Lady Jersey in a sedan chair accompanied by the radical

Samuel Whitbread (junior) on foot, Lord Darlington, Lord Milton, Sir Robert Wilson, Thomas Denman and his wife, Henry Brougham and Mrs Brougham, Mr and Mrs Williams, Mr and Mrs Wilde, the Lord Mayor, Lord William Fitzgerald and Lord Fitzwilliam.[30] This was a good show – in all about twenty ladies and thirty gentlemen, and heavily dominated by reforming Whigs. If, on that occasion, her society friends attempted to persuade her not to attend the Coronation, they did not succeed. She spent the following weeks making her preparations, and having a dress made.

On 19 July the crowds did, in fact, turn up despite the dire predictions of unrest. And that morning Caroline did set out for Westminster Abbey, where the Coronation was to take place. She rode in a yellow state carriage drawn by six bays, attended by her ladies-in-waiting, Lady Anne Hamilton and Lady Hood. The Queen wore a muslin dress, silver brocade petticoat and 'a small purple scarf' with a 'splendid diamond bandeau on her head, with feathers'.[31] Her chamberlain Lord Hood, her old friend Captain Hesse and William Austin rode in the carriage ahead of her. There was no sign of Henry Brougham, who did not support Caroline's action, but who was amongst the spectators, filled with curiosity as to what would happen when she arrived. On the way there were plenty of voices crying, 'The Queen for ever!' but also 'loud whistling'. At one stage Caroline stopped her carriage and looked around, as if not entirely sure of herself, but then the carriage moved on again. At Westminster Abbey the Queen left her carriage and, taking the arm of Lord Hood, walked to the doorway of the West Cloister. The doorkeeper, however, blocked their way. Caroline and Hood next trudged round to the door to the East Cloister. There too she was barred by the doorkeeper, who had been given firm instructions that she should not, at any cost, be let in.

Caroline had with her a ticket for the event which had been sent to her by the Duke of Wellington, who, strangely, seems to have been struck with sympathy for her predicament. This, however, was immaterial, since she refused to enter the Abbey as an ordinary ticket-holder; she would enter only as Queen. Next she called for her carriages and drove round the vast and ancient cathedral towards the door at Poets' Corner – the entrance that was to be used by the royal family. Among the great cheers of the crowds could be heard cries of 'Shame!' Before she reached her destination the Queen appeared to change her mind about her tactics, deciding instead to try to enter nearby Westminster Hall, where many of the Coronation guests were gathering. A pro-government newspaper reported the following exchange with the doorman:

Lord Hood: I present to you your Queen. Surely it is not necessary for her to have a ticket.

Door-Keeper: Our orders are to admit no person without a peer's ticket.

LH: This is your Queen. She is entitled to admission without such a form.

The Queen (smiling but still in some agitation): Yes, I am your Queen. Will you not admit me?

DK: My orders are specific, and I feel myself bound to obey them. (The Queen laughed.)

LH: I have a ticket.

DK: Then my Lord, we will let you pass upon producing it. This will let one person pass but no more.

LH: Will your Majesty go in alone?

(Her Majesty at first assented, but did not persevere.)

LH: Am I to understand that you refuse her Majesty admission?

DK: We only act in conformity with our orders.

(Her Majesty again laughed.)[32]

Miss Elizabeth Robertson was inside the hall when the Queen's attempt at entry was made, and recorded her version of events:

we were electrified by a thundering knock at the Hall door, and a voice without loudly said, 'The Queen – open!' A hundred red pages ran to the door, which the porter opened a little, and from where I sat I had a glimpse of her, leaning on Lord H[ood], followed by Lady H[ood] and Lady Anne Hamilton, standing behind the door on her ten toes, with the crossed bayonets of the sentry under her chin.

The Queen, wrote Miss Robertson, 'was raging and storming and vociferating, "Let me pass; I am your Queen, I am Queen of Britain"'. The Deputy Lord High Chamberlain then appeared and 'with a voice that made all the Hall ring, cried, "Do your duty, shut the Hall door," and immediately the red pages slapped it in her face!'.[33]

Caroline decided to go back to the Abbey, and attempt an entrance at Poets' Corner. Here she encountered Sir Robert Harry Inglis, an official known as a Gold Staff. Inglis had learned half an hour earlier that she was on her way and had run round to block her. He later recorded their conversation: 'Madam,' he said, 'it is my duty to inform your Majesty that there is no place for your Majesty in the royal box, or with the royal family (I forget which).' The Queen replied, 'I am sorry for it.' She then asked how she might get her carriage, and Sir Robert gave instructions for it to be brought up. Then, he wrote, 'I accompanied her Majesty from Poets' Corner across New Palace Yard to Bridge Street.'[34]

Caroline had admitted defeat. She climbed back into her carriage and drove away. There were no great cheers of support from the crowds, just a few cries of 'Shame!' 'Go away!' and 'Go back to Pergami!' It was over. The day and the future belonged to George, whose five-hour Coronation ceremony commenced later in the morning with all the magnificence and pomp that he had ordered for it. He entered at the west door of Westminster Abbey to the sound of the Hallelujah Chorus and a cheering congregation, and staggered up the aisle dragging a splendid crimson velvet train which was decorated with gold stars and was 27 feet long. £24,000 had been spent on his Coronation robes, and £243,000 on the day – and the expenditure was everywhere on display, from the blue and white satin costumes worn by the privy councillors to the King's enormous Spanish hat mounted with ostrich feathers and the long thick curls of the brown wig that sat on his 58-year-old head. The Archbishop of York spoke to remind the King of his duty to preserve the people from the 'contagion of vice' and from a 'general depravity' which was the 'last calamity' that could befall a state. And then George was, finally and without disturbance, crowned.[35]

Caroline, however, was destroyed. Sir Walter Scott wrote that her cause had become 'a fire of straw which was now burnt to the very embers',[36] and Henry Brougham thought that she had 'lost incalculably' for 'getting out of her carriage and tramping about'. Her intention to damage the Coronation, he believed, was 'very bad, but the way of doing it was very, very bad'.[37] The government had spent vast sums on dignifying the Crown and, in the middle of all the splendour, Caroline had behaved with no dignity at all.

That night at Brandenburgh House she seemed aware that she had turned her earlier victory into defeat. 'Her Majesty put on the semblance of unusual gaiety,' wrote Lady Anne Hamilton, but 'while she laughed the tears rolled down her face – tears of anguish so acute that she seemed to dread the usual approach of rest'. When the Queen did retire, at three in the morning, she took a glass of water, added an enormous quantity of the antacid Magnesia, along with a few drops of laudanum. Lady Anne thought the concoction a strange mess, and tried to dissuade her from taking it. But Caroline did so, with the aid of a spoon, and then went to her bed.[38] A few days later Denman observed her with guests 'dancing, laughing and romping, with spirits frightfully overstrained'.[39] She was exhausted and, it was to emerge, seriously unwell.

At the end of July Caroline became 'very sick and had much pain in her bowels'. She seemed 'much surprised' by her illness and did not make a fuss but her old friend Dr Holland was so alarmed that he summoned two other eminent doctors to the house. The medics diagnosed an obstruction of the bowels and believed her condition so grave that they told her that she was dying, and that she should put her papers in order. The speed of events seemed astounding. The Coronation had been just a few weeks earlier, and not a year had passed since the start of her trial.

Lady Anne Hamilton wrote that the Queen astonished those around her 'by her greatness of mind; for her Majesty did not betray the slightest agitation, but immediately and coolly answered, "Oh yes, I understand you; it shall be done"'.[40] That night she stayed up 'burning letters, papers and . . . books' and ordered Hieronymus to burn further documents including her memoirs. In the coming days she saw Brougham, Denman, Wilde and Lushington and made her will. 'She spoke cheerfully, though sensible of her danger,' wrote Denman. She told Stephen Lushington that she 'desired to be buried in Brunswick and wished her tomb to bear no other inscription than 'Caroline of Brunswick, the injured Queen of England'. On 3 August Brougham and Denman were present when, extremely ill but with a firm hand, she signed the will. Then, reported Brougham's friend Thomas Creevey, 'she said with great firmness – "I am going to die, Mr Brougham, but it does not signify."' Brougham responded, "Your Majesty's physicians are quite of a different opinion." "Ah," she replied, "I know better than them. I tell you I shall die, but I don't mind it"'.[41]

In the following days she was in increasing pain, which progressed to produce a delirious state in which she called out and wailed. Death came at twenty-five past ten on the night of 7 August. Lord Hood, who had been with her during the final days, observed: 'I never beheld a firmer mind, or anyone with less feelings at the thought of dying.' Thomas Wilde, who was with her for the final two hours, later told Denman that 'the name of Pergami never passed her lips'.[42] During her illness, though, she had constantly spoken of William Austin, of little Victorine Pergami and of other children to whom she had become close. The fatal condition from which she suffered may have been stomach cancer. At the time, however, the physicians suspected a blockage of Magnesia and rumours flew about that she had been poisoned. *The Times* reported the death of the Queen on 8 August: 'The tragedy of the persecutions and death of a QUEEN is at length brought to its awful close; and thousands – we may say millions – of eyes will be suffused in tears when they shall read in this column that CAROLINE OF BRUNSWICK is no more . . . She died as she had lived, a Christian heroine and a martyr . . .'

On the same day James Catnach rushed out a best-selling broadside with *An Elegy on the* QUEEN printed prominently in enormous letters:

> We have the heart-rending task of announcing to our readers that Caroline, our beloved Queen is no more. She died at 10 o'clock Tuesday night, to the inexpressible grief of the whole British nation . . . From the moment of her illness she entertained no hopes of recovery but observed to those around her that she had undergone many Trials and Troubles, but this would be the last. When the melancholy tidings arrived in town the most poignant grief was visible in every countenance.[43]

The page was adorned with a 'Lament for *Caroline, Rose of England*' – a tear-jerking rhyme about Caroline's passing and reunification in heaven with her daughter Charlotte whilst 'Angels sing to harps of gold'. William Hone produced a squib, *A Slap at Slop*, in which he professed that Caroline had 'died of the dagger of persecution'.[44]

The King, when he received the news of Caroline's death, was on the yacht *Royal George* and about to sail for Ireland – the first visit by a reigning English monarch since Richard II. At first George was not entirely unaffected and 'walked about the cabin the greater part of the night'. Thereafter, however, he was 'gayer than it might be proper to tell', and spent his time 'eating goose pie and drinking whiskey', which he consumed 'most abundantly, singing many joyous songs'.[45] He ordered that the period of official mourning for Caroline be the absolute minimum of three weeks.

The arrangements for Caroline's funeral presented a new crisis for the government. Lord Liverpool was afraid of public unrest more violent than that during the trial, and in particular feared that the Queen's coffin would be purloined and made to lie in state at the Guildhall – the 'capital' of the City of London, and the heart of the Queenite radicals' activity. The Prime Minister decided that the best way to avoid trouble was to convey the body by boat down the Thames to the sea, and from there it could be taken out of harm's way to Brunswick. But the Admiralty objected strongly, believing that the seamen – who had supported Caroline so vehemently during the trial – would block the river with their boats.[46] So a route for the cortège was devised, starting at Brandenburgh House at Hammersmith to the west of London, turning north at Kensington then east at Bayswater, and north of the City, to the north-eastern suburbs and out to Harwich, where a ship would wait for the coffin. This would avoid such sensitive locations as the army barracks at Knightsbridge, the press areas of St Giles, Ludgate Hill and Fleet Street, and the City hotspots at St Paul's and the Guildhall.

It was clear that the Queen's cause was to be revived for the occasion, and that she was, at the end, to be made into a political symbol. Her supporters suggested both the Guildhall and St Paul's as a venue for a forced lying in state for a day – but the Lord Mayor was against the proposal. On the night before the funeral, which was to take place on 14 August, John Cam Hobhouse and Joseph Hume met with other radicals to make plans for the following day. There was a feeling that night that anything might happen, as the funeral route had been kept a secret, and crowds were already gathering and anxious for instructions about where they should go. The press had made clear its outrage that the ministry was, in their view, rushing the Queen's body out of the country, contrary to the wishes of 'the people'.

At six in the morning, in heavy rain, government representatives arrived at Brandenburgh House with a squadron of Oxford Blues who lined up in front of the house facing a hostile horde. Brougham, Lushington and others arrived, along with Hume and Hobhouse. At seven thirty the hearse and sixteen coaches set off into Hammersmith, while the church bell tolled minute time and guns were fired on the Thames. As the procession moved slowly on, the crowds fell in behind, only now learning of the route that had been devised. When they arrived at Kensington Church, at half past nine, the mourners found that the road ahead had been blocked with two vehicles by the Queen's supporters. The procession was brought to a halt right outside William Cobbett's house, which was swathed in black. The crowds now ensured that the two vehicles were joined by others, and a group of people began to dig up Kensington Church Street to make it impassable. The crowds, meanwhile, cried out, 'Through the City! Through the City!'

The hated Life Guards were summoned, arriving to yells of 'No butchers! Kill the buggers!' The Home Office ordered that the attempt to proceed up Kensington Church Street should be abandoned, and the cortège should instead try to cut through Hyde Park, maintaining the ambition to go north and avoid the City. But, at Hyde Park, the crowds had shut the gates – and when the Life Guards tried to open them they were pelted with stones and mud. The cortège moved on to Hyde Park Corner to try to get into the park there, but the way was blocked with market carts; so an attempt was made to proceed up Park Lane – but this too was barricaded and, by now, there was open fighting between the people and the Life Guards. Eventually the cortège forced its way into the park, whereupon the people ran across the grass to block the way out at Cumberland Gate, which gave way to the Edgware Road and the planned northern route.[47]

Henry Brougham was in the procession, pleading with the authorities to let the Queen's coffin go through the City. He wrote that whilst in the park:

> I heard firing and one or two bullets whistled past us. On the first noise I asked [the Queenite army officer Sir Robert] Wilson what it was: 'Oh,' said he, 'it is a noise you are not used to; we are in fire.' Then said I, 'We must get out of it; but perhaps we should do so as soon by going on.' He said, 'Certainly we should not be one whit worse than if we turned round.' So we went forward . . . We escaped without hurt, though one of the bullets struck the carriage. We then got into Oxford Street, and found it crowded with troops, who made us turn into one of the streets leading to the New Road, the great object being to prevent us from getting into the City.[48]

The crowd, he recorded, was enormous and 'furious at the soldiery'.

The situation at Cumberland Gate was, for a time, out of control. The Life Guards attempted to forge a way through despite a heavy downpour of bricks and stones, along with the driving rain. Some soldiers lashed out with their sabres, others fired their pistols. Several men were wounded and two killed – a carpenter, Richard Honey, and a bricklayer, George Francis.

The cortège nonetheless pushed on, but was met with more barricades and more fighting. In the end the Chief Metropolitan Magistrate, Sir Robert Baker, in order to avoid more bloodshed, surrendered to the will of the crowd and allowed Caroline's body to be taken to the City – an act which was to cost him his job. Tory society condemned him for being weak; Harriet Arbuthnot, for instance, was disgusted by his 'folly and cowardice'.[49] From this point on, the procession moved to cries of 'Victory!' – going down the Strand, through Fleet Street and past St Paul's. It finally left the City at five o'clock that night, going East towards Harwich. As at the trial, the confrontation between the will of the government and that of the populace had resulted in the triumph of the people – but this time blood was shed.

The Queen's death produced mixed emotions in Henry Brougham. Over time he had come to believe that she was innocent of the charges against her, and convinced his friend Thomas Creevey that the more he knew Caroline, the more convinced he became that her real obsession was with children (a theory strengthened by Caroline's will, which favoured Victorine and William Austin). Brougham says, wrote Creevey to Miss Ord on 11 August, 'that Pergami's elevation was all owing to her attachment to [the child] Victorine . . . this from Brougham is a great deal, because I think it is not going too far to say that he absolutely *hated* her; nor do I think her love for her Attorney General was very great'. A week later Creevey wrote again: 'And now what do you think Brougham said to me not an hour ago? That if he had gone with the Queen's body to Brunswick, it would have been going too far – it would have been over-acting his part; "*it being very well known that through the whole of this business he had never been very much for the Queen!*" Now upon my soul, this is quite true, and, being so, did you ever know anything at all to equal it?'[50]

In his memoirs, written many years later, Henry Brougham managed to hide the dislike that he had felt for Caroline. Instead he professed to be positively moved by the sight of the 'multitudes' assembled at Harwich and the spectacle of the sea, which was 'covered with boats of every size and kind', their colours being flown at half-mast. 'The contrast of a bright sun with the gloom on every face was striking,' he wrote, 'and the guns firing at intervals made a solemn impression.' He was particularly struck by the sight of a captain in the Royal Navy who had been employed by Caroline on 'dispensing her charities'. The man was weeping 'exceedingly' and wished to accompany the coffin to Brunswick. Brougham watched as 'the crimson coffin slowly descended from the pier', and was borne away to Brunswick. There was, wrote Henry Brougham, 'a kind of national remorse, as well as commiseration, for all that had passed'.[51]

20

AFTERMATH

The crown's a symbol, that the people meant,
To mark their choice, or form of government;
The crown is theirs, and this has been their plan,
To make the *office* sacred, not the *man*:
Hence, if a tyrant on the throne appears,
The place is vacant, and the crown is theirs.

The Right Divine of Kings to Govern Wrong!
Hone and Cruikshank (1821)

There had been no revolution; not even a change of government. But the trial of Queen Caroline did set Britain on the road to political reform. It demonstrated the strength and generality of support for change (despite the loyalist backlash), and jolted the Whigs into the realisation that they must, at last, put the reformers' cause at the heart of their political strategy. During December 1820 and January 1821 Whig leaders organised political meetings throughout the country and the enthusiastic response demonstrated that anti-government feeling was as high as it had been in decades, while pro-reform sentiment remained strong. Neither fact, of course, was reflected in terms of votes in Parliament – and the groundswell of opinion did not affect the business of the Commons or the Lords.

It did, however, change politics in the wider sense. Throughout 1820 the Whig leader, Lord Grey, had been having doubts that his party could ever come to power under the existing method of intriguing in Parliament and bargaining with the King. In short, he believed that the mechanisms for a change in government had broken down, and in April wrote that 'nothing but a strong expression of public opinion calling for a complete change of system' would result in a Whig ministry. Now, after the trial, he spoke publicly on the subject at a county meeting in Northumberland. Even if he were asked to form a government, he said, 'I would not accept it, but upon terms satisfactory to my conscience and honour; and these terms should be nothing short of a complete and total change in the system of government.' With Lord Holland, he now made clear that the lofty Whig aristocrats were ready to make certain compromises with radicals, inside and outside the party, in order to bring about change.[1]

The crisis was not, for many reasons, to come for another decade. But when it did, it was on these terms, and with the Queen Caroline protagonists again to the fore. Lord Grey was the Prime Minister responsible for the Great Reform Act of 1832, and Henry Brougham was in the vanguard of the movement that led to it. Indeed, Brougham is credited with the most popular slogan of the time: 'The Bill, the whole Bill and nothing but the Bill.' William Cobbett, too, was mightily involved. Wellington, whose reaction to public protest during the Queen Caroline agitation had been to ensure that the army was ready to act against the demonstrators, was the Prime Minister before Grey, resisting reform to the end.

In the years between the Queen's trial and the Reform Act there was a mood change in British politics. In 1822 Cobbett wrote:

we owe a great deal to the poor Queen. It was she that pulled down the haughty foes of our freedom more than the rest of us put together. Until she came, scarcely any man dared to say his soul was his own. She raised the people up . . . This nation owes everlasting gratitude to the Queen. It was she that raised us from the very dust. The feeling towards the THING [the establishment] now is much more of *contempt* than *dread*.

It is, of course, necessary to discount for Cobbett's hyperbole. Nonetheless, the politics of the 1820s did seem different. After the trial there was certainly a softening in the Tory style of government. Lord Sidmouth, the ardent advocate of the policy of suppression of seditious sentiment, retired. He had worked long hard days throughout the trial, was fatigued and wished to absent himself from the political stage. He was succeeded at the Home Office by the young Robert Peel, who was to address the central issue that had made the Caroline agitation so dangerous – that of the army and militia. All the time that public protest might be met with sabres and guns there was a danger of an escalation into widespread rebellion. Peel set about defusing that explosive cocktail with the establishment of a police force armed only with truncheons and far more suited to managing public demonstrations and civil disobedience, though this was not to come about until 1829. The suicide of Lord Castlereagh in 1822 was another calming factor. His death meant that the Liverpool ministry could no longer be attacked by reference to the twin demons of oppression, Sidmouth and Castlereagh. At the same time, the government now seemed less willing to use the old methods of suppressing dissent, and the scores of trials brought between 1815 and 1820 for seditious libel, or defamation of the King and his ministers, fell away to a trickle by 1824.[2] In early 1821 George had written to Eldon insisting upon a new wave of prosecutions against 'all the venders of treason and libellers, such as Benbow etc'. But the hard line of the years preceeding the trial was rejected by the ministers.

In short, the Tories were no longer engaged in hostilities with 'the people', and it seemed that one era had ended and another begun. Perhaps this was thanks to the principal achievement of the 1820

agitation – the triumph of public opinion. The government had
clashed with public opinion and lost; and public opinion, as a force,
was now established in British politics for good. It had been on the
march since the French Revolution, glorified as a moral authority, the
voice of truth, liberty and justice. The Queen's trial raised it to its
zenith. Public opinion in 1820 seemed not simply the embodiment of
the wisdom of the people, but also part of the great, unstoppable tide
of history that was to lead to their liberation. It could not keep this
gilded image forever, and by 1832 it was a tarnished thing, representing what was bad about popular sentiment along with what was good.
But it *had*, through the trial, become a power in the land, a force to be
reckoned with and public opinion was now visible on the streets, via
the open political demonstrations by trade societies that continued for
many years after the end of the Caroline Affair.[3]

The Queen's trial also demonstrated that a truly popular press, of
some influence, was at work in Britain. Count the number of newspapers sold, and the figures are not impressive – 10,000 copies being
a 'successful' sales figure for a London paper. But follow the story of
the trial, and a different picture emerges. The stories in the papers
were shouted out in the streets, each paper was read by any number of
people, some were rented out by the hour, others read aloud in coffee
houses and taverns. Then, add to the true penetration of the
respectable press the vast market for satires, cartoons, one-page broadsides and ballads, all commenting on the same event – the trial – and
the contemporary claims that the entire nation was following
Caroline's story do not seem absurd. An intricate news chain was at
work, taking the news, in its many forms, to every town and immeas-
urable numbers of villages. Cobbett, of course, had to go further and
insist that the news of the trial reached every cottage in the kingdom.

At the apex of that system stood *The Times*. The paper's championing of Caroline turned it, for the first time, into the most important
newspaper in Britain, a position it was to hold for more than 150 years.
Its editor, Thomas Barnes, was responsible for the early success. He
maintained the paper's independence from government, nurtured its
relationship with public opinion and in particular with the growing

middle classes. Barnes, in the years after the trial, also developed a close friendship with Henry Brougham, whose influence on *Times'* leaders became notorious. Thus, when the time came, *The Times* campaigned for the Reform Act with as much zeal as it had shown for Caroline, and put pressure on Lord Grey to deliver a degree of democracy that would satisfy the public. Robert Peel described the paper as 'the great, principal, and powerful advocate for Reform'. Thomas Barnes, meanwhile, was described by Charles Greville as 'the most powerful man in the country'. The paper's nickname by then was the Thunderer.

Barnes had taken public opinion, and used it for the success of his great newspaper. The dozens of lesser publishers and editors rushing out broadsides, posters and ballads had a relationship with the public that was closer still. They were, in a sense, the myriad voices that constituted a large part of public sentiment, more like early bloggers than newspaper leader writers. They were the thing itself.

At least, they were the male thing. Women took no part in the printed form of public expression. They made it on to the streets in 1820 and joined the national debate, but ultimately their participation was limited, and it is hard to see the Queen's trial as part of the history of women's liberation. When it was over, the wives and daughters who had joined the Caroline agitation went back into the home, their right to be protected by men made safe by the Queen's triumph. But that was all. The Reform Act in 1832 marked the extension of voting rights to large numbers of middle-class men, but was also the first overt, unequivocal exclusion of women from the political process.[4]

Finally, there is the monarchy. The Queen's trial dragged the King into the gutter. He was insulted, degraded, despised, lampooned and demonised day after day, in hundreds of prints, in defiance of the laws of the land and with more hostility than any British monarch has suffered since. Then, a year later, he was cheered at the Coronation. For someone living in the twenty-first century, there is nothing strange about this – it continues to be the British way with royalty. The public did, and still does, like to demonstrate that its support is not absolute or unquestioning. If royals misbehave, or somehow abuse their

position, the country responds and makes threats. Had Queen
Caroline not triumphed in 1820, it is quite possible that George IV
would have lost the throne. And, who knows, republicanism in Britain
may have had a different history entirely.

ILLUSTRATION LIST

The publishers have made every effort to contact those persons having any rights in the pictures reproduced in this work. Where this has not been possible the publishers will be pleased to hear from anyone who recognises their material.

Integrated Pictures

Frontispiece	Sir George Hayter, circa 1820, National Portrait Gallery
Pages 3, 24, 34, 319	Taken from *The Queen's Matrimonial Ladder*
Pages 56, 109, 146, 165, 179, 223, 235, 247, 272	Taken from *Horrida Bella*
Pages 83, 120, 131	Taken from *The Queen that Jack Found*
Page 95	Taken from *The Queen in the Moon*
Page 187	Taken from *The Green Bag*
Page 204	Taken from *The Queen and Magna Carta*
Page 299	'The Royal Extinguisher', George Cruikshank, 1821, National Portrait Gallery

Plate section

1 Jean Philip, Royal Collection, courtesy of Her Majesty Queen Elizabeth II
2 'A Voluptuary under the Horrors of Digestion', James Gillray, 1792, National Portrait Gallery
3 Sir Thomas Lawrence, Bridgeman Art Library
4 Thomas Heaphy, 1815, National Portrait Gallery

NOTES

ABBREVIATIONS:

RA   Royal Archives
BL   British Library
HO   Home Office
GH   Guildhall
PR   Political Register (Cobbett)

Reportage of the Queen's trial is taken from the transcript published by Robins & Co. in 1820 and edited by Nightingale. Hansard has been used as a supporting text.

1: MARRIAGE

1 Adeane, *The Early Married Life of Maria Josepha, Lady Stanley*, 23.
2 Holland (*Memoirs*), ii, 146.
3 *Malmesbury Diaries*, iii, 153, 159.
4 *Ibid.*, 155, 164.
5 *Ibid.*, 165.
6 *Ibid.*, 165, 171, 179, 180.
7 *Ibid.*, 183.
8 *Ibid.*, 168, 179, 184.
9 *Ibid.*, 168.
10 *Ibid.*, 189.
11 *Ibid.*, 190, 201.
12 *Ibid.*, 208.
13 *Ibid.*, 193, 196.
14 *Ibid.*, 196, 200.
15 *Ibid.*, 215.
16 *Ibid.*, 217.
17 *Ibid.*
18 *Papendiek Journals*, i, 132.
19 Aspinall (*Prince of Wales Correspondence*), i, 5.
20 Brougham (*Historical Sketches*), ii, 2.

21 *Arbuthnot Journal*, i, Introduction, xv.

22 Aspinall (*Prince of Wales Correspondence*), i, 196.

23 Hibbert (*George IV, Prince of Wales*), 51.

24 *The Times*, 'Brighton Uproar', 13 August 1789.

25 Holland (*Memoirs*), ii, 144.

26 *Malmesbury Diaries*, iii, 218.

27 *Ibid.*

28 *Ibid.*, 219.

29 Hibbert (*George IV, Prince of Wales*), 146.

30 *Morning Chronicle*, 10 April, 1795.

31 *Jerningham Letters*, i, 75.

32 David, *Prince of Pleasure*, 169–70.

33 *Morning Chronicle*, 6 April, 1795.

34 Aspinall (*Prince of Wales Correspondence*), iii, 126, 132, 133, 135, 138.

35 *Farington Diary*, ii, 553, 559, 589.

36 Hibbert (*George IV, Prince of Wales*), 150.

37 Richardson (*George IV, A Portrait*), 62.

38 Greenwood, *Lives of the Hanoverian Queens of England*, ii, 260.

39 *Elliot Letters*, iii, 14.

40 Aspinall (*Prince of Wales Correspondence*), iii, 179.

41 *Ibid.*, iii, 191, 197, 204.

2: SEPARATION

1 Aspinall (*Prince of Wales Correspondence*), iii, 179.

2 Nightingale (*Memoirs of Queen Caroline*) (1978) (Introduction), 19.

3 *Elliot Letters*, iii, 33.

4 Granville (*Correspondence*), i, 255.

5 Treasure, *Who's Who*, 222.

6 Stanhope, *Memoirs*, i, 308.

7 MSS Letters of Marchioness of Townshend; Richardson (*The Disastrous Marriage*), 66.

8 *Bury Diary* (1839), iv, 73

9 Nightingale (*Memoirs of Queen Caroline*) (1978) (Introduction), 19.

10 *Berry Journals*, ii, 380.

11 *Bury Diary* (1896), i, 18.

12 Hibbert (*George IV, Prince of Wales*), 208.

13 Granville, *Correspondence*, ii, 204.

14 Fairburn, *Genuine Edition*, 89, 99, 84, 85, 92.

15 *Ibid.*, 95, 96, 111, 112, 181.

16 *Ibid.*, 19, 23, 24, 143.

17 *Ibid.*, 30, 33, 35, 39.

18 Hayward, *Diaries of a Lady of Quality*, 199.

19 Fairburn, *Genuine Edition*, 160–161.

20 PR, 10 June 1820.

21 Manby, *Reminiscences*, 32–3.

22 PR, 263–4.

23 *Ibid.*, 268.

24 *Elliot Letters*, iii, 391.

3: REGENCY

1 Hibbert (*George IV, Prince of Wales*), 273.

2 Aspinall (*Prince of Wales Correspondence*), viii, 52.

3 Smith, E. A. (*George IV*), 134.

4 Shelley, *Letters*, i, 99–100.

5 Gronow, *Reminiscences*, 23.

6 *Bury Diary* (1839), iv, 69.

7 New, *Life of Henry Brougham*, 7.

8 Hazlitt (*Spirit of the Age*), i, 158–9.

9 New, *Life of Henry Brougham*, 49.

10 Aspinall (*Politics and the Press*), 41.

11 *Examiner*, 15 March 1812.

12 *Morning Post*, 18 March 1812.

13 *Examiner*, 22 March 1812.

14 New, *Life of Henry Brougham*, 92.

15 Holland (*Memoirs*), ii, 228.

16 New, *Life of Henry Brougham*, 90.

17 Aspinall (*Letters of the Princess Charlotte*), 181.

18 Brougham (*Life and Times*), ii, 157–163.

19 Austen, *Letters*, 208.

20 Aspinall (*Letters of the Princess Charlotte*), 57.

21 Aspinall (*Politics and the Press*), 307.

22 Aspinall (*Letters of the Princess Charlotte*), 59–60.

23 Brougham (*Historical Sketches*), ii, 22.

24 Mackintosh, *Memoirs*, ii, 259.

25 Murray, *Recollections*, 199.

26 Nicolson, *Congress of Vienna*, 109–10.

27 *Ibid.*, 208.

28 *Ibid.*, 110–11.

29 *Jerningham Letters*, ii, 53.

30 Brougham (*Life and Times*), ii, 208.

31 *Creevey Papers*, i, 197.

32 *Ibid.*, 199.

33 Brougham (*Life and Times*), ii, 227–35.

34 *Ibid.*, 230.

35 *Ibid.*, 254.

36 *Ibid.*, 189.

37 Nightingale (*Memoirs of Queen Caroline*) (1978), 136.

38 Plowden, *Caroline and Charlotte*, 199.

39 Aspinall (*George IV Letters*), ii, 203–205.

40 Hibbert (*George IV, Regent and King*), 98.

41 *Ibid.*, 99.

42 *Croker Papers*, i, 107.

43 Corbett, *A Royal Catastrophe*, 28–9.

44 Lieven (*London Letters*), 34.

45 Brougham (*Life and Times*), ii, 332.

46 BL 11641.f69.

47 Phillips, *Lament of the Emerald Isle*.

48 Martineau, *History of the Peace*, i, 172.

49 Baldwin, *Penroses of Fledborough*, 93.

50 *Ibid.*, 94.

51 Oman, *Gascoyne Heiress*, 93.

52 Holland (*Further Memoirs*), 248.

53 Hermit of Marlow, *Address to the People*, 6.

4: TRAVELS

1 Holland (*Recollections*), 117.

2 Clerici, *A Queen of Indiscretions*, 40.

3 *Ibid.*, 40–41.

4 *Bury Diary* (1896), i, 230.

5 Holland (*Recollections*), 129.

6 Young, *Napoleon in Exile*, 264.

7 Holland (*Recollections*), 129.

8 Young, *Napoleon in Exile*, 267.

9 Melville (*An Injured Queen*), ii, 333.

10 *Ibid.*, ii, 335.

11 Holland (*Recollections*), 146.

12 Wellington (*Supplementary Despatches*), ix, 492.

13 *Ibid.*, 503.

14 *Ibid.*, 401–402.

15 Fraser, *The Unruly Queen*, 262–3.

16 *Bury Diary* (1896), i, 241.

17 Fraser, *The Unruly Queen*, 264–5.

18 *Ibid.*, 266.

19 Clerici, *A Queen of Indiscretions*, 54.

20 *Ibid.*

21 *Ibid.*, 63.

22 Fraser, *The Unruly Queen*, 268.

23 Holland (*Recollections*), 133.

24 *Ibid.*

25 Lucien Bonaparte, *Memoirs*, ii, 91.

26 *Berry Journals*, iii, 46

27 De Boigne, *Memoirs*, ii, 39–40.

28 *Ibid.*, 40.

29 RA Geo/Add 21/102/3.

30 *Ibid.*, 102/4.

31 *Ibid.*, 102/6.

32 *Ibid.*, 102/4.

33 *Bury Diary* (1838), ii, 147.

34 New, *Life of Henry Brougham*, 117.

35 RA Geo/Add 21/102/9.

36 RA Geo 8/1, Bundle 6, 6 August 1815.

37 Melville (*An Injured Queen*), ii, 355.

38 Richardson (*The Disastrous Marriage*), 103–104.

39 RA Geo 8/2, Bundle 8, 9 December 1815.

40 RA Geo/Add 21/102/10.

41 Fraser, *The Unruly Queen*, 284.

42 Huish, *Memoirs of Queen Caroline*, i, 626.

43 Knight, *Passages of a Working Life*, i, 252–3.

44 RA Geo/Add 21/102/11.

45 HO 44/3/163.

46 *Farington Diary*, xvi, 5469.

47 *Ibid.*, 5519.

48 Shelley (Mary), *Letters*, i, 156.

49 Holme, *Caroline, A Biography*, 172.

50 *Ibid.*, 173–4.

51 Melville (*An Injured Queen*), ii, 383.

52 RA Geo/Add 21/10/13.

53 *Ibid.*

54 Marchand, *Byron's Letters*, v, 155.

55 RA Geo 8/2, Bundle 8, 18 October 1820.

56 Holme, *Caroline, A Biography*, 185.
57 *Bury Diary* (1839), iii, 239.
58 Romilly, *Memoirs*, i, 216.
59 *Ibid.*, 216–17.
60 Brougham (*Historical Sketches*), ii, 33.
61 Aspinall (*George IV Letters*), ii, 272–4.
62 *Ibid.*
63 *Ibid.*, 281.
64 RA Geo 8/2, Bundle 8.
65 *Ibid.*
66 Aspinall (*George IV Letters*), ii, 358.
67 *Ibid.*
68 BL Add 38565.
69 *Ibid.*
70 *Ibid.*
71 *Ibid.*
72 *Ibid.*
73 RA Geo 8/2, Bundle 9.
74 *Ibid.*
75 *Ibid.*

5: QUEEN
1 RA Geo/Add 21/102/36.
2 *Creevey Papers*, i, 298.
3 RA Geo 8/2, Bundle 9.
4 New, *Life of Henry Brougham*, 231.
5 BL Add 38565 ffs 109–110.
6 *Ibid.*, f 113.
7 Fraser, *The Unruly Queen*, 344.
8 *Ibid.*, 345.
9 BL Add 38565, 29 March 1820.
10 George, M.D. (*Catalogue of Prints and Drawings*), vol x.
11 BL Add 38565, April 1820.
12 GH Journal 87, f 508.
13 Romilly, *Memoirs*, iii, 103.
14 RA Geo/Add 21/122/43.
15 Stephens, *Hatherley Memoir*, i, 121.
16 Patterson, *Sir Francis Burdett*, i, 326.
17 Reid (*The Peterloo Massacre*), 115.
18 *Ibid.*, 114.

19 *Ibid.*, 149.
20 Bamford, Samuel, *Passages in the Life of a Radical*, i, 208.
21 Patterson, *Sir Francis Burdett*, ii, 491.
22 Hazlitt (*Spirit of the Age*), ii, 238.
23 Cobbett, Anne, *Account of the Family*, 38.
24 *Ibid.*, 40.

6: EXCLUSION
1 *Croker Papers*, i, 159.
2 Castlereagh, *Memoirs and Correspondence*, xii, 211.
3 *Croker Papers*, i, 159.
4 Johnson, *Birth of the Modern World*, 531.
5 Wilberforce (*Life of William Wilberforce*), v, 54 .
6 BL Add 38565.
7 *Ibid.*, f 49.
8 Castlereagh, *Memoirs and Correspondence*, xii, 212.
9 Pellew, *Sidmouth*, iii, 310.
10 Castlereagh, *Memoirs and Correspondence*, xii, 213.
11 *Greville Memoirs*, i, 89.
12 *Croker Papers*, i, 160.
13 Aspinall (*Henry Hobhouse Diary*), 9.
14 BL Add 38565.
15 Aspinall (*Henry Hobhouse Diary*), 10.
16 Pellew, *Sidmouth*, iii, 312, 314–321.
17 Rush, R., *Memoranda* (1845), 267–268.
18 *Manchester Observer*, 4 March 1820.
19 *Republican*, 25 February 1820.
20 HO 40/11.
21 *Ibid.*
22 HO 44/1/218.
23 HO 44/1/215.
24 Pellew, *Sidmouth*, iii, 322.
25 *Ibid.*, 325–6.
26 RA Geo/Add 21/102/37.
27 *Ibid.*
28 Twiss, *Eldon*, ii, 366.
29 Smith, E. A. (*A Queen on Trial*), 25.
30 *The Times*, 25 April 1820.
31 BL Add 78703.
32 BL Add 38284 141.

33 BL Mss Add 78703.
34 RA Geo 8/2, Bundle 9.
35 Knight, *Passages of a Working Life*, i, 258.

7: BROUGHAM
 1 Stewart, *Henry Brougham*, 93–6.
 2 Bourne, *Blackmailing of the Chancellor*, 22.
 3 *Ibid.*
 4 Edgcumbe, *Frances Lady Shelley Diary*, i, 227–8.
 5 Stewart, *Henry Brougham*, 112–13.
 6 Romilly, *Memoirs*, iii, 236–7.
 7 Smith, N. C., *Letters of Sydney Smith*, i, 334.
 8 New, *Life of Henry Brougham*, 232.
 9 BL Add 38565.
10 Brougham (*Life and Times*), ii, 28.
11 Aspinall (*Lord Brougham and the Whig Party*), 106.
12 *Ibid.*, 108.
13 Fraser, *The Unruly Queen*, 355.
14 RA Geo Box 8/2, Bundle 8.
15 BL Add 38285.
16 Brougham (*Life and Times*), ii, 356.
17 BL Add 38565.
18 *Ibid.*
19 *The Times*, 6 June 1820.
20 Brougham (*Life and Times*), ii, 362.
21 *Ibid.*
22 Aspinall (*George IV Letters*), ii, 340–41.
23 Denman, *Memoir*, i, 138–51.

8: AGITATION
 1 HO 44/2/153.
 2 HO 44/2/155.
 3 *The Times*, 6 June 1820.
 4 *Ibid.*
 5 HO 44/2/154–5.
 6 Lieven (*Metternich Letters*), 29.
 7 Spater, *William Cobbett*, ii, 401.
 8 Burney, *D'Arblay Diary*, vii, 349.
 9 Lieven (*Metternich Letters*), 30.
10 Smith, E. A. (*A Queen on Trial*), 38.

11 *Ibid.*, 35.

12 Shelley (Mary), *Letters*, i, 156.

13 Shelley, *Letters*, ii, 801.

14 Stapleton (*George Canning*), 297.

15 Pellew, *Sidmouth*, iii, 328.

16 *Black Dwarf*, 18 June 1820, 808.

17 BL Add 38565.

18 HO 44/2.

19 *Ibid.*

20 Lieven (*Metternich Letters*), 30.

21 *Jerningham Letters*, ii, 168.

22 Stevenson (In: Stevenson (ed.) *London in the Age of Reform*), 121.

23 Smith, E. A. (*A Queen on Trial*), 38.

24 Aspinall (*Henry Hobhouse Diary*, 26); Pellew, *Sidmouth*, iii, 330–31.

25 *Arbuthnot Journal*, i, 23–6.

26 Smith, E. A. (*A Queen on Trial*), 48, 49.

27 *A Letter to Lord Erskine*; BL 8135.

28 Wellington (*Despatches*), i, 127.

29 BL Add 38565.

30 *Greville Memoirs*, i, 100.

31 Smith, E. A. (*A Queen on Trial*), 56.

32 Wellington (*Despatches*), i, 129.

33 *Croker Papers*, i, 110.

34 *Greville Memoirs*, i, 94.

9: NEGOTIATION

1 Melville (*An Injured Queen*), ii, 432.

2 Aspinall (*Lord Brougham and the Whig Party*), 111.

3 Aspinall (*Henry Hobhouse Diary*), 27.

4 *Ibid.*

5 Holland (*Further Memoirs*), 293, 400–403.

6 Aspinall (*Henry Hobhouse Diary*), 28.

7 *Arbuthnot Journal*, i, 23.

8 Wilberforce, *Life of William Wilberforce*, v, 56–7.

9 *Ibid.*, 62.

10 *Ibid.*

11 *Berry Journals*, iii, 244.

12 *Jerningham Letters*, ii, 172.

13 Melville (*An Injured Queen*), ii, 455.

14 Scott, *Familiar Letters*, ii, 84.

15 BL Add 38565.
16 Aspinall (*Henry Hobhouse Diary*), 29.
17 Dixon, *Canning, Politician and Statesman*, 101.
18 Alison, *Lives of Castlereagh and Stewart*, iii, 123.
19 *Arbuthnot Journal*, i, 25.
20 Hinde, *Castlereagh*, 299–301; Stapleton, *George Canning*, 290–92.
21 *Morning Chronicle*, 5 July 1820.
22 Smith, E. A. (*A Queen on Trial*), 78–9.
23 Lieven (*Metternich Letters*), 38–9.
24 *Ibid.*
25 Castlereagh, *Memoirs and Correspondence*, xii, 285.
26 Denman, *Memoir*, i, 163.
27 *The Times*, 6 and 7 July 1820.

10: PUBLICATION

1 *A Peep at the Peers*, 1820.
2 Cobbett, Anne, *Account of the Family*, 52.
3 Cobbett, William, *History of the Regency*, para 441.
4 Melville (*Life and Letters of William Cobbett*), 148–56.
5 *Ibid.*, 158.
6 Graham, *Byron's Bulldog*, 295–6.
7 Nattrass, *Cobbett, Selected Writings*, iv, 251–76.
8 Cobbett, *History of the Regency*, 132.
9 McCalman (*Radical Underworld*), 169.
10 George, M. D., (*Catalogue of Prints and Drawings*), vol x.
11 *A Peep at the Pavilion*, 1820.
12 Stevenson, *London in the Age of Reform*, 128; HO 40/14.
13 Cobbett, Anne, *Account of the Family*, 51.
14 *Arbuthnot Journal*, i, 28.
15 McCalman, *Radical Underworld*, 169; George, M. D. (*English Political Caricature*), 191.
16 McCalman, *Radical Underworld*, 171.
17 *The Political House that Jack Built*, 1820.
18 Hackwood, *William Hone*, 194.
19 *Ibid.*, 241.
20 *Ibid.*, 237.
21 Hone (*Popular Political Tracts*).
22 George, M. D. (*English Political Caricature*), ii, 188.
23 Wood, *Radical Satire*, 14–17, 201–202, 217, 244–5.
24 Hazlitt (*Memoirs*), i, 300.

25 Aspinall (*Henry Hobhouse Diary*),30–31.

26 *Ibid.*, 31.

27 *The Times*, 30 June 1820.

28 *Ibid.*, 3 July 1820.

29 PR, 29 July 1820.

30 *The Times*, 2 August 1820.

31 Parr, *Works of Samuel Parr*, i, 767.

32 Holland (*Further Memoirs*), 288.

33 Field, *Memoirs of Samuel Parr*, ii, 257.

34 Cobbett, Anne, *Account of the Family*, 51.

35 Nattrass, *Cobbett, Selected Writings*, iv, 341–7.

36 Cobbett, William, *History of the Regency*, para 441.

37 Cobbett, Anne, *Account of the Family*, 52.

38 Cole, *Life of William Cobbett*, 249.

11: THE LORDS

1 *The Times*, 18 August 1820.

2 *Courier*, 18 August 1820.

3 Granville, Lady Harriet, *Letters*, i, 155–6.

4 BL Add 41853.

5 HO 44/2/134; HO 44/2/135.

6 Granville, Lady Harriet, *Letters*, i, 155.

7 Huish, *Memoirs of Queen Caroline*, ii, 515.

8 *Creevey Papers*, i, 306–307.

9 *Ibid.*, 309.

10 Graham, *Byron's Bulldog*, 300.

11 Granville, Lady Harriet, *Letters*, i, 161.

12 Melville (*An Injured Queen*), ii, 508.

13 RA Geo Add 10/1.

14 Granville, Lady Harriet, *Letters*, i, 156.

15 *Creevey Papers*, i, 310.

16 Greville, *Memoirs*, i, 105.

17 Denman, *Memoir*, i, 164.

18 Granville, Lady Harriet, *Letters*, i, 157.

19 Hutchinson, *Letters*, 195–6.

20 Granville, Lady Harriet, *Letters*, i, 154.

21 *Jerningham Letters*, ii, 174.

22 Graham, *Byron's Bulldog*, 296.

23 Moore, *Memoirs*, iii, 149.

24 Denman, *Memoir*, i, 149.

25 *Ibid.*

26 *Berry Journals*, iii, 236.

27 *Ibid.*, 239.

28 *Ibid.*

29 *Oxford Dictionary of National Biography*, 2004.

12: PROSECUTION

 1 Smith, E. A. (*A Queen on Trial*), 78.

 2 Lieven (*Metternich Letters*), 56.

 3 HO 44/1/77–8.

 4 *Newspaper Readers*, 1820.

 5 *Courier*, 20 August 1820.

 6 *Newspaper Readers*, 1820.

 7 *Cobbett's Answer*, 1820.

 8 Hunt, Leigh, *Correspondence*, i, 156.

13: FOREIGNERS

 1 Bagot, *George Canning*, ii, 100.

 2 *Queen's Case Stated*, 1820; BL 8135.

 3 *Ibid.*

 4 Colley, *Britons*.

 5 *Royal Letter Bag*, 1820.

 6 *Ibid.*

 7 Graham, *Byron's Bulldog*, 295–6

 8 RA Geo 8/2.

 9 Brougham (*Historical Sketches*), ii, 30.

10 Granville, Lady Harriet, *Letters*, i, 194.

11 George, M. D. (*Catalogue of Prints and Drawings*), vol. x.

12 RA Geo 11/1, Bundle 32D.

13 *Italian Liars*, 1820.

14 Fox, *Journal*, 41.

15 Hutchinson, *Letters*, 196.

16 *The Times*, 23 August 1820.

17 Granville, Lady Harriet, *Letters*, i, 160.

18 Fox, *Journal*, 42.

19 *Black Dwarf*, August 1820.

20 Denman, *Memoir*, i, 165.

21 Lieven (*Metternich Letters*), 51.

22 *Ibid.*, 56.

23 RA Geo Add 10/1, Bundle 5.

14: WOMEN

1 Lieven (*Metternich Letters*), 51.
2 *Ibid.*
3 Boynton, *Scandal and Society*, 44.
4 *Ibid.*
5 Granville, Lady Harriet, *Letters*, i, 169, 175.
6 Lieven (*Metternich Letters*), 51.
7 Granville, Lady Harriet, *Letters*, i, 171.
8 *King's Treatment*, 1820.
9 *Ibid.*
10 Address (*Nottingham, 26 July 1820*).
11 *Ibid.*
12 Granville, Lady Harriet, *Letters*, i, 178–9.
13 HO/2/156.
14 *Courier*, 20 August 1820.
15 *Ibid.*, 2 September 1820.
16 Lieven (*Metternich Letters*), 51.
17 *Arbuthnot Journal*, i, 35.
18 *Doll Tear-Sheet*, 1820.
19 Granville, Lady Harriet, *Letters*, i, 175.
20 *British Trio*, 1820.
21 *Glorious Deeds of Women*, 1820.
22 *Queen's Case Stated*, 1820.
23 MacDonald, *The Queen Caroline Affair*, 101.
24 Fulford, *Romanticism and Masculinity*, 161–8.
25 Smith, E. A. (*A Queen on Trial*), 108.
26 *Ibid.*, 102.

15: INVESTIGATION

1 Lieven (*Metternich Letters*), 54.
2 Aspinall (*George IV Letters*), ii, 361–3.
3 *Ibid.*
4 *Ibid.*, 363.
5 Lieven (*Metternich Letters*), 57
6 Denman, *Memoir*, i, 165–7.
7 Aspinall (*George IV Letters*), ii, 366, 369.
8 RA Geo 11/3.
9 *Ibid.*, Bundle 37.
10 RA Geo/Box 11/2, Bundle 32 H.
11 RA Geo/Box 11/3, Bundle 36.

12 *Ibid.*

13 RA Geo Box 10/1, Bundle 5.

14 RA Geo Box 12/3, Bundle 41.

15 RA Geo Box 10/1, Bundle 5.

16 RA Geo Box 11/3, Bundle 37.

17 RA Geo Box 12/3, Bundle 42.

18 RA Geo Box 11/2, Bundle 33.

19 *Ibid.*, Bundle 37.

20 *Ibid.*, Bundle 36.

21 RA Geo Box 10/2, Bundle 10.

22 RA Geo Box 11/3, Bundle 36.

23 *Ibid.*

24 RA Geo Box 12/3, Bundle 41.

25 RA Geo Box 11/1, Bundle 32.

26 RA Geo Add 11/1, Bundle 32C.

27 *Ibid.*

28 *Ibid.*

29 *Ibid.*

16: CONVULSION

1 Smith, E. A. (*A Queen on Trial*), 114.

2 *Ibid.*

3 *The Times*, 7 October 1820.

4 *Anne Boleyn and Caroline of Brunswick Compared*, 1820.

5 Lieven (*Metternich Letters*), 61.

6 Hobhouse, John Cam, *Recollections*, 31.

7 Pellew, *Sidmouth*, iii, 332.

8 HO 44/3/159.

9 HO 44/2.

10 HO 44/3/171.

11 Pellew, *Sidmouth*, iii, 330.

12 Prothero, *Artisans*, 137.

13 *Ibid.*, 14–2.

14 Tracts 1820–1821; BL 8135.e.4.

15 *Ibid.*

16 *Ibid.*

17 *Addresses*, 1820.

18 *Ibid.*

19 *Periodical Press*, 24.

20 Barker, H., *Newspapers*, 53–64.

21 Rush, R., *Memoranda* (1833), 243, 247.

22 *Newspaper Readers*, 1820.

23 Wilberforce, *Life of William Wilberforce*, v, 66.

24 Shepard (*Street Literature*), 72.

25 BL Add 38565.

26 Shepard (*John Pitts*), 53.

27 *England's Lamentation*, BL.

28 Rush, R., *Memoranda* (1845), 347.

29 *Arbuthnot Journal*, i, 38.

30 Brougham (*Life and Times*), ii, 405.

17: DEFENCE

 1 *Greville Memoirs*, i, 105.

 2 Denman, *Memoir*, i, 169.

 3 RA Geo 11/3, Bundle 37.

 4 *Creevey Papers*, i, 321–2.

 5 *Arbuthnot Journal*, i, 40.

 6 *Berry Journals*, iii, 256.

 7 *Ibid.*

 8 *Ibid.*, 256–7.

 9 Granville, Lady Harriet, *Letters*, i, 182.

10 Aspinall (*George IV Letters*), ii, 371.

11 *Courier*, 7 October 1820.

12 Granville, Lady Harriet, *Letters*, i, 184.

13 *Ibid.*, i, 185.

14 *Creevey Papers*, i, 324.

15 *Ibid.*, 323.

16 Granville, Lady Harriet, *Letters*, i, 186.

17 *Courier*, 17 October 1820.

18 *Creevey Papers*, i, 323.

19 Lieven (*Metternich Letters*), 62.

20 *Creevey Papers*, i, 324.

21 *Ibid.*

22 Huish, *Memoirs of Queen Caroline*, ii, 605–606.

23 *Ibid.*, ii, 608.

24 *Ibid.*, ii, 609–10.

25 Lieven (*Metternich Letters*), 63.

26 *Creevey Papers*, i, 326.

27 Melville (*An Injured Queen*), ii, 529–30.

18: RESOLUTION

1 *Creevey Papers*, i, 331.

2 Smith, E. A. (*A Queen on Trial*), 122.

3 *Arbuthnot Journal*, i, 47.

4 *Colchester Diary*, iii, 181

5 Lieven (*Metternich Letters*), 68.

6 *Creevey Papers*, i, 336.

7 *Ibid.*, i, 332.

8 BL Mss Add. 56541.

9 *Ibid.*

10 *Creevey Papers*, i, 337.

11 Lieven (*Metternich Letters*), 40.

12 *Creevey Papers*, i, 339.

13 *Arbuthnot Journal*, i, 52.

14 Cobbett, William, *History of the Regency*, para 446.

15 Melville (*An Injured Queen*), ii, 502.

16 *Ibid.*, ii, 510.

17 Ziegler, *Life of Addington*, 390.

18 Brougham (*Life and Times*), ii, 408–10.

19 PR, 18 November 1820.

20 Lieven (*Metternich Letters*), 74.

21 *The Times*, 13 November 1820.

22 PR, 1820, 447.

23 *The Times*, 14 November 1820.

24 *The Gentleman's Magazine*, November 1820.

25 Melville (*An Injured Queen*), ii, 512.

26 Wickwar, *Struggle for Freedom*, 164.

27 Rush, R., *Memoranda* (1845), 347.

28 Melville (*An Injured Queen*), ii, 511.

29 Cobbett, William, *History of the Regency*, para 446.

30 Penrose, *Benjamin Haydon*, 249.

31 Richardson (*The Disastrous Marriage*), 192.

32 Smith, E. A. (*A Queen on Trial*), 153.

33 *The Traveller*, 11 November 1820.

34 *Glasgow Herald*, 18 November 1820, MacDonald, *Queen Caroline in Scotland*, 103.

35 *Norwich Courier*, 18 November 1820.

36 *The Traveller*, 18 November 1820.

37 Laqueur, *Queen Caroline Affair* (In *Journal of Modern History*, vol. 54, 432.).

38 *Traveller*, 19 November 1820.

39 *The Times*, 18 November 1820.

40 Pellew, *Sidmouth*, iii, 332.

41 *Traveller*, 20 November 1820.

42 Melville (*An Injured Queen*) ii, 513–14.

43 *Croker Papers*, i, 175.

44 Pellew, *Sidmouth*, iii, 334–6.

45 *The Times*, 30 November 1820.

46 Lieven (*Metternich Letters*), 76.

47 Hackwood, *William Hone*, 234–5.

48 Pellew, *Sidmouth*, iii, 336.

49 RA Geo Box 8/16.

50 *The Queen in Danger*, 1820.

51 *Black Dwarf*, 30 November 1820.

19: BACKLASH

1 *Black Dwarf*, 27 September 1820, 444.

2 Brougham (*Life and Times*), ii, 419.

3 Cobbett, William, *History of the Regency*, para 448.

4 Pellew, *Sidmouth*, iii, 336.

5 Newton Dunn, *The Man Who Was John Bull*, 122.

6 *Ibid.*, 125–6.

7 *Ibid.*, 130, 141.

8 *Letter from the King*, 1821.

9 Melville (*An Injured Queen*), ii, 519–20.

10 Spater, *William Cobbett*, ii, 408; Melville (*Life and Letters of William Cobbett*), ii, 179–80.

11 Ra Geo/22504.

12 RA Geo/22491–2.

13 RA Geo/22510.

14 RA Geo/22511–2.

15 RA Geo/22524.

16 Pellew, *Sidmouth*, iii, 336–7.

17 *Arbuthnot Journal*, i, 64.

18 Melville (*An Injured Queen*), 536–7.

19 Nightingale (*Last Days of Queen Caroline*), 88–9.

20 *Arbuthnot Journal*, i, 69.

21 BL Add 38565.

22 RA Geo Box 8/2, Bundle 13.

23 *Ibid.*

24 *Ibid.*

25 *Ibid.*

26 *Ibid.*

27 *Ibid.*

28 Hibbert (*George IV, Regent and King*), 190.

29 RA Geo Box 8/2, Bundle 13.

30 *Ibid.*

31 Nightingale (*Memoirs of Queen Caroline*) (1822), iii, 129.

32 Hibbert (*George IV, Regent and King*), 202–203.

33 Richardson (*The Disastrous Marriage*), 207–208.

34 Fraser, *The Unruly Queen*, 8.

35 Hibbert (*George IV, Regent and King*), 13.

36 Lockhart, *Life of Sir Walter Scott*, vi, 317.

37 *Creevey Papers*, 361–2.

38 BL Mss Add 78703.

39 Denman (*Memoir*), i, 187.

40 Hamilton, Anne, *Secret History*, ii, 11.

41 *Creevey Papers*, ii, 21.

42 Fraser, *The Unruly Queen*, 460–61.

43 *Elegy on the Queen*, 1821.

44 *A Slap at Slop*, BL.

45 Smith, E. A. (*A Queen on Trial*), 193.

46 Prothero, *Artisans*, 147.

47 *Ibid.*, 148–50.

48 Brougham (*Life and Times*), 11, 426.

49 *Arbuthnot Journal*, i, 114.

50 *Creevey Papers*, ii, 26.

51 Brougham (*Life and Times*), ii, 428.

20: AFTERMATH

 1 Mitchell, Austin (*Whigs in Opposition*), 152–5.

 2 Twiss, *Eldon*, ii, 413.

 3 Prothero, *Artisans*, 142.

 4 Tuite, *Domesticity*, 132.

SELECT BIBLIOGRAPHY

MANUSCRIPTS
Royal Archives
British Library, Add Mss and Place Newspaper Collection
University College London, Brougham Mss
Sheffield Archives, Fitzwilliam Papers
Guildhall Archives

NEWSPAPERS AND JOURNALS
Black Dwarf, *Cobbett's Weekly Political Register*, *The Courier*, *The Examiner*, *The Gentleman's Magazine*, *Glasgow Herald*, *Hampshire Chronicle*, *John Bull*, *Leeds Mercury*, *London Gazette*, *The Observer*, *Manchester Observer*, *Morning Chronicle*, *Morning Herald*, *Morning Post*, *News*, *Norwich Courier*, *Sun*, *The Republican*, *The Times*, *The Traveller*, *True Briton*, *The Republican*, *Annual Register*, *Edinburgh Review*, *New Times*, *Patriot Bristol Mercury*

SELECTED BROADSIDES AND PAMPHLETS
Address of the Female Inhabitants of Nottingham, with Her Majesty's Answer. G. Harvey, London, 1820.
Address of the Married Females resident in the Parish of St Mary-le-bone, etc. London, 1820.
Answer to the Attorney General's speech. William Cobbett, London, 1820.
The British Seamen and their Beloved Queen. J. Pitts, London, 1820.
Brave Alderman Wood (*Queen Caroline – The British Seamen and their Beloved Queen*). Catnach, London, 1820.
Caroline and the Italian Ragamuffins!!! John Fairburn, London, 1820.
Derry Down Triangle! J. Tyler, London, 1820.
Doll Tear-Sheet. London, 1820.
Glorious Deeds of Women! London, 1820.
The Great Milan Leech. William Benbow, London, 1820.
The Green Bag, Or, A Dainty Dish to Set Before a King. J. Robins & Co., London, 1820.

Green Bag Oddities, Or, Give the Devil his Due. J., Tyler, London, 1820.

Horrida Bella, Pain and Penalties Versus Truth and Justice, William Benbow, London, 1820.

Italian Liars, Witnesses against our Queen. John Fairburn, London, 1820.

The King's Treatment of the Queen shortly stated to the people of England. William Hone, London, 1820.

Letter from Her Majesty the Queen to the King, William Hone, London, 1820.

Long Live Queen Caroline. (*Britons Claim her as your Queen!!*) J. Pitts, London, 1820.

More Loyal Addresses!!! Salmagundi, Or All the world at Hammersmith!!! A jeu d'esprit for October, 1820. Robins and Sons, London, 1820.

Non Mi Ricordo. J. Pitts, London, 1820.

Non Mi Ricordo. William Hone, London, 1820.

On the Return of Queen Caroline to England. J. Fairburn, Jun. London, 1820.

A Peep at the Pavilion, Or, Boiled Mutton with Caper Sauce at the Temple of Joss. E. Wilson, London, 1820.

A Peep at the Peers, William Benbow, London, 1820.

The Periodical Press of Great Britain and Ireland, Or, An Inquiry into the State of the Public Journals. Hurst, Robinson & Co., London, 1824.

The Printers' Address to the Queen. William Hone, London, 1820.

The Queen and Magna Carta, Or, The Thing that John Signed. Thomas Dolby, London, 1820.

Queen Caroline and the British Trio. Bull, Pat & Sawney. Thomas Dolby, London, 1820.

The Queen's Case Stated. William Hone, London, 1820.

The Queen in the Moon. Grove & Co., London, 1820.

The Queen that Jack Found. John Fairburn, London, 1820.

A Slap at Slop and the Bridge-Street Gang. William Hone, London, 1821.

The Political House that Jack Built. William Hone, London, 1819, 1820.

The Royal Extinguisher: Or, The King of Brobdingnag & the Lilliputians. George Humphrey, London, 7 April 1821.

The Royal Letter Bag; Containing Familiar Epistles from Royal Personages . . . Thomas Dolby, London, 1820.

The Spirit of Despotism. William Hone, London, 1821.

A Warning Letter to His Royal Highness the Prince Regent, from the Reverend Lionel Berguer, T. & J. Allman, London, 1819.

PRINTED

Adeane, Jane H.: *The Early Married Life of Maria Josepha, Lady Stanley.* Longmans and Co, London, 1899.

Alison, Sir Archibald: *Lives of Lord Castlereagh and Sir Charles Stewart* (3 vols). Blackwood, Edinburgh and London, 1861.

Arbuthnot Journal: *The Journal of Mrs Arbuthnot 1820–1832*. Edited by Francis Bamford and the Duke of Wellington (2 vols). Macmillan and Co Ltd, London, 1950.

Archer, John E.: *Social Unrest and Popular Protest in England, 1780–1840*. Cambridge University Press, 2000.

Aspinall (*George IV Letters*): Aspinall, A. (ed.), *The Letters of King George IV, 1812–1830* (3 vols). Cambridge University Press, 1938.

—— (*Henry Hobhouse Diary*): Aspinall, A. (ed.), *The Diary of Henry Hobhouse (1820–1827)*. Home and Van Thal, London, 1947.

—— (*Letters of the Princess Charlotte*): Aspinall, A. (ed.), *Letters of the Princess Charlotte 1811–1817*. Home and Van Thal, London, 1949.

—— (*Lord Brougham and the Whig Party*): Aspinall, A. (ed.), *Lord Brougham and the Whig Party*. Manchester University Publications, 1927.

—— (*Prince of Wales Correspondence*): Aspinall, A., (ed.), *The Correspondence of George, Prince of Wales, 1770–1812* (8 vols). Cassell, London, 1963–71.

Aspinall, A.: *Politics and the Press c. 1780–1850*. Home and Van Thal, London, 1949.

Asquith, Ivon: *James Perry and the Morning Chronicle, 1790–1821*. University of London, 1973.

Austen (*Letters*): *Jane Austen's Letters*. Collected and edited by Deirdre Le Faye. The Folio Society, London, 2003.

Aylmer, Edward: *Memoirs of George Edwards . . .* J. Tallis, London, 1820.

Bagot, Josceline Fitzroy (ed.): *George Canning and his Friends* (2 vols). John Murray, London, 1909.

Baldwin, Rev. A. B. (ed.): *The Penroses of Fledborough Parsonage. Lives, Letters and a Diary*. A. Brown and Sons, Hull, 1933.

Bamford, Samuel: *Passages in the Life of a Radical* (2 vols). Simpkin, Marshall and Co, 1844.

Barham, R. H. Dalton: *The Life and Remains of Theodore Edward Hook*. Richard Bentley, London, 1849.

Barker, Hannah: *Newspapers, Politics and English Society 1695–1855*. Longman, London, 1999.

Barnes, J. C. F.: *Popular Protest and Radical Politics: Carlisle, 1790–1850*. University of Lancaster, 1981.

Bawn, J. P.: *Social Protest, Popular Disturbances and Public Order in Dorset, 1790–1838*. University of Reading, 1984.

Behrendt, Stephen C. (ed.): *Romanticism, Radicalism and the Press*. Wayne State University Press, Detroit, c. 1997.

Behrendt, Stephen C.: *Royal Mourning and Regency Culture: Elegies and Memorials of Princess Charlotte*. Macmillan Press, London, 1997.

Berridge, Kate: *Vigor Mortis: The End of the Death Taboo*. Profile Books, London, 2001.

Berry Journals: *Extracts of the Journals and Correspondence of Miss Berry, 1783–1852*. Edited by Lady Theresa Lewis (3 vols). Longmans, Green and Co, London, 1865.

Berry Papers: *The Berry Papers, Being the Correspondence Hitherto Unpublished of Mary and Agnes Berry, 1763–1852*. Edited by Lewis Melville. John Lane, London, 1914.

Bickely, Francis (ed.): *The Diaries of Sylvester Douglas, Lord Glenbervie* (2 vols). Constable, London, 1928.

Bindman, David: *The Shadow of the Guillotine: Britain and the French Revolution*. British Museum Publications, London, 1989.

Blinkinsop, Vicesimus (Theodore Hook): *Tentamen: Or an Essay towards the History of Whittington*, (*A Satire on Sir Matthew Wood*). William Wright, London, 1820.

Bonaparte, Lucien: *Memoirs of the Private and Political Life of Lucien Bonaparte, Prince of Canino*. Translated from the French (2 vols). Henry Colburn, London, 1818.

Bourne, Kenneth: *The Blackmailing of the Chancellor: Some intimate and hitherto unpublished letters from Harriette Wilson to her friend Henry Brougham, Lord Chancellor of England*. Lemon Tree Press, London, 1975.

Boynton, Lindsay: 'Scandal and Society', *Squanderous and Lavish Profusion: George IV, his Image and Patronage of the Arts*. Edited by Dana Arnold, 1955.

Briggs, Asa: *Press and Public in Early Nineteenth-century Birmingham*. Oxford, 1948.

British Trio: *Queen Caroline and the British Trio, Bull, Pat and Sawney* (*A Song in Defence of Queen Caroline*). Thomas Dolby, London, 1820.

Brougham, Lord Henry: *Historical Sketches of Statesmen who Flourished in the Time of George III* (3 vols (Series)). Charles Knight and Co, London, 1839.

——: *The Life and Times of Henry Lord Brougham Written by Himself* (3 vols). William Blackwood and Sons, Edinburgh and London, 1871.

Brown, Richard: *Revolution, Radicalism and Reform: England, 1780–1846*. Cambridge University Press, 2000.

Buckingham and Chandos, Duke of: *Memoirs of the Court of George IV 1820–1830* (2 vols). London, 1859.

Burney, Fanny: *Diary and Letters of Madame d'Arblay*. vol. 7, 1813–1840. Edited by Charlotte Frances Barrett. 1846.

Bury, Lady Charlotte: *Diary Illustrative of the Times of George the Fourth*

Interspersed with Original Letters from the Late Queen Caroline and from various other Distinguished Persons (2 vols). Fourmestraux and Co, Paris, 1838.

——: *Diary Illustrative of the Times of George the Fourth Interspersed with Original Letters from the Late Queen Caroline, the Princess Charlotte and from various other Distinguished Persons* (4 vols). Henry Colburn, London, 1839.

——: *The Court of England under George IV. Founded on a Diary Interspersed with Letters written by Queen Caroline and various other Distinguished Persons* (2 vols). John MacQueen, London, 1896.

Castlereagh, Robert Stewart, 2nd Viscount: *Memoirs and Correspondence of Viscount Castlereagh*. Edited by his brother, Charles Vane, Marquess of Londonderry (12 vols). Henry Colburn, London, 1848–53.

Christie, Ian R.: *Stress and Stability in Late Eighteenth-century Britain: Reflections on the British Avoidance of Revolution*. Clarendon Press, Oxford, 1984.

Clare, John: *The Letters of John Clare, 1793–1864*. Edited by Mark Storey. Clarendon Press, Oxford, 1985.

Clark, Anna: *Queen Caroline and the Sexual Politics of Popular Culture in London, 1820*. Representations No. 31. 1990.

Clerici, Graziano Paolo: *A Queen of Indiscretions. The Tragedy of Caroline of Brunswick Queen of England*. Translated by Frederic Chapman from the Italian. The Bodley Head, London; John Lane Company, New York, 1907.

Cobbett, Anne: *Account of the Family*. William Cobbett Society, 1999.

Cobbett, William: *History of the Regency and Reign of King George the Fourth* (2 vols). William Cobbett, London, 1830.

Cole, G. D. H.: *The Life of William Cobbett*. Collins, London, 1924.

Colley, Linda: *Britons, Forging the Nation, 1707–1837*. Yale University Press, London, 1992.

Collison, Robert: *The Story of Street Literature: Forerunner of the Popular Press*. Dent, London, 1973.

Cookson, J. E.: *Lord Liverpool's Administration: The Crucial Years 1815–1822*. Scottish Academic Press, Edinburgh and London, 1975.

Corbett, Vincent: *A Royal Catastrophe, The Death in Childbirth of the Princess Charlotte of Wales*. 1985.

Crane, R. S. and Kaye, F. B.: *A Census of British Newspapers and Periodicals 1620–1800*. Chapel Hill, 1927.

Creevey Papers: *The Creevey Papers, A Selection from the Correspondence and Diaries of the Late Sir Thomas Creevey MP* (2 vols). Edited by The Right Hon. Sir Herbert Maxwell Bart MP LL.D FRS. John Murray, London, 1903.

Croker Papers: *The Croker Papers. The Correspondence and Diaries of the Late*

Right Honourable John Wilson Croker LL.D, FRS (3 vols). Edited by Louis J. Jennings. John Murray, London, 1884.

Darvall, F. O.: *Popular Disturbances and Public Order in Regency England.* Oxford University Press, London, 1934.

David, Saul, *Prince of Pleasure, The Prince of Wales and the Making of the Regency.* Little, Brown and Company, London, 1998.

Davis, Michael T. (ed.): *Radicalism and Revolution in Britain, 1775–1848: Essays in Honour of Malcolm I. Thomis.* Macmillan, Basingstoke, 1999.

De Boigne, *Comtesse: Memoirs of the Comtesse de Boigne.* Edited from the original MS by M Charles Nicollaud (3 vols). William Heinemann, London. 1907.

De Stael-Holstein, A: *Letters on England.* London, 1825.

Demont, Louise: *Journal of the Visit of Her Majesty the Queen to Tunis, Greece, and Palestine.* Translated by Edgar Garston. T. and J. Allman, London, 1821.

Denman (*Memoir*): *Memoir of Thomas, First Lord Denman formerly Lord Chief Justice of England* (2 vols). Edited by Sir Joseph Arnould. Longmans, London, 1873.

Dickinson, H. T. (ed.): *Britain and the French Revolution, 1789–1815.* Macmillan, Basingstoke,1989.

Dinwiddy, J. R.: *Radicalism and Reform in Britain, 1780–1850.* Hambledon, London, 1992.

Dixon, Peter: *Canning, Politician and Statesman.* Wiedenfeld and Nicolson, London, 1976

Doll Tear-Sheet: *Doll Tear-Sheet alias The Countess 'Je ne me rappelle pas', a match for 'Non mi ricordo'* . . . London, 1820.

Edgcumbe, Richard (ed.): *The Diary of Frances Lady Shelley 1787–1817.* (2 vols). John Murray, London, 1912.

Elliot Letters: *Life and Letters of Sir Gilbert Elliot, First Earl of Minto, from 1751 to 1806* (3 vols). Edited by his great-niece, The Countess of Minto. Longmans, Green and Co, London, 1874.

Emsley, Clive: *Britain and the French Revolution, 1789–1848.* Longman, Harlow, 2000.

Fairburn: *Fairburn's Genuine Edition of the Book including The Defence of Her Royal Highness, The Princess of Wales, as prepared by Mr Spencer Perceval.* John Fairburn, London, 1813.

Farington Diary: *The Diary of Joseph Farington* (16 vols). Published for Paul Mellon Centre for Studies in British Art by Yale University Press, Newhaven and London, 1978–84.

Field, Rev. William: *Memoirs of the Life, Writings and Opinions of the Rev. Samuel Parr* (2 vols.). London, 1828.

Foote, Jesse: *A Letter on the Necessity of a Public Inquiry into the Cause of the Death of Her Royal Highness Princess Charlotte and her Infant*. (Pamphlet). London, 1817.

Fox, Celina (ed.): *London – World City 1800–1840*. London, 1992 .

Fox, Henry Edward: *The Journal of the Hon. Henry Edward Fox, afterwards Fourth and Last Lord Holland, 1818–1830*. Edited by the Earl of Ilchester. Thornton Butterworth, London, 1923.

Fraser, Flora: *The Unruly Queen, The Life of Queen Caroline*, Macmillan, London, 1996.

Fulford, Roger: *The Trial of Queen Caroline*. B. T. Batsford, London, 1967.

Fulford, Tim: *Romanticism and Masculinity: Gender, Politics and Poetics in the Writings of Burke, Coleridge, Cobbett, Wordsworth, De Quincey and Hazlitt*. Macmillan, Basingstoke, 1999.

George, Mary Dorothy: *Catalogue of Personal and Political Satires*, British Museum, 1935–54.

——: *English Political Caricature (1798–1832). A Study of Opinion and Propaganda* (2 vols). Clarendon Press, Oxford, 1959.

Gilmartin, Kevin: *Print Politics: The Press and Radical Opposition in Early Nineteenth-century England*. Cambridge University Press, 1996.

Gilmour, Ian: *Riot, Risings and Revolution: Governance and Violence in Eighteenth-century England*. Hutchinson, 1992.

Golby, J. M. and Purdue, A. W.: *The Civilisation of the Crowd: Popular Culture in England, 1750–1900*. Batsford, London, 1984.

Graham, Peter W. (ed.): *Byron's Bulldog – The Letters of John Cam Hobhouse to Lord Byron*. Columbus, Ohio State University Press, 1984.

Granville (*Correspondence*): *Lord Granville Leveson Gower (First Earl Granville), Private Correspondence 1781–1821*. Edited by his daughter-in-law Castalia, Countess Granville (2 vols). John Murray, London, 1916.

Granville, Lady Harriet: *Letters of Harriet, Countess Granville 1810–1845* (2 vols). Edited by The Hon. F. Leveson Gower. Longmans and Co, London, 1894.

Greenwood, Alice Drayton: *Lives of the Hanoverian Queens of England* (2 vols). G. Bell and Sons Ltd, London, 1911.

Greville, Charles Cavendish Fulke: *The Greville Memoirs, 1814–1860* (8 vols). Edited by Lytton Strachey and Roger Fulford. Macmillan, London, 1938.

Griggs, E. L.: *The Collected Letters of Samuel Taylor Coleridge* (6 vols). Oxford University Press, 1956–1971.

Gronow Reminiscences: *Captain Gronow, His Reminiscences of Regency and Victorian Life 1810–60*. Edited by Christopher Hibbert. Kyle Cathie Limited, London, 1991.

Hackwood, William: *William Hone, His Life and Times*. T. Fisher Unwin, London, Leipsic, 1912.

Halévy, Elie: *A History of the English People in the Nineteenth Century*. Translated by E. I. Watkin and D. A. Barker, etc. (6 vols). Ernest Benn, London, 1949–52.

Hamilton, Lady Anne: *Secret History of the Court of England, from the Accession of George the Third until the Death of George the Fourth* (2 vols). W. H. Stevenson, London, 1832.

Hansard: *Hansard's Parliamentary Debates, First Series*.

Harling, Philip: *The Law of Libel and the Limits of Repression. The Historical Journal*, vol. 44, Issue 01 March 2001.

Harral, Thomas: *Anne Boleyn and Caroline of Brunswick Compared: In an Address to the People of England*. London, 1820.

Harris, Robert: *Politics and the Rise of the Press: Britain and France, 1620–1800*. Routledge, London, 1996.

Harrison, Mark: *Crowds and History, Mass Phenomena in English Towns, 1790–1835*. Cambridge University Press, 1988.

Hawes, Frances: *Henry Brougham*. Jonathan Cape, London, 1957.

Hayward, A., QC (ed.): *Diaries of a Lady of Quality from 1797 to 1844*. Longmans, London, 1864.

Hazlitt, William: *Memoirs of William Hazlitt* (2 vols). Richard Bentley, London, 1867,

———: *The Spirit of the Age; Or, Contemporary Portraits* (2 vols). A. and W. Galignani, Paris, 1825.

Henderson, Tony: *Disorderly Women in Eighteenth-century London: Prostitution and Control in the Metropolis, 1730–1830*. Longman, London, 1999.

Hermit of Marlow (Shelley): *An Address to the People on the Death of the Princess Charlotte. The Hermit of Marlow*. Compton and Ritchie, London, 1817.

Hibbert, Christopher (ed.): *Greville's England: Selections from the Diaries of Charles Greville 1818–1860*. Folio Society, London, 1981.

Hibbert, Christopher: *George IV, Prince of Wales 1762–1811*. Readers Union, Newton Abbot, 1973.

———: *George IV, Regent and King 1811–1830*. Allen Lane, London, 1973.

Hill, Bridget (compiler): *Eighteenth-century Women, An Anthology*. Allen and Unwin, London, 1984.

Hinde, Wendy: *Castlereagh*. Collins, London, 1981.

Hindley, Charles: *Curiosities of Street Literature, with a New Introduction by Leslie Shepard* (2 vols). The Broadsheet King, London, 1966.

———: *The History of the Catnach Press*. C. Hindley, 1887.

——: *The Life and Times of James Catnach (Late of Seven Dials) Ballad Monger*. London, 1878.

Hobhouse, John Cam (Baron Broughton): *Recollections of a Long Life* (6 vols). Edited by his daughter, Lady Dorchester. John Murray, London, 1909.

Holland (*Memoirs*): *Memoirs of the Whig Party During My Time*. Holland, Henry Richard, Lord (2 vols). Edited by his son: Holland, Henry Edward, Lord. Longmans, London, 1854.

—— (*Further Memoirs*): *Further Memoirs of the Whig Party 1807–1821 with Some Miscellaneous Reminiscences*. Holland, Henry Richard, Lord. Edited by Lord Stavordale. John Murray, London, 1905.

—— (*Recollections*): *Recollections of Past Life*. Holland, Henry, Sir. President of the Royal Institution of Great Britain, Physician in Ordinary to The Queen. Longmans, Green and Co, London 1872.

Holme, Thea: *Caroline: A Biography of Caroline of Brunswick*. Hamish Hamilton, London, 1979.

Hone, J. Ann: *For the Cause of Truth: Radicalism in London, 1796–1821*. Clarendon Press, Oxford, 1982.

Hone, William: *Hone's Popular Political Tracts: Consisting of The House that Jack Built, Queen's Matrimonial Ladder, Non mi ricordo . . .* William Hone, London, 1825.

——: *Second Trial: The King Against William Hone*. London, 1818.

Hope, Valerie: *My Lord Mayor – Eight Hundred Years of London's Mayoralty*. London, 1989.

Hudson, Derek: *Thomas Barnes of The Times*. Cambridge University Press, 1943.

Huish, Robert: *Memoirs of Queen Caroline, Queen Consort of England from the earliest period of her Eventful Life* (2 vols). Thos Kelly, London, 1821.

Hunt, James Henry Leigh: *The Autobiography of Leigh Hunt*. Smith, Elder and Co, London, 1885.

——: *The Correspondence of Leigh Hunt* (2 vols). Edited by Thornton Hunt. Smith, Elder and Co, London, 1862.

Hunt, Tamara: *Morality and Monarchy in the Queen Caroline Affair*. Albion XXIII, 1999.

Hutchinson, Sara: *The Letters of Sara Hutchinson from 1800 to 1835*. Edited by Kathleen Coburn. Routledge and Kegan Paul, London, 1954.

Ingrams, Richard: *The Life and Adventures of William Cobbett*. HarperCollins, London, 2005.

Jackson, Mason: *The Pictorial Press, Its Origin and Progress*. Hurst and Blackett, London, 1885.

Jerningham Letters: *The Jerningham Letters (1780–1843)* (2 vols). Edited with Notes by Egerton Castle MA, FSA. Richard Bentley, London, 1896.

Kent, David A. and Ewen, D. R. (eds): *Regency Radical: Selected Writings of William Hone*. Michigan, 2003.

Knight, Charles: *Passages of a Working Life During Half a Century: With a Prelude of Early Reminiscences* (3 vols). Bradbury and Evans, London, 1864.

———: *The Old Printer and the Modern Press*. London, 1854.

Koss, Stephen: *The Rise and Fall of the Political Press in Britain* (*Volume 1 – The Nineteenth Century*). Hamilton, London, 1981.

Laqueur, Thomas W.: 'The Queen Caroline Affair: Politics as Art in the Reign of George IV', *Journal of Modern History*, 1982.

Lever, Tresham (ed.): *The Letters of Lady Palmerston*. John Murray, London, 1957.

Lieven (*London Letters*): *Letters of Dorothea, Princess Lieven, during her Residence in London, 1812–1834*. Edited by Lionel G Robinson. Longmans, London, 1902.

——— (*Metternich Letters*): *The Private Letters of Princess Lieven to Prince Metternich 1820–1826*. Edited by Peter Quennell. John Murray, London, 1948.

——— (*Unpublished Diary*): *The Unpublished Diary and Political Sketches of Princess Lieven, together with some of her letters*. Edited by Harold Temperley. Jonathan Cape, London, 1925.

Lillywhite, Bryant: *London Coffee Houses*. George Allen and Unwin, 1963.

Lockhart, John Gibson: *The Life of Sir Walter Scott* (10 vols). Edinburgh, 1902.

Lyttelton Sarah: *Correspondence of Sarah Spencer Lady Lyttelton, 1787–1870*. Edited by her great-granddaughter, The Hon. Mrs Hugh Wyndham. John Murray, London, 1912.

MacDonald, Catriona: 'Abandoned and Beastly?: The Queen Caroline Affair in Scotland', *Twisted Sisters: Women, Crime and Deviance in Scotland since 1400*. 2002.

Mackintosh (*Memoirs*): *Memoirs of the Life of The Right Honourable Sir James Mackintosh* (2 vols). Edited by his son Robert James Mackintosh. Edward Moxon, London, 1835.

Madden, Lionel and Dixon, Diana (compilers): *The Nineteenth-century Periodical Press in Britain. A Bibliography of Modern Studies, 1901–1971*. Garland, London, 1976.

Malmesbury Diaries: *The Diaries and Correspondence of James Harris, First Earl of Malmesbury* (4 vols), 1844. Edited by Third Earl of Malmesbury. Richard Bentley, London, 1844.

Malmesbury, James Howard Harris: *Memoirs of an Ex-Minister: An Autobiography by James Howard Harris, Third Earl of Malmesbury*. Longmans, London, 1884.

Manby, George William: *Reminiscences*. Sloman, Yarmouth, 1859.

Marchand, Leslie (ed.): *Byron's Letters and Journals* (12 vols). John Murray, London, 1973–1994.

Martineau, Harriet: *A History of the Thirty Years' Peace: AD 1816–1846* (4 vols). George Bell and Sons, London, 1877.

McCalman, Iain (ed.): *An Oxford Companion to the Romantic Age: British Culture, 1776–1832*. Oxford University Press, 1999.

McCalman, Iain: *Radical Underworld: Prophets, Revolutionaries and Pornographers in London 1795–1840*. Cambridge University Press, 1987.

McWilliam, Rohan: *Popular Politics in Nineteenth-century England*. Routledge, London, 1998.

Melville, Lewis (ed.): *Life and Letters of William Cobbett in England and America* (2 vols). John Lane, London, 1913.

Melville, Lewis: *An Injured Queen, Caroline of Brunswick* (2 vols). Hutchinson and Co, London, 1912.

Mitchell, Austin Vernon: *The Whigs in Opposition, 1815–1830*. Clarendon Press, Oxford, 1967.

Moore, Thomas: *Memoirs, Journal and Correspondences of Thomas Moore* (8 vols), London, 1853.

Mori, Jennifer: *Britain in the Age of the French Revolution, 1785–1820*. Longman, Harlow, 2000.

Murray (*Recollections*): *Recollections from 1803 to 1837*. The Hon. Amelia Murray. Longmans, London, 1868.

Nattrass, Leonora (ed.): *William Cobbett, Selected Writings* (6 vols). Pickering and Chatto, London, 1998.

Nattrass, Leonora: *William Cobbett: The Politics of Style*. Cambridge University Press, 1995.

New, Chester, *The Life of Henry Brougham to 1830*. Clarendon Press, Oxford, 1961.

Newton Dunn, Bill: *The Man Who Was John Bull: The Biography of Theodore Edward Hook 1778–1841*. Allendale, London, 1996.

Nicolson, Hon. Sir Harold George, KCVO, *The Congress of Vienna. A Study in Allied Unity 1812–1822*. Constable and Co Ltd, London, 1946.

Nightingale, Joseph: *Memoirs of the Public and Private Life of Queen Caroline*. Edited and Introduced by Christopher Hibbert. The Folio Society, London, 1978.

——: *The Last Days of Queen Caroline*. J. Robins and Co, London, 1822.

O'Connell, Sheila: *The Popular Print in England 1550–1844*. British Museum Press, London, 1999.

Oman, Carola: *The Life and Diaries of Frances Mary Gascoyne-Cecil 1802–1839*. Hodder and Stoughton, London, 1968.

Palmer, Stanley: *Police and Protest in England and Ireland, 1780–1850*.

Cambridge University Press, 1988.

Papendiek Journals: *Court and Private Life in the Time of Queen Charlotte: Being the Journals of Mrs Papendiek, Assistant Keeper of the Wardrobe and Reader to Her Majesty*. Edited by her grand-daughter, Mrs Vernon Delves Broughton. Richard Bentley and Son, London, 1887.

Parr, Samuel: *The Works of Samuel Parr with Memoirs of his Life and Writings, and a Selection from His Correspondence* (8 vols). Edited by John Johnstone. London, 1828.

Patterson, M. W.: *Sir Francis Burdett and His Times (1770–1844)* (2 vols). Macmillan, London, 1931.

Pellew, George: *The Life and Correspondence of the Right Hon. Henry Addington, First Viscount Sidmouth* (3 vols). John Murray, London,1847.

Penrose, Alexander (ed.): *The Autobiography and Memoirs of Benjamin Robert Haydon 1786–1846*. G. Bell and Sons, London, 1927.

Phillips, Charles: *The Lament of the Emerald Isle [upon occasion of the death of Princess Charlotte]*. W. Hone, London, 1817.

Philp, Mark (ed.): *The French Revolution and British Popular Politics*. Cambridge University Press, 1991.

Prothero, I. J.: *Artisans and Politics in Early Nineteenth-century London: John Gast and His Times*. Dawson, Folkestone, 1979.

Quinault, R. and Stevenson, J. (eds): *Popular Protests and Public Order: Six Studies in British History, 1790–1920*. George Allen and Unwin, London, 1974.

Read, Donald: *Press and People, 1790–1850. Opinion in Three English Cities*. Edward Arnold, London, 1961.

Reid, Robert: *The Peterloo Massacre*. William Heinemann, London, 1989.

Richardson, Joanna: *George IV: A Portrait*. Sidgwick and Jackson, London, 1966.

——: *The Disastrous Marriage. A Study of George IV and Caroline of Brunswick*. Jonathan Cape, London, 1960.

Rickword, Edgell (ed.): *Radical Squibs and Loyal Ripostes: Satirical Pamphlets of the Regency Period, 1819–21*. Adams and Dart, Bath, 1971.

Rogers, Nicholas: *Crowds, Culture and Politics in Georgian Britain*. Clarendon Press, Oxford, 1998.

Romilly (*Memoirs*): *Memoirs of the Life of Sir Samuel Romilly, written by Himself; with a Selection from his Correspondence* (3 vols). Edited by his sons. John Murray, London, 1840.

Royle, Edward and Walvin, James: *English Radicals and Reformers 1760–1848*. Harvester, Brighton, 1982.

Royle, Edward: *Revolutionary Britannia? Reflections on the Threat of Revolution in Britain, 1789–1848*. Manchester University Press, 2000.

Rudé, George: *The Crowd in History: A Study of Popular Disturbances in France and England, 1730–1838*. Lawrence and Wishart, London, 1981.

Rush, Richard: *Memoranda of a Residence at the Court of London*, 1833.

Schweizer, Karl and Black, Jeremy (eds): *Politics and the Press in Hanoverian Britain*. Mellon, 1989.

Scott, Walter, Sir: *Familiar Letters of Sir Walter Scott* (2 vols). Edited by David Douglas. David Douglas, Edinburgh, 1894.

———: *The Journal of Sir Walter Scott*. Edited by John Guthrie Tait and William Mathie Parker. London, 1939–1950.

Sharpe, Reginald R.: *London and the Kingdom* (3 vols). Longmans, London, 1894–1895.

Shelley (*Letters*): *The Letters of Percy Bysshe Shelley* (2 vols). Edited by Roger Ingpen. Sir Isaac Pitman and Sons Ltd, London, 1912.

Shelley, Mary (*Letters*): *The Letters of Mary Wollstonecraft Shelley*. Edited by Betty T. Bennett (3 vols). The John Hopkins University Press, Baltimore and London, 1980.

Shepard, Leslie: *John Pitts: Ballad Printer of Seven Dials, London, 1765–1844* . . . Private Libraries Association, Pinner, 1969.

———: *The History of Street Literature*. David and Charles, Newton Abbot, 1973.

Smith, E. A.: *A Queen on Trial: The Affair of Queen Caroline*. Sutton, London, 1993.

———: *George IV*. Yale University Press, New Haven and London, 1999.

———: *The House of Lords in British Politics and Society, 1815–1911*. Longman, London, 1992.

Smith, N. C. (ed.): *The Letters of Sydney Smith* (2 vols). Clarendon Press, Oxford, 1953.

Sommerville, Charles John: *The News Revolution in England: Cultural Dynamics of Daily Information*. Oxford University Press, 1996.

Spater, George: *William Cobbett: The Poor Man's Friend* (2 vols). Cambridge University Press, 1982.

Stanhope (*Memoirs*): *Memoirs of the Lady Hester Stanhope as Related by Herself in Conversations with her Physician* (3 vols). Henry Colburn, London, 1845.

Stanhope, John: *The Cato Street Conspiracy*. Jonathan Cape, London, 1962.

Stapleton, Augustus Granville: *George Canning and his Times*. London, 1859.

Stephano, Celina: *Adventures of a Greek Lady, the Adopted Daughter of the Late Queen Caroline* (2 vols). London, 1849.

Stephens, W. R. W. (ed.): *A Memoir of the Right Hon William Page Wood, Baron Hatherley* (2 vols). Richard Bentley, London, 1883.

Stevenson, John (ed.): *London in the Age of Reform*. Blackwell, Oxford, 1977.

———: *Popular Disturbances in England, 1700–1832*. Longman, London, 1992.

Stewart, Robert: *Henry Brougham 1778–1868: His Public Career*. Bodley Head, London, 1985.

Taylor, David: *The New Police in Nineteenth-Century England*. Manchester University Press, 1997.

Thompson, Edward Palmer: *The Making of the English Working Class*. Gollancz, London, 1980.

Thomson, Anthony Todd, FLS: *The Authentic Medical Statement of the Case of Her Royal Highness the Late Princess Charlotte of Wales* (pamphlet). London, 1817.

Treasure, Geoffrey (ed.): *Who's Who in Late Hanoverian Britain. (1789–1837) Being the Seventh Volume in the Who's Who in British History Series*. Shepheard-Walwyn, London, 1997.

Twiss, Horace: *The Public and Private Life of Lord Chancellor Eldon* (3 vols). John Murray, London, 1844.

Vernon, James (ed.): *Re-reading the Constitution: New Narratives in the Political History of England's Long Nineteenth Century*. Cambridge University Press, 1996.

Vernon, James: *Politics and the People: A Study in English Political Culture, 1815–1867*. Cambridge University Press, 1993.

Wahrman, Dror: *Imagining the Middle-Class: The Political Representation of Class in Britain c. 1760–1840*. Cambridge University Press, 1995.

Wardroper, John: *The World of William Hone*. London, 1997.

Webster, Sir Charles: *The Foreign Policy of Castlereagh, 1812–1815. Britain and the Reconstruction of Europe*. G. Bell and Sons, London, 1950.

Wellington, Field Marshal Arthur Wellesley, Duke of: *Despatches, Correspondence and Memoranda* (8 vols) 1819–1832. Edited by his son, the Duke of Wellington. John Murray, London, 1867–1880.

——: *Supplementary Despatches, Correspondence and Memoranda*. Edited by his son, the Duke of Wellington. Volume the Ninth [April 1814 to March 1815]. John Murray, London, 1862.

Wickwar, William H.: *The Struggle for the Freedom of the Press, 1819–1832*. Allen and Unwin, London, 1928.

Wilberforce, R. I. and S. W.: *The Life of William Wilberforce* (5 vols). John Murray, London, 1838.

Wilkinson, George Theodore: *An Authentic History of the Cato Street Conspiracy*. Thomas Kelly, London, 1820.

Wilks, John: *Memoirs of Her Majesty, Queen Caroline . . . Consort of George IV, King of Great Britain* (2 vols), London, 1822.

Wilson, Ben: *The Laughter of Triumph: William Hone and the Fight for the Free Press*. Faber & Faber, London, 2005.

Wood, Marcus: *Popular Satire in Early Nineteenth-century Radicalism, with Special Reference to Hone and Cruikshank*. University of Oxford, 1989.

——: *Radical Satire and Print Culture, 1790–1822*. Clarendon Press, Oxford, 1994.

Woodward, Sir Ernest Llewellyn: *The Age of Reform, 1815–1870*. Clarendon Press, Oxford, 1962.

Worrall, David: *Radical Culture: Discourse, Resistance and Surveillance, 1790–1820*. Harvester, Wheatsheaf, London, 1992.

Young, Norwood: *Napoleon in Exile: Elba 1814–1815*. Stanley Paul and Co., London, 1914.

Ziegler, Philip: *A Life of Henry Addington, First Viscount Sidmouth*. Collins, London, 1965.

INDEX